THE "I" OF THE CAMERA

Originally published in 1988, *The "I" of the Camera* ha in the literature of film. Offering convincing alternative approaches that have gained most prominence in academ Rothman challenges readers to think about film in adven more open to movies and our experience of them. In essays examining particular films, filmmakers, genres, a flects on such matters as film violence, eroticism, and t American film. Rothman argues compellingly that mo philosophical perspective of American transcendentalis contains all of the essays that made the book a bench It also includes fourteen essays, written subsequent publication, as well as a new foreword. The new ch the scope of the volume, fleshing out its vision of film h the author's critical method and the philosophical pers

before the
w
cession
00222785
01347720

William Rothman is Professor of Motion Pictures and irector of the uate Program in Film Study at the University of Miami. He has taught at Harvard University, New York University, and for three years served as Director of the International Honors Program on Film, Television and Social Change in Asia. He is the author of numerous books and essays on aspects of film.

E Book version available

CAMBRIDGE STUDIES IN FILM

GENERAL EDITORS

William Rothman, *University of Miami*
Dudley Andrew, *Yale University*

Cambridge Studies in Film is a series of scholarly studies of high intellectual standards on the history and criticism of film. Each book examines a different aspect of film as a social and cultural phenomenon, setting standards and directions for the evaluation and definition of film scholarship. Designed for both film enthusiasts and academic readers, the series is international in scope of subject matter and eclectic in terms of approach and perspective. *Cambridge Studies in Film* provides a foundation in the theory and philosophy of the emerging visual media that continues to shape our world.

SELECTED TITLES FROM THE SERIES

The Cinema of Satyajit Ray, by Darius Cooper
Documentary Film Classics, by William Rothman
John Huston's Filmmaking, by Lesley Brill
Projecting Illusion: Film Spectatorship and the Impression of Reality, by Richard Allen
Interpreting the Moving Image, by Noël Carroll

THE "I" OF THE CAMERA

Essays in Film Criticism, History, and Aesthetics

SECOND EDITION

WILLIAM ROTHMAN
University of Miami

PUBLISHED BY THE PRESS SYNDICATE OF THE UNIVERSITY OF CAMBRIDGE
The Pitt Building, Trumpington Street, Cambridge, United Kingdom

CAMBRIDGE UNIVERSITY PRESS
The Edinburgh Building, Cambridge CB2 2RU, UK
40 West 20th Street, New York, NY 10011-4211, USA
477 Williamstown Road, Port Melbourne, VIC 3207, Australia
Ruiz de Alarcón 13, 28014 Madrid, Spain
Dock House, The Waterfront, Cape Town 8001, South Africa

http://www.cambridge.org

© William Rothman 2004

This book is in copyright. Subject to statutory exception
and to the provisions of relevant collective licensing agreements,
no reproduction of any part may take place without
the written permission of Cambridge University Press.

First published 2004

Printed in the United States of America

Typeface Sabon 9.75/12.5 pt. *System* LaTeX 2ε [TB]

A catalog record for this book is available from the British Library.

Library of Congress Cataloging in Publication Data
Rothman, William.
The "I" of the camera : essays in film criticism, history, and aesthetics / William Rothman. – 2nd ed.
p. cm. – (Cambridge studies in film)
Includes bibliographical references and index.
ISBN 0-521-82022-7 – ISBN 0-521-52724-4 (pb.)
1. Motion pictures. I. Title. II. Series.
PN1995.R68 2003
791.43–dc21 2003048464

Page xxix is a continuation of the copyright page.

ISBN 0 521 82022 7 hardback
ISBN 0 521 52724 4 paperback

To Kitty

Contents

Foreword to the Second Edition		*page* ix
Preface to the First Edition		xix
Acknowledgments		xxvii
Notes on the Essays		xxix
1	Hollywood Reconsidered: Reflections on the Classical American Cinema	1
2	D. W. Griffith and the Birth of the Movies	11
3	*Judith of Bethulia*	17
4	True Heart Griffith	29
5	The Ending of *City Lights*	44
6	*The Goddess*: Reflections on Melodrama East and West	55
7	*Red Dust*: The Erotic Screen Image	67
8	Virtue and Villainy in the Face of the Camera	74
9	Pathos and Transfiguration in the Face of the Camera: A Reading of *Stella Dallas*	87
10	Viewing the World in Black and White: Race and the Melodrama of the Unknown Woman	96
11	Howard Hawks and *Bringing Up Baby*	110
12	The Filmmaker in the Film: Octave and the Rules of Renoir's Game	122
13	*Stagecoach* and the Quest for Selfhood	139
14	To Have and Have Not Adapted a Film from a Novel	158

15 Hollywood and the Rise of Suburbia 167

16 Nobody's Perfect: Billy Wilder and the Postwar American Cinema 177

17 *The River* 206

18 *Vertigo*: The Unknown Woman in Hitchcock 221

19 *North by Northwest*: Hitchcock's Monument to the Hitchcock Film 241

20 The Villain in Hitchcock: "Does He Look Like a 'Wrong One' to You?" 254

21 Thoughts on Hitchcock's Authorship 263

22 Eternal Vérités: Cinema-Vérité and Classical Cinema 281

23 Visconti's *Death in Venice* 298

24 Alfred Guzzetti's *Family Portrait Sittings* 304

25 The Taste for Beauty: Eric Rohmer's Writings on Film 321

26 *Tale of Winter*: Philosophical Thought in the Films of Eric Rohmer 325

27 The "New Latin American Cinema" 340

28 Violence and Film 348

29 What Is American about American Film Study? 358

Index 381

Foreword to the Second Edition

When Beatrice Rehl, my friend and editor at Cambridge University Press, told me that Cambridge considers *The "I" of the Camera* to be one of its most successful books on film and invited me to prepare a new edition, I leapt at the opportunity. I was delighted that Cambridge – which can boast of more worthwhile film books than perhaps any other publisher – considers *The "I" of the Camera* to be a milestone in the history of film study and also a work that remains vital and relevant to shaping the future of the field.

This second edition of *The "I" of the Camera* contains all fifteen of the essays – with newly made and greatly improved frame enlargements – that were included in the volume when it was originally published in 1988. I have also added no fewer than fourteen essays – enough new material to have made a separate volume of its own. All the additional essays were written subsequent to the book's original publication. They range from critical studies of particular films ("*The Goddess*: Reflections on Melodrama East and West," "*Stagecoach* and the Quest for Selfhood," "Visconti's *Death in Venice*"), filmmakers ("Nobody's Perfect: Billy Wilder and the Postwar American Cinema"; "The Villain in Hitchcock" and "Thoughts on Hitchcock's Authorship"; "Philosophical Thought in the Films of Eric Rohmer" and the foreword to the American edition of Rohmer's *The Taste for Beauty*) and movements or genres ("Eternal Vérités: Cinéma-Vérité and Classical Cinema," "The 'New Latin American Cinema,'" "Viewing the World in Black and White: Race and the Melodrama of the Unknown Woman") to more general reflections ("Hollywood and the Rise of Suburbia," "Violence and Film," "What Is American about American Film Study?).

What I wrote in my original preface articulates my reason, as well, for putting together this expanded collection of essays:

By publishing all of these essays under one cover, I hope to make them readily available and also more approachable, for although their prose is untechnical and as clear as I know how to make it, their way of thinking about film, which is also a way of viewing film, a way of viewing film as thinking, will be unfamiliar to many readers. My hope is that reading the essays together will help impart familiarity with their way of thinking. But another aim in putting these essays together is to make their way of thinking *less* familiar – more provocative, more critical, more demanding. This is writing that calls upon the reader to think about movies, which means, in part, thinking about the hold movies have over us. This in turn means, in part, thinking about why we resist thinking about movies, why such resistance is, as it were, natural. (This thought, too, it may be natural to resist.)

When I wrote these words fifteen years ago, I was registering my conviction that *The "I" of the Camera* was capable of challenging readers to think about film in more adventurous ways, ways more open and responsive to what movies themselves have to say, and more open and responsive to our experience of them. I was also registering my expectation that my book would meet with resistance within the field of film study. It did.

In 1988, academic film study was in the grip of the doctrine that its legitimacy could be established by only the "higher authority," the field called "theory." The reign of theoretical systematizing over film study, which has now more or less definitively come to an end, was at its most repressive. Students were taught that, to think seriously about film, they first had to break their attachments to the films they loved. It was an unquestioned doctrine within the field that movies were pernicious ideological representations to be resisted and decoded, not treated with the respect that is due to works of art capable of instructing us how to think about them. It was another dogma that the human figures projected on the movie screen were mere "personas," discursive ideological constructs, not people. Yet another was that the world projected on the screen was itself an ideological construct, not real; and, indeed, that so-called reality was such a construct, too.

The "I" of the Camera presented – and still presents – an alternative to these skeptical views. That is the basis of both the book's historical significance and its continuing relevance to the field of film study. Aspiring to an Emersonian philosophical perspective, these essays, individually and collectively, urge us to speak about film in our own human voices, in words accountable to our own experience but unsanctioned by any "higher authority." They also stake out a critical method or discipline, a practice of close reading underwritten by the philosophical principle that we cannot understand a film's worth, or its meaning, by applying a theory that dictates to us what we are to say, but only by acknowledging the film's understanding of itself. No wonder the book met with resistance from a field that was rigidly intolerant to all alternatives to the theoretical frameworks that dictated its agenda!

When I was a Harvard undergraduate in the early 1960s, so-called analytical philosophy was the prevailing school of thought in American academic philosophy (as, on the whole, it still is). But analytical philosophy was long past the heroic era of Gottlob Frege or the young Ludwig Wittgenstein or even the Vienna School of the 1920s, with its grand ambition of grounding mathematics and even science – indeed, all human knowledge – in logic, hence in philosophy. When I made my decision to major in philosophy, logical positivism had long since failed, and analytical philosophy had drastically lowered its sights. It still came with the territory for philosophy professors and their students to assume an air of arrogant superiority to each other, as well as to those benighted souls who lacked professional training in philosophical analysis. But academic philosophy in America had come to view itself as a technical discipline, and a minor one at that, reduced to conceptual "mopping up," like the Emil Jannings character, the once-proud doorman, in F. W. Murnau's *The Last Laugh*.

Viewed from within the Harvard Philosophy Department in the early 1960s, in short, philosophy had a most unexciting future. Philosophy also had no relevant past except for the cautionary tale of the failure of its once-heroic dream to provide the foundation for all knowledge. Although it was the beauty of mathematical logic that first drew me to major in philosophy, the downbeat mood within the Harvard Philosophy Department perversely appealed to me. (Years later, I learned that the favorite film of the professor who first inspired me to enter philosophy was *Gilda*. He loved to dream about Rita Hayworth, but what he loved most about her was her unattainability.) I was a child of the existentialist 1950s, and in an absurd, meaningless universe, philosophy, that most absurd and meaningless of all absurd and meaningless endeavors, seemed somehow sublime to me.

My attitude toward philosophy changed when Stanley Cavell arrived at Harvard during my junior year and I began working closely with him. I embraced the revolution in philosophy, effected from *within* the analytical tradition, signaled by Ludwig Wittgenstein in *Philosophical Investigations*, as Cavell taught me to read that seminal work, and by J. L. Austin, Cavell's own professor of philosophy, in his investigations of ordinary language. As I made clear in my Honors Thesis, written under Cavell's supervision, Wittgenstein's *Philosophical Investigations* meant to me, among other things, that philosophy and science were different enterprises, to be assessed by different criteria. Nor was philosophy simply to be equated with constructing arguments, presenting and defending theses, or erecting theoretical systems. An exemplary philosophical activity is one that aspires to achieve a perspective – at one level, a perspective of self-reflection – that enables a certain kind of understanding to be reached.

During my senior year at Harvard College, Cavell invited me to enroll in a graduate seminar in aesthetics he was offering that focused on the aesthetics of film. (In *The World Viewed*, he describes this seminar and the role that what he takes to be its failure played in his decision to write his brilliant and beautiful little book about film.) To me, this seminar was anything but a failure. It inspired me to stay on at Harvard to work with Cavell as a doctoral student. Ultimately, I wrote a dissertation that presents an analysis of the concept of expression – to this day, I rely on its ideas – that uses film as its primary example of an artistic medium and uses Hitchcock's *Notorious* as its primary example of a film.

Before Cavell's arrival at Harvard, I was already thinking about film. He helped me to understand that I was doing philosophy – and *why* it was philosophy – when I thought about film the way I was thinking about it. To understand this was to understand something about philosophy, something about film, and something about the potential fruitfulness – indeed, the necessity – of their marriage. It was also to understand something about myself. For the first time, I knew that I was not drawn to philosophy, as I liked to imagine, because it was perfectly meaningless to me. In reality, philosophy meant the world to me. Thinking philosophically about film was – and is – my true vocation.

I can pinpoint the moment this understanding crystallized. Christmas week 1972. Snow on the streets of Manhattan. I was standing in front of a bank of elevators in the lobby of the Waldorf-Astoria Hotel (ironically, the location of one of the darkest hours in American film history; it was at a meeting at the Waldorf that Hollywood formulated its plans for the blacklist). The annual meeting of the American Philosophical Association was in full swing. The job interviews – my reason for being there – were on the 31st floor. An elevator door opened, but before I got to it, it closed. Another door opened. Again, it closed before I got to it. This happened a third time, and a fourth. Finally, it penetrated my ivory dome that I must not have wanted to let the interviewers on the 31st floor force me to pigeonhole my work in terms of the conventional categories of academic philosophy. So I made tracks, went to a movie, and, within a week, had sent out 200 letters to colleges with film programs. The next fall, I started teaching film in the Cinema Studies Department at New York University and returned to Harvard three years later to teach at the newly built Carpenter Center, not quite knowing whether I was coming or going, but certain that I was charting my own path of discovery and self-discovery.

Philosophy's concerns have never been separable from the concerns of ordinary human beings living on Earth. Hence the concerns of philosophy have also found expression, historically, in arts such as literature, painting, and theater, as in the deep affinity between philosophical skepticism, as it figures centrally in the writings of Descartes, and their exact contemporary, Shakespeare's tragedies and late romances. In the 1930s and 1940s, the concerns of philosophy and Hollywood movies similarly converged. In the so-called classical Hollywood cinema, characters are forever engaging in philosophical dialogues that sustain serious conversations about such matters as what constitutes a conversation, or a marriage worth having, or a community that keeps faith with the ideas on which America was founded. These movies are also forever meditating on the conditions of their own medium.

Yet as the fledgling field of film study turned to European systems of thought in an effort to secure its legitimacy as an intellectual discipline, that unreflective condescension toward film already almost universal among American intellectuals became more firmly entrenched than ever. By 1988, it had become an unassailable doctrine of academic film study in America that popular movies could not possibly exemplify serious ways of thinking, but only ways of *not* thinking; they could be instruments only of "dominant ideology," which we need no help from the films themselves in order to understand, that is, decode. The field assumed that it could know with certainty, on the basis of some theory or other, that Hollywood movies, and Hollywood itself, could be only a machine, an apparatus, whose effects on viewers had to be analyzed objectively, where "objectivity" begins – and ends – with disengagement from one's ordinary experience as a viewer. But what if film is, as it were, inherently subversive – subversive, for example, of the ideology that holds that subjectivity and objectivity are absolutely separable, as if there were not always a medium between them? (In the history of Western philosophy, this ideology can be traced back to Cartesian dualism. It underlies the Saussurian linguistics, based on the opposition between "signifier" and "signified," that, in the heyday of the stultifying influence of semiology on film study, left so many film students bewitched, bothered, and bewildered.) Then an approach to the study of film that begins by denying a priori the possibility that movies are self-conscious would have the inevitable consequence of subverting their subversiveness, denying what is genuinely thought provoking – historically and ontologically – about film.

As *The "I" of the Camera* attests, during the 1970s and the 1980s, a turbulent period for the field of film study, I was never tempted to turn to semiology or Althusserian Marxism or Lacanian psychoanalysis to make my work more "scientific." As I said, Wittgenstein's *Philosophical Investigations* (and, I might add, the writings of Nietzsche, the later Heidegger, the Americans Emerson and Thoreau) meant to me that philosophy and science were different enterprises to be assessed by different criteria. Nor was I tempted to turn to the new theoretical frameworks that promised – or the field imagined that they promised – to make film study more rigorous by bringing it into alignment with *systems* of thought. Rather, the more I studied the films I cared most about, the more I felt confirmed in my view that they were thinking seriously – thinking philosophically, as I put it in *Hitchcock – The Murderous Gaze*, my first book – about matters that I was thinking about, too. What *constitutes* a movie's thoughtfulness or self-awareness, however, is not easy to say. Finding a way to say it, nonetheless, was a central goal of my Hitchcock book. It is an abiding goal of all the essays in *The "I" of the Camera*, old and new. Hence the aptness of the book's title.

The reign of theoretical systematizing over film study is over, as I have said. Yet it remains the case that the theoretical writings that are presented to film students as exemplary all apply theoretical systems *to* films. The essays in *The "I" of the Camera* do not proceed this way. It is a feature of many of these essays, indeed, that at a certain point what I think of as the emotional temperature of the prose rises, and the writing climaxes and concludes, on philosophical principle, not with a recapitulation of the essay's main claims and arguments, but with a charged description of a philosophically meaningful moment of a film, as I experience it.

In some of the original essays in *The "I" of the Camera*, a note of anger may occasionally be heard – an expression of my growing sense of alienation from a field that was losing sight of what to me was most thought provoking about movies. When I sat down fifteen years ago to write a preface to the volume, I had every intention of rebutting, point by point, the theoretical positions that were, by my lights, leading the field astray. In the preface I actually composed, however, anger is absent, as it is absent from the essays I composed especially for the book ("D. W. Griffith and the Birth of the Movies," "True Heart Griffith," "The Ending of *City Lights*," "*The River*"). Those essays, and the preface as well, are among my favorite pieces in *The "I" of the Camera*. They now seem to me the best instances I had produced, up to 1988, of the kind of philosophical writing about film that I love and believe in. I am also aware that they are among the pieces in the book that readers within the field of film study have found most difficult to recognize as examples of film theory at all.

In part because of the resistance *The "I" of the Camera* has encountered, most readers today remain as unfamiliar as ever with the way of thinking philosophically about film that my writing champions. Nonetheless, I hope and expect that the book will no longer meet with the degree, or kind, of resistance that it originally encountered. The reign of theoretical systematizing over film study has ended, as I keep saying (hoping that I'm not whistling in the dark). The publication, in altered circumstances, of this second edition promises to give my book a second chance, or, to be more accurate, to give the field a second chance to respond to these essays, to address their ideas, methods, and critical claims, and to assess the potential usefulness, to the serious study of film, of the philosophical perspective they aspire to achieve.

Preface to the First Edition

In 1982, *Hitchcock – The Murderous Gaze* was published, the culmination of a project that had occupied me for ten years.[1] During that period, I had published other essays on films and filmmakers. These had appeared in widely scattered journals, and at the time I submitted the Hitchcock manuscript I resolved to collect them in one volume, along with a number of papers presented at conferences but never published. *The "I" of the Camera* is the product of that resolution, although half its essays were written in the intervening five years, in part with the aim of making the volume less a collection and more a real book.

There are differences of style and emphasis between the earlier and later essays, but they are unified by a consistent reliance on the close reading of sequences to back up the claims made about the filnis, a consistent *practice* of close reading, and a consistent commitment to reflecting on what that practice reveals about film. Taken together, these essays survey film history from early Griffith almost to the present day. From this survey, a picture of the history of film emerges, at least in outline – a picture that acknowledges the centrality of films that reflect philosophically on the mysterious powers and limits of their medium.

Through extended readings of five characteristic films, *Hitchcock – The Murderous Gaze* attempted to arrive at an understanding of Hitchcock's authorship and its place in the history of film. At the same time, the book was an investigation of the *conditions* of film authorship, a critique (in the Kantian sense) of film as a medium of authorship. However incessantly the death of the author may be proclaimed, the fact is that there are film authors. But what is it to be an author in the medium of film? What is authorship, what is a medium, what is film?

[1] William Rothman, *Hitchcock – The Murderous Gaze* (Cambridge, MA: Harvard University Press, 1982).

In its reflections on authorship, *The "I" of the Camera* is a companion piece to *Hitchcock – The Murderous Gaze*. It contains essays on two Hitchcock films ("*Vertigo*: The Unknown Woman in Hitchcock" and "*North by Northwest*: Hitchcock's Monument to the Hitchcock Film") that complement and extend the readings in the Hitchcock book. It also contains essays that attempt to sketch perspicuous picture of the work of a number of other exemplary film authors, most notably D. W. Griffith ("D. W. Griffith and the Birth of the Movies," "*Judith of Bethulia*," and "True heart Griffith"), Howard Hawks ("Howard Hawks and *Bringing Up Baby*" and "To Have and Have Not Adapted a Film from a Novel"), Charles Chaplin ("The Ending of *City Lights*") and Jean Renoir ("The Filmmaker in the Film: Octave and the Rules of Renoir's Game" and "*The River*").

In negotiating the treacherous conceptual waters surrounding authorship, both books draw continually on the analysis of the concept of expression worked out in "Three Essays in Aesthetics," my doctoral dissertation in philosophy.[2] To say that Hitchcock expresses himself in his films is to say that he is revealed by them and also that he declares himself in them. Beyond this, through his acts of making films, he fulfills himself, becomes more fully who he is, creates himself. It is possible to know Hitchcock through his films because he is the creation of the films as surely as he is their creator. But this does not mean that the Hitchcock made knowable in these films is a fiction of the films' texts, that the real Alfred Hitchcock remains unknowable. The Hitchcock the films make knowable is the human being of flesh and blood. (This is part of what Hitchcock's famous cameo appearances declare.)

That we may know Hitchcock through his films may seem impossible, but it is no more impossible than that human beings are capable of expressing themselves in any other medium, are capable of expressing themselves at all. It is a fact that human beings are capable of revealing and declaring and creating themselves. Yet this fact is also a mystery. *The "I" of the Camera* takes this mystery to be, historically, one of the central themes of film. Hitchcock's films, and the other films I write about, develop this theme by creating intimate, mysterious relationships between the camera and the camera's "subjects," the human beings who dwell within the world of the film (they are also the stars who present themselves to the camera and are revealed by it), and equally intimate and mysterious relationships between the camera and the author, the "I" the camera represents. (The camera also represents the viewer. Does it, then, always serve two masters?)

[2] William Rothman, "Three Essays in Aesthetics" (unpublished dissertation, Harvard University, 1973).

Authorship is only one of the central concerns of *The "I" of the Camera*. Two essays ("Virtue and Villainy in the Face of the Camera" and "Pathos and Transfiguration in the Face of the Camera: A Reading of *Stella Dallas*) study the ways in which theatrical melodrama is transformed by the role of the camera and what that transformation reveals about film and its traumatic break with theater. "*Red Dust*: The Erotic Screen Image" reflects on the erotic dimension of film's awesome power. "Alfred Guzzetti's *Family Portrait Sittings*" explores the camera's role in cinéma-vérité and the relationship between "documentary" and "fiction." "Hollywood Reconsidered: Reflections on the Classical American Cinema," which opens this volume with an overview of the history of film, addresses the question (among others), What is American about American film?

By publishing all of these essays under one cover, I hope to make them readily available and also more approachable, for although their prose is untechnical and as clear as I know how to make it, their way of thinking about film, which is also a way of viewing film, a way of viewing film as thinking, will be unfamiliar to many readers. My hope is that reading the essays together will help impart familiarity with their way of thinking. But another aim in putting these essays together is to make their way of thinking *less* familiar – more provocative, more critical, more demanding. This is writing that calls upon the reader to think about movies, which means, in part, thinking about the hold movies have over us, This in turn means, in part, thinking about why we resist thinking about movies, why such resistance is, as it were, natural. (This thought, too, it may be natural to resist.)

Most of what I understand about resistance to thinking about movies I learned the old-fashioned way, in the classroom. But it was also in the classroom that I learned that this resistance may be overcome, or, even better, put to use.

All of the pages that follow bear the mark of almost twenty years of lecturing about film, beginning at Harvard when I was a graduate student in philosophy, then continuing at the University of California at Berkeley and Wellesley College. I was Assistant Professor in Cinema Studies at New York University before I returned to Harvard, where I taught film history, criticism, and theory from 1976 to 1984, the period in which most of these essays were written. My practice in the classroom is an essential source of this writing, and it is important that I characterize it.

In a typical classroom session, I spend at least half the time going through one or more sequences with an analyzer projector or video player that allows me to stop the film at any time, fixing the image and keeping it on the screen. Taking the passage line by line, gesture by gesture, expression by expression, shot by shot, I speak about what is on the screen (and what is significantly absent) at each moment, what it reveals, what motivates it, and how it affects the viewer's experience. I speak about what every viewer sees and also about what I have come to see that other viewers may not see (Hitchcock films, especially, are crisscrossed with private jokes and other "secrets" that are nonetheless in plain view). In short, I perform a reading of the sequence, moment by moment, and I invite others in the room to interject at any time with a remark or a question that adds to or revises or challenges my reading or proposes an alternative reading.

Usually the sequence is from a film I have viewed with the class the night before, have read about in the critical literature, and have previously known (viewed with an audience and also studied, moment by moment, on an editing table). Increasingly, over the years, it is a film I have also previously taught. I enter the classroom already knowing much of what I am going to say. I am already prepared with a reading, but I am also always prepared to revise that reading by testing it in class. In the classroom, I am also always thinking – thinking out loud in front of the class and in front of a film that is holding all of us in its spell even as I speak. I am making discoveries – and inviting others to make discoveries, and they *are* making discoveries – here and now in the face of the power of film. (And the reading I have already prepared is itself woven from discoveries originally made, or at least made to be tested, in the classroom.) The deepest of these discoveries are about the mysterious hold film has over viewers. They are about what viewers ordinarily pass over in silence, and about that silence.

What goes on in the darkness of a movie theater, like what goes on behind the closed doors of a classroom, is open to all who are present, yet is at the same time intimate and private. Ordinarily, even when a film ends and the lights go on and we resume our ordinary lives and our ordinary conversations, we do not break the silence of our communion in the face of the film. Films speak to us in an intimate language of indirectness and silence. To speak seriously about a film,we must speak about that silence, its motivations and depths; we must speak about that to which the silence gives voice; we must give voice to that silence; we must let that silence speak for itself. This is an important part of what I learned – and learned to achieve (at least when the stars were with me) – while thinking out loud in front of a class.

In the classroom, we are all engaged in a common enterprise. I am the lecturer, but I am also a student being initiated, initiating myself, in thinking about film. Over the years, the thinking that goes on in the classroom has fed innumerable conversations outside the classroom. These conversations have deepened the sense of a common enterprise and in turn fed the thinking in the classroom. And it is from this thinking and talking and listening in and out of school that the writing in this book emerged.

In a sense, this writing attempts to recapture the magic of those hours in class and those conversations out of school. It is animated by a wish that underlies all writing, perhaps, and is certainly a wish (*the* wish?) that underlies film: the wish to keep the past before us, however inadequate we may be to bring it back to life. Yet in another sense those classroom sessions and conversations, however magical, were only rehearsals for this writing. Indeed, what made them magical was never separable from the fact of my writing, from its promise that I was committed to thinking things through, to working toward formulations that, however subject to revision, however provisional, I would unprovisionally be prepared to call my own, to make available, to publish.

My authority in the classroom has always borrowed on this promise, as has my participation in the conversations that have sustained my thinking, conversations inspired by the shared vision of a community of writers, understood in the widest sense of men and women dedicated to making their mark. Such a promise can be kept, such a debt made good, only by writing.

Writing must establish its own authority, but writing with authority about film poses particular problems, problems that are at once literary and philosophical. Thinking out loud in front of a classroom, one can trust to the film itself to make everyone present mindful of what a film *is*. The written word cannot in this way join writer and reader in the face of the film. Writing can only invoke (call upon the reader to remember) or evoke (call upon the reader to imagine) the power of film and the particularity of an individual moment on film. In attempting this, the writer's primary tool is description, although frame enlargements provide a useful supplement.

In class, there are occasions when I stop the film in order to speak and other occasions when I stop the film in order to remain silent, allowing the moment to resonate in everyone's thoughts. (Often I do not know before I push the button whether I am going to speak or remain silent.) In any truly artful "sequence reading" performed in the classroom, one speaks only when the silence itself calls for giving voice to it. When the silence speaks in its own voice, the art is in listening. Every such masterful sequence reading is a study in the limits of what can be said. It is also a study in the limits of what goes without saying. What the *possibility* of such mastery reveals is that the limits of language and the limits of film coincide. That is, there is a boundary between them, and it is possible for a sequence reading to discover this boundary, even survey part of it.

When one performs a sequence reading in the classroom, there is a clear distinction between speaking and being silent, a distinction drawn automatically, as it were, every time one opens one's mouth. In writing about a sequence, however, even when the words are supplemented by frame enlargements, it is necessary to describe what is on the screen at a particular moment in order to make a remark about it at all or even in order to let it pass without remark. In writing, description is a form of speech, but it is also a form of silence. In order for writing to survey the boundary between speech and silence, that boundary – like the power of film and the particularity of the moment of film – must be invoked or evoked by the writing itself, by its voices and silences.

The sequence readings in this book set this challenge for themselves: to describe every individual moment in all its dramatic power and its psychological depth while also conveying the power and depth of the succession of moments out of which the sequence – and ultimately the whole film – is composed.

The challenge is also to make every individual remark – every philosophical remark occasioned by a particular moment – rigorously accountable both to the film and to my own experience while also making these remarks succeed each other with inexorable logic. The goal is a piece of writing that sustains each of its interweaving lines of thought until it comes to an end, perhaps by reaching a conclusion. That it is possible for a sequence reading to sustain thinking that is at once spontaneous and strictly logical is a significant and inherently unpredictable fact about writing, about thinking, and about film. To the degree that I have achieved such writing in *Hitchcock – The Murderous Gaze* and in the present essays, I have made the sequence-reading form my own, one that enables me to express myself, to say what I have to say about the films I write about. And what I have to say about these films is that they have something to say and that they say it.

A deconstructionist, in rejecting the possibility of such an achievement, might well embrace the sequence reading as the ideal medium for demonstrating that film – like writing, like speech, like thought itself – can never be coherent, intact, whole, can never take full possession of its cacophony of silences and voices. My readings present an alternative to this skeptical vision (although I relish as much as any deconstructionist the opportunities for free association, epigrams, jokes, paradoxes, digressions, parenthetical remarks, and so on, afforded by the sequence-reading form).

When I read a sequence, I put my own words to the thoughts of the camera's subjects and to the author's thoughts. I give voice to these thoughts, although all I have to go on are the views framed by the camera, views from which the author is absent and which present the camera's subjects only, as it were, from the outside. My assertions are claims to have achieved – and claims that the film has achieved – something that a skeptic would take to be impossible, and I make such claims in order to assert what I find most astonishing, revolutionary, transfiguring, about the films I study. At one level, this is their extreme self-consciousness, the depth of their thoughts about the "I" of the camera. As I read them, these films are *thinking*; they are thinking about thinking, and they are thinking about film, meditating on the powers and limits of their medium.

Film, a medium limited to surfaces, to the outer, the visible, emerges in these films' meditations as a medium of mysterious depths, of the inner, the invisible. "The human body is the best picture of the human soul," Wittgenstein writes in *Philosophical Investigations*, expressing his wonder – wonder is always his starting point – that we have so much as the *idea* that other minds are inaccessible to us, separated from us by an unbridgeable barrier.[3] Wittgenstein's ambition is nothing less than to overcome skepticism by an acknowledgment of the everyday, effecting a fundamental transformation of the central tradition of Western thought. Film participates in this enterprise by demonstrating that the "barrier" of the movie screen – like the boundary between invisible and visible, inner and outer, subjective and objective, female and male, imaginary and real, silence and speech – is not really a barrier at all, however natural it may be to envision it as one, and by wondering what this "barrier" then is.

[3] Ludwig Wittgenstein, *Philosophical Investigations* (New York: Macmillan, 1953), p. 178.

Acknowledgments

This book is deeply indebted to so many people that I cannot hope to present an accounting here. There are three people whom I must single out, however, for without them it would not exist at all.

Marian Keane was my close collaborator on almost every film course I taught at Harvard. Harvard called her my "Teaching Fellow," but she was really my fellow teacher. Our almost daily conversations during the years I was writing these essays were essential, irreplaceable sources of energy and commitment and ideas, not to mention laughs. Every time I asked her to read a draft of an essay, I was rewarded (and the reader of this book will be rewarded) by her suggestions and criticisms. This book is also indebted to her writings about film, from which I have greatly profited, as have all her readers.

Stanley Cavell and I worked together extremely closely during the years I was teaching film at Harvard. We had innumerable conversations about film and related matters; we avidly read each other's writing. Whenever we could, we attended each other's classes, and we jointly taught a course on film comedy. Long before my return to Harvard, he had been my doctoral advisor, and I thought of myself – I still think of myself – as his student. But one thing one learns by being a student of Stanley Cavell is that a student is not a disciple. We have separate visions; we see eye-to-eye, but from different slants. That he has learned from me as I have learned from him, that he is as interested in my writing as I am in his, that a teacher is also a student, are also things he taught me, somehow having a faith in education so deep as to enable him to find a way to ram such ideas through my thick skull. This book owes an immeasurable debt to Stanley Cavell for his teaching, his writing, and the example he sets by the civilized way he lives his life.

Kitty Morgan, my wife, has likewise taught me more than I once thought it possible for one person to learn from another. She understood before I did how important publishing this book was to me and would not allow me to abandon the project. Without the benefit of her encouragement, support, inspiration, and companionship, I would long ago have run out of spunk.

Notes on the Essays

Chapter 1. "Hollywood Reconsidered: Reflections on the Classical American Cinema" was presented at the Symposium on Film and Intercultural Communication at the 1985 Hawaii International Film Festival. I wish to register my appreciation to Wimal Dissanayake and Paul Clark for inviting me to participate in that exceptionally rewarding dialogue between Asian and American filmmakers and critics. "Hollywood Reconsidered" was published in the *East–West Film Journal*, 1(1): 36–47 (December 1986).

Chapter 2. "D. W. Griffith and the Birth of the Movies" appeared in *Humanities* (the journal of the National Endowment for the Humanities), 6(4): 17–20 (August, 1985).

Chapter 3. "*Judith of Bethulia*" is a revised version of an unpublished paper initially written in 1976.

Chapter 4. I wrote "True Heart Griffith" in 1987 to balance the otherwise skewed picture of Griffith that would have emerged from this book had my remarks on *Judith of Bethulia* and *The Birth of a Nation* been left to stand on their own.

Chapter 5. "The Ending of *City Lights*" was written in 1986 for inclusion in the first edition.

Chapter 6. "*The Goddess*: Reflections on Melodrama East and West" was presented at the Symposium of the Hawaii International Film Festival, 1989, and at the China Institute, New York, in 1990. It was published in Wimal Dissanayake, ed., *Asian Film Melodrama* (New York and Cambridge, England: Cambridge University Press, 1993).

Chapter 7. "*Red Dust*: The Erotic Screen Image" is a version of a paper presented at the convention of the Society for Cinema Studies, 1976.

Chapter 8. "Virtue and Villainy in the Face of the Camera" was presented at a 1982 Symposium on Film and Melodrama at the Whitney Humanities

Center, Yale University. Thanks to Professor Norton Batkin, who organized the event. The symposium was a challenging exchange of views.

Chapter 9. "Pathos and Transfiguration in the Face of the Camera: A Reading of *Stella Dallas*," conceived as a companion piece to "Virtue and Villainy in the Face of the Camera," was presented at the 1983 convention of the Society for Cinema Studies and published in *Raritan Review*, 3(3): 116–35 (Winter 1984).

Chapter 10. "Viewing the World in Black and White: Race and the Melodrama of the Unknown Woman" was presented at the 23rd Annual Conference on Literature and Film, Florida State University, 1998.

Chapter 11. "Howard Hawks and *Bringing Up Baby*" was presented at the Film and University Conference held in 1975 at the Graduate Center of the City University of New York.

Chapter 12. "The Filmmaker in the Film: Octave and the Rules of Renoir's Game" was written for a collection of essays edited by Ellen P. Wiese, who made a number of suggestions that led to many changes and improvements in the piece. The collection was published as a special issue of *The Quarterly Review of Film Studies*, 7(3): 225–36 (Summer 1982).

Chapter 13. "*Stagecoach* and the Quest for Selfhood" was published in Barry Grant, ed., *John Ford's Stagecoach* (New York and Cambridge, England: Cambridge University Press, 2003).

Chapter 14. "To Have and Have Not Adapted a Film from a Novel" appeared in Gerald Perry and Roger Shatzkin, eds., *The Modern American Novel and the Movies* (New York: Ungar, 1978), pp. 70–80. I am grateful to Gerald Peary for his constructive criticism of a draft of the essay.

Chapter 15. "Hollywood and the Rise of Suburbia" was presented at the Symposium of the Hawaii International Film Festival, 1987, and was published in the *East–West Film Journal*, 3(2): 96–105 (June 1989).

Chapter 16. A version of "Nobody's Perfect: Billy Wilder and the Postwar American Cinema" was presented at the Annual Meeting of the American Society for Aesthetics, 2002, and published in *Film International*, 1(1): 36–47 (Winter 2003).

Chapter 17. "*The River*," was written as I was about to depart for my second visit to India. As a study of the cinema of Jean Renoir, it complements "The Filmmaker in the Film: Octave and the Rules of Renoir's Game." In its reflections on the ambiguous relationship between fiction and documentary in the medium of film, it is a companion piece to "Alfred Guzzetti's *Family Portrait Sittings*."

Chapter 18. "*Vertigo*: The Unknown Woman in Hitchcock" was published in Joseph H. Smith and Willima Kerrigan, eds., *Images in Our Souls: Cavell, Psychoanalysis, Cinema*, Vol. 10 of Forum for Psychiatry and the Humanities Series (Baltimore: Johns Hopkins University Press, 1987), pp. 64–81.

Chapter 19. "*North by Northwest*: Hitchcock's Monument to the Hitchcock Film" was read at the 1980 session of the English Institute and published in *The North Dakota Quarterly*, 51(3): 11–24 (Summer 1983).

Chapter 20. "The Villain in Hitchcock" was presented at the Annual Meetings of the Society for Cinema Studies, 2002, and published in Murray Pomerance, ed., *BAD: Infamy, Darkness, Evil, and Slime on Screen* (New York: SUNY Press, 2003).

Chapter 21. "Thoughts on Hitchcock's Authorship" was written for the Hitchcock Centenary Symposium at New York University, 1999, and was published in Richard Allen and S. Ishii Gonzales, eds., *Hitchcock: Centenary Essays* (New York and London: British Film Institute, 1999).

Chapter 22. "Eternal Vérités: Cinema-Vérité and Classical Cinema" was presented at the Beyond Document Symposium, Carpenter Center, Harvard University, 1993. It was published in Charles Warren, ed., *Beyond Document* (Middletown, CT: Wesleyan University Press, 1991).

Chapter 23. "*Visconti's Death in Venice*" was presented at the Annual Meeting of the American Society for Aesthetics, 1990.

Chapter 24. "Alfred Guzzetti's *Family Portrait Sittings*" appeared in *The Quarterly Review of Film Studies*, 2(1): 96–113 (February 1977).

Chapter 25. "The Taste for Beauty: Eric Rohmer's Writings on Film" was published as the Foreword to the American edition of Eric Rohmer, *The Taste for Beauty* (New York and Cambridge, England: Cambridge University Press, 1989.)

Chapter 26. "*Tale of Winter*: Philosophical Thought in the Films of Eric Rohmer" was presented at the Annual Meeting of the American Society for Aesthetics, 1999, and published in *Filmhäftet*, (Summer 2001).

Chapter 27. "The 'New Latin American Cinema'" was presented at the Intercultural Communication Conference, University of Miami, 1995, and published in *Film and Philosophy* (Winter 1997).

Chapter 28. "Violence and Film" was presented at the Annual Meeting of the University Film and Video Association, 1999. It was published in David Slocum, ed., *Violence in American Film* (New York and London: Routledge, 2001).

Chapter 29. "What Is American about American Film Study?" was presented at the Symposium of the Hawaii International Film Festival, 1991, and published in Wimal Dissanayake, ed., *Asian Film Melodrama* (New York and Cambridge, England: Cambridge University Press, 1993).

THE "I" OF THE CAMERA

CHAPTER 1

Hollywood Reconsidered:

Reflections on the Classical American Cinema

America's experience of film is virtually unique in that in almost every other country, the impact of film cannot be separated from the process or at least the specter of Americanization. In America, film in no sense represents something external; it is simply American. But what is American about American film?

For a decade or so after the first film exhibitions in 1895, film shows presented a grab bag of travelogues, news films, filmed vaudeville acts, trick films, and gag films. The audience for film in America was disproportionately urban and was made up of recent immigrants, largely from Eastern Europe. (The extent to which that was true is a subject of some contention among film historians.) In a sense, film has been involved, even in America, in a process of Americanization – "naturalizing" recent arrivals, teaching them how Americans live (and also breaking down regional differences, a process that television has taken over with a vengeance). However, following the sudden growth of nickelodeons in 1908, exhibitions were skewed to be more "upscale." The theatrical narrative – especially adaptations of "legitimate" novels and stage plays – became the dominant form of film in America, as it has remained to this day. Griffith's early films made for the Biograph Company were clearly intended for an audience of Americans who, like Griffith himself, could take for granted the fact, if not the meaning, of their Americanness.

Of course, the question of the Americanness of American films is complicated by the fact that in every period, foreigners played major roles in their creation. From Chaplin to Murnau to Lubitsch to Lang, Hitchcock, Renoir, Ophuls, Sirk, and Wilder, many of the most creative "American" directors have been non-Americans, at least when they began their Hollywood careers. This is almost equally true among stars, screenwriters, and producers.

Reprinted: See "Notes on the Essays."

Indeed, there are entire genres of American film, such as film noir and the thirties horror film (with their influence of German expressionism), that can seem to be hardly American at all.

But then again, virtually all Americans either are born as non-Americans or are recent descendants of non-Americans. One might think that there could be no such thing as a specifically American culture, but that is not the case. In the nineteenth century, for example, what is called transcendentalism – the philosophy of Emerson and Thoreau, the stories and novels of Hawthorne, Melville, and Henry James, the poetry of Whitman – is quintessentially American. However, this example underscores a distinctive feature of American intellectual and cultural life. There was no nineteenth-century French philosopher approaching Emerson's stature, but had there been, young French men and women today, as part of the experience of growing up French, would be taught his or her words by heart and learn to take them to heart. But in the process of growing up American, young men and women are not taught and do not in this way learn Emerson's words or the value of those words. Americans, as compared with the English or French or Chinese or Japanese, are unconscious of the history of thought and artistic creation in their own country – unconscious of the sources, American and foreign, of their own ideas. Nonetheless, through mechanisms that are at times obscure, American ideas such as those of Emerson remain widespread and powerful in America. It is one of Stanley Cavell's deepest insights, to which I shall return, that Hollywood film of the thirties and forties is rooted in, and must be understood in terms of, the American tradition of transcendentalism. That this is so and that Americans remain unconscious that it is so are equally significant facts about American culture.

Some may challenge the American pedigree of American transcendentalism, arguing that it is only a belated flaring of a worldwide Romantic movement whose genesis had nothing to do with America, but grew out of the Transcendental Idealism of the German Immanuel Kant, who in turn built on the work of Locke, Hume, and Berkeley in Great Britain, Leibniz in Germany, and Descartes in France. Emerson and Thoreau, voracious readers, were conscious of these sources, but conscious as well that although Romanticism was a source of their own thinking, America in turn was a central source of Romanticism. It is no accident that Kant's *Critique of Pure Reason* was contemporaneous with the creation of the United States of America or that Descartes – Shakespeare's contemporary – was writing at the time of the founding of the first French and English colonies in America.

The American and foreign roots of nineteenth-century American philosophy and literature cannot be disentangled: This is part of what makes that work so American, as is the fact that it takes the identity of America to be a central subject. What America is, where it has come from, and what its destiny may be are central themes through which American culture has continually defined itself. In the crucial period from 1908 to the country's entrance into World War I, the period when narrative film was taking root, American film took up this question of America's identity, culminating in *The Birth of a Nation*, the film that definitively demonstrated to the American public the awesome power that movies could manifest. Indeed, in the work of D. W. Griffith, the dominant figure of American film during those years, America's destiny and the destiny of film were fatefully joined.

Griffith started out with an idealistic vision: America's destiny was to save the world, and film's destiny was to save America. By the time of *The Birth of a Nation*, however, he had drawn closer to the more ambiguous, darker visions of Hawthorne, Poe, and Melville. He had made the disquieting discovery that in affirming innocence, the camera violates innocence; however idealistic their intention, movies touch what is base as well as what is noble in our souls. This knowledge, with which he struggled his entire career, is Griffith's most abiding – if least recognized – legacy to American film.

In *Indian Film*, a landmark study, Erik Barnouw and S. Krishnaswamy shrewdly insist that neither historians nor sociologists can give us precise answers regarding the impact of film on society. They limit themselves to a qualified endorsement of the claim, made on the occasion of the twenty-fifth anniversary of the Indian film industry, that film "has unsettled the placid contentment of the Indian masses, it has filled the minds of youth with new longings, and is today a potent force in national life."[1] In other words, although we may well never fully understand film's efficacy in causing or resisting social change in India, we can at least say that film has been centrally involved in the process by which Indian society has adapted itself to modern ideas. In the clash between modern ideas and orthodox Hindu canons on such matters as untouchability and the role of women, film in India (at least until recent years) has been allied, implicitly or explicitly, with the forces of modernity.

Griffith's attitude toward modern ideas, especially concerning the role of women, was ambivalent. That ambivalence was most pointedly expressed in the tension between his flowery, moralistic intertitles and the dark mysteries he conjured with his camera. Griffith combined a Victorian conviction that it was proper for women to be submissive with a profound respect for the intelligence, imagination, and strength of the women in his films. And what remarkable women he had the intuition to film! As I ponder Griffith's

[1] Erik Barnouw and S. Krishnaswamy, *Indian Film* (Oxford University Press, 1980), p. 102.

spellbinding visions of Lillian Gish, Mae Marsh, Blanche Sweet, and others, I am struck equally by the voraciousness of his desire for women and his uncanny capacity to identify with them.

After the war, the American film industry grew to international dominance. The postwar Hollywood in which Griffith struggled fruitlessly to reclaim his preeminence clearly allied itself with the libertarian spirit of the "Jazz Age." But with all their glamour and spectacle, their Latin lovers, flappers, and "It" girls, Hollywood films of the twenties never really made clear what that spirit was, nor it sources, nor the grounds of its opposition to orthodox ideas, nor the identity of the orthodoxy it was opposing. Following the withdrawal or repression of Griffith's seriousness of purpose, the years from the end of the war to the late twenties are the obscurest period in the history of American film.

We are taught that that was the "Golden Age of Silent Film," the age when film became a glorious international art and language. Yet those were also the years when Hollywood's power over the world's film production, and its hold on the world's film audiences, came closest to being absolute. Strangely, except for the occasional cause célèbre, such as von Stroheim's *Greed*, the magnificent comedies of Chaplin and Keaton, and Murnau's *Sunrise* (which, together with Chaplin's *City Lights*, provided the swan song for that era), no American film of that period still has an audience (beyond a core of hardened film buffs), even among film students.

Coming at a time of creative crisis, the simultaneous traumas of the new sound technology and the Great Depression (which brought about changes in studio organization and ownership) disrupted the continuity of American film history. There was an influx of personnel – directors, actors, writers, producers – from the New York stage (and, increasingly, from abroad, as political conditions worsened in Europe). By and large, the Broadway imports (unlike the Europeans) were unlettered in film. They approached the new medium with ideas whose sources were to be found elsewhere than in the history of earlier film achievements. Then again, "the talkies" were a new medium for everyone, even for movie veterans for whom filmmaking had been their education.

When Hollywood movies began to speak, no one could foresee the new genres that would emerge. It took several years of experimentation, of testing the limits, before a new system of production was securely in place and a stable new landscape of genres and stars became discernible. The release of *It Happened One Night* in 1934, the first year of rigid enforcement of the Production Code, can be taken to inaugurate the era of what has come to be known as "the classical Hollywood film."

Such films as *It Happened One Night*, for all their comedy, revived Griffith's seriousness of moral purpose and his original conviction that film's awesome power could awaken America, in the throes of a nightmare, to its authentic identity. Or perhaps it is more accurate to say that classical Hollywood films leapfrogged Griffith to link up directly with nineteenth-century American transcendentalism.

It was Stanley Cavell who first recognized the implications of this. In his seminal book *Pursuits of Happiness*,[2] Cavell defined a genre he named "the comedy of remarriage" (the central members of this genre include: *It Happened One Night, The Awful Truth, Bringing Up Baby, His Girl Friday, The Philadelphia Story, The Lady Eve*, and *Adam's Rib*).

In remarriage comedies, men and women are equals. They have equal rights to pursue happiness and are equal spiritually – equal in their abilities to imagine and to demand human fulfillment, as Cavell puts it. In these films, happiness is not arrived at by a couple's overcoming social obstacles to their love, as in traditional comedy, but by facing divorce and coming back together, overcoming obstacles that are between and within themselves.

Indian film, in siding against orthodox Hinduism, and Japanese film, in siding against feudal consciousness, endorse the claim that women have the right to marry for love. There are classical Hollywood films – *Camille* is one that comes to mind – in which feudal attitudes and religious orthodoxy obstruct the course of love, but such films typically are set in the past and set elsewhere than in America. American society, as presented in the remarriage comedies, already sanctions the right of women to marry and even to divorce for reasons of the heart. It is marriage itself, the nature and limits of its bond, that is at issue in these films – at issue, that is, philosophically.

Cavell understands the women of these films, played by the likes of Katharine Hepburn, Claudette Colbert, Irene Dunne, and Barbara Stanwyck, as being on a spiritual quest, like Thoreau in *Walden*, Emerson in his journals, and the poet in Whitman's "Song of the Open Road." A non-American source he cites is Nora in Ibsen's *A Doll's House*, who leaves her husband in search of an education he says she needs but she knows he cannot provide. The implication, as Cavell points out, is that only a man capable of providing such an education thereby could count for her as her husband. The woman of remarriage comedy is lucky enough to be married to a man like Cary Grant or Spencer Tracy who has the capacity, the authority, to preside over her education, her creation as a new woman.

[2] Stanley Cavell, *Pursuits of Happiness: The Hollywood Comedy of Remarriage* (Cambridge, MA: Harvard University Press, 1981).

In "Psychoanalysis and Cinema: The Melodrama of the Unknown Woman," a paper Cavell delivered in 1984 at a forum on psychiatry and the humanities, he goes on to ask himself:

> What of the women on film who have not found and could not manage or relish relationship with such a man, Nora's other, surely more numerous, descendants? And what more particularly of the women on film who are at least the spiritual equals of the women of remarriage comedy but whom no man can be thought to educate – I mean the women we might take as achieving the highest reaches of stardom, of female independence as far as film can manifest it – Greta Garbo and Marlene Dietrich and at her best Bette Davis?[3]

This question leads Cavell to discover a second genre of classical Hollywood film, which he calls "the melodrama of the unknown woman" (*Blonde Venus, Stella Dallas, Random Harvest, Now, Voyager, Mildred Pierce, Gaslight, Letter from an Unknown Woman*).

One cost of the woman's happiness in the comedies is the absence of her mother (often underscored by the attractive presence of the woman's father), as well as her own failure to have children, her denial as a mother. In the melodramas, the woman does not forsake motherhood and is not abandoned to the world of men. No man presides over her metamorphosis, and it leads not to the ideal marriages the comedies teach us to envision but to a possible happiness apart from or beyond satisfaction by marriage. As in the remarriage comedies, it is not society that comes between a woman and a man – not, for example, the threat of social scandal or a law that can be manipulated to separate her from her child. Rather, it is the woman's absolute commitment to her quest to become more fully human.[4]

In "Virtue and Villainy in the Face of the Camera," I argue that *Stella Dallas* – one of the films Cavell includes within the genre of the melodrama of the unknown woman – in no way glorifies a woman's submission to a system that unjustly denies her equal right to pursue happiness. My understanding of the film, like Cavell's, rejects the generally accepted critical view that such melodramas affirm a woman's noble sacrifice of her happiness, that they affirm that there are things more important than a woman's

[3] Stanley Cavell, "Psychoanalysis and Cinema: The Melodrama of the Unknown Woman," in Joseph H. Smith and William Kerrigan, eds., *Images in Our Souls: Cavell, Psychoanalysis, Cinema* (*Forum for Psychiatry and the Humanities*, Volume 10, 1987) (Baltimore: Johns Hopkins University Press), pp. 11–43.

[4] Cavell notes that this feature distinguishes films in this genre from *Madame Bovary* and *Anna Karenina*. It may also be pointed out that it equally distinguishes the American melodramas from the films of Kenji Mizoguchi in Japan, which might seem to offer a parallel. Actually, Ozu's films probably have a more intimate kinship with the American films.

happiness. When Stella, standing outside in the rain, unseen, watches her daughter's wedding through a window and then turns away with a secret smile, she is not a figure of pathos, but a mysterious, heroic figure who has transformed herself before our very eyes, with no help from any man in her world. This is a transcendental moment of self-fulfillment, not self-sacrifice.

Through such genres as the remarriage comedy and the melodrama of the unknown woman – and, by extension, the whole interlocking system of genres that emerged in the mid-thirties – classical Hollywood films inherited the Victorian faith in the marvelous and terrifying powers of women and fulfilled a deep-seated nineteenth-century wish by placing a "new woman" on view.

In the decade or so after 1934, Hollywood films were intellectually of a piece, like network television today. The diverse genres were not in ideological opposition, but derived from a common set of ideas and a common body of knowledge – at one level, knowledge about the medium of film. But by the mid-forties, that commonality began to break down. Although extraordinary films like *Adam's Rib, Letter from an Unknown Woman*, and *Notorious* continued to keep faith with the classical Hollywood vision, a regressive tendency was ascendant.

I think of film noir, for example, as regressive because it disavows the vision of classical Hollywood melodramas and comedies without addressing their ideas. In *Double Indemnity*, there is a moment that is emblematic of this failure. As Fred MacMurray is struggling to kill her husband, Barbara Stanwyck sits silently in the front seat of the car. The camera captures the look on her face, which is meant to prove that she is the incarnation of evil. Yet in the face of the camera, she remains unknown to us, like Stella Dallas (also Barbara Stanwyck, of course) when she turns away from watching her daughter's wedding and smiles a secret smile. *Stella Dallas*, like other classical Hollywood melodramas and comedies, interprets the unknownness of the woman as an expression of her humanity, hence of our bond with her, forged from within. *Double Indemnity*, withdrawing from that understanding without acknowledging it – an understanding about women, about humanity, about the camera and the medium of film – interprets the woman's unknownness as a mark of her inhumanity, which makes it rightful for Fred MacMurray to kill her – alas, too late – at the end of the film.

By the fifties, American movies were divided on ideological grounds in ways that mirrored the political divisions – and, unfortunately, the debased political rhetoric – of a country racked by the paranoia of the McCarthy era. Within each of the major fifties genres, "liberal" and "conservative" films struck opposing positions, as Peter Biskind argues in *Seeing Is Believing*, his study of Hollywood films of the period.[5] But except for a number of directors of the older generation, such as Ford, Hawks, and Hitchcock, the classical Hollywood voice – and conscience – had fallen silent.

Hollywood's audience was fragmenting. The older generation, once the audience for classical Hollywood films, stayed home and watched television. Why the men and women of this generation abandoned movies, or were abandoned by movies, is no less a mystery than why they once demanded movies that spoke to them with the greatest seriousness. Surely they could not really have believed that America in the fifties fulfilled the transcendental aspirations expressed by the movies they had taken to heart. Yet they opted for television's reassurance that what was happening now was not really passing them by, that they were plugged into a human community after all. At the same time, rock 'n' roll (with its seductive promise of breaking down barriers now), not film (in which a screen separates the audience from the world of its dreams), fired the imagination of the young. The fate of film in America, and the longing to become more fully human that it expressed, hung – and still hangs – in the balance.

In the fifties, a new generation of American directors, Nicholas Ray perhaps the most gifted among them, made the "generation gap" their subject in films that, identifying with the young, dwelled on such matters as the failure of American fathers to pass on something of value to their sons. An avant-garde attempted to create a new American cinema – unfortunately, without undertaking to learn the first thing about the old. "Method acting" struggled to infuse film with an authenticity that was eluding it, as did cinema-vérité documentary in the sixties. But despite this activity, Hollywood tended to drift farther from its sources and from even the memory of its past achievements. America was losing a knowledge it has not since reclaimed, as witness the creative crisis today facing a film industry mostly intent on producing products that are the moral equivalent of video games – films that parody our perilous existence as human survivors even as they deny that anything important is at stake.

When I say that knowledge has been lost, I certainly mean to imply that there has been a failure of education and, in turn, of criticism. Even today, film students in America are taught (and most contemporary film criticism underwrites this) to dismiss remarriage comedies like *It Happened One Night* as mere "fairy tales for the Depression" and to despise melodramas like *Stella Dallas* for their supposedly regressive attitude toward women.

It is especially poignant that the recent upsurge in feminist film criticism has so far remained less than fully attentive to the depth of the feminism

[5] Peter Biskind, *Seeing Is Believing* (New York: Pantheon Books, 1983).

of classical Hollywood films. In part, this blindness testifies to the current extent of the dogmatic acceptance, within academic film departments, of a number of seductive but flawed theories. Especially influential among feminist film critics is Laura Mulvey's theory that classical Hollywood films subordinate women to the status of objects of the camera's male gaze. Accepting this premise, feminist criticism has failed to recognize that the camera in classical Hollywood films cannot simply be identified with the authority of the patriarchal order. Rather, the films take up and explore the implications of one of Griffith's central discoveries about the camera, also one of the deepest sources of film's universal appeal: In its passivity and its agency, its powers of creation and the limits of those powers, the camera is male *and* female. (This is one of the central themes of *Hitchcock – The Murderous Gaze.*)

The blindness of criticism to the achievements of American film goes deeper than the transient influence of any particular theory. After all, I have been suggesting that until the publication of *Pursuits of Happiness* forty years after the films were released, no critic had even articulated what the remarriage comedies – among the most popular films ever made – were really saying.

The gap that needs to be accounted for is not between readings like Cavell's and the ways audiences have experienced these films (I do not believe there is such a gap) but between the ways we experience films and the ways we ordinarily speak about them. What makes this gap possible is the fact that movies address matters of intimacy and do so in a language of indirectness and silence. From the beginnings of film history, what it is that actually takes place within and among silent viewers in those darkened halls has been a mystery. In the thirties and forties, film was the dominant medium of our culture, and yet public discourse about film (no doubt this was true of private conversation as well) virtually never attempted to probe the truth of our experience of movies. But perhaps this should not surprise us, for it simply underscores the fact that movies expressed ideas that had no other outlet in our society. Except within the discourse of films themselves, America's experience of film, its knowledge of film, has always been and remains primarily unarticulated, unconscious. If we are to understand film's impact on society, this knowledge must be brought to consciousness. Criticism must finally fulfill its role.

Movies exercise a hold on us, a hold we participate in creating, drawing on our innermost desires and fears. To know a film's impact, we have to know the film objectively. To know a film objectively, we have to know the hold it has on us. To know the hold a film has on us, we have to know ourselves objectively. And to know ourselves objectively, we have to know the impact of the films in our lives. The idea of a criticism that aspires to be at once objective and rooted in the critic's experience (yet another idea whose American and non-American sources cannot be disentangled) is one that Stanley Cavell has taught me to associate with the names of Kant, Emerson, Thoreau, Kierkegaard, Nietzsche, Freud, Heidegger, and Wittgenstein – and Cavell himself. Such criticism forsakes the wish – without denying the depth of its motivation – to find a "scientific" methodology that would give us an unchallengeable place to stand outside our own experience. It is a central tenet of American transcendentalism that such a place must always be illusory: We cannot arrive at objective truth without checking our experience.

Feeling legitimized by the latest "postmodernist critical methodologies," too many academic film critics today deny their experience of classical Hollywood films, refuse to allow themselves to take instruction from them. Predictably, the resulting criticism reaffirms an attitude of superiority to the films and their audiences. Echoing a long-familiar strain in American cultural life, such criticism furthers rather than undoes the repression of these films and the ideas they represent.

We critics can play our part in undoing that repression only if we perform our acts of criticism in the spirit of classical Hollywood films. Like the Cary Grant character in *The Philadelphia Story*, we need the sagacity to demand to determine for ourselves what is truly important and what is not.[6] Equally needed is the capacity Grant reveals in *Bringing Up Baby* when he makes up for his lack of worldliness by announcing to Katharine Hepburn, in the final moments of the film, the truth of his experience of their day together: He never had a better time in all his life. We cannot play our part in reviving the spirit of the films we love without testifying, in our criticism, to the truth of our experience of those films: We never had a better time in all our lives.

[6] For an appreciation of the relevance of this example and the example that follows, I am indebted to Marian Keane's "The Authority of Connection in Stanley Cavell's *Pursuits of Happiness*," *Journal of Popular Film and Television*, 13(3):139–50 (Fall 1985), the most insightful and reliable essay concerning Cavell's writing about film.

CHAPTER 2

D. W. Griffith and the Birth of the Movies

Film was not invented to make movies possible. The Lumière brothers' first public screening in 1895 was the culmination of innumerable technical developments that finally allowed films to be made and projected, but the invention of film did not immediately give rise to movies as we know them. Within ten years, film had become a sizable industry and medium of popular entertainment, but news films, travelogues, films of vaudeville acts, trick films, and gag films were the dominant forms. Even as late as 1907, dramatic narratives constituted only one-sixth of the "product."

The turning point came in 1908. With the sudden growth of nickelodeons, respectable theaters intended primarily for the screening of films, producers turned to such "legitimate" fare as adaptations of novels and stage plays, and the dramatic narrative became the dominant form of film, as it has remained to this day. It was at this critical – and rather mysterious – juncture that the technology of film decisively linked up with the incipient idea of movies. Not entirely coincidentally, it was in 1908 that David Wark Griffith directed his first film.

Griffith was a struggling actor from Kentucky, no longer young, with fading dreams of attaining immortality as a playwright. In desperation, he accepted work with the American Biograph Company as a movie actor. When Biograph needed a new director, he stepped in.

In the next five years, working for Biograph, Griffith directed over five hundred short dramatic films in every imaginable genre – an inexhaustible treasure trove for students of film.

In 1913, Griffith took his next fateful step, breaking with Biograph when the company refused to release his *Judith of Bethulia* as a feature-length film. Striking out on his own, he produced as well as directed a series of extraordinary features culminating in *The Birth of a Nation* (1915), the

---

Reprinted: See "Notes on the Essays."

film that definitively demonstrated to the world how powerful movies could be.

The Birth of a Nation was an astounding commercial success, but controversy surrounded it from the beginning. It was embraced by the resurgent Ku Klux Klan, and the NAACP rallied opposition, attempting to have the film banned. Griffith was shocked at the accusations that his film inflamed racial hatred; by all accounts, that was not his conscious intention. As if in defense against such charges – some would say in atonement – he sank all his profits from *The Birth of a Nation* into *Intolerance*, a colossal, majestic film, but a commercial debacle.

Deeply in debt, Griffith struggled the rest of his life to regain financial independence. In the years after the end of World War I, he made a number of his greatest films, *Broken Blossoms, True Heart Susie* (my personal favorite), *Way Down East*, and *Orphans of the Storm* among them. Yet he never reclaimed his position and power in the film industry.

Movies had become a giant corporate business, centered in Hollywood, with a rationalized system of studio production to which Griffith never fully adjusted. It became increasingly difficult for him to find backing for his projects, and by the last years of his life he was a pathetic figure haunting Hollywood, abandoned by the industry that owed him so much. But this is not the place to dwell on the melancholy denouement of the Griffith story.

Griffith's years at Biograph were like Haydn's years at Esterhazy. Churning out two films a week for over five years provided endless opportunities for experimentation. If an idea didn't work the first time, he tried it again – and again. To study the evolution of Griffith's Biograph films from 1908 to 1913 is to witness movies being born – year by year, month by month, week by week.

Film students once were taught that Griffith single-handedly invented what is loosely called "the grammar of film" – continuity cutting, close-ups, point-of-view shots, iris shots, expressive lighting, parallel editing, and the other techniques and formal devices that movies have employed for almost a century. Recent scholarship has made it clear that Griffith did not actually originate any of the inventions that once had been credited to him. Precedents have been found for all his innovations. Although his films were intimately involved in that complex process, Griffith was not the "prime mover" in the development and institution of the set of rules and practices that constitute the grammar of the movies.

Yet the more I ponder film's mysterious history, the deeper my conviction of Griffith's centrality. Without Haydn, the symphony would have developed, but without the examples of Haydn's symphonies and quartets and sonatas, and without the ideas about music manifest in those examples, Beethoven would not have become the Beethoven we know. Without

Griffith, movies would have developed their grammar, and Hollywood would have become Hollywood but Chaplin would not have become Chaplin, nor Hitchcock Hitchcock, nor Renoir Renoir. The same can be said for Murnau, Dreyer, von Stroheim, Eisenstein, Ford, or von Sternberg. Griffith's centrality does not reside in a legacy he left to all subsequent movies, but in the inheritance he passed on to the greatest filmmakers of the succeeding generation. To them, Griffith was inescapable. From the period in which movies as we know them were born, it was Griffith's work alone that fully demonstrated the awesome power of the film medium, and it was Griffith's ideas about the conditions of that power that demanded – indeed, still demand – a response.

What movies are and what gives them their power are questions that vexed society at a time when the movies were fighting off their first attacks from would-be censors. Griffith's Biograph films are affirmations of the power of movies – and veiled (sometimes not so veiled) allegories justifying his unleashing of that power.

Consider *A Drunkard's Reformation* (1909), for example, a fascinating early Biograph film. It tells a story about the power of theater, but movies are what Griffith really has in mind. A young girl persuades her alcoholic father, who beats her whenever he is intoxicated, to go with her to a temperance play called *A Drunkard's Reformation.* At the theater, Griffith cuts back and forth between the actors on stage and the father and daughter in the audience. Gradually, the father begins to recognize himself in the drunkard on stage. As the stage father takes a drink and begins to beat his little girl, the father in the audience watches in fascination. His daughter views him warily out of the corner of her eye. Conscious of the play's intoxicating hold over him, she is afraid that theater, like whiskey, will release the monster within him. With the grace of God, this does not happen. Rather, the unfathomable power of theater brings him to his senses and saves his soul.

Griffith's Biograph films declared their innocent intention: to tap the awesome power of film in the hope of saving souls. By the time of *The Birth of a Nation*, however, Griffith's vision had grown darker, as is revealed in the remarkable sequence in which Mae Marsh, ignoring warnings, goes out alone to draw water from the spring. In a natural setting that dwarfs the merely human, Gus, a "renegade Negro," views Mae Marsh as she is absorbed in viewing a squirrel playing in a tree. Griffith cuts from a long shot of the girl to an iris insert of the squirrel. (This is not, strictly speaking, a point-of-view shot, but our view and hers do not essentially differ.)

He cuts back to the delighted and unself-conscious girl, then to a shot, notable for its expressionism, of Gus coming into the foreground to get a better view of something off screen that has struck his attention.

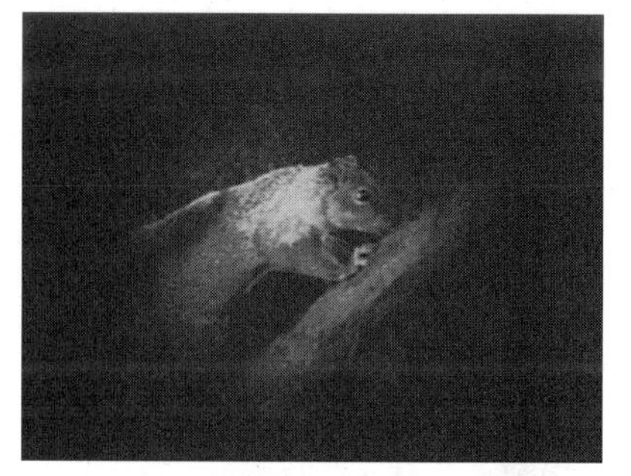

Registering the menace of Gus's gaze, the next shot of Mae Marsh is closer than the preceding view of her. Again, though, it is not literally a point-of-view shot. Nor is it inflected, expressively, with Gus's erotic desire.

Griffith cuts again to the playful squirrel and then back to the girl, delectable and frighteningly vulnerable in her unself-conscious absorption. In this context, the cut to the expressionistically composed tight close-up of Gus is deeply disturbing.

Gus is intoxicated by his views of the innocent girl. The twisted branches turn the frame into an expressive metaphor for the monstrous forces within him that his intoxication threatens to liberate.

In Griffith's dramaturgy, deeply indebted to Victorian melodrama, innocence and monstrousness are eternally at war for possession of the human soul. In the present sequence, Griffith explicitly links the act of viewing to both these opposing forces. But is our viewing, and Griffith's, innocent or monstrous?

The innocent girl is vulnerable to Gus – and vulnerable to the camera. In affirming innocence, the camera violates innocence; this is the most

disquieting discovery Griffith passed on to his successors. However innocent their intention, movies emerge out of darkness.

Monstrousness threatens to possess Gus; yet he is not a villain. A dupe of the ambitious mulatto Lynch, himself a victim of Stoneman, the twisted, hypocritical carpetbagger, Gus is a figure of pathos, like the lunatic in *A House of Darkness* (1913).

In this late Biograph film, one of Griffith's most transparent allegories about art's powers of redemption, a lunatic is intoxicated by his views of an innocent woman (Griffith's expressionistic framing of Gus's viewing recalls his framing of the lunatic here).

Wild-eyed, the lunatic advances on the woman. Providentially, at the critical moment, the sound of piano playing drifts in from another room. Music, like theater in *A Drunkard's Reformation*, has the power to save men's souls. The beautiful melody calms the lunatic and saves him – and the woman – from the darkness within. In *The Birth of a Nation*, however, Providence does not intervene to avert the tragedy.

Overcoming or surrendering to the monstrous forces within himself, Gus steps forward from his place as a secret viewer and presents himself to Mae Marsh. Heartbreakingly, he declares his love for her and proposes marriage. Reacting in horror, the terrified child flees. Gus runs after her, desperately trying to reassure her that he means no harm. She climbs to the top of a cliff, with the frenzied Gus close behind. When he steps forward again, apparently to stop her from leaping, she jumps to her death.

Moments later, the Little Colonel (Henry Walthall) comes upon his dying sister. Realizing what has happened, he stares into the camera, his face an expressionless mask.

Walthall, a magnificent actor, plays this as a scene out of Shakespearean tragedy, not melodrama. In his anguish and his despair, he dedicates himself to vengeance; this is what Walthall's acting, under Griffith's direction, expresses. His look to the camera calls upon us to acknowledge his guilt, not his innocence, for he knows in his heart that he has no right to condemn Gus – because he himself at this moment, with the camera as witness, guiltily embraces the dark, monstrous forces within himself.

The last third of *The Birth of a Nation*, with its nightmarish inversion of Griffith's cherished values, follows from this guilty moment. The vengeful Ku Klux Klan, emerging out of darkness, does not and cannot restore the rightful order. All it can do is allow our nation to be born; it cannot save its soul. The burden of *The Birth of a Nation* is that America was born with blood on its hands. Its soul remains to be saved.

Griffith's masterpiece casts movies, as well as America, in shadow. Vanished is his faith that movies will be our salvation. How could they be, when they emerge out of darkness?

Griffith's films after his break with Biograph no longer claim for themselves the power of salvation. Their aspiration is more modest: to help keep alive, during dark times, the distant dream of a world to come in which innocence may be restored to its rightful throne.

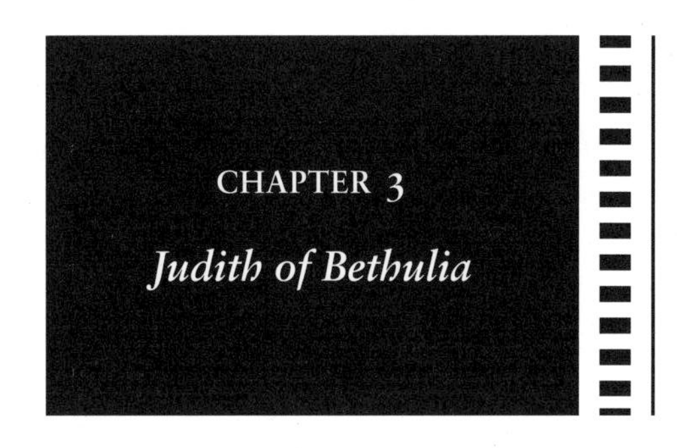

Judith of Bethulia (1913) was D. W. Griffith's first feature-length film. Griffith devoted extraordinary energy and attention to its making. Indeed, he broke irrevocably with the Biograph management, for whom he had directed over five hundred short films, by his refusal to shorten it or to release it as two separate two-reelers. The last film of Griffith's long and productive association with Biograph, it remained, in his own estimation, one of his very best films.

Everything points to the conclusion that *Judith of Bethulia* is a key film in Griffith's career. Indeed, it is a film of considerable compositional complexity, thematic directness, and cinematic artistry. In addition, it highlights a fundamental strain in Griffith's filmmaking, perhaps carrying it to the furthest extreme of any of his films. Thus, *Judith of Bethulia* helps provide a perspective on Griffith's work as a whole. Yet the film has received virtually no critical attention.

I shall proceed by first sketching the film's narrative (the division into sections is my own).

I. *Idyllic Prologue*: The film begins with a prologue depicting the life of the peaceful community of Bethulia. The first shots are of the well outside the city's walls. We see, for example, the innocent flirting of the young lovers, Naomi and Nathan (Mae Marsh and Robert Harron). Then the stout walls of the city are shown, and only then the marketplace within the walls of the city. Judith, the widow of the hero Manasses, is introduced. This prologue ends with a shot of the great "brazen gate" that guards the entrance to the city.

II. *The Assyrian Threat*: The Assyrians, led by Prince Holofernes, capture Bethulia's well. Naomi is among the prisoners taken. The Assyrians attempt

---

Reprinted: See "Notes on the Essays."

to storm the walls, but are repelled. In the Assyrian camp, Holofernes is enraged. He is not placated by the bacchanalian revel staged to please him. There is then a renewed all-out attempt to storm the city's walls and penetrate its gate. A pair of shots (one of the defenders and one of the attackers) is repeated three times, then followed by a shot of Judith watching and then a shot of Holofernes waiting. Then a new pair of shots of defenders and attackers – closer and more dynamic – is intercut with the shot of Judith, now visibly more excited, and the shot of the intent Holofernes. We then get still closer and more violent shots of defenders and attackers, and a wild fusillade of shots encompassing all the setups thus far used in the sequence. Finally the shot of Judith is followed by the image of a giant battering ram brought into place against the gate. Yet the gate holds.

III. *The Siege*: Holofernes takes counsel. The Assyrians lay Bethulia under siege. There are scenes of suffering within Bethulia (for example, doling out water to thirsty Bethulians). The people come to Judith, imploring her to lead them. She is in despair, but then she has a vision of "an act that will ring through the generations." (We are not shown Judith's vision.) She dons sackcloth and ashes and then bedecks herself in her "garments of gladness." At the Assyrian camp, Holofernes takes out his impatience and frustration on his captains. Judith, veiled, leaves for the Assyrian camp to carry out her mysterious plan.

IV. *The Seduction*: Judith enters Holofernes's tent and begins the process of seducing him. Enticingly evading his touch, she finally leaves his tent (" . . . his heart ravished with her"). There is prayer in the Bethulian marketplace. Holofernes's eunuch comes to Judith's tent to announce that Holofernes is ready to see her and that she should prepare herself. A title tells us what we can in any case see: Judith is aroused by the prospect of the impending encounter. Shots of Holofernes are intercut with other shots: Judith in excited anticipation; a desperate Pickett's Charge–like attempt by the Bethulians to reach the well, leading to renewed fighting at the walls; the separated Naomi and Nathan. Holofernes dismisses his erotic slave dancers (" . . . Famous Fish Dancers from the illustrious Temple of Nin"). Judith, faltering in her resolve, catches sight of her loyal old retainer and prays for strength. The eunuch summons Judith. In Holofernes's tent, Judith seductively entices Holofernes to drink, refilling his chalice until he collapses, dead drunk. Seeing him helpless, she hesitates, momentarily cradling his head. Then Griffith cuts to images of dead Bethulians, fallen in the attempt to retake the well, and suffering in the marketplace of Bethulia. Griffith cuts back to Judith, who raises Holofernes's sword to strike; then Griffith cuts to the exterior of the tent.

V. *The Bethulians's Triumph*: When the Assyrians discover that their leader has been killed, there is chaos in their ranks. In the marketplace of Bethulia, Judith triumphantly unwraps the severed head of Holofernes. The Bethulian soldiers, transformed, pour out of the city's gate, defeat the Assyrians, and raze their camp. Naomi and Nathan are reunited.

VI. *Epilogue*: Judith passes through the marketplace. The Bethulians bow before her. She walks out of the frame.

Any discussion of *Judith of Bethulia* might well begin with a reflection on the character of Judith, in particular, her sexuality. In the context of Griffith's work, Judith's sexuality is noteworthy in two general ways: its "womanliness" and its "manliness." In contrast, for example, to Mae Marsh in *The Birth of a Nation,* Judith is very much a woman, although Blanche Sweet was only fifteen years old at the time. Judith's womanliness has three aspects.

1. *Judith's womanly beauty*. Griffith presents Judith's womanly beauty directly to the viewer. Griffith gives us images of Judith that are neither his Victorian "Madonna" idealizations nor his patented depictions of "dear" girlish behavior (jumping up and down with enthusiasm, and the like). Nor are they the "familiar" representations so common in Griffith's work (the presentation of Nathan and Naomi is, in this sense, "familiar," with the camera asserting a patriarchal authority over its subjects, exposing their tender cores, treating them as children). In the shots of Judith in sackcloth and ashes, the usual dematerializing effect of Griffith's makeup is eliminated in shots that anticipate Carl Dreyer's *The Passion of Joan of Arc* in their acknowledgment that a woman's face is made of flesh.

Certain shots of Judith preparing to seduce Holofernes, and engaged in that seduction, reflect a frank acknowledgment (again, rare in Griffith's images of women) that a woman has a body made from flesh that includes, say, armpits and breasts.

2. *Judith's knowledge of sexuality*. Complementing Judith's beauty are her knowledge and mastery of every stage of seduction. Her womanly confidence in her own sexuality is manifest in her peacocklike strutting, dressed in her "garments of gladness" in the full ensemble, her beauty

enticingly veiled, and in the knowing way she parts her veil. Judith’s hands, especially, become instruments of seduction. The focus on hands, effected by the use of the frame line as well as costuming and gesture, is one of the main strategies of the film. Judith’s womanhood is expressed in her hands, and Holofernes’s manhood is concentrated in his. For example, when he comes to the entrance of Judith’s tent, he enters the frame hands-first.

When Judith enters his tent for the first time, each stage of the seduction is registered in a pose or gesture of their hands. The erotically charged images of Holofernes’ hand reaching for Judith’s tantalizingly withheld hand are intercut with the Bethulians, begging for water, imploringly holding out their hands.

When Judith kills Holofernes, his death is registered by the cessation of movement of his hands (shades of Hitchcock’s *Blackmail*). It is Judith’s hands, now transformed, that wield the sword.

3. *Judith’s desire.* When the Assyrians make their all-out attempt to penetrate the great brazen gate, the battle is imaged symbolically as an attempted rape: Bethulia is, as it were, a woman threatened with violent penetration. The title summing up the sequence makes the underlying parallel all but explicit: “Yet Holofernes could not batten down the brazen gate nor make a single breach.” The climax of the sequence is the appearance of the terrible, revelatory image of the giant battering ram.

The shots of fighting, cut in a crescendo of intensity, are intercut with repeated shots of Holofernes waiting in his tent and Judith watching the battle from her window. The shots of Judith and Holofernes are linked in their composition.

Throughout the film, in fact, the left side of the frame tends to be dominated by either Judith's presence or Holofernes' presence, implying the bond between them.

The spectacle, climaxing in the image of the battering ram, fills Judith with ever-increasing excitement. When Judith subsequently places herself in Holofernes's hands, pretending to offer herself, but really meaning to kill him, she finds herself sexually drawn to his majestic, bull-like presence. He has inflamed her passion even before they meet.

Despite Judith's intentions, she is sorely tempted not to kill Holofernes but to surrender her body to him. It is not that, in her intoxication with her enemy, she is motivated by the idea that he is good (as is, for example, the Mountain Girl, infatuated with Belshazzar, in the Babylonian story of *Intolerance*). A title declares " . . . And Holofernes became noble in Judith's eyes," but Griffith is using "noble" in accordance with the pseudobiblical language characteristic of most of the titles in the film ("Nathan could scarce refrain from going to the succor of Naomi" is among the more risible examples) and means nothing more than "splendid." In Holofernes' tempting presence, Judith does not think in moral terms at all, and it is not any idea of marriage or family that inflames her.

That the wiles of the "paint-and-powder brigade" have the power to tempt and/or deceive good men is a basic fact of life in Griffith's narrative universe. It is the strategy of these worldly women to excite eligible men, while at the same time presenting a falsely innocent face to the world. In *True Heart Susie* (1919), William is disillusioned when he learns Bettina's true nature. It is perhaps only in *The White Rose* (1923) – arguably the Griffith film that is most fully worked out thematically – that Griffith presents a good man inflamed by the erotic presence of a woman he knows to be "bad." But the presentation of the good Judith drawn to the splendid yet brutal Holofernes is perhaps unique in all of Griffith's films in its acknowledgment, and acceptance, of the dark side of a woman's sexual desire.

Judith is every inch a woman, yet the second noteworthy aspect of her sexuality is that the people of Bethulia call upon her to act as their leader – that is, as Griffith understands it, to assume a man's role. While Judith watches the spectacle of the battle, she is visibly aroused, as though part of her desires the Assyrians' penetration. But she is also racked with guilt. She wants to answer the Bethulians' call, but she feels powerless to lead them in battle. It is in this state, compounded of arousal and despair, that Judith has her first vision – a vision that, significantly, Griffith withholds from the viewer, although the presentation of holy visions is one of his specialties (as witness, for example, *The Avenging Conscience, Home Sweet Home*, and even *The Birth of a Nation*).

Acting on her vision, Judith puts on her "garments of gladness" and goes to Holofernes as though she were his bride. To complete her envisioned act, she must harden herself, conquering her own desire. Thus, a fateful struggle takes place in Holofernes's tent. How is the outcome of this struggle determined?

Providentially, Judith catches sight of her loyal old retainer. This is nicely presented in a deep-focus shot with Judith in the foreground, the retainer in the background, and a smoking censer in the right foreground. Visually, the censer is linked with the well outside Bethulia's gate – directly by its shape and inversely by the water/fire opposition that runs through the film.

This shot is intercut with the representation of a simultaneous event: the ambush of a group of brave Bethulians who try to draw water from the captured well. This kind of crosscutting in Griffith's work implies a virtual psychic connection. Although Judith cannot actually see this display of barbarism, the sight of the retainer at this moment is functionally equivalent to such a view, serving to make Judith mindful of her people's suffering. A spasm of disgust passes through Judith – disgust for her own body sinfully drawn to the agency of her people's suffering, I take it. She prays to the Lord for strength.

Judith talks Holofernes into dismissing his eunuch so that she can be his sole "handmaid" for the night. Alone with Holofernes in his tent, she finds herself again inflamed with desire. Repeatedly, she fills his chalice and goads him into drinking himself into a state of intoxication. For a moment, she cradles his head in her arms, but then a second vision comes to her. The cinematographer Karl Brown describes this moment:

> His highest objective, as nearly as I could grasp it, was to photograph thought. He could do it too. I'd seen it. In *Judith of Bethulia*, there was a scene in which Judith stands over the sleeping figure of Holofernes, sword in hand. She raises the sword, then falters. Pity and mercy have weakened her to a point of helpless irresolution. Her face softens to something that is almost love. Then she thinks, and as she thinks, the screen is filled with the mangled bodies of those, her own people, slain by this same Holofernes. Then her face becomes filled with hate as she summons all her strength to bring that sword whistling down upon the neck of what is no longer a man but a blood-reeking monster.[1]

Actually, what Griffith shows here is not, as it were, natural thought, but a God-given vision. When Judith is transformed by this second vision, the manhood passes out of Holofernes' hands and animates hers.

In Griffith's imagery, the city of Bethulia itself undergoes a parallel sexual metamorphosis. The climactic image of the rout of the Assyrians is a shot of the triumphant Bethulians pouring out of the brazen gate. In reversal of the earlier images of Bethulia as a woman, Griffith here images the city as a potent man.

Judith of Bethulia centers on the dramatic struggle within Judith – spiritual, yet imaged in sexual terms and mirrored by the armed struggle between the Bethulians and the Assyrians – to perform an act that appears to deny her womanly nature. How can this struggle, and specifically its triumphant and liberating resolution, be reconciled with the affirmation, fundamental to Griffith's work, of an order in which sexuality can be fulfilled naturally only through love within a marriage?

To begin to answer this question, it is necessary to reflect on Griffith's understanding of the natural history of a woman. When a woman grows from an infant and baby and becomes a girl, she simultaneously starts to play with dolls and begins to develop (at first unaware) the ability to attract men. When she comes of age and blossoms into a young woman, the

[1] Karl Brown, *Adventures with D. W. Griffith* (New York: Farrar, Straus & Giroux, 1973), p. 12.

change is twofold. Unless tutored in the wily ways of the paint-and-powder brigade (as is, for example, Mae Marsh in *The White Rose*; Lillian Gish, by contrast, is constitutionally unable to master the simplest wile), she continues to act in public as a girl. But she knows that her girlishness now veils her womanhood, a mystery never to be betrayed.

In defending her "trust" – her virgin womanhood – she is prepared to fight like a man. Only within the privacy and sanctuary of a marriage may she reveal herself as a woman. Her mystery now revealed, what follows naturally is that she becomes transformed into a mother. Her womanhood fulfilled, her trust now passes from her own body to the walls of her home, which enclose and protect her baby, as her womb once did. Evil threatens, no longer rape, but its equivalent, violence to her baby. Now she will fight like a man to protect her home.

The paint-and-powder brigade is made up of women who display their womanhood in public, although what they reveal is not womanhood in all its mystery and beauty but only a monstrous caricature: When a woman betrays her trust, she loses her true beauty. It follows logically that womanliness in Griffith's films – unlike girlishness, manliness, or motherhood – is ordinarily invisible, or at least out of bounds for the camera. How can womanliness be filmed, without violating its sanctity? But then what makes Griffith's presentation of Judith possible?

As a childless widow, Judith is no longer a girl, and she is no virgin: She has been initiated into the life of marriage, has revealed her womanhood and given her trust. (If a Griffith virgin were granted Judith's vision, she would not understand it.) Yet she remains childless, denied that natural fulfillment of a woman.

Is Holofernes the man who can fulfill Judith? Griffith takes great pains to present Holofernes as a majestic figure. In general, Griffith's visual treatment of men, the ways in which his camera differentiates among, for example, Henry Walthall, Robert Harron, Richard Barthelmess, Lionel Barrymore, Donald Crisp, Joseph Schildkraut, Ivor Novello, and Walter Huston, is as crucial to his filmmaking as his treatment of women. It was no mean feat to transform slight Henry Walthall into such an imposing figure. This is attested to by Karl Brown. At his first meeting with Billy Bitzer, the cinematographer of *Judith of Bethulia*, Bitzer at first scoffed when Brown offered himself as an assistant. As Bitzer and Griffith were about to depart, Brown pleaded: "'Please, Mr. Bitzer! I know I'm not wanted, but before you go, will you *please* tell me how you managed to make Hank Walthall look so big in *Judith of Bethulia*?' He stopped and stared at me. I continued recklessly. ' . . . If you'll please tell me, I won't ever bother you any more, honest I won't.' His face softened into kindness. 'Sure, be glad to. But it'll take a little time. Report for work at nine tomorrow and I'll show you what you have to do.'"[2]

Holofernes' bull-like majesty and the power of his armies – crystallized in the image of the giant battering ram – arouse Judith. If Holofernes is fully a man – one who can take the place of her dead husband – then he can fulfill Judith in the natural way, and she need not carry out her plan. But, of course, Holofernes does not pass this test. If he were fully a man, he would have succeeded in penetrating the gate of Bethulia.

When Judith succeeds in enticing Holofernes to drink himself into a stupor, she knows that he cannot satisfy her. (For Griffith, any man who drinks to intoxication always thereby exposes a weakness of character that is also a sexual weakness.) Her realization of her power over him shatters the illusion of Holofernes' manhood and frees Judith from her temptation.

For a moment, she cradles his sleeping head in her arms, as if her womanly nature tempts her to view him as the child she so passionately desires, or to imagine bearing his child. This temptation cannot be defeated by any display of power over him, but only by another God-given vision: a vision of the death and suffering that Holofernes has wrought on Bethulia.

Once Holofernes' monstrousness is exposed, Judith's womanhood no longer protects him from her. She becomes transformed. Wielding the sword like a man, she slays the monster and cuts off his head, symbolically castrating him. (Like Judith's first vision, this unnatural act is not – cannot be – framed by Griffith's camera.) When she displays the severed head in the marketplace, she acts as Bethulia's triumphant leader, revealing – to her people and to us – that she has assumed her dead husband's place. This revelation is the climax of the film.

By surrendering herself to her visions, Judith assumes a woman's role, as Griffith understands it, in relation to the power that grants her vision. The moment at which she unmasks Holofernes, the moment at which she gives herself completely to this higher power, is the moment of her fulfillment as a woman. Yet, paradoxically, this is also the moment at which she performs a man's act, is transformed into a man. This paradox is fundamental to Griffith's understanding of what it is to be a woman. When her trust is threatened, a true woman reveals that she possesses a man within her.

The man within Judith is Manasses. But although their marriage proves still to be alive, does it remain issueless? Is she left unfulfilled as a woman

[2] Karl Brown, *Adventures with D. W. Griffith* (New York: Farrar, Straus & Giroux, 1973), p. 12.

after all? The film's answer is that Judith's act gives life to the city itself. Judith has become the mother of Bethulia.

Reborn, the city is transformed. Bethulia's soldiers have at last become men: They storm out of the city's gate to rout the disordered Assyrian forces. Naomi and Nathan are reunited, their fruitfulness assured.

This rebirth in turn transforms Judith. Her transformation is reflected in the final shot of the film. In the marketplace, within Bethulia's walls, she passes into, through, and out of the frame. No one looks directly at her. Everyone bows before her. She no longer lives in the city, whose inhabitants are now all as her children. She dwells in a higher realm. She is no longer even the camera's subject.

This final shot invokes the characteristic closing of a Griffith film: a family united within its home – except, of course, that at the end of *Judith of Bethulia* the mother and father are both absent from the frame. This final shot also completes the series of equations between Judith's sexuality and the city of Bethulia. Bethulia is no longer a woman threatened by violation, and no longer a man; it is finally a home (whose walls are the symbolic equivalent of its mother's fulfilled sexuality).

Thus, the film's dramatic struggle is articulated in terms that are, after all, consistent with the laws of Griffith's narrative universe, and the character of Judith can be accounted for in Griffithian terms. Nonetheless, the film's drama, particularly in its resolution, remains extraordinary in Griffith's work. This is reflected in the fact that Judith's act, though inspired by holy visions, is in no sense Christian.

The general point that the film's resolution is not Christian – is, indeed, specifically pre-Christian – is crucial to understanding the place of this film in Griffith's work. *Judith of Bethulia* is Griffith's major Old Testament film.

The grounding of *Judith of Bethulia* in Old Testament tradition and morality is everywhere manifest. The central strategy of identifying a woman's sexuality with a city, for one thing, is familiar from the Old Testament. But also, the outcome of Judith's struggle is not that she softens and forgives Holofernes, redeeming the tyrant through love; her act of retribution for her people's suffering equals Holofernes' acts in its harsh cruelty. The film's eye-for-an-eye spirit may be seen, at one level, to determine the system of doubling – with symbolic equivalences and reversals – so characteristic of the film. The Assyrians cut off Bethulia from its water supply, and their tents are razed by flames. Holofernes attempts to penetrate Bethulia's gate with his battering ram, and Judith slays him with the sword. Judith's retainer doubles Holofernes' eunuch. And so on. This system of doubling in turn is linked to the doubling of the Judith/Holofernes and the Judith/Manasses pairs, and by the doubling of both by the Naomi/Nathan pair, by the doubling of the city and its captured well, and, most important, by the doubling of Judith and Bethulia.

Judith's consciousness serves as a field of battle for higher forces; up to a point, this reflects the general Griffith dramaturgy, laid out most explicitly in *Dream Street* (1921). Under the all-seeing Morning Star, the symbolic drama of *Dream Street* unfolds, motivated by the figures of the demonic violinist (whose mask of sensual beauty hides a face only an orthodontist could love) and a beatific preacher. The former's mad fiddling has the power to whip mortals into a Dionysian frenzy, whereas the latter's calm voice speaks in Apollonian strains.

The pre-Christian world of *Judith of Bethulia*, however, has no Morning Star to oversee it. This world is ruled by the Hebrew deity, who calls upon Judith to perform an act of violence, not an act of forgiveness; to harden, not soften.

Judith's motherhood is unnatural, for Griffith, in the sense that it is not Christian. It is perhaps only in *Abraham Lincoln* (1930) that Griffith presents a heroic act true to both Old Testament and New Testament morality: The modern-day Abraham gives birth to a nation, not through a liberating, triumphant, but unnatural sexual fulfillment, but through a Christian act of sacrifice.

The presentation of an un-Christian act as heroic is unusual in Griffith's work, but it does not in itself undermine the Christian identity of Griffith's camera. In telling this story of a pre-Christian world, Griffith's camera is freed from certain constraints, because the characters are not Christians, but other constraints remain. Thus, Griffith can film Judith in all her womanliness without betraying his principles, but he cannot show us her vision of the act that will "ring through the generations," or the unnatural act itself.

Of course, by refraining from showing us that vision or that act, Griffith at the same time strongly serves the interests of his narrative, investing the film with a central enigma (What is Judith planning to do?) and suspending its solution (What has Judith done?), intensifying the film's climax.

Thus, although Griffith does not violate his Christian morality in the depiction of Judith's struggle and the resolution of that struggle, that morality does not by itself account for the film, for the nature of Griffith's implication in this pre-Christian world (and the implication of his camera) remains to be determined. But that determination cannot be achieved apart from a critical account of the relationship, in Griffith's work, between his Christian moralizing and his violent eroticism. The latter emerges in a uniquely pure form in *Judith of Bethulia*, in part because it is his major film that asserts no Christian moral. But Griffith could never, in any case, negate his violent eroticism simply by asserting a moral. The tense and complex relationship between these conflicting strains dominates Griffith's work. It manifests itself in various guises: as an opposition between the theatrical and the poetic/transcendental; between the realistic and the dreamlike; between the representation and the symbolization of events; between the extreme linearity of the parallel-edited suspense sequences and a film's organic composition as a whole. It is this tension, above all, that engenders the specific density and texture of Griffith's films and accounts for their form.

CHAPTER 4

True Heart Griffith

After D. W. Griffith broke with the American Biograph Company over his wish to release *Judith of Bethulia* as a feature-length film, his output was divided between large-scale epics and more unassuming productions that show him in a different and in many ways more appealing light (although Griffith's greatest films, such as *The Birth of a Nation*, succeed as intimate dramas as well as epics). Of these deceptively modest films, *True Heart Susie* (1919) and the more famous *Broken Blossoms*, made in the same year, are the most charming, the most assured, and the most lovable. *True Heart Susie* is also one of Griffith's most prophetic meditations on the medium of film.

Susie (Lillian Gish) grows up in the small town of Pine Grove. (The film calls this Indiana, but who could doubt that Griffith is thinking of his native Kentucky?) She has been raised by her "Aunty" (Loyola O'Connor, whom Griffith loved to cast as a matronly woman bearing on her shoulders all the suffering of the ages), always expecting to marry William (Robert Harron) when the time comes. But when will he understand that she is the love of his life and claim her with a kiss?

Not wishing to stand in the way of William's making a name for himself, Susie sells her beloved cow and anonymously gives William the money that enables him to go to college (although Susie, who wins the school spelling bee, is obviously the better student of the two).

College, at once exhilarating and sobering, seduces William and fires his ambition. He gives little thought to Susie, who waits faithfully at home. When he returns from college, he falls for Bettina, a wily big-city girl who is visiting an aunt in Pine Grove. He assumes a position as the town's minister – his real ambition is to win fame as a writer – and chooses Bettina, not Susie, for his wife.

Reprinted: See "Notes on the Essays."

The marriage is an unhappy one, but William suffers in silence, dedicating himself to his ministry. Suffocated in the role of minister's wife, Bettina begins to sneak off to "wild" parties. One stormy night, Bettina "thoughtfully" goes out to get William a book he needs – but mainly to go to a party. When she loses her key and is caught in the rain, she knocks on Susie's door, tells her the truth, and prevails upon Susie to let her spend the night – and to lie to William for her. It turns out that Bettina, poor thing, has caught a chill. She dies, as Griffith's title not unsympathetically sums her up, "a little unfaithful," letting William believe that she caught her death procuring his book. In memory of this "service," he vows never to let another love enter his life. Only later, when Aunty informs him about Susie's sacrifice in sending him to college and one of Bettina's friends confesses to him how guilty she feels for her involvement in the party that claimed his wife's life, does he release himself from his vow. At last, he declares to Susie that he has loved her all his life, and they kiss.

True Heart Susie opens with the title "Is real life interesting? ... Every incident is taken from real life," followed by a dedication to the women who suffer "pitiful hours of waiting for the love that never comes." The film's claim for the reality of its incidents is tempered by its acknowledgment that its story departs from the romantic scenario as it unfolds in the lives of the true-hearted women (rhetorically, Griffith embraces them within his audience) whose pitiful waiting is not finally rewarded as is that of Susie. Indeed, Susie is doubly rewarded: William at last comes to know her, and all along she is known by Griffith and by us. In the face of the camera, Lillian Gish stands in for all the unknown Susies in the world to whom *True Heart Susie* offers not only pity but also a genuine, respectful appreciation.

That is, the film begins by declaring its reality to be authentically real and yet transfigured – transfigured, we might say, by the medium of film. This acknowledgment, sustained throughout the film, enables *True Heart Susie* to avoid the overblown and naive rhetoric of, say, *Intolerance* and to strike a fully satisfying narrative tone reminiscent of Jane Austen (hardly a name one usually associates with Griffith). One of Jane Austen's central achievements is the creation of a voice for herself as narrator, at once objective and delicately ironic, that fully registers the intimacy of her relationship with her characters. In *True Heart Susie*, perhaps uniquely in Griffith's work, indeed in the entire silent cinema, the titles consistently achieve such a voice.

In most of his films, Griffith composes at least some titles in a stilted, flowery diction that declares these pronouncements to be from "on high." Such titles are denials that the film's author is human, disavowals of the human feelings and attachments that Griffith's camera so eloquently expresses as well as reveals. In *True Heart Susie*, there is no conflict between camera and narrative voice: Griffith's titles declare that he is, in all essential ways, no different from the people who live within the world of his film.

One manifestation of Griffith's intimate bond with the world of *True Heart Susie* is the transparency of his identification with the obtuse figure of William. When William's first story, with which he hopes to make his mark as a writer, is accepted for publication, the letter of acceptance from the big-city publisher is not a little condescending in its praise of the story's "quaint characterizations." Through this letter, Griffith speaks volumes about the gap between William's sensibility (as revealed by the camera) and that of the publisher, a gap of which William has as yet little inkling. There is a gap here as well between William and Griffith, who is ruefully wise to the irony that *True Heart Susie* will gain much of its acceptance by virtue of the condescension of those who will prize its characterizations as merely quaint rather than true. But the gap between William and Griffith is also a reflection of their bond. William's naiveté and foolishness once were Griffith's own, *True Heart Susie* implies: William is a figure out of Griffith's past, Griffith as he once was.

It is not just William whom Griffith knows this intimately. One of the unprecedented achievements of Griffith's work as a whole is the creation of remarkably intimate relationships between his camera and the extraordinary women who are its dearest subjects. In *True Heart Susie*, Griffith "identifies" as deeply with Lillian Gish/Susie as with Robert Harron/William, and in this respect the film is characteristic of his work, not exceptional.

Griffith's bond with Susie is apparent in his handling of the film's opening sequence, the Friday afternoon spelling class. After correctly spelling the word "cry," William has the misfortune of drawing "anonymous" (this choice of word is a nice ironic touch). Susie turns her eyes toward him, knowing he is misspelling the word, looks toward the teacher, and then steps forward to take her turn. Upset, William raises his hand as if to lodge a protest. Aware of his feelings, Susie again looks toward him, deliberating whether or not to misspell the word on purpose. (All this, the camera effortlessly reveals to us.) As the teacher looks on beaming, Susie spells the word correctly. The deflated William lowers his hand, and he and Susie switch places, her eyes fixed on his as she steps around him.

Throughout this passage, Susie's inner conflict is perspicuous to a camera intimately attuned to her intelligence, her pride, her willfulness, her yearning for respectability, and her love of William. And Griffith gives voice to her feelings – and to his own sympathetic affection for her – with a priceless title: "Susie, like the girl in the verse: '*I'm sorry that I spelt the word, I hate to go above you. Because,*' the brown eyes lower fell, '*Because, you see, I love you.*'"

Griffith's ability to "get inside" Susie is also manifest at the beginning of this sequence when he introduces her with the title "the plain girl." It is not that Griffith is asserting that Susie is plain – Griffith can see what the camera reveals to us, that this is no plain-Jane, this is Lillian Gish, one of the world's great beauties. He is giving voice to Susie's image of herself, invoking Susie's inner voice. Again and again in *True Heart Susie*, Griffith's titles voice characters' ways of thinking about themselves and the events in which they are enmeshed. There is always a gap between the voices in such titles and Griffith's own voice; yet these titles also seem animated from within, as if they were remembered voices, voices out of the past or out of a dream. Again, it is as if Griffith is remembering who he once was and wondering what has become of him.

Griffith's intimate bond with Susie is no less eloquently acknowledged in those sequences in which he allows the camera's revelations to stand without authorial comment. I am thinking, for example, of the Chaplinesque passage in which Susie walks down a country lane and sees William and Bettina together (they don't see her) and the even more heartrending sequence in which Susie, believing that William is ready to propose to *her*, walks into William's house only to find Bettina in his arms.

In the former passage, there is a cut from a three-shot to Susie, and the camera holds on her. At once drawn to the spectacle and recoiling from it, she closes her eyes, stares again, looks away, looks back, turns her gaze away, turns back.

We imagine ourselves in Susie's place, and our heart goes out to her. We need no title to understand what she is feeling. In lieu of a title giving voice

to Susie's feelings – or his own – Griffith cuts to Susie at home that evening, alone with her diary, then to the words she is writing: "Perhaps after all will wait until spring" (to marry William). Susie's words say all. Or, rather, they say nothing, and allow us (given what the camera has revealed to us about her) to read everything between the lines.

When, in the latter sequence, Susie opens the parlor door and sees William embracing Bettina, Griffith again frames the three in a long-shot.

Griffith cuts to Susie silently struggling with herself to pull her eyes away, then to a shot that functions like a shot from her point of view (to the last stages of his career, Griffith resisted the true point-of-view shot), then back to the anguished Susie in a closer framing.

In a reprise of the long three-shot setup, Susie lowers her gaze and leaves. Griffith cuts to her in the hallway, then frames her in an intimate medium close-up against the wall. Within this frame, which is held for what seems an eternity, Susie smiles, laughs nervously, distractedly runs her finger over her lips, anxiously casts her gaze toward the door, despairingly looks down, and, finally, before fleeing from the house, stares in panic right into the camera.

Throughout this agonizing passage and its equally grueling sequel (Aunty makes Susie return to William's house, where she suffers through his announcement that he has "taken her advice" and is now engaged to Bettina), Griffith refrains from using any titles that do not simply relay what a character says. Again, we know Susie's feelings by taking in the camera's revelations and by imagining ourselves in her place. Again our heart goes out to her. Griffith breaks his silence only after the final image of this complex sequence fades out, and then only with the terse title "The merry wedding bells." This is followed by shots of Susie sadly beholding Bettina in her wedding gown, helping the bride with her train, and finally collapsing when the newlyweds depart in their carriage.

The bitter irony in the word "merry" is Griffith's sole verbal acknowledgment that he feels for Susie as we do. Otherwise, he allows her suffering to pass in silence, as if his feelings go without saying. This reticence is powerful testimony to the limits of language, the eloquence of silence – the eloquence of Griffith's silence and of Susie's, which is also the eloquence of Lillian Gish on film.

But what "goes without saying" here? Surely, it is Griffith's wonderful love for Susie and equally wonderful capacity to imagine himself in her place. Griffith's love for Susie also has a dark side, however (as always with Griffith, as always with film).

When she comes upon William and Bettina embracing, Susie's suffering takes the form of a paralyzing self-consciousness, a terror of being viewed (Is not this terror also rage?) as she now stands revealed. It is not simply the possibility of being viewed by William that paralyzes her, but of being viewed by anyone, because she is afraid to face herself at this moment, to face her terror and rage. Hence the profundity of Griffith's strategy for conveying the nature and unfathomable depth of Susie's suffering: He simply positions her against a wall and films her becoming more and more self-conscious. We are viewing Susie's self-consciousness, acted out by Lillian Gish with Griffith's direction or perhaps his withholding of direction. But at another level, this is no act; we are viewing Lillian Gish's real self-consciousness in the face of the camera. When this self-consciousness culminates in casting a desperate look to the camera, actress and character are joined in this gaze.

And director and actress are joined in the understanding that in the medium of film, self-consciousness is consciousness of the camera – consciousness of the self as the camera reveals it, consciousness of the self the camera represents. The camera not only reveals self-consciousness but also is its source: The camera represents the gaze of others that paralyzes Susie, and it also represents her inner gaze, in the face of which her naked, vulnerable self stands exposed.

Susie's anguished self-consciousness is the camera's visible mark – Griffith's mark, our mark – on her: This is the darkness in what "goes without saying" about the passage. With the words "The merry wedding bells," Griffith declares his love for Susie, which is his love for Lillian Gish, but he is speaking to us, not to her, and is also acknowledging his continuing responsibility for her suffering – the responsibility of his silence. In turn, this guilt is Griffith's deepest bond with William.[1]

In a crucial sequence early in the film, William, strolling in the woods with Susie, carves their initials on a tree trunk and almost kisses her. As he leans toward her, her lips are pursed and her eyes closed in ecstasy, but William and Susie do not come together. It is as though there were an invisible barrier between them. Then, suddenly self-conscious, he hesitates and pulls back.

By flashbacks and subtle invocations of the framings within this sequence, passage after passage echoes this moment at which William fails to cross the barrier, to claim Susie (for example, when William departs for college, when he returns, and when, knowing he has made a mistake in his own marriage, he advises Susie with a heavy sigh to be sure she chooses the right mate).

[1] There is an essay yet to be written, complementary to the present chapter, that meditates on Susie's guilt as well as William's guilt and studies the bond between Griffith and Gish not by addressing his strategies for filming her but her strategies for declaring herself to – and withholding herself from – the camera. She understands the camera as deeply as he does. Griffith is the director, but the camera is not simply "his": The camera's mark is on Gish, but her mark is on the camera as surely as Griffith's is. In the face of the camera, Gish declares her love for Griffith, which is as wonderful as his love for her. Yet this woman's love, like this man's, also has a dark side.

It is William's mysterious failure, which haunts the entire film, that must be undone if the lovers are to be united – and it is miraculously undone at the end of the film. Is the moment of William's failure also a moment of Susie's failure? Throughout the film, William's silence bears responsibility for Susie's suffering. Does her silence bear responsibility for his guiltiness, hence bear its own burden of guilt?

In *Broken Blossoms*, too, there is a kiss that does not take place, but when Richard Barthelmess refrains from kissing Lillian Gish, it is not a failure but a heroic gesture. Barthelmess consummates his sublime love in the only way open to him (he is, after all, a "Yellow Man"), by renouncing his desire. Griffith underscores the nobility of that renunciation (Does he also call it into question?) by intercutting the near kiss with a barbaric prizefight. When William does not kiss Susie, he is not being noble; he is failing to acknowledge his love. His is a catastrophic failure whose consequences are immensely cruel to Susie and to himself, and even crueler – indeed, fatal – to Bettina. Yet William's failure does not undermine Griffith's attachment to him. Indeed, he reserves his most affectionate title for this terrible, painful moment: "Of course, they don't know what poor simple idiots they are – and we, who have never been so foolish, can hardly hope to understand – but –."

Using the word "we," Griffith steps forward, explicitly referring to himself. He ironically identifies himself – as he identifies me, as he identifies you – as someone who has "never been so foolish" and hence cannot "hope to understand" the likes of Susie and William who don't know what "poor simple idiots they are." Of course, Griffith really means that he has been – and perhaps still is – so foolish, that he does understand. Despite its remarkable playfulness, this title does not disavow the gravity of the moment.

Rather, it delicately expresses a philosophical resignation toward the condition of being human, and toward two features in particular of this condition: the feature that human beings are fated to expose their limitations at every moment, and the feature that, for human beings, youth dies. Griffith, that monumental but forbidding founding father of the art of film, is rarely thought of as delicate, affectionate, playful, or philosophical; yet these are all qualities he possesses.

With this title, Griffith is declaring his human bond with Susie and William and calling upon us to acknowledge that we share this bond as well. We, too, were once "poor simple idiots," were we not? And the question Griffith asks himself (What has become of me?) is a question he calls upon us to ask ourselves as well. Have we really changed?

The medium of film grants us a perspective from which we can recognize the follies to which the camera's subjects appear blind. In Griffith's understanding, film has a miraculous capacity to reveal truth; yet human beings have always possessed this power to transfigure reality. Susie and even the oblivious William ultimately come to know themselves as the camera enables us to know them, to see themselves as they are revealed in film's transfiguring light. We all have the power to recognize what we have become, Griffith is saying, to look back on the roads we have walked, to choose a new path. That human beings deny this power is, for Griffith, the tragedy, or at least the pathos, of history.

Part of Griffith's irony, then, is that we are "poor simple idiots" like Susie and William, and part of the irony is that human beings, "poor simple idiots" though they may be, are never as blind as they appear. As revealed by the camera, Susie and William know the truth in their hearts even when they act as though they do not. For example, when William hesitates and then self-consciously pulls away without kissing Susie, he knows (as she does) that this kiss was to have sealed the pledge of eternal love signified by their initials on the tree. He knows that his self-consciousness means that he does, not that he does not, really love this woman. He knows what is at stake, which is why this moment has the power to come back to haunt him. Self-conscious in the face of the camera, conscious that his own self is a mystery to him, he – like Susie – is conscious of the camera, attuned to the mystery it represents, which here manifests itself in the invisible barrier separating him from the love of his life. In the last reel of *True Heart Susie*, Griffith invokes this mystery with extraordinary intensity.

Having arranged to sleep alone in the spare room, Bettina sneaks out to a party. Griffith cuts from Bettina dancing to Susie solicitously tucking in her beloved Aunty, then to William, lying alone in bed, troubled. He gets up and walks down the hall to the room where he thinks his wife is sleeping. He hesitates uneasily in front of the closed door. Deciding not to go in, he returns to his room and stares out the window, deep in thought. We know what is on his mind. He is thinking about, longing for, Susie. At this moment, Griffith cuts to the object of William's desire. Illuminated as if by an inner glow, Susie is weeping at her window, pitifully "waiting for the love that never comes."

Then Griffith cuts to a shot that serves to represent Susie's view (although it could just as well be William's). The only light in this frame comes from the window, a rectangle of light in the midst of darkness, the bars of the window forming a cross. Symbolically, this window, or the light that shines through it, invokes the powers of good that, in Griffith's dramaturgy, are in eternal war with the powers of evil. (Evil is personified in *True Heart Susie* not by Bettina but by the seductive, mustachioed stranger William believes to be the anonymous benefactor who pays the college tuition.) Like the "Morning Star" that presides over the world of *The White Rose*, this window represents the true love, the faith, that joins Susie and William in spirit. Of course, what joins them is also what keeps them apart: William will always be true to his marriage vows, and Susie will never step between husband and wife. The illuminated window stands in for their dream of a better world, a glorious world in which love is fulfilled and faith rewarded, but it also brings home that it is a dream, brings home the unhappy conditions of their lives as they really are. Yet in the world of *True Heart Susie*, a world transfigured by the medium of film, what keeps Susie and William apart has the power to unite them, or reunite them, in the end.

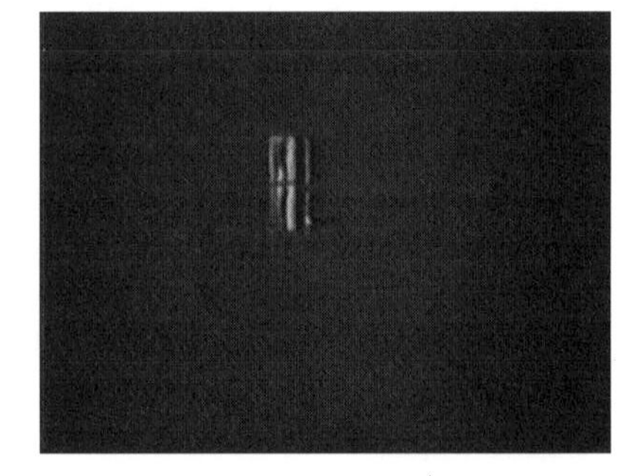

This vision of an illuminated frame-within-the-frame, crossed by shadows and surrounded by darkness, serves as a perfect emblem for the film frame and for film's transfiguring light. It is a positive counterpart to *The Birth of a Nation's* invocations of film's demonic power, Griffith's declaration that film is also divine. But this passage embeds a disquieting reminder of film's dark side as well. The union of Susie and William requires a miraculous intervention, and this miracle exacts a human price. It is precisely at this moment, as if in ironic answer to Susie's and William's Christian prayers, that the heavens open and poor Bettina catches her death.

When Bettina is dropped off at home after the party, she discovers that she has lost her key. She goes over to Susie's house, tells Susie about the party, and implores Susie to let her spend the night – and to lie for her. The title "But True Heart Susie . . ." is followed by a medium close-up of the two women in Susie's bed. Bettina seems asleep, but Susie, her face an inscrutable mask, is wide awake, looking intently at this woman she has every motivation to hate. Susie's hand clenches into a fist, and she seriously contemplates striking Bettina. Instead, she cradles her feverish rival, rests Bettina's head on her breast, and lies awake beside Bettina, taking comfort in her presence, as if they were sisters.

In Susie's eyes, Bettina is not a villainess, whatever her failings, but a fellow human sufferer. Susie forgives Bettina, and *True Heart Susie* calls upon us – as it calls upon Griffith – to follow her edifying example. And yet, for Susie to be happy, Bettina must die.

The Birth of a Nation tells the story of a nightmarish war, of cycles of revenge, of wounds that never heal. *True Heart Susie*, despite its dark side, is a film about forgiveness. Susie forgives Bettina, and in the great closing sequence, she forgives William for his years of silence.

The sequence begins with a frame devoid of human figures, the curtained window forming a frame-within-the-frame. Holding a watering can, Susie appears within this window. Griffith cuts to a more intimate framing, within which she lowers her head and weeps.

In the original longer setup, Susie bravely pulls herself together – but without looking up – and begins watering, nurturing, the flowers. Just then a shadow – the silhouette of a man – appears in the right foreground. Susie reacts with a start to this apparition, as if she were seeing a ghost.

Griffith cuts to William, framed in courtly profile. A title presents his solemn words: "I've learned the truth."

Susie clasps the watering can to her breast, then self-consciously covers her face with it, protecting herself from William – and from the camera.

The silhouette draws closer to Susie in the frame. In panic, she drops the can and withdraws, uncovering a graceful floral arrangement that turns the "empty" frame-within-the-frame into a harmonious still life. Then William enters the frame in the flesh and crosses to the far left of the screen.

A title reads "Is it too late, Susie? I know now I have loved you all my life." Then William steps closer to the window at precisely the moment she reenters the frame-within-the-frame. Her movement left to right in the background precisely matches his in the foreground, as if they were mirror images.

For a long moment, they stand face to face, staring at each other. They come so close, but do not touch each other, as if a pane of glass separated them, no less palpable a barrier for being invisible. Everything about Griffith's filming of this moment enhances the uncanny impression that William is a viewer beholding Susie projected on a movie screen.

Susie's doubting eyes are peeled to his as William leans yet closer. Still with a trace of disbelief, she purses her lips in anticipation of the kiss she has imagined all these years. Her eyes shut, and at last the barrier is bridged, the kiss happens, the dream comes true!

Susie opens her eyes, as if astonished at the miracle, but also as if conscious that someone may be watching, and Griffith tactfully cuts to a longer, more discreet frame, within which the kiss gracefully continues.

The film ends with the title "And we may believe they walk again as they did long years ago," followed by a hallucinatory vision of Susie and William, children again – even Susie's beloved cow has come back to life! – walking down the familiar country road into the depths of the frame. This "happy ending" is also a reminder that such happiness, in our lives, remains a dream.

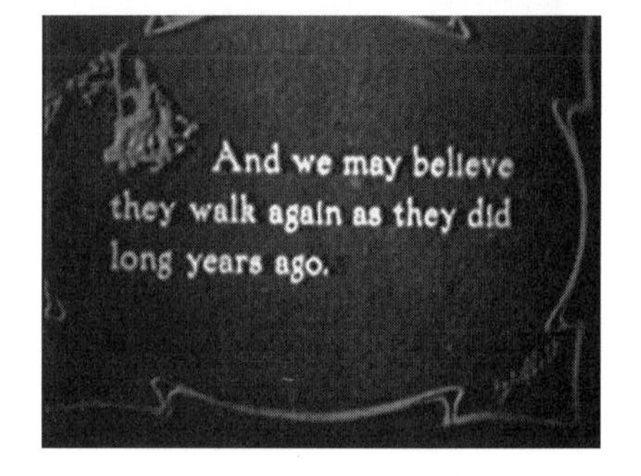

When William appears before Susie as a ghostly apparition and

then enters the frame in the flesh, it is as if a dead man comes to life before her eyes, a shadow assumes substance. It is also as if William steps into, or out of, the world of a film, crossing the barrier represented by the screen. When he declares his love and Susie forgives him, Griffith is saying, William is created, and Susie, too, dies and is reborn. And Griffith discovers a deep inner connection between the mysteries of creation, forgiveness, and love and the mystery at the heart of film. By envisioning creation, forgiveness, and love in terms of crossing the barrier separating film from reality, *True Heart Susie* anticipates the ending of *City Lights* and provides deep inspiration for classical Hollywood genres of the thirties and forties, such as the remarriage comedy and the melodrama of the unknown woman.

CHAPTER 5
The Ending of *City Lights*

Charlie Chaplin and Buster Keaton, the two greatest creators of silent-film comedy, arrived at diametrically opposed strategies for discovering comedy in the conditions of film. What a sublime accident of fate!

As an actor, Chaplin is perfectly expressive, whereas Keaton is famous for his inexpressiveness (more accurately, for the rigorous limits he places on the expressions he allows himself). Chaplin seems always to be performing for an audience whose love he craves, whereas Keaton characteristically seems unconscious of having an audience. Keaton incarnates a comical character who is naturally earnest, guileless, innocent, like a Kafka protagonist. In particular, he never smiles; that is, he finds nothing funny. Chaplin on screen, by contrast, laughs often, and his laughter frequently is addressed openly to the camera. Keaton almost never declares, or even expresses, desire, whereas Chaplin's passions are always manifest, although Chaplin, unlike Keaton, is also a master of deception, a seducer. Filmically, their styles are opposed as well. The way the world appears is essential to Keaton's films, but not Chaplin's. Chaplin the performer is at the center of his world, whereas Keaton is on the outside looking in. Keaton makes his gags with the camera, Chaplin with his performance on camera.

Keaton's comedy, as I understand it, turns on one joke, at one level a joke on the medium of film. We might say that the Keaton character wishes for a viewer's relationship with the world. That role he finds natural, as we do. Unlike us, though, who are called upon only to view a Keaton film, he finds it impossible to view the world for more than a few moments at a time. To survive (and also to win the woman, which is always his ostensible goal), he must continually act. But human actions do not come naturally to him, although he follows all the rules. He seems not to have a native comprehension of ordinary behavior, not because he lacks intelligence, but

---

Reprinted: See "Notes on the Essays."

because ordinary human beings have desires that he does not seem to have, or at least is unaware of having. Of course, the author of the film, who arranges "accidents" precisely to force him to act in the world whether he wants to or not, hence who keeps distracting him from his contemplations, is also Keaton: This is the joke, the constant irony in Keaton's films, perhaps most profoundly registered in *Sherlock, Jr.*, when he steps into the world of the film-within-the-film that he is viewing. The medium of film allows Keaton to be his own straight man.

If the wish to be free to view the world is at the heart of the Keaton figure on screen, then in order to lead us to affirm our bond with that figure, Keaton the filmmaker must create images – and images of himself! – so satisfying that we will be tempted to give up the world to view them. Keaton's comedy turns on one joke. At one level, it is a joke on the medium of film, or film's joke on him and us. The transcendental moments do not have the moral dimension of Griffith's transcendental moments. For Griffith, the transcendental realm is one in which our relationships with other human beings are fulfilled, not denied; Griffith must have disapproved of Keaton's films, which are torn between fulfilling and mocking our wish to view rather than inhabit the world. They mock romance, but they are also romances. They seem profoundly skeptical about the possibility of being a dual citizen of the real world (the only world in which romantic dreams can be fulfilled) and the transcendental realm. Indeed, Keaton implies something darker: that we human beings are cut off from both realms, are not at home in the world, but also are not free to contemplate it from the outside because we are continually thrust into existence. Keaton discovers in the conditions of film a perfect medium for rendering an existential despair that is the ironic underpinning to the optimism of his stories. Life is hell, for Keaton, but for the grace of film and the epiphanies it alone makes possible.

His secret wish to be a viewer is at the heart of Keaton's comedy. At the heart of Chaplin's comedy is the wish to end his separation from the world. The conditions of the medium serve Chaplin as a metaphor for the barriers that human beings long to overcome in their quest to become fully human. Chaplin is not a spectator wishing to contemplate the world's design; he is a performer who takes pleasure in the applause of his audience. Viewing fills him with longing, not satisfaction. What he longs for, viewing cannot provide, and neither, in the end, can contact with an audience.

Yet it is complicated. Chaplin is a performer, but he performs for audiences within the world of the film, and he also performs for the camera, for us, for himself as audience. Chaplin the performer, his camera's inescapable subject, is a mask for Chaplin the director, the man behind the camera, and vice versa. Chaplin controls the camera, and this is something to be declared not to an audience within the world of the film but to us. But what are his real feelings about us, and ours about him? He wants us to love him, but is this only an expression of his disdain for us? (In *The Circus*, for example, he has disdain for all audiences but one – the woman he loves – and perhaps – if so, even the camera is not in on this secret – even for her.) And do we really love Chaplin, or would we reject him if he stepped forward into our presence and declared himself to us? Not despair, but a passionate wish and a palpable terror are at the heart of Chaplin's films: the wish and terror of overcoming the barrier for which film is a metaphor, the wish and terror of making or allowing a dream to become real. In the ending of *City Lights*, as I understand it, he declares this wish and faces this terror by, in effect, calling upon us to imagine that no screen separates him from us.

Keaton's films declare themselves to be transcendent, heavenly designs, as though only the pleasures offered by film, not ordinary human satisfactions, make life worth living. Chaplin, by contrast, dwells on the impossibility of being perfectly satisfied, or giving perfect satisfaction, by film. To Chaplin, film does not, even ironically, represent salvation. In heaven, Chaplin will not cross the street to see – much less to make – a film. Yet it is no accident that film is his medium. Reflecting on himself, Chaplin reflects on film as surely as Keaton does. Although his films may not be "cinematic" in the usual sense of the term, in the ending of *City Lights*, made when the silent film was given up for dead, Chaplin creates one of the profoundest of all meditations on the nature of the film medium.

To the accompaniment of a bittersweet melody (composed by Chaplin himself), the sequence opens with a shot of "the Girl" (Virginia Cherrill) in a flower shop – *her* flower shop – busily putting together a floral arrangement. (Evidently, her eyesight has been restored.) Her back is to the plate-glass window behind her, which dominates the background. She is oblivious to the world we view through that window, the busy street with its traffic and its pedestrians going about their business. In her absorption, she is vulnerable to being viewed without her knowledge by someone on the other side of the window (as she is vulnerable to our view).

There is a cut to the street corner outside, a location and framing already filled with resonance in the film. The Little Tramp rounds the corner and enters the frame, walking without the customary Chaplin élan. Having served his time in prison for a crime he did not commit, having resigned himself to never again seeing the woman he loves (whose sight-saving operation he had secretly made possible), he is melancholy.

We return to the unsuspecting Girl, framed in a longer shot, her back still to the window, through which we now view a limousine pulling up in front of the shop. An elegantly dressed young gentleman steps out and walks through the door. Only then does the Girl turn away from her floral arrangement to greet the customer. For a moment, they face each other at opposite ends of the frame.

Framed in medium close-up, she stares at his handsome face with a look of hopeful expectation, but all he says is, "I'd like to order some flowers." She is brought back from her reverie – her fantasy that he is the one, the Prince Charming of her dreams, whose chivalrous gift enabled her sight to be restored. Her grandmother appears – she works with the Girl in the shop – and takes from Prince Charming the slip of paper on which his order is written, and he leaves.

In a medium long-shot, the Girl, breathing deeply, stares blankly toward the camera. Concerned, her grandmother goes to her side. "Why, what's the matter, child?" The mood of her reverie still lingering, the Girl sits down. "Nothing, only I thought he had returned." The grandmother hugs her a bit (consolingly? encouraging the dream? resignedly?) and goes off to begin filling the order, leaving the Girl alone to dream in the face of the camera.

Meanwhile, on the street, a crowd of pedestrians is massed at the traffic light, waiting for it to change. When they begin to surge across the street, the camera pans right, going against the grain of this movement in a declaration of its autonomy. It continues moving on its own until it frames the window of a pawnshop. The Tramp, still deep in gloom, enters the frame and looks into the pawnshop window.

The two newsboys who have been tormenting the Tramp throughout the film (perhaps not entirely unaffectionately) spot him and grin. One of the boys loads up a peashooter.

The Tramp, hit by the pea, looks down, rubbing the back of his head, then sees the boys – but he is too dispirited to take chase.

Still staring in the direction of the boys, and thus not noticing where he is, the Tramp approaches the flower-shop window, which has a large arrangement on display (the Girl cannot be seen in this frame). Another pea strikes him in the head, and he angrily shakes his finger, but the boys only laugh.

There is a cut to a longer framing. The boys in the foreground, in combination with the lamppost and the pedestrians, obscure the Tramp from our view.

But as he moves screen left and the pedestrians move off to the right, the Girl is revealed through the window, absorbed in her floral arrangement and her dream.

One of the boys shoots another pea and then returns to his pal's side, affecting innocence (and eclipsing the Girl from view). Again the Tramp wags an ineffectual finger at them. Then, his eyes to the ground, he resumes his morose walk, the boys staring mischievously after him, waiting for their next opening. Suddenly, the Tramp freezes. The music soars to a new height of sentiment, and there is a cut to the Tramp's point of view: a rose lying in the gutter, discarded and forlorn.

As the Tramp stoops and picks up the rose, one of the boys snatches a piece of cloth protruding through a split in his pants. Almost upended, the Tramp wheels around and grabs it back. The boy and his pal scamper off. The Tramp takes two leaping steps after them, the camera reframing with his motion, but then he gives up the pursuit. But by its movement, the camera reveals the Girl, who has been watching this scene with great amusement, an amusement that momentarily pulls her out of her longing. (Perhaps this is the first time since her operation – the first time in her life? – that she gives herself to laughter.) Unknowingly, then, the Tramp wins the Girl as an audience, exactly as he wins the audience under the big top in *The Circus*. The circus audience laughs at the Little Tramp's "antics" without realizing that he isn't being funny at all, that he is in dire distress. In Chaplin's work, this myth of the

origins of comedy in a clown's broken heart and the blindness of his audience plays a central role. It is complemented by his frank admissions (as in *The Pilgrim*, for example, when the Tramp-turned-minister acknowledges his parishioners' applause after a rousing rendition of the David-and-Goliath story) that he loves to perform, to win an audience's heart by making it laugh.

In a quintessentially Chaplinesque bit of business, the Tramp pulls off something that had just gotten stuck to the sole of his shoe, and the Girl, laughing, expresses her appreciation to her grandmother at her side.

Framed at a slightly different angle, the Tramp keeps moving screen left, all the time staring back at the boys, toward whom he gestures futilely. Through the window, we see the Girl's attention divided between arranging the flowers and watching the antics of this clown, who delicately blows his nose with the cloth, folds it neatly, and inserts it into the pocket of his tattered evening coat. Then, to the great glee of his audience on the other side of the glass, he crowns his "act" with another quintessentially Chaplinesque gesture: As the music cadences, he gives his smartly folded handkerchief a pat worthy of a Beau Brummel. Having performed this affirmation that his dignity is intact, he is ready once more to venture forth into the world.

There is silence as we cut to a remarkable shot framed from within the shop. The Girl is in the lower foreground, her face turned away from the camera, so that all we see is the back of her head (which initially blocks the Tramp's rose from our view). Through the window, she views the Tramp as we do, as though she were separated from him, as we are, by a screen.

The Tramp begins to raise his hand as though to savor the fragrance of the rose (which is below the frame line) before resuming his wandering. This is when he sees her. Between the almost imperceptible movement of his hand and the ever-so-slight motion of her head as she recoils from his strangely intense stare, the rose is revealed in the frame.

At just this moment, too, the bittersweet music again starts up. The Tramp's eyes widen, and a gloriously dopey grin spreads over his face.

The Girl is transfixed by his gaze, but as she tries to make sense of what she is seeing, bewilderment takes over as the dominant strain in her reaction. Then she pulls her hand away and, deliberately denying the mystery, turns back to her grandmother and says, "I've made a conquest!"

When we cut back to the previous framing, the Girl is now turned toward the camera and away from the Tramp, who is still standing motionless, flower in hand, grinning.

In effect, the Girl has directed her scoffing remark to us, has made us her confidants. (Although we do not share her position, at least we are located at her side in the flower shop, separated from this man by a sheet of glass.) She turns back to face him just as a petal falls from his rose. Then another petal drops. Then another.

Seeing the falling petals, she gestures to the Tramp (this glass is also a barrier to speech) and, holding up a fresh rose, indicates that he should enter the shop. She says something to her grandmother, who hands her a coin, which she holds up along with the rose.

As the Girl rises and heads for the door, the Tramp suddenly panics. He wheels around, meaning to make tracks, his movement and hers perfectly synchronized in the frame.

There is a cut to outside the shop, where the camera reframes with the Tramp as he tries to get away before the Girl reaches his side. But then he stops and turns toward her. The scene freezes into a tableau. The Tramp is on the left, his body poised to flee, but his face expressing his desperate longing to stay and make the woman he loves fall in love with him as he really is. The Girl is on the right, holding up the coin, which occupies the center of the frame. When the coin fails to entice him to return, she tries the rose. Dancing its part in an enchanted ballet, his hand moves with infinite slowness, reaching gracefully across the frame to accept the gift of the flower.

Then she again holds up the coin. When he still shows no interest in it, she steps toward him, closing the distance between them. Taking his arm, she pulls him into the center of the frame.

In an oblique shot of the Girl viewed over the Tramp's shoulder (the framing clearly differentiating his perspective from that of the camera), she places the coin in his hand, closes his fingers over it, and pats them with the affection due a child. All the while, she chatters away like a Griffith ingenue, yet looks deeply into his eyes. Whether her eyes recognize the look in his eyes or her hand (for so many years, her only eyes) remembers the touch of his hand, suddenly the Girl knows, her knowledge expressed both in her eyes and in the tender way her hand begins stroking his. A close-up isolates their hands in the frame.

For a moment, her hand closes his in its grasp. Then, tenderly, but with heartbreaking tentativeness, it follows the path of his arm toward his shoulder. The camera, taking its lead from her knowing hand, reframes until we view the Tramp's face – famously, he is holding the rose between his teeth. His eyes betray his excitement and his dread.

Terrifyingly, her hand withdraws, momentarily breaking contact, and she asks, "You?" The Tramp nods. She touches her hand to her heart. Pointing to his eyes, he asks a question, which is really an answer: "You can see now?" She nods her head. "Yes, I can see now." Choking back sobs, she presses his hand against her heart and smiles bravely.

We cut to a medium close-up of Chaplin, with only the edge of the Girl's hair visible in the frame; it feels very much like a shot from her point of view. His hand is still raised to his mouth, his rose still between his teeth, his gaze still locked with hers, his eyes still filled with dread and terror. And yet – he beams, he smiles, he laughs, as though struck by the realization of how irresistibly funny this wonderful, terrible moment is. Then the scene fades out, and his face is engulfed in darkness.[1]

In describing this last moment, I am no longer willing to refer to this human figure as "the Tramp." It is *Chaplin*, this human being of flesh and

[1] Woody Allen models the ending of *Manhattan* on that of *City Lights*. When Mariel Hemingway says that he has to accept the fact that people change and has to learn to trust people, we get a sustained close-up of Allen, grudgingly admitting that she is right. But his rueful admission is to himself, by extension to us, and not to her. Her reaction to this acknowledgment is not at issue, as though there were no question of her love for him, the only question being whether or not, when she changes, she will fall out of love with him. But what entitles Allen to take this woman's love for granted? (That they have "great sex," as he puts it, is not sufficient grounds. Besides, how can he be so certain that their sex is "great" for her too? How can he know that she is not an actress?) Even at this moment, Allen remains the center of his universe. This shot frames Allen's judgment on his own persona and proclaims the birth of a new Woody Allen. Yet despite its apparent self-deprecation, it reaffirms, it does not question, Allen's old claim to be the sole authority (even though it appears to invest that authority in a woman). In other words, he has not really changed. *Manhattan* is his impassioned plea to his audience to let him change, to let him cast off his comical *shlemiel* persona. If we keep him from changing, he tells us, that is no laughing matter. Yet he remains maddeningly blind to what we can clearly see: that his genius, like Chaplin's, is for comedy, and that his comical persona is an inescapable and inexhaustible subject for him, indeed his only subject.

blood, who stands exposed in this frame, revealed in his mortality and his desperate longing to be loved. This revelation by the camera is also a declaration of the camera, a declaration by the film's author that he *is* the pathetic Little Tramp. Chaplin completes his design by stepping forward.

With this gesture, Chaplin calls upon us to imagine something very specific: that he has stepped out of the world of the film and into our presence, that no "window" separates us, no screen. Chaplin calls upon us to imagine, in other words, that the medium of film is no barrier. (Viewed in these terms, this moment is the exact counterpart to the great passage in Buster Keaton's *Sherlock, Jr.* in which Keaton literally steps into the world of the film-within-the-film he is viewing.) To envision this in the medium of film is to envision – this is a utopian fantasy and a terrifying one – the overcoming of all the barriers that human beings have created to ward off the knowledge that human happiness rests in human hands.

Why does Chaplin not follow this shot with a shot of the Girl's reaction? To show her reaction here would be to speak for her on the subject of what is in her heart about him. In part, Chaplin refrains from doing this because he cannot say what this shot reveals about his nature, about who he really is. Is he worthy of love?

This is a real question, and a deep one. The Tramp is not merely a pathetic victim. After all, he has exploited the Girl's blindness, deceiving her into fostering a dream that he knows cannot come true – unless he is the lover of her dreams. (That Chaplin is not guileless is part of what it means that he is a mime. Innumerable Chaplin gags involve sudden transformations designed to make guilty behavior appear innocent.)

Chaplin has every reason to belive that by revealing himself in this way, he is cruelly disillusioning this woman, destroying her dream. It may be said, in his defense, that he did not engineer this revelation, which is the product of a series of accidents. Yet if he is a victim of these accidents, he is also their perpetrator. He is the author of the film who has presided over all these "accidents" with this end in view.

The Tramp, in his sensitivity, his noble spirit in the face of suffering, his humanity, is someone we love. But this figure is also Chaplin's mask, created through his performance and also his control over the camera. He presents himself as the Little Tramp, but all the time he is the director in control – manipulative, cold, inhuman. That the Tramp himself has a murderous aspect increasingly becomes of interest to Chaplin, whose films come to dwell more and more on this split in his self. (That the Tramp is also a monster is the central point of *The Great Dictator*, for example, in which Chaplin undertakes to play not only a Tramp-like Jewish barber but that arch monster, Adolph Hitler.)

Once we recognize Chaplin's unfathomable power, we understand that it is not only the Girl's love (or ours) that is in doubt. By revealing himself, he risks discovering that he has no place in her dream, but also the equally terrifying possibility that this real woman possessed of sight has no place in *his* dream. (Perhaps he loved her for her blindness.)

To show the Girl's reaction would also be to dictate to us what we are to feel, and this, too, Chaplin refrains from doing. He chooses, rather, to allow us no way of imagining what might follow this moment – apart from imagining ourselves in her place. That is, in the same gesture by which Chaplin calls upon us to imagine that he has stepped out of the world of the film, he also calls upon us to imagine that we find ourselves within that world, not outside and safely screened from it.

By calling upon us to imagine that the screen is not a barrier, Chaplin calls upon us to reflect on the limits of the medium of film and to ask ourselves whether or not we wish for those limits to be transcended. Do we wish for the Tramp to be real, if that means we must give our love to a human being of flesh and blood? This is a philosophical question about the human capacity for love and for avoiding love. It is also a question of the greatest possible personal concern to Chaplin: *City Lights* declares that he stakes his whole existence on our answer. In the film's final frame, Chaplin stands in for every one of us; yet by assuming his place, he declares his separateness from us. It would not be possible for any of us to stand in for him in this frame.

Whether we accept or reject Chaplin at this moment, something dies, and something is born, in our relationship with him. In the end, perhaps, film is not funny for Chaplin. Perhaps we have failed him, and he has destroyed our dreams. Perhaps film connot bring about salvation, but rather confirms the worst about our condition. And yet, just before the final fade-out, Chaplin does, miraculously, laugh.

CHAPTER 6

The Goddess

Reflections on Melodrama East and West

In China, as in Japan and India, film represents a radical discontinuity in traditional culture. But film represents a radical discontinuity in Western, and specifically American, culture as well. Even in the West, and even in America, all films, no matter how "traditional" their cultural sources, were motivated by, and motivated, radically new ideas and forms of life. In America, these ideas and forms of life, however new, had sources within America's own cultural traditions. My belief is that the same was true in China: Chinese film was "Western," but it was also Chinese in its forms and its sources. Nor is it possible to make a sharp distinction between what is Chinese and what is Western, what is "inside" or "outside" the Chinese cultural tradition, just as it is not possible to draw such a line in the case of the West, or of America.

The transcendentalism of Emerson and Thoreau is a central source of popular American movie genres. Their roots in American transcendentalism are essential to what makes American films American. But transcendentalism in America, a late American flowering of European Romanticism, also is a reflection of, and a reflection on, the great impact of the introduction to the West of Asian religion, philosophy, and art. That is, Hollywood romantic comedies and melodramas have "Eastern" as well as "Western" sources. They mark American culture's ongoing conversation with itself, which is also a conversation sometimes brutal with China (and with the rest of Asia as well). In the same fashion, Chinese films mark China's conversation with the West, and with America, which is also Chinese culture's ongoing conversation with itself.

Wu Yonggang, the director of *The Goddess* (*Shen nu*) (1934), spent several years in Hollywood before returning to China to work within the Shanghai industry. Clearly, his film has an extreme technical sophistication and self-consciousness that invite comparison with films of the Hollywood director who most obviously influenced and inspired him: Josef von Sternberg. Like *Blonde Venus*, the von Sternberg melodrama that is especially closely related to it, *The Goddess*, a late silent film, evidences a mastery of the forms and techniques that constitute the "classical" style, a style we sometimes identify with Hollywood but that is also international.

This does not make *The Goddess* any less Chinese. Noël Burch argues, to quite perverse effect (and David Bordwell, in his work on Ozu, is inclined to go along with him to a large extent) that the "Japanese-ness" of a Japanese film can be a function only of its systematically violating "Western codes," especially of editing, as if Japanese films that do not violate Western editing codes cannot possibly also uphold Japanese aesthetic traditions or revise them from the inside. But Japanese filmmakers have proved themselves capable of using Western codes no less idiomatically than American or European filmmakers (even if they have sometimes revised them in the process), have equally made the conventions of classical cinema their own without betraying their Japanese-ness. Then why think of these conventions as exclusively Western, alien to Japan (or China, or India)?

If *The Goddess* evidences a mastery of classical style in general, it is equally masterful in its use of the specific forms and strategies of a particular genre that, likewise, we sometimes identify with Hollywood but that is also international: the romantic melodrama that Stanley Cavell so evocatively names "the melodrama of the unknown woman." This genre encompasses such American exemplars as *Stella Dallas, Now, Voyager*, and *Letter from an Unknown Woman*. Again, the great example directed by von Sternberg is *Blonde Venus* – like *The Goddess*, a film about a mother reduced to prostitution by her commitment to raising her young son.

Cavell traces the close logical relationship between the melodrama of the unknown woman and the genre of romantic comedy he calls "the comedy of remarriage." In American comedies like *It Happened One Night, The Awful Truth, The Philadelphia Story*, or *Adam's Rib*, a woman finds her voice, is fulfilled, through the attainment of a new kind of marriage, one characterized as a conversation between equals, the whole process also interpreted as one of her education and interpreted as well as a political allegory about the fulfillment of the American dream of creating a new America, an ideal human community, a utopia.

The melodramas of the unknown woman, too, center on a woman's quest for selfhood, but in this genre the woman attains – or fails to attain – fulfillment, not through an ideal marriage, which is for one reason or another barred to her, but on her own, or only with the help of the world of women, forsaking or transcending marriage. These films do not glorify a woman's suffering, her victimization, as is conventionally supposed. Like the remarriage comedies, they are dedicated to the proposition that nothing on earth is more important than a woman's self-fulfillment and happiness in the world.

The remarriage comedy is a genre for which Americans seem to have a unique aptitude. (Why films of this genre have virtually never been made outside the United States is an intriguing question, although certain factors are obviously pertinent. For one thing, comedies of remarriage require, as a condition, that in certain circumstances divorce be an option for men and women; in the 1930s, the heyday of the genre, precious few societies satisfied this condition.) Every national cinema, by contrast, has a tradition of films intimately related to the American melodramas. But what is the relationship of, say, a Chinese melodrama like *The Goddess* to its American counterparts? How do cultural differences manifest themselves in the ways the conditions of such a genre are interpreted and developed?

Before this question is addressed it will be helpful to pause to sketch the narrative of the film.

The Goddess tells the story of a Shanghai prostitute struggling to bring up her young son on her own. The woman encounters a gangster who moves in, uninvited, and becomes her pimp. At a certain point, she tries to break away and get a job in a factory, but finds no work. So she accepts the situation, bowing to the brutal reality that she needs money to support her son.

Years pass, but mother and son still enjoy a pure, innocently joyful, intimacy. All these years, she has been hiding some of her earnings in a chink in the wall. The gangster suspects, but has never found, the secret cache. Now that the boy is old enough, she enters him in a fancy private school, lying about the boy's father.

Her son's education proceeds apace. She is happy, despite her compromises, and despite the fact that other mothers spread rumors and the other boys continually pick on him.

In the first of the film's great tear-jerking sequences, all the parents are gathered in the school auditorium for a student talent show. Two little girls finish their spectacularly cute song and dance routine, and then our little hero sings a poignant song about a poor newsboy and his aging parents. As he sings, the other mothers gossip in each other's ears, his own mother anxiously looks on, and, no doubt, handkerchiefs rustle and tears flow tears in darkened movie theaters all over Shanghai.

The rumors reach the schoolmaster in the form of an anonymous letter. He undertakes an investigation, in the course of which he visits the boy's mother at home, where he spots a telltale polka-dot dress hanging on a coatrack. He also bears witness to this woman's genuine commitment to her son's education. Her love and commitment shine through most dazzlingly when she declares the truth about herself in a passionate "aria" that leaves the schoolmaster speechless with astonishment. (Cavell has pointed out that such an aria of "self-nomination," to use Peter Brook's term, is an obligatory scene in the American melodramas of the unknown woman.)

The schoolmaster recommends to the board that the boy be allowed to remain in school. Fearing scandal, the board members vote him down, upon which he submits his resignation. When she receives the letter informing her of her son's expulsion, she resolves that they will escape to some faraway place. This is when she discovers that the gangster has stolen her money. In a rage, she goes to his gambling den and demands her money. For a moment, he seems perplexed, even a bit frightened, by her intensity. Then, dismissing his uncanny sense that this woman possesses a terrifying power, he regains his composure and tells her, with his usual leer, that he has already spent the money. In disbelief and fury, she pounds his chest with her fists. As he turns to leave, dismissing her, she grabs a bottle. The camera assumes his position and recedes from her, its movement matching the gangster's as he walks toward the door. She advances on the receding camera and strikes out violently with the bottle, attacking this brutal man and symbolically attacking the camera as well.

The schoolmaster visits her in prison. He tells her that he will raise her son as his own. Alone again in her cell, she has a vision of her son, smiling and happy – her one ray of hope, as a title puts it.

Having viewed *The Goddess* in China a number of years ago, I have carried with me ever since a memory of Ruan Lingyu's sad eyes. I thought I remembered that she played a submissive victim, but this was my memory playing tricks. She plays a woman who is sad much of the time – she has much to be sad about – but she is strong, and never meekly submits to anything. We view her in the throes of a wide range of powerful feelings, culminating in her two extraordinary explosions of emotion: she kills her gangster pimp/lover, she tells the truth to the schoolmaster, and declares herself with astonishing passion and authority.

Throughout *The Goddess*, Wu Yonggang's camera lingers on his star as lovingly and "excessively" as von Sternberg's on Dietrich, and Ruan Lingyu emerges as fully Dietrich's equal in extravagant, breathtaking beauty.

Yet there is a striking difference. Ruan Lingyu is like Marlene Dietrich minus the theatricality. When von Sternberg says "You have to understand that I am Dietrich," he is asserting both that she is nothing without him and that he is nothing without her. Film's creation of Dietrich is the creation of von Sternberg; these beings are inextricably intertwined, and woman and man participate equally in their creation. By contrast, Wu Yonggang and Ruan Lingyu are separate beings.

Early in *The Goddess*, the woman looks at herself in the mirror and puts finishing touches to her hair and makeup before going out to walk the streets. Wu Yonggang does not cut to frame her in the mirror. If this were a von Sternberg film, we would surely be shown, and would linger over, the star's reflected image looking inscrutably yet provocatively right into the camera, at once a "fetish" and a subject mocking our guilty wish to reduce her to an object. In contrast to Dietrich, Ruan Lingyu is not "objectified" or "fetishized." The camera does not relate to her in a guilty way, nor is she guilty of complicity with a guilty camera.

In the face of the camera, Ruan Lingyu is innocent in a way Marlene Dietrich is not, or claims (theatrically?) that she is not. To be sure, she, too, is no virgin. The film makes no bones about the way this "Goddess" makes her living. No Hollywood film even of the pre-Production Code era is so explicit about prostitution. She does not enjoy selling her body, but she is no "fallen woman." She does not feel – and the film does not imply that she should feel – corrupted or defiled or sinful or somehow responsible for the cruelties the world inflicts on her and her innocent son. In the eyes of the camera, and in her own eyes, she remains pure. Except for the schoolmaster, we never see a man, even the gangster, touch her with desire. (A corollary of this is that, when she smites the gangster by her own hand, no blood is drawn.)

When *The Goddess* is compared with *Blonde Venus*, it is striking that "romance" in the Western sense seems virtually nonexistent in the Chinese film. This woman is not searching for fulfillment through love; what she dreams of is her son's fulfillment, which is interpreted as his education. *The Goddess* gives no thought to the boy's real father, as if he had none. Nor is there any sense, as there is in *Blonde Venus*, of a romance (incestuous, Freudian) between mother and son, despite the extraordinary physical intimacy that prevails between them (for example, in the wonderful sequence in which the son teaches his mother the gymnastic exercises he learned at school. Imagine if this had been Marlene Dietrich, with von Sternberg directing!)

The only moments in *The Goddess* that strike this American male viewer as erotic occur in the woman's two encounters with the schoolmaster. He is drawn to her first by compassion and then by awe at her moral character, but he is also moved, repeatedly, to touch her.

When the schoolmaster pays a visit to her home as part of his investigation, there is a charged moment at which, apparently solicitously, he reaches out to put his hand on her shoulder, but she turns and pulls out of the frame, leaving his hand dangling for a long moment. During this awkward moment we – and he – cannot help but be aware that he feels a strong desire to touch her (however we may interpret this desire).

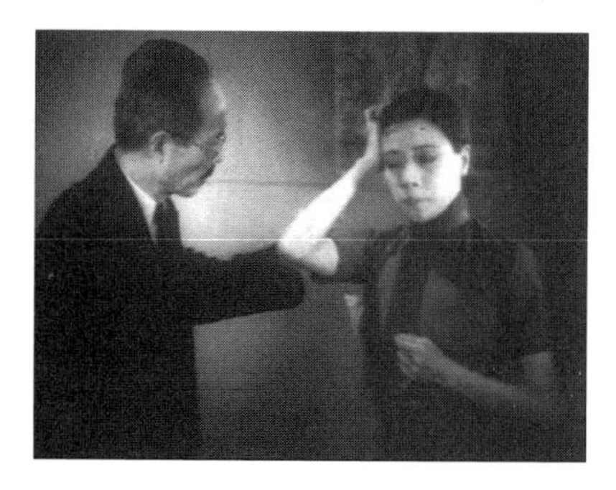

When, a few moments later, the schoolmaster pats her son's head just after she strokes the boy's hair, we again feel the schoolmaster's desire to be touching *her*, which he does – in close-up – before he makes his exit.

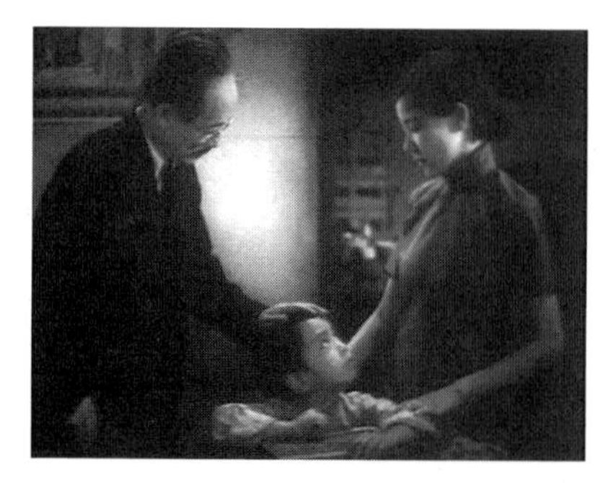

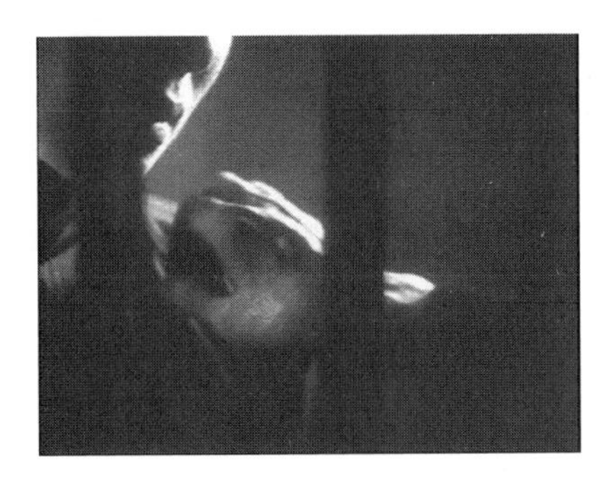

We sense this desire even more strongly at the end of the film, when he visits her in prison. This powerfully emotional sequence climaxes in a close-up, gloriously composed and lit, of the man's hand reaching through the bars, tenderly touching the woman's shoulder.

His desire to touch her seems to go beyond mere kindness, as if there-were a – secret – passionate bond between them. But the schoolmaster has the self-discipline to sublimate his desire (as has, for example, the heroic cadre in the face of his passionate young recruit in Xie Jin's *The Red Detachment of Women*). Without a capacity for passion, and without the self-discipline to transcend it, he would not be worthy to raise this woman's son as his own. Yet the possibility is not even considered, as it would be if this were an American film, that he might offer to marry her.

What astonishes the schoolmaster is this woman's noble, selfless dedication to her son's education. Is it that she wants her son to "get ahead," wants him to acquire the trappings of respectability and its attendant privileges? No. The schoolmaster, in making his case to the board (interestingly, they are dressed Chinese style whereas he is impeccable in his Western suit), makes it clear that, in this corrupt society, a school's reputation is no true measure of its ability to provide a real education. True education cannot be separated from ethical practice and moral authority. What ultimately matters is not one's place in society, for society has lost its values, but one's moral character – a fine Confucian, and Emersonian, doctrine (as is the film's idea that, whoever the boy's father is, society is responsible, we are all responsible, for his education).

In the corrupt Shanghai of *The Goddess*, the brutal gangster occupies a "low" position in the social hierarchy, yet he wields great power. That he represents the film's link, even its equation, between male sexuality and brute force, the rule of the fist, is the implication of a striking shot that envisions his would-be victims symbolically trapped between his legs. The film makes a further connection, perhaps equation, between the rule of the fist (hence male sexuality) and capitalist exploitation: The factories in which workers labor like slaves are framed to emphasize their conspicuously phallic smokestacks, and the Shanghai skyline itself, repeatedly invoked by the director, is a row of phallic towers.

In any case, the brutal gangster is not the cruelest villain in the world of *The Goddess*. At least he is vibrantly alive, and at least he is no hypocrite. More contemptible are the cowardly men on the school board and the hypocritical women – they would feel at home in W. C. Fields's Lompoc – who encourage their children to mock a virtuous woman and her innocent son.

In identifying and condemning the brutal exploiters and the hypocrites who betray the true spirit of education, *The Goddess* passes judgment on virtually all of Shanghai society. In this world, virtue is compelled to stand alone, joined only by the camera (only by the director, and, by us).

In the chapter "Virtue and Villainy in the Face of the Camera," I argue that in the American films that followed those of Griffith, virtue cannot declare itself, cannot be declared, except through the agency of the camera, and that the camera, always also an instrument of villainy, cannot "nominate" innocence without at the same time violating it. In *Blonde Venus*, the camera's relationship to Dietrich is linked to that of her villainy-tainted husband. The camera's relationship to Dietrich is also linked to her son's relationship to her. At one level, this son is innocent, like the son in *The Goddess*. But *Blonde Venus* declares him also to be implicated in the world's villainy (as is the camera, as is the viewer, as is the author, as is the act of storytelling itself, as is film's art of projecting a world). At one level, the whole film springs from this "innocent" boy's desire. Villainy and innocence, the camera and its subject, are, in *Blonde Venus*, two faces of one god, or goddess, as inseparable as creation and destruction.

The Goddess, by contrast, implies that its woman and boy are perfectly innocent, untainted, as is their intimacy with each other, as is the camera's intimacy with their intimacy. Viewing them on screen, together or apart, we experience an innocent pleasure, a joy, foreign to our experience of American movies. In a sense, the camera relates to Ruan Lingyu not as a father (as Griffith's camera relates to Lillian Gish, for example) but as a son, perhaps as this innocent son grown up but retaining his filial piety.

The schoolmaster, like the camera, views this woman as an ideal mother – indeed, as his mother. As I have suggested, in *Blonde Venus*, too, the camera can be viewed as assuming the role of Dietrich's son. But *Blonde Venus* emphatically does not locate the mother/son relationship, or the camera's relationship to that relationship, in a region of purity separate from the "real world" of exploitation and cruelty, as *The Goddess* does.

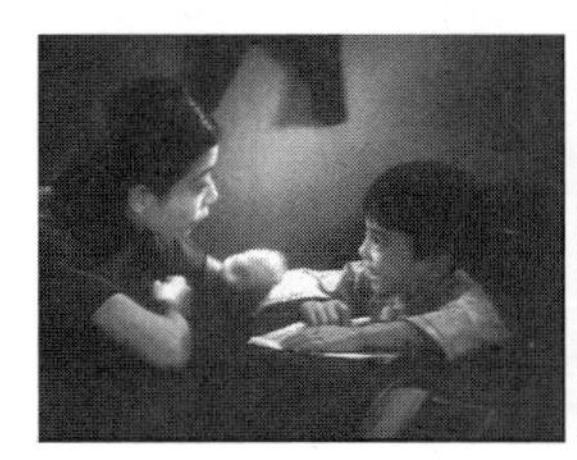  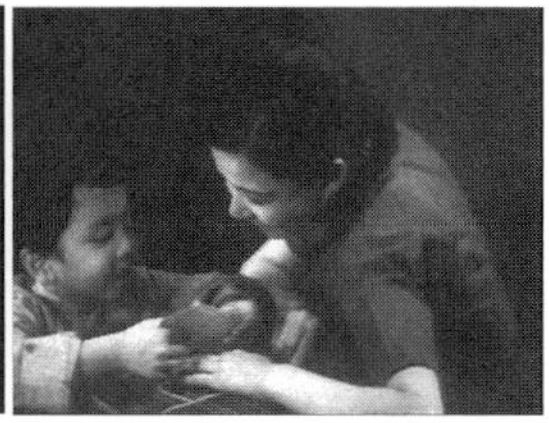

When we view the joyful intimacy between mother and son in *The Goddess*, the film's implication is not that what we are glimpsing is an Eden from which they must inevitably be banished for their sins. Nor are we viewing a "phase" that must inevitably succumb to raging Oedipal conflicts. The implication, rather, is that their love will never lose its innocence and joyful intimacy no matter what their fates in an unjust world, no matter what compromises the world may force them to make in other regions of their lives. No doubt we too lead compromised lives, yet *The Goddess* aspires to touch a region of purity within us when it invokes such visions of innocence, an innocence that – astonishingly, if we are familiar with only American melodramas – the camera does not threaten to violate.

In some respects *The Goddess* seems a more progressive revision of the American film melodrama. I am thinking of the features I have mentioned such as the film's unflinching acknowledgment of the woman's prostitution, the way the film shows her intimacy with her son without making it seem problematic, the fact that film does not impose a phony "love interest" on her. Yet all these features also have a regressive aspect to them, throwing into relief the feminism of the classical American cinema. American melodramas are about a woman's quest for self-fulfillment when the option of marriage to Cary Grant or Spencer Tracy is ruled out – a marriage that is at once a romantic dream come true and a conversation between equals. In *The Goddess*, the woman never looks to a man for her self-fulfillment because she is not on a quest to fulfill her self. True, she is not in quest of a self because she does not doubt she already has or is a self. But she does not have doubts on this score because she knows her mission in life is to provide her son with an education.

But it is complicated. Although the woman's final vision is of her son, *The Goddess* presents this vision in the context of its acknowledgment and affirmation of the woman herself: The woman envisions her son, but we envision her envisioning her son. This boy is the ideal subject of education, but it is Ruan Lingyu who is the ideal subject of Wu Yonggang's camera. This woman, mediated by film, is at the heart of *The Goddess*, as Dietrich, mediated by film, is at the heart of *Blonde Venus*. Taken literally, *The Goddess* affirms a woman's self-denial, but as a film, it affirms that woman's self, just as the great Hollywood melodramas affirm the selfhood of the women who are their central subjects.

*The Godde*ss does not endorse "the patriarchy" any more than does *Blonde Venus* or any of the other American unknown-woman melodramas. Quite the contrary, *The Goddess* decisively attacks it, although it does so in the name of an ideal father, the schoolmaster, and the values he endorses. These happen to be the values he finds to be perfectly incarnated – and articulated – by an ideal mother. For the sake of acknowledging the values this woman represents, this man is willing to renounce his social position (although not, perhaps, to take off his tie), his privileged place in a degraded, corrupt social hierarchy. What does this woman value? Astonishingly, the film incorporates into its remarkable closing sequence a vision of what she holds most dear, as she envisions it alone in her prison cell.

When the schoolmaster visits her in prison, he swears he will look after her son as if he were the boy's real father. Then he leaves, and she is alone in her cell. Framed in medium long- shot, her head is bowed. Then she looks up with a hopeless expression. Her arms dejectedly at her side, she turns and makes her way to a bare table, the camera reframing with her. There she sits, stroking her arm with her hand, her slumped posture poignantly expressing her dejection.

There is a cut to a medium close-up. Looking down and screen left, she strokes her hair and turns her face as if to look at something offscreen to the right. Then the expressionlessness that is the perfect expression of her inner desolation miraculously gives way to an ecstatic look.

A title says, in effect, that she has left only one ray of hope. Then we see her in medium shot at the far left of the frame, looking toward the blank, dark background. Suddenly, as if projected onto a screen, her little boy appears in the right background of this frame. He meets her gaze – and the camera's – with a heartbreaking smile of innocence and hope, a vision real enough and unreal enough to move us, as it moves his mother, to tears. Then the vision fades out, and the woman turns almost to face the camera, closes her eyes, sighs, slightly lowers her head, raises her head again but without opening her eyes, sighs once more, and still keeps her eyes closed as our vision of her, too, fades out and the final title appears.

So this film about education is also engaged in education, identifying and affirming what it holds to be of value in a way open only to the medium of film. Indeed, like the ending of *Stella Dallas*, the ending of *The Goddess* is also an invocation of our condition as viewers, a declaration of the medium of film. It interprets our condition as one of solitary confinement: Film is our bridge to a world of hope, a world that, *The Goddess* reminds us, is not, or is not yet, real (will it ever be?). The film does not offer a practical way of changing society so as to make this vision real. All it does – perhaps all a film can do – is keep alive, or breathe life into, such a vision, such a hope, of a better world.

The ending of *The Goddess* does not feel "happy" like the ending of *Blonde Venus* or even *Stella Dallas*. The vision the film leaves us with is, in the end, that of a virtuous woman cast off by an unjust world. Yet, because all this woman has lived for is her son's education, this is a vision of happiness. This woman is happy, but only as long as she keeps her vision alive by closing her eyes, by shutting out the world.

Our vision of her, too, in the end fades out. The film ends, as all films must end, and we are left alone, imprisoned in a cruel, unjust world. We can keep alive our vision of this woman only if we, too, "shut our eyes." This is, at one level, what *The Goddess* calls upon us to acknowledge.

The *Goddess* contains several surefire "tear-jerking" passages, yet there is a reticence characteristic of the film that is quite different from the hyperbolic expressions of emotion usually associated with movie melodramas.

Partly, this has to do with the fact that no physical threat is established. The gangster's threat is that he will harm her son. Yet when the film uses parallel editing to create suspense (for example, when it cuts back and forth between the board meeting and the gangster's search for the hidden money), or when the camera self-consciously calls attention to itself by framing a view of the woman through the gangster's legs, or by composing images of factories that emphasize their phallic smokestacks, or by assuming the gangster's literal position, making the woman's attack on him a symbolic attack on the camera as well), Wu Yonggang's camera does declare that it possess a capacity for violence, for villainy, as surely as does von Sternberg's. But in *The Goddess*, the camera's capacity for villainy somehow does not keep it from invoking visions of innocence that it does not even threaten to violate.

It is as if *The Goddess* divides the role of the camera (the role of the author, the role of the viewer) between two regions, one guilty and one innocent, one compromised and one pure, one public and one private. A happy marriage between public and private is a central aspiration of American films. At one level, bridging the gap between these two regions is what *The Goddess*, too, is centrally about: It is what distinguishes the heroic schoolmaster from the hypocrites on the school board. At another level, though, the film does not even contemplate bridging this gap: Keeping these regions separate is what allows the camera to invoke virtue without threatening to violate it.

In a sense, then, *The Goddess* is implicated in the hypocrisy it attacks, the duplicity of isolating one's public from one's private self. Perhaps such a compromise is inevitable in the China of Chiang Kai-shek, or Mao, or Deng Xiaoping, or Jiang Zemin. (And what about the America of George Bush?) But if it is inevitable, how will China ever change?

Is *The Goddess* a call for a social revolution? It is and it is not, I take it. Insofar as it is not, the film affirms the value of keeping one's eyes closed so that one's imagination can be free. Insofar as it is, it is not Mao's revolution that *The Goddess* calls for, but one akin to the new American revolution envisioned by the remarriage comedies and melodramas of the unknown women of the American cinema – a revolution that affirms the values represented by the schoolmaster and his Goddess. Call these the values of education. As I am writing these words, China is torn in a struggle between a hypocritical party and a generation of young people in quest of an education. Whatever the film's compromises, we cannot be in doubt on which side *The Goddess* stands.

CHAPTER 7

Red Dust

The Erotic Screen Image

Red Dust, released by Warner Brothers in 1932, and directed by Victor Fleming, opens with a kind of prologue that introduces the Clark Gable character and establishes the setting: Gable is foreman of a large rubber plantation an arduous day's trek from Saigon (amazingly, everyone in the film pronounces it "Say-gon"). A monsoon is approaching, and Gable is furious that so many of the trees have been tapped too young (good rubber cannot be made from such trees).

Jean Harlow arrives by boat, expecting to leave when the boat does. She first manifests herself as an offscreen voice, and then is seen from Gable's point of view. Gable is sullen in her presence. His elderly friend (Tully Marshall) chides him for not recognizing a natural playmate in this beautiful young woman. This sets the stage for the most entertaining scene in the film, Harlow drawing upon her repertory of techniques of wit to break down Gable's sullenness: for example, by relating how Roquefort cheese is made (by slapping the sheep – "Ewes, don't you call them?" – around the udders), although she never gets the full story out; by mocking Gable for his sulking ("I'll go peacefully, officer," she says, as though she were a prostitute and he a cop).

Harlow takes it as her task to make Gable laugh, and when she finally succeeds, he pulls her toward him and opines that she is not so bad after all. Then the camera pans to a squawking parrot, invoking a sexual act not explicitly shown. (*Red Dust*, made two years before rigid enforcement of the Production Code began, need not hedge the issue of whether or not the couple has sex. Contrast, for example, the famous cut to the airport tower in *Casablanca*.)

When her boat has to chug back to Saigon for repairs. Harlow's overnight stay stretches to a month. Finally, the boat returns. As she boards it, she

---

Reprinted: See "Notes on the Essays."

tries to coax from Gable some acknowledgment that he feels something for her. Thinking that she is hinting that she wants to be paid, he hands her money. The sequence concludes with a glorious image of Harlow that represents her reaction to Gable's dismissive gesture. This shot both captures – in soft-focus, idealized, haloed form – Harlow's great beauty (a beauty that, it is a point of the shot, does not awaken Gable's desire, or if it does, he does not recognize it) and confirms her humanity, accords her a psychology grounded in a sense of alienation and privacy with which we may identify.

First introduced from Gable's point of view, Harlow's own point of view is now authorized by the film. This shot does not impute carnal desire to her; nor is it designed to arouse the viewer erotically, although she is, as I have suggested, posed, lit, and framed so as to bring out her beauty to the full – a beauty that is here declared to be spiritual. Harlow's reaction reveals, for example, her awareness that Gable does not even understand that his gesture constituted a slap in the face. She refrains from returning Gable's cruelty in kind. She simply wants this man to acknowledge her.

It might be noted that the Production Code was soon to undermine the basis of Harlow's screen persona. This persona is crystallized in her trademark platinum hair. A *Photoplay* feature on Harlow's beauty secrets notes that "Jean's platinum halo has probably aroused more comment and curiosity than any one feature of any star." Naturally described as a "halo," it is an emblem of her purity of spirit and her longing for love and acceptance. But as platinum, bleached, it marks her as a fallen woman. She is, at the very least, no virgin, and the world is inclined to treat her as a tart. One way she responds to this treatment is by deliberately acting vulgar, making herself ugly. This is the dominant strain in her performance in *Dinner at Eight* (1933), for example. Harlow's alienation is the basis of her wit.

Why won't Gable acknowledge Harlow, and why does he fail to be excited by her? A clue arrives on the next boat. The new assistant foreman (Gene Raymond) arrives, and we share Gable's immediate reaction to him: This is a mouse or a boy, not a man – such a wimp will never make it on the plantation. Then we also share Gable's initial view of the figure implicated in Raymond's lack of manliness: Raymond's wife (Mary Astor), who is an intolerable, snobbish bitch.

Raymond plunges to his nadir when he is stricken with fever. Up to the point of crisis, Gable continues to speak and act in ways contrived to shock

Astor, calling her to task for being there, uninvited, and indeed for existing at all. (Only later are we given the skeleton of a psychological explanation for Gable's excessively harsh treatment of Astor: His mother, unable to take the robust life here, died on the plantation.) But when the crisis comes, Gable nurses Raymond through his fever.

Witnessing this, Astor apologizes for failing to recognize Gable's altruism. Gable renews his provocative tack, implying that her apology is itself a product of her spoiled rich-girl attitude. Further, he asserts that his act was not really altruistic, but was motivated by the perception that she was attracted to him. She slaps him hard in the face, and their relationship is transformed.

That this slap gives birth to Gable's passionate desire for Astor is confirmed by what follows: As a tiger roams on the edge of the compound, Astor prepares for a bath, while Gable secretly spies on her. His desire is aroused, and he knows it; she desires him, but she has no knowledge of such matters, does not recognize the passion welling up within her.

Thus we read the following sequence, in which Gable takes Astor on a tour of the plantation, as his deliberate seduction of her. As part of their tour, he shows her various stages in the production of rubber (for example, showing through a microscope how raw rubber, when assaulted by chemicals, "stiffens into an indignant mass"). The tour is interrupted when the monsoon suddenly breaks. Astor's bewildered reaction is clearly double: Her "What's happening?" refers to the monsoon, consistently referred to as "she," but it also refers to the storm within, the inner tempest of her passionate desire. The storm is both an agent of Astor's sexual arousal and a metaphor for it. (This is, of course, conventional enough.) She may be married, but Astor now finds herself erotically aroused for the first time. And Gable, her first real man, literally sweeps her off her feet and carries her to the compound.

Here we are given our second reaction shot of Harlow, who watches as Gable carries Astor into his room. With her platinum hair blown by the storm and rendered luminous by the lightning, Harlow is once again radiantly beautiful. But this soft-focus, idealized, yet humanized, image of Harlow (one that is given to us, but is available to no one in the world of the film) again represents no one's desire, nor is it designed to convey an erotic charge to the viewer. It stands opposed to our next view.

Within this frame, Gable is very much in the background, setting off Mary Astor, who is seen, as it were, from within the bounds of decency. This transgressive image solicits our gaze to pass pleasurably over the perfect form of her features (her nose, ears, and lips), her smooth skin, her taut neck and arms, her swelling breasts. Her movements further accentuate the sensation the image gives us of her body as made of flesh, and her face a fleshly part of her body, its features carnal regions rather than instruments of expression. In this image, she seems entirely consumed by sexual desire. Astor’s carnality, and not her soul or her mind or her heart, is what the shot declares and embodies. Astor’s earlier snobbish behavior is at least for a moment cast off, leaving not an individual, but an object and subject of desire.

Typically, Mary Astor plays, in movies, characters who act aloof, although these characters often have so little self-awareness that they are unaware that this is an act. When Astor’s act is exposed on film, she is typically interpreted – as she is in *Red Dust* – as a woman whose only wish is, to paraphrase Kenneth Anger’s quotation from Astor’s real-life diary, “to have the living daylights fucked out of her.”[1] Astor’s aloof act is declared, in films like *Red Dust*, to mask a terrifying, all-consuming sexual desire. *The Maltese Falcon* pierces through to a further intuition about Astor: that her displays of insatiable lustfulness, masked by her aloof act, are themselves theatrical. Yet instead of meditating on the mystery of this woman’s nature (in particular, her motivations in so theatricalizing her sexuality), *The Maltese Falcon*, anticipating film noir, regressively explains this theatricality away, interpreting it as villainy. It fails to appreciate (and *Red Dust* even fails to recognize) the spirit of irony and the wit with which Mary Astor participates in the animation of her screen persona. Jean Harlow’s wit is about alienation in the face of the world; Astor’s wit is about alienation from oneself.

The Mary Astor figure is the object of Gable’s desire, but *Red Dust* does not allow him to win her in the end. The remainder of the film chronicles the events in the course of which Gable comes to renounce his desire and to accept Harlow as his mate.

Having sent Raymond to a distant part of the plantation so as to have freer access to his wife, Gable finally goes to the far-off outpost where the

[1] Kenneth Anger, *Hollywood Babylon* (New York: Dell, 1981), p. 274.

poor guy has been hopelessly screwing things up. Ostensibly, he goes there to shoot a marauding man-eating tiger, but his real intention is to announce to the cuckolded husband that Gable and the wife are in love with each other. Yet in the presence of this nice boy who looks up to him for being decent as well as for possessing the prowess to shoot tigers, Gable cannot bring himself to do what he came to do. Distraught by the discovery that there are limits to how low he is willing to sink, he leaves immediately upon killing the tiger, saying nothing. (After Gable's departure, Raymond is told about his wife's affair.)

Back at the compound, Gable and Harlow team up to perform a charade intended to make Astor think that he was deceiving her all along, that he was never in love, but only using her. Astor is so upset that she loses control and shoots Gable. When her husband arrives, he actually believes the story that she joins with Harlow and Gable in concocting to explain the spectacle that greets him.

Husband and wife depart together. Astor, for so long unaware of desire, has become disillusioned by desire. And the very gesture by which Gable frees Astor to leave with her husband at the same time denies his desire. It also declares his knowledge and acceptance of his bond with Harlow. Whether he desires her or not, he now knows she is the right mate for him. As the film's epilogue confirms, their relationship is like that of innocent children, who have fun playing games together. Then is their bond not grounded in desire?

Gable, wounded, lies in bed while Harlow reads to him a bedtime story about a bunny rabbit. When his playful fingers hop a little too suggestively for the spirit of the story, she jestingly chastises him. This depiction of their relationship is stripped of any suggestion of sexual desire between them. If they are to make love, the film allows us to imagine it only as an extension of their childish play, their playful denial of desire.

There are two conceptions of sexuality that *Red Dust* sets in opposition. The first is embodied in the relationship between Gable and Astor: sexuality as a brute passion, a storm arousing and aroused by violent nature. All of the animals that appear or are alluded to in the film (the tiger that leaps as Astor's passion wells up within her; the tiger Gable shoots; the parrot; most comically, the "ewes, don't you call them" that the makers of Roquefort cheese slap around) invoke this conception of sexuality as animalistic. The monsoon itself, a "she," has already been described in its link to Astor's passion. Perhaps most extreme, there is the link between the process of arousing human erotic passion and the processes by which rubber and cheese are produced. All three processes are described in identical terms;

in each, "slapping around" and the consequent indignant stiffening are crucial steps. And, of course, Gene Raymond, who will never grow into a real man, has been, like so many rubber trees (if this isn't stretching a point), "tapped too young." Such repetition and structuring of motifs, though almost never discussed in the critical literature, is an entirely characteristic aspect of Hollywood films of the thirties. (This aspect is polished to its greatest brilliance in the work of Howard Hawks.)

The second conception, embodied in the Gable–Harlow relationship, is the contrasting idea of sexuality as good clean fun, an innocent child's game untainted by desire.

It seems plausible to speculate that the rigid enforcement of the Production Code in 1934 suppressed the depiction of sexuality as a brute passion in Hollywood films, and with it any explicit representation of sexual desire. The positive aspect of that repression was the creation of conditions favorable to the development of the remarriage comedy, initiated in 1934 by Frank Capra's *It Happened One Night*, also starring Clark Gable. The Gable–Harlow relationship anticipates Gable's relationship to Claudette Colbert in the Capra film, except that Colbert, like the heroines of all the remarriage comedies, harbors a Mary Astor within her. (Or perhaps we might say that Colbert is an Astor figure who harbors a Harlow within her. After all, like Astor in *Red Dust*, Colbert in *It Happened One Night* starts out, in her relationship with Gable, acting the part of a snobby bitch.)

Sexuality is not only *represented* on film, of course; movies are themselves *sexy*, incorporating forms that excite the viewer sexually or quasi-sexually (the latter qualification is intended to register the intimate links between eroticism and violence on film). Understanding the ways in which movies have been charged erotically and the ways in which these erotic forms may be, and have been, used by viewers (for example, as material for private erotic fantasies, themselves variously integrated into viewers' forms of life) is essential for any complete account of the movie both as a social institution and from the perspective of the evolution of its forms.

It might be assumed that rigid enforcement of the Production Code inhibited the practice of creating erotic screen images, but matters are not that simple. For one thing, representations of explicitly sexual relationships may or may not be filmed erotically. Miriam Hopkins's pre-1934 films emphasize and articulate her sexuality. Her persona on screen is that of an idealist who is also a lustbox; her consciousness of her dual nature is poisoned by her loathing for her own fallenness, which is what, to her, her body signifies. Hopkins's body functions as a sign of her sexuality, but she is virtually never filmed the way Mary Astor is in *Red Dust*; images of Miriam Hopkins on screen are almost never rendered erotic.

On the other hand, erotic images can be placed within a narrative context that disavows their connection with sexual arousal. (Such a distinction may readily be brought to bear on the photographs in any issue of *Playboy*.) My impression is that such is indeed the rule in those Hollywood films of the late thirties that employ erotic images. The most intensely erotic Hollywood screen figure of the late thirties is Simone Simon, Jean Renoir's first choice for the role of Christine in *The Rules of the Game*. But Simone Simon's Hollywood films characteristically declare her erotic presence to be presexual (as, for example, in the thirties remake of *Seventh Heaven*). I cannot think of a single Hollywood film made between 1934 and 1940 that employs erotically rendered images and declares them to be representations of sexual desire. In this sense, *Red Dust* is very much a pre-Production Code film.

Part of the importance of this line of thought is that it gives us yet another reason to reject the often-made claim that the "classical" Hollywood movie developed as a clear-cut extension of "bourgeois" nineteenth-century realism (as though we already knew how to think about that). The truth is that, from Griffith on, movies have been and continue to be no less intimately involved with the rendering of erotic images than they are with processes of "identification."

Traditional accounts of the "sex symbols" in Hollywood's history, like everything else about the private history of the public institution of movies, stand in need of revision. If we continue to pursue this subject, we should expect surprises. After all, who would surmise, or remember, that in *Red Dust* the camera possessed carnal knowledge of the prim Mary Astor, but not the legendary sex symbol Jean Harlow?

The idea of photographing actions and stories came about with the development of techniques proper to film. The most significant of these, you know, occurred when D. W. Griffith took the camera away from the proscenium arch, where his predecessors used to place it, and moved it as close as possible to the actors.

– Alfred Hitchcock[1]

For Hitchcock, "pure cinema" was born when Griffith's camera crossed the barrier of the proscenium. This transgression freed film to discover a natural subject in theater, in the interpenetration of theater and the world reflected in the familiar ambiguity of the English word "acting." Theatricality is theater's natural condition; the candid or unself-conscious can be depicted, in theater, only by acting. But when Griffith's camera broke the barrier of the proscenium, it assumed the capacity, as a matter of course, to unmask theatricality. In movies, the camera routinely distinguishes between gestures and expressions that are candid and those that are staged.

Film's opposition between the theatrical and the nontheatrical is grounded in, and grounds, its conventional ways of presenting human beings in the world. Typically, the camera alternately frames its human subject within public and private spaces. The frame of the "objective" shot is a stage on which a human being performs, subject to view by others in his or her world. Within the frame of the reaction shot, the subject views the spectacle of the world, expresses a private reaction, and prepares the next venture into the public world. Point-of-view and reaction shots together combine to effect the camera's penetration of his or her privacy. The human subject of the camera alternates tensely and hesitantly between acting and viewing in preparing entrances onto the world's stage, performing, and withdrawing again into a privacy to which only the camera has access.

[1] François Truffaut, *Hitchcock* (New York: Simon & Schuster, 1967), p. 40.

Reprinted: See "Notes on the Essays."

To sustain film's opposition between the theatrical and the candid, movies developed a mode of acting that is distinct from stage technique. In the face of the camera, the movie actor must appear unself-conscious; no way of acting in the theater corresponds to this look of unself-consciousness, and no audience can stand in for a camera in registering it.

Film's massive appropriation of nineteenth-century theatrical forms, most importantly melodrama, must not blind us to its fundamental break with theater. Griffith's films owe almost everything to theatrical melodrama; yet they undermine theatrical melodrama by placing the viewer in an intimate relationship, unavailable to a theater audience, with human beings who inhabit a world and hence cannot in themselves be pure exemplars of virtue or villainy. And they also bring to the fore the encounters between the camera and the human subjects whose privacy it penetrates, encounters for which theatrical melodrama knows no equivalent.

In the theatrical melodramas of the nineteenth century, as Peter Brooks argues in *The Melodramatic Imagination*, the nightmare struggle for the liberation of virtue is won when innocence is publicly recognized in a "movement of astonishment," and evil – with its own lesser power to astonish – is driven out. Theatrical melodrama is a drama of recognition, and acts of what Brooks calls "self-nomination" play an essential role. "The villain ... at some point always bursts forth in a statement of his evil nature and intentions."[2] The heroine, too, announces her moral identity by declaring "her continued identification with purity, despite contrary appearances."[3]

In theatrical melodrama, good and evil can and must declare themselves. How can good and evil be declared in films? This is the question I address in what follows. My motivation is to gain insight into the conditions under which, in movies, human beings are presented and present themselves, that is, to gain a deeper understanding of what becomes of human beings on film.

In *Double Indemnity*, there is a moment at which Barbara Stanwyck's evil is meant to be unambiguously declared. As Fred MacMurray is struggling to kill her husband, she sits silently in the front seat of the automobile. The camera frames her closely, capturing a clear view of the look on her face.

[2] Peter Brooks, *The Melodramatic Imagination* (New Haven, CT: Yale University Press, 1976), p. 37.

[3] Ibid., p. 38.

This is the one moment in *Double Indemnity* when we are privileged to view the look that Stanwyck's stepdaughter saw years before, the look that stamped her stepmother as evil in her eyes. It is a serious weakness of the film that at this moment it comes up with no more definitive way of demonstrating that this woman is evil. Stanwyck looks almost toward the camera, but her eyes are vacant, as if she were absorbed in a private reverie. How could this look – how could any look the camera might capture – show that this woman – we know Barbara Stanwyck as a noble heroine (*Stella Dallas*), a lead in romantic comedy worthy of marrying Henry Fonda (*The Lady Eve*), and a decidedly admirable professional actress from Brooklyn – is absolutely evil? It may not be nice that she is in a trance while her husband is being murdered in a plot she instigated, but it does not make her a villain.

What is missing at this moment is an act of self-nomination. Stanwyck does not declare her moral nature here; indeed, she never does so in the film. An example that immediately springs to mind of a villain announcing his moral identity – and this is surely a moment of astonishment – occurs in *The Thirty-nine Steps* when the villainous Professor Jordan raises his hand to reveal that the top joint of his little finger is missing.

Note that just before the moment of revelation, Hitchcock frames the Professor and Hannay in such a way that we see – and see that Hannay does not see – the Professor give a start on Hannay's words "I believe she was coming to see you about some Air Ministry secrets."

Hence, when the Professor turns to face Hannay and says, calmly, "Did she tell you what the foreign agent looked like?" we know he is dissimulating like a villain.

But not only villains dissimulate. It is a running joke, and more than a joke, in *The Thirty-nine Steps* that the innocent Hannay must put on act after act, must slip into role after role, in order to assert his innocence.

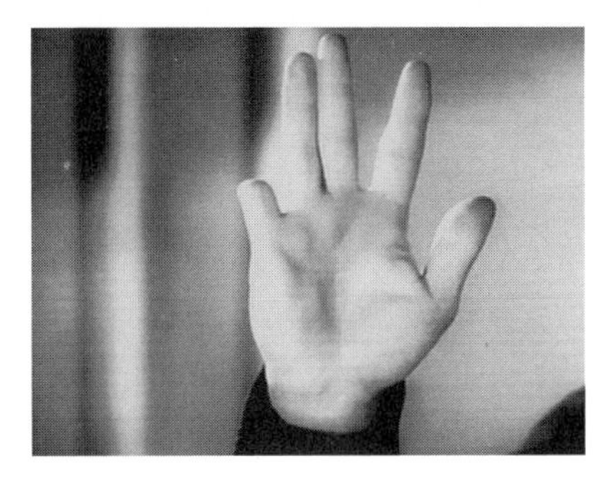

It is only at the moment he shows his hand that the Professor unmasks himself. Then the astonishing view the Professor authors and presents to Hannay is matched by an equally astonishing view Hitchcock authors and presents to us.

The implication of these matched gestures is that there is a link between the villain and Hitchcock (both are authors of views), as there is a link between Hannay and us (both are viewers). We might also say that the gesture is the camera's. It is this view framed by the camera that shows Hitchcock's hand. The camera is revealed at this moment as an instrument of villainy.

In Hitchcock's films – and not just in films by Hitchcock – there are incessant suggestions that the camera is an instrument of villainy. This passage from *The Thirty-nine Steps* exemplifies one form these suggestions take: the assertion of a link or equivalance between the villain's gesture and a gesture of the film's author. Two passages from *The Lodger* exemplify a second form: the camera's assumption of the villain's literal position.

First is the film's opening shot, a view of a terrified woman from the perspective of her murderer, a villain we never get to view. Second is our introduction to the lodger (Ivor Novello), who may or may not be a murderer. Before we view his face, the camera assumes his perspective – one that has, from the opening, been associated with the villain – as he approaches the front door of the house and reaches his hand into the frame to grasp the knocker.

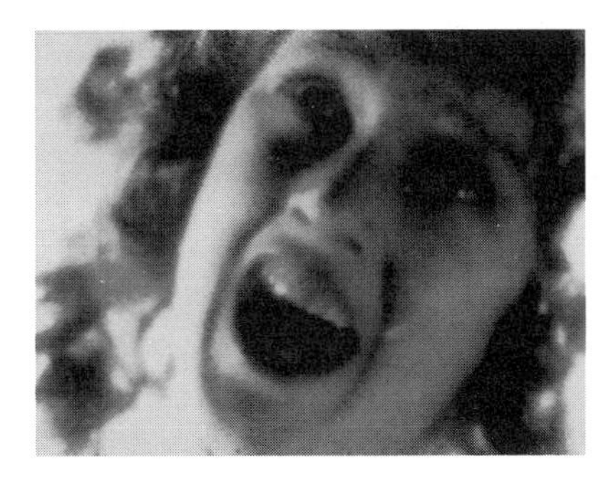

Closely related to these two examples are those passages in which Hitchcock frames a human figure in such a way as to make him a kind of symbolic stand-in for the camera. This occurs, for example, when the lodger first enters the house. In this frame, Novello is the camera's subject, but he also stares into the depths of the space, possessing it with his gaze.

When the Professor unmasks himself, he authors a view that declares his moral identity, and Hitchcock matches this with a view that reveals *his* bond with the villain. When the camera assumes the villain's place, by contrast, it is not the camera's status as an instrument of authorship but its passive aspect that is revealed. At such moments, villainy is invoked, all right, but it is linked with the act of viewing, not with the authoring of views. Hence, these moments are akin to the passages in Hitchcock's films – and again, not just in Hitchcock's films – that portray guilty acts of viewing (for example, the crofter in *The Thirty-nine Steps* or Norman Bates in *Psycho*).

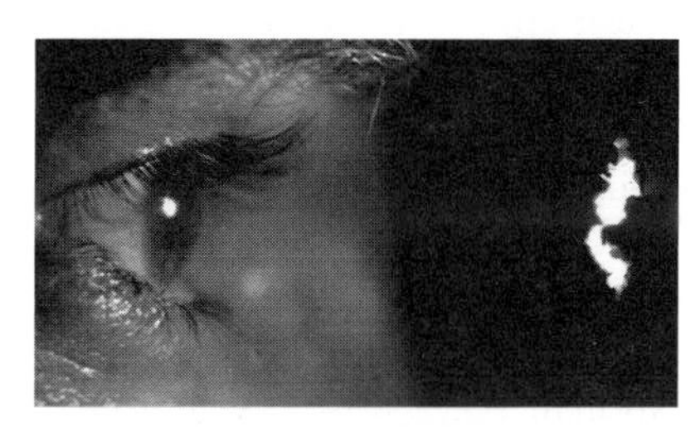

These have, as their ancestor, the extraordinary shot in *The Birth of a Nation* of Gus, the "renegade Negro," intoxicated by what he sees, guiltily viewing the innocent Mae Marsh as she, in turn, is absorbed in viewing a playful squirrel.

These are not examples of a villain's self-nomination. At these moments, the human representative of evil within the world of the film

stands revealed not by his own gesture but by the camera, which links his villainy to his guilty act of viewing.

There is a third general way of revealing the camera's link with villainy. I am thinking of those moments when a villain unmasks himself, or appears to unmask himself, by looking directly into the camera. For example, at just the moment in *The Lodger* when our suspicion is at a height that Ivor Novello is a murderer, he gives the camera a look that appears to confirm that he is guilty.

When a villain meets the camera's gaze, he presents himself to be viewed by the camera. We view him without his "false face," and we are astonished. He reveals himself to be an author of views like the Professor, but the view whose authorship he claims is presented to us, not to someone within the world of the film – and it is our view of *him*.

Yet this gesture is also akin to the camera's suggestions that the act of viewing is villainous. Meeting the camera's gaze, he reveals his knowledge of our viewing; this look by which he unmasks himself denies our innocence. And what is perhaps most significant about this double-edged gesture is that it appears to be at once a gesture by the camera and a gesture by the camera's subject. Their gestures appear not only to match but to be one and the same.

In speaking of a gesture that appears to be both the villain's and the camera's, I have in mind such passages as the ending of *Psycho*, when Norman Bates/Tony Perkins raises his gaze directly to the camera and grins.

Hitchcock and Norman/Perkins appear to be conspirators of such intimate complicity that a distinction can hardly be drawn between them. In effect, the film's author has become one with the human subject of his camera. Norman/Perkins has become a mask for Hitchcock, one of Hitchcock's stuffed birds; in turn, the grinning Norman/Perkins has been impressed indelibly on our idea of who Hitchcock is.

But consider a passage from *The Beloved Rogue*, a silent film starring John Barrymore as François Villon and Conrad Veidt as the king of France.[4]

In this scene, Villon succeeds in making the king his dupe, convincing him that he has such magical powers that the king dare not execute him. But Barrymore goes beyond the dramatic needs of the scene by presenting a knowing, villainous look to the camera.

This look to the camera is astonishing, and it is easy to imagine that it equally astonished the film's director, Alan Crosland. Crosland's camera nowhere performs a gesture that matches Barrymore's suggestion here that the film's hero has a capacity for evil. Barrymore has appropriated – and undermined – the director's – and the camera's – authority.

There are, in turn, cases in which the camera undermines the authority of a figure who appears to nominate himself as a villain. For example, when the lodger looks at the camera, he appears to be unmasking himself, but this is followed by a shot from his point of view that places him within the audience at a fashion show. Here a look we took to be a villain's self-nomination is given an innocent explanation: This is only a spectator; this is only the look of a spectator. (Then again, perhaps this spectator is not innocent. Perhaps no spectator is.) Thus, a view that seemed clearly legible has turned ambiguous and enigmatic. Indeed, the sequence leaves us only with a question about the camera's motivation, coupled with a demonstration that, for all we know, this human being – and perhaps any human being – may be capable of villainy. That is, the passage confronts us with the limits of our access to the world of a film: We cannot take for granted that the camera will reveal to us – even that it can reveal to us – innocence or guilt in human beings. The role of the camera undermines the very basis of theatrical melodrama.

At the end of *Psycho*, as we have seen, Norman Bates/Tony Perkins fixes the camera in his gaze and grins: Again, a villain appears to be unmasking himself, with the camera's complicity. But then, "mother's" mummified face is momentarily superimposed over (surfaces from under?) his living face.

Whoever or whatever we take Norman Bates/Tony Perkins to be, Hitchcock's extraordinary gesture declares, he is no villain of theatrical melodrama. In *The Murderous Gaze*, I interpret this composite figure, this being possessed by death, as emblematic of the condition of all human beings on film:

[4] For introducing this passage to me, and showing me how to think about it, I am grateful to Marian Keane, who has been studying this film in the context of her doctoral dissertation on John Barrymore, which I am awaiting with eager anticipation.

> The camera fixes its human subjects, possesses their life. They are reborn on the screen, creatures of the film's author and of ourselves. But life is not fully breathed back into them. They are immortal but they are always already dead. The beings projected on the screen are condemned to a condition of death-in-life from which they can never escape. What lures us into the world of a film may be a dream of triumphing over death, holding death forever at bay. But . . . the world of a film is not a private island where we may escape the conditions of our existence. At the heart of every film is a truth we already know: we have been born into the world and we are fated to die.[5]

For Hitchcock, film ultimately turns out to be not a medium of melodrama but the medium perfectly suited to express a vision of human existence as an imprisonment from which there is no imaginable escape. Hitchcock's films are no more tragedies or comedies than theatrical melodramas are, but they are also not theatrical melodramas. Their underlying vision undermines theatrical melodrama, for there are no villainous human beings responsible for creating what it is this film lays bare that is intolerable in the human condition.

Villainy is integral to Hitchcock's vision, but it emerges from and expresses a perfectly human dream of escaping from the real conditions of human existence. The camera can "nominate" a villain only by nominating itself. The camera becomes evil's only real exemplar, but theatrical melodrama requires that evil manifest itself perfectly in human form. Villains in theatrical melodrama are the creation of an occult force; in films they are, in part, the creation of the camera.

Perfect human representatives of evil are not real; human beings wish for them and theatrical melodrama is motivated in part by that wish. But the camera reveals that human beings are only human. When they appear inhuman, as they often do in films, the camera (which human beings also wish for) participates in creating that inhumanity. Evil, understood as an occult force that exists apart from human beings and their creations, has no reality in the face of the camera.

What I am suggesting, as I wade through these deep waters, is that film not only undermines theatrical melodrama but also provides a particular way of understanding its motivation. Of course, theatrical melodrama has its opposing vision, which provides in turn its own interpretation of film – its interpretation, that is, not of film's motivation but of its nature: Film is evil.

But now it is time to turn to virtue or innocence and how it might be declared – or declare itself – in films.

[5] William Rothman, *Hitchcock – The Murderous Gaze* (Cambridge, MA: Harvard University Press, 1982), p. 341.

In *Pursuits of Happiness*, Stanley Cavell invokes Matthew Arnold in elucidating the claim that in remarriage comedies like *The Philadelphia Story* film has found one of its great subjects:

> There is a visual equivalent or analogue of what Arnold means by distinguishing the best self from the ordinary self and by saying that in the best self class yields to humanity. He is witnessing a possibility or potential in the human self not normally open to view, or not open to the normal view. Call this one's invisible self; it is what the movie camera would make visible.[6]

A film like *The Philadelphia Story* stakes itself on the claim that the camera has the power to reveal virtue or innocence in any human subject – to participate in making it visible. In the comedies Cavell studies, the camera's power to reveal the "invisible self" enables romance to contain the threat of melodrama. The remarriage comedies, like the Hitchcock thrillers, discover in the camera – film's instrument of villainy – the means to undermine theatrical melodrama, which demands the conviction that there are persons whose exemplification of good or evil is absolute, human beings who know their moral identity and have the power of naming it.

We have seen that the camera can single out a human subject as a villain, an exemplar of evil, but only by revealing (in the same gesture) that this figure's villainy cannot be separated from his or her bond with the camera. Then can the camera also compellingly single out a human exemplar of virtue, and, if so, what does this reveal about the camera?

In *The Birth of a Nation* sequence we have considered, Gus's guilty viewing is contrasted with Mae Marsh's innocent viewing. Her absorption in her views of the squirrel reveals her girlish innocence, her guiltlessness, but it hardly makes her the astonishing heroine of theatrical melodrama who declares her moral identity. What the sequence establishes, rather, is her vulnerability. But is the camera, in this sequence, innocent like Mae Marsh or guilty like Gus? True, the camera does not exactly assume Gus's point of view, does not exactly present to us his guilty views, the way it presents to us views of the squirrel that are effectively indistinguishable from her girlish views. In this sequence, the camera frames no views that are fully charged with Gus's desire. When it frames Gus's staring eyes, the camera links villainy with the act of viewing, but not with its own viewing. Griffith's camera attempts to disavow its implication in villainy; yet to us this implication – this connection between Gus and the camera – is manifest.

[6] Stanley Cavell, *Pursuits of Happiness: The Hollywood Comedy of Remarriage* (Cambridge, MA: Harvard University Press, 1981), p. 158.

In sequences like this, "virtue" is really vulnerability, or we might call it "virginity." The camera's revelations of Mae Marsh's innocence are also violations of that innocence. It is a small step from such violations to the pornography of those Griffith passages in which the camera, in effect, acts as the very instrument of a woman's terrorization (for example, the famous scenes in *Broken Blossoms* in which Lillian Gish, framed closely, hysterical from fear of her brutal father, appears brutalized by the camera itself). Then it is another small step to films like *Stella Dallas*, which are often called melodramas, although there is no villainous human figure responsible for the noble heroine's suffering. Such films are examples of what becomes of theatrical melodrama on film, with the camera appropriating the villain's role, serving as agent – as well as observer – of the heroine's anguish. Yet in *Stella Dallas*, the camera at the same time plays an essential role in her liberation, her transfiguration.

In general, it seems clear to me that when the camera designates a heroine as virtuous in the same gesture by which it reveals, yet disavows, its own implication in villainy, this declaration has no authority. The woman designated, however "noble," is not a heroine, but a victim. As in *Double Indemnity*, what seems missing is an act of self-nomination, in this case performed by the heroine.

There is a problem, however, in conceiving of such acts on film. A heroine cannot unmask herself, because she wears no mask. Then how can she declare herself to the camera? What can she do, in the face of the camera, that will reveal her virtue, other than enduring the camera's gaze?

"Enduring the camera's gaze" is how I think of our final poignant vision of Margaret, the crofter's wife, in *The Thirty-nine Steps*. She does not confront the camera, and indeed she gives no outward sign that she knows she is being viewed. Yet she is not absorbed like Mae Marsh nor oblivious; I view her as knowingly bearing the burden of the camera's gaze, the way she knowingly bears the burden of her husband's brutality.

A less inhumane way the camera can declare an exemplar of virtue is by designating representative human beings as judges and letting these representatives' judgments stand as conclusive. In such a case, the camera need not claim the authority to recognize perfect virtue; all it need claim is the power to nominate qualified witnesses. To be qualified, one need be no hero or heroine; all one need be is manifestly human. To declare its subject human, in this sense, all the camera need do is make visible that subject's invisible self, and this is something the camera does have the power to do.

A textbook example of this strategy occurs in the James Whale version of *Show Boat*. In the sequence I have in mind, Helen Morgan, now pathetically reduced in station, is auditioning. As she begins the song "Bill," the camera frames her squarely and holds this framing, compelling her to endure its gaze for a painfully long time.

Finally, there is a cut to the once-skeptical impresario, who nods approval – to our great satisfaction – to someone offscreen, and a cut to the piano accompanist, who firmly nods his agreement. The tension broken, we cut to an "objective" three-shot. When we now return to the original frontal framing, its effect is completely transformed. We are now Helen Morgan's appreciative audience, not her judges; the verdict is in. For the remainder of the song, Whale cuts back and forth between ever closer and more ravishing views of this woman and shots of all the people in the theater, from janitors to dancers, gathering around the singer one by one – a community joined in astonishment at the beauty of her performance, sign of the beauty of her soul.

A second humane way the camera can declare an exemplar of virtue is by paying its respects by withdrawing its gaze. Films abound in gestures of this kind: for example, the camera's withdrawing to satisfy Thomas Mitchell's wish to die alone in *Only Angels Have Wings*; the camera's cutting away from Emil Jannings at the climax of his humiliation in *The Blue Angel*; the camera's respecting the privacy of Frank Morgan's suicide in *The Shop Around the Corner*; the camera's withdrawal from the heroine at the end of Carl Dreyer's *Gertrud*.

Can an exemplar of virtue declare himself or herself by meeting the camera's gaza? Here I think of the moment near the end of *Dinner at Eight* when Marie Dressler, learning of John Barrymore's suicide, looks right into the camera. (Four months after this shot was taken, Marie Dressler, the era's most popular star, was dead.)

It is not that Dressler presents herself to the camera, like a villain; at this moment, she endures the camera's gaze, like a heroine. She is in no trance, but perfectly clear-eyed. Then what does she see in the face of the camera? (What she sees, I take it, is essentially what we see when we view Norman Bates at the end of *Psycho*.) We are viewing no perfect exemplar of an occult moral force here, no heroine of theatrical melodrama; we are viewing a human being mindful of a mortality we can see stamped on Marie Dressler's face. This moment of her recognition of her humanity is also the moment of our recognition of it. It is a moment exemplary of the camera's capacity to render the invisible self visible. Like the ending of *Psycho*, then, this moment undermines the basis of theatrical melodrama.

Perhaps the most astonishing of all examples of this power of the camera is the passage from Jean Renoir's *Grand Illusion* in which a kind old German prison guard gives a harmonica to Jean Gabin, who is near the breaking point from solitary confinement.

The sequence opens on a tin dish filled with inedible-looking food. The camera tilts up and pans left across a stone wall. It holds on Gabin's face, which reveals a look of despair such as belonged, in films of the thirties, to only this beloved French star.

Having demonstrated this man's capacity to endure its gaze, the camera humanely withdraws, reframing to take in the guard's entrance. The guard immediately reveals his humanity, shows he is qualified as a judge. Seeing Gabin's haunted look, he vainly tries to offer solace by giving the prisoner a comradely pat on the shoulder.

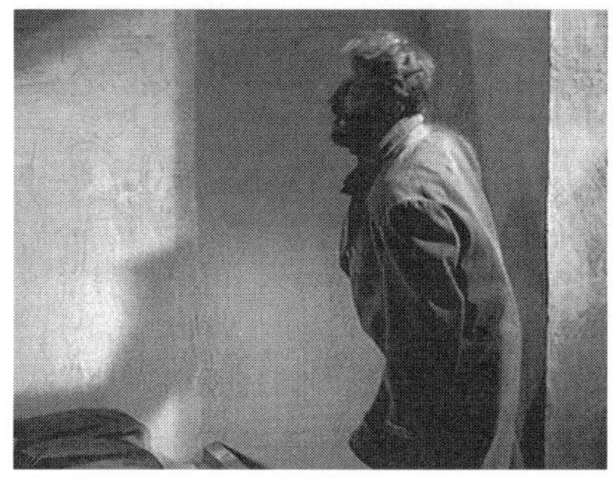

Gabin responds with an angry tirade. When the camera reframes to exclude the stunned guard, this underscores that he has momentarily become a horrified spectator and Gabin a spectacle. At the same time, the camera has the calm assurance to wait out the storm.

Gabin finally sits, and the guard gives him a harmonica on the chance he might comfort himself with music. When the guard quietly leaves, he passes through the frame and the camera does not even mark his exit. Has this human being simply been forgotten?

It is unimaginably satisfying when Renoir's camera withdraws from Gabin and cuts to the guard outside the door awaiting a sign. And it can make life seem worthwhile that the camera now reveals that the guard – starving for music – is immediately transported by the tune Gabin plays.

When he recognizes the song ("Frou-frou"), he knows that Gabin – whose nature is to pursue women – has come back to life. The guard is satisfied – satisfied that his own capacity for happiness is still alive and that he has lightened this stranger's burden. And Renoir shows how much he respects this human judge by allowing him to speak for the film when he says, to another guard who was wondering what was going on, "The war has gone on too long."

My point about this sequence is that Renoir's camera employs all the strategies available to it for rendering respect for its human subjects without falsely denying the camera's capacity for inhumanity. Perhaps part of Renoir's point is that melodrama has gone on too long.

CHAPTER 9

Pathos and Transfiguration in the Face of the Camera

A Reading of *Stella Dallas*

In *The Melodramatic Imagination*, Peter Brooks argues that in theatrical melodrama, human exemplars of good and evil can and must declare themselves.[1] In the original theatrical melodramas of the early nineteenth century, heroine and villain declare their moral natures. Announcing themselves to be human exemplars of the occult forces of good and evil, they perform acts of "self-nomination." But in films, human beings never stand revealed by their own gestures alone. They are always also revealed by the camera.

As I show in the preceding chapter, the camera can "nominate" a human subject as an exemplar of evil only by revealing at the same time that this figure's villainy is inseparable from the camera's bond with him or her – that is, only by nominating *itself* as well, and thereby implicating the film's creators and viewers. When human beings appear inhuman in films, as they often do, the camera is instrumental in creating their inhumanity. Understood as theatrical melodrama understands it, as an occult force existing apart from human beings and their creations, evil has no reality in the face of the camera.

If the camera is an exemplary instrument of villainy, how can it single out an exemplar of goodness? Starting at least with Griffith (and perhaps this has a precedent in American theatrical melodrama as opposed to the French examples Brooks studies), "virtue" in films is typically reduced to innocence and in turn to vulnerability. The assertions of Mae Marsh's "virtue" in *The Birth of a Nation*, for example, are the camera's demonstrations of her innocence. They are also violations of that innocence, despite Griffith's strenuous attempts to disavow his own implication in villainy. However "noble" the "Little Sister" may be, she is a victim, not a self-knowing,

[1] Peter Brooks, *The Melodramatic Imagination* (New Haven, CT: Yale University Press, 1976), p. 37.

Reprinted: See "Notes on the Essays."

powerful heroine in Brooks's sense. She is pathetic, and nothing exemplifies her pathos more than her violation by the camera.

In King Vidor's *Stella Dallas* (1937), there is no evil character responsible for the suffering of Stella (Barbara Stanwyck), although there is all too much cruelty in Stella's world, much inhumanity in which the camera is implicated. Consider, for example, the extraordinary sequence at the posh resort frequented by her daughter's college classmates and their families.

Looking for the mother of the young man Laurel has been dating, Stella enters the hotel shop, all dolled up like a floozie, but – it would appear – thinking herself dressed in high style. Laurel and her date are sitting together at the counter of the adjoining ice-cream parlor, sipping sodas, but mother and daughter do not see each other. Stella, deporting herself in an outrageously affected manner that she seems to take to be genteel, makes a spectacle of herself, unknowingly, it seems.

Stella seems too oblivious to hear, and Laurel is too wrapped up with her date to attend to, the wisecracks the other students exchange about this vulgar woman "dressed like a Christmas tree." Only when one of her classmates says whom the woman had been looking for does Laurel look up at the big mirror behind the counter and see her mother, who still does not notice her.

Laurel rushes out, unable to face an encounter. She is upset because she understands her own vulnerability, in the world of such privileged snobs, but also, I take it, because, for the first time, she sees her mother through others' eyes. Recognition of her own vulnerability coincides with a terrifying onset of knowledge of her mother's vulnerability, hence of her own power over her mother. Laurel is terrified of revealing to her mother that she appears vulgar not only in the eyes of these contemptible strangers but also in her own daughter's eyes.

In this sequence, then, we "identify" not with Stella but with the gazes that cruelly expose her. Much of the sequence is filmed with Stella in the background, reflected in the mirror. This striking composition underscores the status of this mirror as a "surrogate screen" like the movie screen early in the film and the window at the end. (In *The Lady Eve*, reversing and perhaps parodying this sequence, Preston Sturges puts a mirror in Barbara Stanwyck's hands and gives her sole access to – and control over – what it reflects.) The camera mercilessly frames a vision of Stella that would mortify her were she to possess it herself. (I am leaving aside the alternative interpretation that her self-presentation here is calculated.) Later she will, in effect, gain access to this vision, and she will, symbolically, die although she will also come to life again.

Our sense of Stella's vulnerability here is inseparable from her seeming obliviousness of how others see her, and it is exacerbated by her conviction that no one has a surer grasp of appearances than she. Her lack of self-consciousness, crystallized in her obliviousness of the camera, is a condition of that "vulgarity" that is inseparable from her innocence. Exposing her vulgarity entails violating that innocence, and the camera is instrumental in this villainy.

Positing Stella as noble while violating her innocence by rendering her pathetic seems the cornerstone of this film's strategy for moving its audience to tears, but this by itself is not sufficient. Viewed as pathetic, lower than we, and noble, higher than we, Stella is not a figure with whom we identify. Because her feelings are not ours, the film needs a way of incorporating feelings we can share and communicating those feelings to us. But whose feeling is to be communicated to us? In films, feeling to be communicated to the viewer can be expressed by the camera; more typically, as I argue in the preceding chapter, it is expressed by an inhabitant of the film's world, who is, in effect, designated as a representative of humanity.

After the debacle in the ice-cream parlor, Laurel insists – with no explanation – that her mother take her home. As Stella and Laurel lie in their separate berths on the train, voices filter in from the next compartment: Two of Laurel's classmates are joking about the vulgar woman who made such a spectacle of herself. Laurel is sick with dismay at the possibility that her mother may have overheard these words. Stella has indeed overheard, but when Laurel leans into her compartment, she pretends to be asleep. Not knowing if her mother really overheard the voices, Laurel snuggles up to her, receiving comfort and revealing her desire to give comfort. This is a touching gesture through which Laurel emerges neither as noble nor as pathetic, but as human. Yet what underpins the film's communication of Laurel's human feeling to us is, again, its seeming exposure of Stella's vulnerability. In the face of this pathetic figure we affirm our community with Laurel – a community in which poor Stella has no place.

In the following sequence, too, we are moved to an affirmation of community from which we exclude Stella. Stella visits Helen, the woman her husband Stephen now loves. Pretending that she finds Laurel an "inconvenience," she offers to give her up. Helen is not taken in and recognizes what she calls Stella's "selflessness." We perceive Helen's emotion less in her face (much of the time she is turned away from the camera) than in her voice: Behind the "excessive" evenness of her tone and precision of her choice of words we can discern her effort to keep from breaking down, an effort that reveals itself in tiny hesitations. Tenderly, Helen reaches out to offer comfort, but this contact makes Stella uneasy, and Helen holds back. She hesitates in part because she knows she is implicated in Stella's pain – is, indeed, its source. What crowns Stella's astonishing selflessness in Helen's eyes is precisely, I take it, that Stella shows no sign of hating her.

In judging Stella to be selfless, Helen views her as being better than she is. In the presence of this exemplar Helen feels humbled, and Helen's feeling, not Stella's, is communicated to us. We are moved that Helen appreciates Stella, and moved as well that Helen grieves to be unable to reach Stella, to comfort her. Helen's attunement with the camera only underscores, for us, Stella's obliviousness of how she appears in Helen's eyes, and our eyes. Yet again, it seems, underpinning Helen's emotion and ours is the camera's violation of Stella's innocence, its rendering of her as pathetic. This rendering culminates in the film's ending, which also radically undermines it.

The closing sequence is prefaced by an exchange between Laurel and Helen. Just before the wedding, Helen comes upon Laurel at the window, sees that she has been crying, and divines what is troubling her. Laurel had always imagined that even if distance prevented her mother from attending the wedding, she would at least send word. Helen, her faith in Stella's selflessness intact, asks Laurel if she can really believe that any distance in the world would keep her mother away if she knew about the wedding. Laurel, accepting Helen's implication that her mother does not know, repeats, in a whisper, "No distance in the world. . . . "

As if motivated by these words invoking the mystery of Stella's absence, there is a cut to a magisterial shot of the street in front of the house, the camera craning down and in. The effect of this declaration of the camera is extraordinary; it is as if a higher power manifests itself. Stella makes her appearance only in the next shot (it is on a more human scale) of the hubbub in the street. It takes us a moment to pick Stella out of the crowd, but the camera unhesitatingly follows her as she makes her way to the fence, from which, through a large window – Helen has seen to it that the curtains are open – she can view the ceremony as though it were projected on a movie screen.

Once she assumes this station, the body of the sequence begins, alternating shots of Stella viewing and shots of what she views. All the family – except Stella, of course – is in place: Stephen, Helen, Laurel, and the young stiff she is marrying. Everyone is absorbed in the ceremony, which means that no one looks at the camera, no one sees Stella looking. Stella is spellbound, but shows no expression, as the wedding begins.

Helen seemed to speak for the film when she reassured Laurel that her mother loves her so much that if she only knew about the wedding, nothing would keep her away. We are called upon to accept her judgment that Stella is noble and to share her view of Stella as pathetic. ("Couldn't you read between those pathetic lines?" she asks Stephen when he takes at face value Stella's note announcing her intention of marrying her old friend Ed. Stephen, like every character incarnated by John Boles, is singularly incapable of reading between any lines.) When Stella bridges all earthly distance and finds her way to the window, this appears to confirm her nobility and her pathos. Surely it breaks Stella's heart to remain outside at her daughter's wedding, but she makes this sacrifice because she is selfless. If we take this loving mother's exclusion to be unnecessary or misguided, that only intensifies her pathos.

This phase of the sequence, in which Stella does not express what she is thinking or feeling, is brought to a close when a policeman orders her to move on. She implores him to let her stay a little longer. He looks through the window, sees what she is viewing, and lets her continue. With Stella, we view the conclusion of the ceremony, culminating in the couple's kiss.

This kiss – the happy ending – is what Stella was waiting to see, and it provokes her, for the first time, to a reaction. As a tear rolls down her cheek, she diverts her gaze, looking down and away. The tear reveals that she is moved; yet her lowered gaze also veils her feelings, as though from someone watching. She gives what can be described only as a

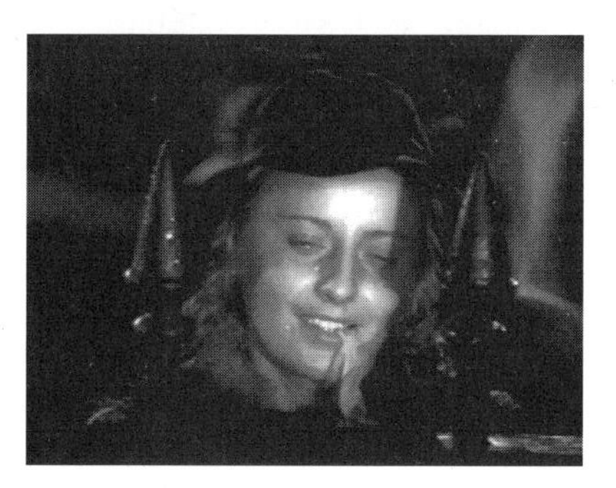

secret smile – a smile that guards its secret source. Then she looks up, her face transfigured. Her smile now openly shows her happiness. Yet this smile that announces her feeling also keeps her secret.

As she walks jauntily away from the window and toward the camera, we get a clear view of the look of happiness on her face. It is on this look that the image fades out and the film ends – and we, as satisfied as Stella, file out of the theater and into the night.

No doubt, were Helen magically empowered to view what we have viewed, she would take Stella's happy look to confirm that motherhood is a woman's highest (indeed, only) calling, and she would take Stella's transfiguration as a sign – miraculously granted by the unearthly power that presides over this world – that acts of sacrifice bring their own reward. To Helen, Stella's happiness would signify the all-importance of being inside. Helen would deny the possibility that Stella is happy *not* to be inside, happy to be free from marriage and motherhood, to be free to view this world from outside as we do. Then, too, Stella's secret smile anticipates her turning away from the window, as though what makes her happy is not viewing the world rather than living in it but feeling free from all attachments to the world, even the attachments of a viewer.

Expressively, the final fade-out, which engulfs Stella in blackness, can be viewed as figuring her death, but Helen would also deny the possibility that Stella is happy to be free to die.

There is a mystery to Stella's transformation. Her jaunty walk now is the walk of the "old" Stella! Yet we thought she had shed that identity, that it had died for her after she overheard Laurel's classmates' derisive talk about the "painted woman." The last time we saw this "old" Stella it was really a "new" Stella putting on a performance intended to make Laurel think that her mother did not really love her. The Stella who has the power to enact her old self as a role could, perhaps, play any role, but now this Stella, too, has died and been reborn. Does the jaunty walk reveal that Stella has been transformed back to her original identity, or is she *playing* the old Stella again?

If Stella is acting, who is the woman performing this act, why has she chosen this role, and for what audience is she performing?

One possible answer to the last of these questions is that she is performing for herself. Another possibility: for no audience in her world; that is, for the camera. When Stella lowers her gaze as though she were being watched and smiles her secret smile, she is acknowledging the camera, acknowledging the "higher power" that manifests itself in the commanding crane shot that echoes Laurel's whispered "No distance in the world . . . ," and acknowledging how she appears in our eyes. Thus transfigured by the power to acknowledge the camera, hence to acknowledge herself, she is no longer the innocent woman vulnerable to the camera's violation.

But perhaps Stella never really was the pathetic figure we took her to be: perhaps she always knew herself better than we knew her, and perhaps all along we have failed to acknowledge her. Perhaps when she presented herself at the hotel, for example, she knew perfectly well that her outfit violated "respectable" taste and was deliberately affronting snooty sensibilities, although without weighing the consequences for Laurel of this theatrical gesture. (After all, the "old" Stella made all of her daughter's dresses, and no less an authority than Helen is impressed by Laurel's wardrobe.)[2]

At this moment, in other words, we must recognize that we do not know Stella and have never really known her. We have no more grounds for judging the "new" Stella to be noble than we had for taking the "old" Stella to be pathetic. We do not know what has brought her back to life. We do not know what makes this woman happy, and in the face of her happiness we do not know what to feel. Then why does this ending give us such deep satisfaction that we, too, smile through our tears?

Most "tearjerkers" center on the suffering of a noble heroine. *Stella Dallas* is among those that tell the story of a woman who has to choose between the pursuit of her own happiness and the happiness of her daughter. The original version of *Imitation of Life*, directed in 1934 by John Stahl, is a roughly contemporary film of this type in which the heroine gives up the love of her life for the sake of her daughter's happiness. In *Stella Dallas*, it seems, for the sake of her daughter's happiness the heroine gives her daughter up – an even higher sacrifice, if motherhood is understood as women's highest fulfillment. But both films appear to assert that a heroine must sacrifice her own happiness for the sake of *something*. This claim that there are things more important than a woman's happiness has something to do with why such films seem to us so problematic, even offensive, why there may seem to be something wrong with them not only aesthetically but also morally.

I have not, in my remarks about *Stella Dallas*, explicitly addressed this moral revulsion, but my reading is, in part, a response to it. It is generally

[2] Stanley Cavell helped me to recognize that Stella's behavior can consistently be interpreted in these terms.

supposed that films like *Stella Dallas* glorify a woman's submission to a system that unjustly deprives her of her equal right to pursue happiness. These heroines embrace their suffering in gestures posited as noble. Their gestures of self-sacrifice are meant to move us. We are meant to affirm our community with all who endorse them.

Perhaps such a description is accurate for Stahl's *Imitation of Life*, although I do not wish to prejudge this issue here. What can be said unequivocally is that *Stella Dallas* declares itself not guilty of such villainy. The film's mysterious and ambiguous ending leaves us not knowing what the heroine has become and not knowing what to feel in the face of her happiness. Stella has been transformed – or has transformed herself – before our very eyes, unveiling at last that power and mystery the camera discovers in Barbara Stanwyck in *The Lady Eve* and *Double Indemnity*.

Understood in these terms, *Stella Dallas* reveals its especially intimate relationship to the genre Stanley Cavell calls "the remarriage comedy," whose underlying myth is also about the creation of a new woman. There are differences, of course, that would have to be accounted for in any full study of these matters. One feature of the remarriage comedy is that the woman's relationship with her father is of great importance, whereas her mother is literally or figuratively absent. Cavell argues that this feature derives from the genre's source in Shakespearean romance, especially in *The Winter's Tale*. Another feature is that the central couple is childless. *Stella Dallas* negates both of these features, but perhaps a more fundamental difference is that no man in *Stella Dallas* plays the role of, say, Cary Grant in *The Philadelphia Story*: No man presides over Stella's creation. Stephen tries to tutor Stella, but she rejects his instruction. What she comes to learn is something he cannot teach and indeed does not know. It is a private matter between this woman and the camera.

In *Woman and the Demon: The Life of a Victorian Myth*, Nina Auerbach argues that there is one central, although unacknowledged, myth that underlies all expressions of Victorian culture: a myth about woman's astonishing powers of metamorphosis or rebirth. Everywhere in Victorian culture she finds fragmentary reflections of this myth, but nowhere a full and explicit statement of it.[3] The Victorians aspired to create and yet recoiled from creating (or even compellingly representing) a "new woman" who would freely express the divine and demonic powers Victorians fervently believed that women possessed. Cavell suggests that the remarriage comedy reveals a historical stage in the development of the consciousness of women.

[3] Nina Auerbach, *Woman and the Demon: The Life of a Victorian Myth* (Cambridge, MA: Harvard University Press, 1982).

Auerbach's book suggests a way of interpreting this stage as a response to the innermost concerns of nineteenth-century culture.

Speculating on the fate of this Victorian myth in the twentieth century, Auerbach uses Marilyn Monroe as a paradigm of movie stardom and concludes that movie audiences are obsessed with the mortality of stars rather than their divinity. But it is a mistake to turn directly to the era of the breakdown of classical Hollywood without considering the period of the movies' greatest flourishing, when stars were viewed as human *and* immortal, and film's inheritance – and transformation – of Victorian culture was most manifest.

Putting the Auerbach and Cavell theses together, it seems plausible to suggest that when remarriage comedies envision the creation of the "new woman," or when Stella Dallas/Barbara Stanwyck smiles her secret smile in the face of the camera, film is inheriting a Victorian faith in the marvelous and terrifying powers of women. Beyond this – and however this assertion may ultimately need to be hedged or qualified – the medium of film at last allowed perhaps the deepest of all Victorian aspirations to be fulfilled. By placing the "new woman" on view, films awaken us from the Victorian dream or nightmare and close the book of the nineteenth century.

CHAPTER 10

Viewing the World in Black and White

Race and the Melodrama of the Unknown Woman

In *Contesting Tears*, Stanley Cavell identifies a genre of romantic melodrama he calls "the melodrama of the unknown woman" (taking this name from *Letter from an Unknown Woman*, one of the definitive films of the genre). The films he identifies as members of this genre include *Blonde Venus; Camille; Stella Dallas; Show Boat; Now, Voyager; Gaslight*; and *Letter from an Unknown Woman*. The starting point of this essay is the observation that all of these melodramas that are set in America – and innumerable other American melodramas as well – include at least one African American in their cast. Some play minor roles. Some are all but invisible. They are nonetheless present. Starting from the hypothesis that this is not a coincidence, but rather constitutes a significant feature of a genre of American film melodramas, in this chapter we explore some implications of this feature on our understanding of classical genres and broach the question of the relation of gender and race within the American cinema as a whole.

I wish to emphasize the exploratory nature of this essay, which raises more questions than it answers, and barely scratches the surface of complex, and sensitive, matters. In speaking about race in our culture, even more than in speaking about gender, it is best to proceed with caution, and with humility. Who has standing to speak about such matters, and on what grounds, are questions all Americans must take seriously.

Now, Voyager

I begin with *Now, Voyager*, a melodrama with an African American character whose presence seems incidental. Blink, and you miss him. He's a man called Samson, and he appears when Charlotte, the Bette Davis character, arrives at Cascade after her mother's death, and for the first time meets Tina, the young daughter of Jerry, the love of Charlotte's life. In the published screenplay, Miss Trask, a teacher at the school, orders him to take

Charlotte's suitcase, but he never appears on screen. In the film, it is Charlotte who asks Miss Trask whether Samson can get her bags from the car. Miss Trask orders him to do so, and he heads out the door, wordlessly.

Irving Rapper, the film's director, handles the moment so as not only to render this black man all but invisible, but to *declare* his invisibility. Samson is invisible to Charlotte, who keeps staring at little Tina, whom she is seeing for the first time, even as he enters the frame, completely eclipses Tina from view, tips his hat (but without looking at Charlotte), is eclipsed by Charlotte, and then unceremoniously exits the frame.

The next shot, too, seems deliberately designed to declare Samson's invisibility. It begins as a shot of Charlotte, and only when she moves toward Tina, and Samson moves toward the door, do we realize that he has been in the frame all the time, eclipsed by Charlotte from our view. As Samson nears the door, the camera reframes with Charlotte, so as produce, again, his unceremonious exit.

In a film that is all about visibility and invisibility, knownness and unknownness, this carefully choreographed passage brings home that Samson is invisible to his world, as Charlotte has been. There is a kinship or affinity between the black man and the "unknown woman." And yet there is a crucial difference between them. This passage declares a fact about society in the world of the film, which is also a fact about the real American society of the forties, that there exist human beings like Samson who are condemned to unknownness by the color of their skin, who are not free to be anything but invisible, who have no say in the matter. And it also declares a fact about melodrama, or about movie melodramas such as this, that in opening our eyes to one woman's heroic quest for selfhood, we risk closing our eyes to others who are not allowed her freedom to change. Charlotte has the power to pass judgment upon the world, to judge the world to be unworthy to judge her. What gives her this power is her willingness to choose to be invisible like Samson if her quest for selfhood calls for that. The world does not allow Samson this choice.

Stella Dallas

Stella Dallas is another film in which the presence of an African American character, in this case Stella's black maid, Gladys (Lillian Yarbo), can appear merely incidental. Again, though, by virtue both of an inner bond with the heroine and a difference in their horizons of possibilities, the black character plays a crucial role in defining who the "unknown woman" is.

In the pathos-filled birthday party scene, Gladys is a sympathetic coconspirator with Stella. She helps set things up so as to make the best possible impression on the expected guests, and on Laurel, who marvels that her mother was able to do it all. Gladys senses as quickly as anyone that no guests are actually coming, and her sympathy for Laurel, and for her mother, is apparent. At one point, Stella reminds Gladys that when the guests arrive she should refer to Laurel as "Miss Laurel" (Gladys replies with an exaggerated "Yes *Ma'am*"). But most of the time, when the two women are alone, neither puts on airs, and Gladys feels free to call Stella "Stel." Crucially, Gladys appreciates Stella's taste. When she first lays eyes on Stella all dressed up for the party, she *loves* her outfit. And when Stella, concerned, comments that Laurel is always telling everyone how beautiful her mother is, Gladys says, in all honesty, "Honey, you can sure live up to it!" (To this, Stella replies, "If I live through this thing, I'm going to get myself another corset" and leaves the room, and the camera registers Gladys's appreciative amusement.)

Gladys and Stella seem such good friends that it comes as a shock, some time later, when Laurel comes home from a visit with her father and his friend, the newly widowed Helen, calls for Gladys, and Stella tells her, matter of factly, that she isn't here any more, that she had let Gladys go, explaining "What did I need with anybody around?" She adds, "You know what I did? I saved enough money out of her wages to pay a deposit on a fur coat for *you*." (Earlier, Stella had mused to Gladys that she would give anything to see Laurel in a fur coat.)

Like Samson, Gladys is not a stereotype, like most of the maids played in thirties films by Hattie McDaniel, Louise Beavers, or Butterfly McQueen (however, these vivid performers, in their vividly different ways, also transcend these stereotypes) as well as by the less well-known Lillian Yarbo. Gladys is given no demeaning "business," and comes across as an intelligent, well-mannered, and warm human being. Her evident humanity underscores the fact, however, that she hardly so much as exists as a character. We learn nothing about her life (Where is she from? Is she married? Does she have children? Does she have dreams and aspirations of being something more than a white woman's maid?). We do not learn how she came to be hired, or what becomes of her when, in the darkest days of the Depression, Stella fires her.

It seems that the film takes this character for granted – takes for granted that Stella takes her for granted, takes for granted that we will not give a moment's thought to her fate, not let her distract us from our absorption with Stella. But what if the realization does dawn on us that this woman's fate is as important as Stella's? Then we may well feel like rebuking Stella, and the film, and the genre of melodrama it exemplifies, and, perhaps, ourselves, for being so indifferent to this woman. But over the years, I have learned the danger of underestimating this remarkable film. I do not doubt, in fact, that King Vidor's film *means* such a realization to dawn on us, *means* us to feel rebuked, *means* us at some point to recognize that in opening our eyes to Stella's unknownness we were closing our eyes to the unknownness of others. (And do we really know, in any case, that Stella is as indifferent as she seems to be? After all, she is putting on an act for Laurel's benefit; she doesn't want her daughter to know how much she really worries about money.) That is the film's point, or part of the point, in including this African American character, acknowledging her humanity, and then treating her as if she were disposable.

Within the body of criticism that has grown up around *Stella Dallas*, an impulse has repeatedly surfaced to rebuke Stella, not for being too selfish, but for being too selfless, for being so devoted to her daughter's happiness that she is indifferent to her own. And the impulse has repeatedly surfaced to rebuke the film, and the genre of melodrama it exemplifies, for endorsing the idea that women should sacrifice themselves for the sake of others. My own understanding of the film, like the reading Cavell presents in *Contesting Tears*, is that those who view Stella as selfless are assuming that they know something about her they really do not know, are denying her unknownness, the way the world does, and in that way are denying her selfhood. The film repudiates such denials. At the end of the film, Stella achieves a philosophical perspective that allows her to transcend society's view of her. Stella is outside because she chooses to be, because society as it stands – a society that judges people by their appearance – is not to her taste, does not live up to her standards. Gladys's presence in the film serves to remind us why the world merits Stella's disapproval.

Blonde Venus

In Josef von Sternberg's 1932 film *Blonde Venus*, the earliest of the "unknown woman" melodramas Cavell identifies, there are two African American characters. One is Viola, whom Helen, the Marlene Dietrich character, hires as a nanny when she first goes on the lam with her son. Viola seems so forgettable that I had, in fact, forgotten her. The other is Cora, played unforgettably by the great Hattie McDaniel in an early screen performance.

Cora is a friend who helps Helen when she is destitute and hiding from the police. A character played by Hattie McDaniel can hardly be invisible, of course, or, for that matter, silent. This is the film in which McDaniel first displayed that no-bullshit wit that is so much a part of her screen persona and that makes her a natural friend to Dietrich (who does not at all feel humiliated by being destitute, because, in her judgment, society, not she, is really on trial).

In *Toms, Coons, Mulattos, Mammies and Bucks*, Donald Bogle, usually so appreciative of Hattie McDaniel, strangely detects in von Sternberg's *Blonde Venus* an attempt "at first to pass [her] off as a humorless, less jolly version of Louise Beavers." He goes on,

> The film stars Marlene Dietrich as a Depression heroine driven to shame by her poverty. Fleeing her husband who fights for custody of their young son and carrying the boy with her, Dietrich hides out in a small Southern town where she is befriended by a congenial local mammy. Not only does mammy McDaniel supply provisions and moral support, but she also serves as a lookout, quick to warn Dietrich before the detectives close in. The down-and-out heroine has come to rely on the servant as her last friend, and once again the prehumanized black domestic is the true and trusted companion out to aid the white world, not harm it.[1]

[1] Donald Bogle, *Toms, Coons, Mulattoes, Mammies & Bucks: An Interpretive History of Blacks in American Films, 4th ed.* (New York and London: Continuum, 2001), p. 83.

But of course in *Blonde Venus* Dietrich is anything but a "Depression heroine driven to shame by her poverty." As we have noted, she does not regard her poverty as shameful. In her eyes, women driven to poverty are not degraded or fallen; in their outcast state, they are members of what in *Morocco* the Dietrich character calls "the foreign legion of women." She thinks of these women as her sisters. ("You don't look like those other women," the dumb cop who is in her trail says to her. "Give me time," she replies.) Like every member of this sisterhood, Dietrich is all too aware of the powerful forces the "white world" can bring to bear. But she does not accept that world's claim to have *moral* authority. It is she who passes judgment on the world, not the world that passes judgment on her. And her power to pass judgment is anchored by her unknownness, her outsideness, a condition that links her with her black sister.

Cora is not a "mammy," by the way, although she does put on a mammy act to determine whether the stranger who has shown up in town is a cop or simply a white man "browsing around." Cora is not Helen's servant, she is her friend. In aiding Helen, she is not, as Bogle suggests, acting to aid the white world. She is aiding a woman who accepts her as a sister, a woman she accepts as a sister, a woman who is a fugitive from the white world, which in *Blonde Venus* is also the patriarchy. Having said that Dietrich and McDaniel are like sisters, however, I must also point out that the film acknowledges a distinction between them. They are sisters under the skin, but one woman's skin is white, the other's black, and, in the judgment of the world, which has the force of Law behind it, this makes them unequal. In the film, as in the real America of the thirties, the world as it stands is a man's world as surely as it is a white world. A white woman is free in a way her black sister is not, but Helen is not free the way her husband is; she is not free to keep her son. No woman can really be free in such a world. Freedom, for Helen, is an illusion. Yet, however illusory her freedom, she does have the power, as her black sister does not, to transform herself in the eyes of the world, to be reborn, to emerge from a gorilla skin to the beat of jungle drums and assume a new identity as "the Blonde Venus."

And in the end she has the power to return to reclaim her son, to tell her story to him the way he wishes her to tell it, to keep the story – the illusion, the world – going.

In a melodrama like *Blonde Venus*, which hinges on the power of an "unknown woman" to judge a world that claims to judge her, the heroine's acceptance of her outsideness is the source of her freedom, her powers of metamorphosis, which are denied to the black woman. Again, an African American character participates in defining the heroine's condition by virtue of their kinship, the fact that they are sisters under the skin, and their difference, which is only skin deep but makes all the difference to the world.

Show Boat

In *Show Boat*, Julie (Helen Morgan) is a tragic mulatto figure. The daughter of a white father and a black mammy, she keeps her "black blood" a secret. But she has inherited her natural gift to be a "leading lady" on the stage (but not in real life). Inheriting her gift for singing, Julie also inherits songs that have been handed down from mammy to mammy, songs that revolve around the idea that it is natural for a woman like her to love one man all her life. Young Magnolia (Irene Dunne), daughter of the showboat owners, does not have a drop of Negro blood, but she and Julie have a special bond, an affinity both women recognize. Magnolia, like Julie, possesses that unknownness essential for singing "Negro songs," and essential, in general, for success on the stage. (The film, by the way, touches on the idea that the world of theater, like the world of "only make believe," is a world that allows what society otherwise does not allow. Like the show business world in *The Jazz Singer*, like the theater world of the thirties, the world of James Whale's film is a world capable of reconciling what remains unreconcilable in the real world.)

If one "only makes believe," one's dream can come true – but only in "make-believe." One must also face facts. In the world as it stands, in *Show Boat*, the happy ending that is possible for Magnolia is not possible for Julie. For Magnolia to succeed, Julie, more her mother than her biological mother is, has to withdraw (Stella Dallas withdraws). But there is also an isolation in Julie's temperament – in the temperament of any woman destined for the stage – that makes her *wish* to withdraw, to remain outside.

In addition to the mulatto Julie, who passes as white, *Show Boat* also contains black characters, most notably those played by Paul Robeson and

Hattie McDaniel. No less than McDaniel in this film, the Robeson character is no doubt a stereotype: the shiftless, lazy, good-for-nothing black man. But it is worth noting that when something he cares about is at stake, he does, much to his wife's surprise, put himself out, as he does when Magnolia is in the throes of a dangerous childbirth and he braves the raging Mississippi to find help. (In aiding Magnolia, he is not acting to aid the white world; her bond with Julie marks Magnolia as black.) It is not that he is lazy by nature; rather, as a matter of principle, he "suits himself," as he declares in his duet with McDaniel. He has a philosophy of life, in other words, a philosophy he learned from "Ol' Man River' (or "Ribber," as Robeson impeccably enunciates it in his show-stopping song) himself.

In this production number, the camera treats Robeson differently from the other singers in the film. Irene Dunne and Allan Jones sing to each other, in shot – reverse shot or in profile.

Helen Morgan, when she sings her great number "Bill," is so absorbed within the world of the song that she can be framed in an almost frontal close-up without our ever sensing either that she is performing for the camera as an audience or that its presence makes her uncomfortable.

Filming Robeson, the camera frames him tightly, too, and nearly frontally, as he sings to no one within the world of the film. Unlike Helen Morgan, though, it seems to take effort for him to avoid meeting the camera's gaze. His eye line repeatedly, and uneasily, crosses the axis. We sense the pleasure Robeson takes in his performance, his wish to present himself theatrically. We also sense his inhibition in the face of the camera, his unwillingness or inability to address the camera directly.

Donald Bogle writes, in a fine passage,

> In all [Robeson's] movies, audiences were aware of his great bulk and presence. His eyes gleamed. His smile was brilliant and infectious, often revealing the complete joy of the actor as he sang, sometimes masking an ambivalent, ironic side of his personality. But always Robeson used his smile to draw his audience to him.[2]

And yet, when he finishes his definitive performance of "Ol' Man Ribber," Robeson cannot help smiling with satisfaction, but this smile is not addressed to the film's audience, or to any audience within the world of the film. He has no one to whom he can address this smile. It is this condition of isolation, imposed upon him by a world that will not look a black man in the eye, that is declared by the camera's placement.

Imitation of Life

In *The Negro in Films*, a book published in the forties, Peter Noble writes that in the 1934 version of Fannie Hurst's novel *Imitation of Life*, "Louise Beavers appeared as the self-effacing, faithful, kind-hearted epitome of the worst type of 'mammy' role." He goes on,

> All she desired, it seemed, was to be able to serve her mistress well, and "to have a big funeral with white horses" when she died.... As *Literary Digest* remarked, "Obviously, [Peola, Delilah's daughter, played by Fredi Washington] is the most interesting person in the cast. Her drama is the most poignant, but the producers not only confine her to a minor and carefully handled subplot, but appear to regard her with distaste. They appear to be fond of her mother, because she is the meek type of old-fashioned Negro that, as they say, "knows his place," but the daughter is too bitter and lacking in resignation for them.[3]

[2] Ibid., p. 99.

[3] Peter Noble, *The Negro in Films* (London: Skelton Robinson, 1949), p. 62.

Peola, Daniel Leab writes in the same vein in *From Sambo to Superspade*, is simply an updated version of the tragic mulatto of nineteenth-century melodrama and early silent film. As was the case with her predecessors, mixed blood can bring nothing but sorrow. And the movie delineates Peola in the same terms that had always defined the mulatto stereotype. While Delilah's mammy figure is treated sympathetically if condescendingly, the character of Peola has virtually no redeeming features.[4]

Donald Bogle goes further:

> *Imitation of Life*'s great contradiction, its single subversive element, was the character Peola... Originally, Peola had been conceived as a tragic mulatto type, the beautiful girl doomed because she has a "drop of Negra blood." But as played by Fredi Washington, Peola became a character in search of a movie. With eyes light and liquid and almost haunted, Miss Washington made Peola a password for non-passive resistance. "Mama," she cried, "I want the same things in life other people enjoy." The line was the film's great one, its simplest and most heartfelt. To obtain the equality she wants, Peola has to rebel against the system. Peola was the New Negro demanding a real New Deal. But as *The New York Times* pointed out in its review of the film, "The photoplay was content to suggest that the sensitive daughter of the Negro woman is bound to be unhappy if she happens to be able to pass for white." The explanation for Peola's rebellion is simply that she wants to be white, not that she wants white opportunities. Her weeping by her mother's casket was Hollywood's slick way of finally humiliating her, its way of finally making the character who had run away with herself conform to the remorseful mulatto type.[5]

All these writers, in affirming Peola, find a need to rebuke Delilah and indict the film for endorsing Delilah's way of thinking. As Bogle puts it, Louise Beavers' Delilah was

> ...a combination of tom and aunt jemimah magnified and glorified in full-blown Hollywood fashion. But she introduced to the 1930s audience the idea of black Christian stoicism. "Bow your head," she tells daughter Peola. "You got to learn to take it. Your pappy kept beating his fists against life all his days until it eat him through." In its historical perspective, this Christian stoicism – particularly because Beavers was able to make movie patrons believe that she herself believed it – "elevated" the Negro character in films by endowing him with Christian goodness far exceeding that of any other character.... Of course, the irony of this stoicism was that it made the Negro character more self-effacing than ever and even more resolutely resigned to accepting his fate of inferiority.[6]

[4] Daniel J. Leab, *From Sambo to Superspade: The Black Experience in Motion Pictures* (Boston: Houghton Mifflin, 1976), p. 108.

[5] *Toms, Coons, Mulattoes, Mammies & Bucks*, pp. 59–60.

[6] Ibid, p. 59.

This misses the point of the film, however. Without question, *Imitation of Life* expects us to love Delilah, as does the film's protagonist Bea, played by Claudette Colbert (in a role that counterpoints her role in *It Happened One Night*, the earliest of the remarriage comedies, made in the same year). But the film does not expect us to embrace Delilah's way of thinking. Indeed, Delilah is as unfathomable to us as she is to her daughter, or for that matter to Bea. Unlike Delilah, we do know what Peola wants, we know why she wants it, we want it too, as does Bea. We do not blame Peola for thinking the way she does. But neither do we blame Delilah for not being able to fathom her daughter's thinking.

At first, Bea thinks she understands Delilah's way of thinking, because she thinks that Delilah simply thinks the way any mother thinks. But in thinking this, Bea does not take into account Delilah's conviction that mammies are different from mothers. As the film goes on, Delilah becomes more and more a mystery to Bea. Bea discovers a wonderful example of the unfathomable difference between them in Delilah's reaction to her offer to give her 20 percent (!?) of the profits from the sale of pancakes made according to Delilah's secret recipe, a recipe handed down to her by her own mammy. Delilah expresses her wish not to own her own home; she would rather continue looking after Bea and Jessie, Bea's daughter. Bea reacts to Delilah's reaction with that sense of affectionate but superior amusement – a mode we see again and again in *It Happened One Night* – so characteristic of Claudette Colbert on screen. To Bea, as to us, Delilah is a woman so innocent that she is terribly vulnerable; she needs to be protected from a world beyond her ken.

In Delilah's view, mothering, like making pancakes (or, in *Show Boat*, singing Negro songs), comes naturally to a black woman; the knowledge of how to be a mammy was passed down to her from her own mammy, who learned it from her own mammy before her. But if mothering comes naturally to a black woman, how come her daughter reacts to her in this unnatural way? What mammies know, Delilah believes, is that a mammy's love, like Christ's love, is unconditional. Hence Donald Bogle sees her as the embodiment of "Christian stoicism." And yet when her daughter "unborns" herself from her, as she puts it, Delilah's stoicism fails. Believing that mothering comes naturally, not knowing how her daughter can react to her in this unnatural way, she is pushed beyond her capacity to endure. She does not have the spiritual strength to bear such suffering, she says. (The implication is not that a white mother would have the spiritual strength she feels she lacks, but that if a white mother were disavowed by her daughter, that would not constitute the same kind of ordeal, because a white mother's love is not absolute the way a mammy's love is.) For Peola to pass for white, to reject her own mother, is for her to go against God's wishes, Delilah believes, because God made her black. And yet God also made Peola the way she is, gave her a nature her own mother cannot comprehend. In despairing of life here on earth, in forsaking the world for the sake of a great funeral, Delilah is asserting her faith in God, but she is also rejecting the world that God, in his infinite wisdom, created.

Again, *Imitation of Life* does not rebuke Peola for rejecting her mother's way of thinking. After all, the film rejects it, too. And yet Delilah's way of thinking, unfathomable though it may be, profoundly affects everyone in the film. For example, when Peola leaves school and writes to her mother that she never wants to see her again, Bea, knowing how much it means to Delilah, goes off to track Peola down and to try to get her to change her mind. It is while Bea is away on this mission that Jessie falls in love with the man that, unbeknownst to her, is the love of her mother's life. And it is after Delilah's funeral that Bea, acting on the lesson she feels the tragedy has taught her, decides to reject this man's proposal, or, rather, to defer accepting it until such a time that her daughter falls out of love with him.

It might seem that, by making this decision, Bea has come to embrace Delilah's way of thinking, that she is now thinking like a mammy, not a mother. But that is not so. For one thing, Delilah always thought it unnatural for Bea not to desire to remarry, and immediately recognizes Bea's Mr. Right when he finally comes along. For another, Bea makes her decision in the hope of avoiding Delilah's fate. She acts out of a genuine understanding of her daughter's desire, not an inability to understand her daughter. Besides, she acts to satisfy her own desire as well. For she takes pleasure in being close to Jessie, and the film ends in anything but a mood of resignation. Bea and Jessie are together, looking forward to a bright future, even as Bea reminisces to her daughter about the very scene between them, now long ago, that constituted the film's opening. When this scene – so reminiscent of the ending of *Blonde Venus* – now fades out, as several earlier scenes had done, it creates an uncanny sense that the film's opening scene is about to fade in, as if this were the beginning of the film, not the end, as if the whole film had been a story told – and about to be told again – by this mother to her daughter.

The point I am trying to make, and I apologize for my inelegance in groping for it, is that *Imitation of Life* does not condemn Peola for rejecting her mother's way of thinking. But neither does it condemn Delilah for failing to understand her daughter. Peola loves her mother no less than her mother loves her. And in the end Peola is not humiliated. Bea remarks, after she witnesses Peola's terrible break with her mother, that she has witnessed a tragedy. But *Imitation of Life* is not a tragedy. A tragedy has no villain.

But in this film there is a villain. Society, the world as it stands, is to blame for Delilah's death and Peola's unhappiness. The film does not advocate that we beat our fists against life, which is what drove Peola's father to his death. But neither does it advocate that we passively accept the world as it is, much less that we abandon the here and now for the sake of the hereafter, as Delilah does. The world must be changed. We must change the world. Otherwise we are all to blame.

Imitation of Life, for all its sympathy for Delilah, does not endorse her "Christian stoicism." The film has a social consciousness it is often thought to lack. That is the import of two remarkable moments we would do well to ponder.

One is the great passage, early in the film, when Delilah rings Bea's doorbell, thinking she has placed a "help wanted" ad for a "girl." Bea's young daughter falls into the bathtub and begins crying, and her mother, alarmed, runs upstairs to see if her baby has been hurt. Delilah waits downstairs, concerned for Bea's baby and also for her own child, because she is in desperate need of a job. John Stahl, the film's director, frames Delilah through the bars of the balustrade, creating a strikingly Hitchcock-like composition.

Surely this shot is making a statement about racism, the statement that this black woman's lot – any black woman's lot – is to be unfree. Note, however, that at the very moment the film is declaring Delilah's condition as a black woman to be one of imprisonment, Delilah is smiling. She is smiling, presumably, because as a mother – or as a mammy – she is happy to hear that baby Jessie is O.K. But she is also smiling, presumably, because it is clear to her at this moment that this woman, herself a mother, will not turn her or her child away. That is, being unfree is a mother's lot, as it is a black person's lot.

The other passage concludes with Delilah pondering the mystery that some people are born white and some black, when there is no real difference between them that justifies treating them so differently. Because it can't be the Good Lord's fault that human beings are judged by the color of their skin rather than by the content of their character, who is to blame, Delilah wonders, staring into the camera with a bewildered look that makes me think of Patricia Collinge in *Shadow of a Doubt*, unable or unwilling to put

two and two together, when she ponders the mystery that for a second time in as many days her daughter narrowly escaped death.

Delilah is too innocent, or too oblivious, to point a finger. But the film is not. What we know, what Delilah does not, is that society is to blame, we are to blame, we are all responsible.

In an excellent piece on Howard Hawks's *Man's Favorite Sport?* Molly Haskell argues that innumerable details of the film fall into place the moment it becomes obvious that fishing stands in for man's true "favorite sport," the pursuit of women.[1] The dialogue takes on a quality of persistent double entendre. Situations, gestures, and images disclose a graphic sexual underside, and a whole reading of the film as sexual allegory is invited.

Bringing Up Baby has a comparable structure of doubleness. Thus the film's opening: Cary Grant, atop a brontosaurus skeleton, is thinking. He is pondering the correct placement and function of the bone he is holding, but he is thinking about something else as well. He is about to marry Miss Swallow, to enter a state that brooks "no domestic entailments of any kind." The brontosaurus will be their only baby: Marriage to Miss Swallow means no sex. Cary Grant is pondering the correct placement and function of another "bone."

Line after line refers to Grant's "precious" bone, his "rare" bone, the bone which, Katharine Hepburn tries to impress on the terrier George, they so badly need. All of this reaches one absurdly logical conclusion when Grant finds himself unable to shake the name "Mr. Bone."

The mythical term "intercostal clavicle" itself conspires with this doubleness. This reconstructed brontosaurus is a creature with a clavicle – hence presumably its head, even its mind – between its ribs. Grant is pondering a gap between the ribs (the one from which Katharine Hepburn no doubt springs) that calls for a bone to fill it. Then, too, Hepburn has a leopard in something like the way in which Grant has a bone.

[1] Molly Haskell, "*Man's Favorite Sport?* Revisited," in Joseph McBride, ed., *Focus on Howard Hawks* (Englewood Cliffs, NJ: Prentice-Hall, 1972), pp. 135–8.

Reprinted: See "Notes on the Essays."

Dialogue, names, situations, gestures, even formal compositions are motivated by the demands of this doubleness. *Bringing Up Baby*, like *Man's Favorite Sport?* presents a story "straight," but it also exhibits a systematic doubleness, clustering around key equivalences or principles of substitution that invite an allegorical reading. Part of my claim here is that the same can be said about every Howard Hawks film.

Critical writing on Hawks remains dominated by the idea that he is a "functional" director: Hawks pared down his cinematic technique and subordinated it to the service of telling a story. This idea is frequently allied with a picture of the director that limits even Robin Wood's insightful book on Hawks's films: Hawks as the paradigm of the unself-conscious American action director. Viewed in this light, Hawks's films appear straightforward, unintellectual, of value because they spring from a simple vision of the world presented with integrity and professional skill, but a vision held unself-consciously, instinctively.

Yet early in his career, Hawks was on record as believing that there were only two important filmmakers in Hollywood: Hawks and von Sternberg. From the first, Hawks thought of his work as standing above nearly all other American films in ambition and achievement. My own sense is that Hawks's films are, as a group, perhaps the most cerebral and specifically brilliant in the whole Hollywood canon.

Hawks's early sound films, such as *Scarface* and *Twentieth Century*, bear the mark of a man who is brilliant and knows it. The celebrated device in *Scarface* of marking each murder sequence with an "X" approaches the status of a gratuitous display of cleverness and virtuosity. The bowling-alley execution, with its perfect strike and "X" on the scoresheet, is Hawks's as well as Tony's coup.

Hawks does eschew Hitchcock-like "identification effects," as well as conspicuously expressive lighting and compositions, complex montages, elaborate camera movements, Fordian pictorialism, and flash-backs and elaborate narrative devices. Most Hawks films, composed of frames, nearly all of which are flat, cluttered, and dark, avoid pictorialism to the point of courting ugliness. The incipient antipictorialism of *Bringing Up Baby* eventually leads to *Gentlemen Prefer Blondes*, with its deliberate clashing of garish colors.

John Belton and others have persuasively demonstrated Hawks's attentiveness to the externalizations of the dramatic or comic events acted out in front of the camera. Clothing, bodily bearing, details of social groupings in a spatial environment, and the most minimal nonverbal gestures all disclose dramatically significant details to Hawks's camera. If Hitchcock's camera asserts its presence and its independent power (for example, to "get inside the character's head"), Hawks's camera appears neutral. Yet it consistently picks up dramatically significant, expressive details and renders them perspicuous.

Hawks's discernment of significant detail is never clearer than in his handling of reactions. A reaction shot discloses to the viewer a character's response to what he or she has just seen. The response framed in the conventional reaction shot is transparent and unambiguously identifiable.

Hitchcock developed his own alternatives to the conventional reaction shot, such as what might be called the "reactionless" shot. For example, James Stewart in *Rear Window* and *Vertigo* repeatedly discloses no visible response to what he witnesses; these reaction shots do no more than testify to the fact that he has borne witness to what we too have seen.

One characteristic Hawksian reaction shot, by contrast, reveals such a complex of emotions that although we can readily identify the constituents of the character's reaction, we cannot sum up that response and give it a name. (Sometimes, particularly in *The Big Sleep*, Hawks places such a complex reaction within a deep-focus framing, not cutting to a separate shot.) Such a reaction shot implies a total intimacy between character and viewer. Yet despite, or perhaps because of, that intimacy, the character retains a privacy in the face of the camera.

This technique can be observed in as early a Hawks film as *A Girl in Every Port*, and we see it in *Bringing Up Baby*. I am thinking of the close-up of Hepburn (the first close-up in the film) responding to Grant's revelation of his engagement ("Engaged? To be married?").

How could we hope to sum up the welter of emotions that cross her face in the brief duration of this shot, in the course of which she resolves to pursue this man until he catches her? Despite our intimate understanding of her feelings at this moment, she retains her independence and her air of irreducible mystery. The importance of this moment is underscored by its contrast to the close-ups of Grant that Hawks gives us (for example, covered with feathers after Baby's attack on the chickens, or resigned to being unable to get a word in edgewise). Grant's face reveals not an impenetrable free resolve but an all-too-identifiable impotence.

Hawks, like Griffith, Hitchcock, and Renoir, has a whole repertory of signs that continually reappear, deepening in resonance, in film after film. And Hawks sustains his practice of composing each film around a single central symbol or cluster of symbols.

Fire. The lighting of cigarettes is a much-commented-on ritual in Hawks's films whose sexual underside has been noted. Fire, in general, and heat are linked with this motif: the fire in *Only Angels Have Wings* and *Ball of Fire*; the hothouse in *The Big Sleep*; the spark of electricity that destroys the Thing; the attempt by Marilyn Monroe and Jane Russell in *Gentlemen Prefer Blondes* to humiliate Elliot Reed by turning the heat up in his stateroom.

Flowers. In *Twentieth Century*, John Barrymore sticks Carole Lombard in the ass with a hatpin in order to inspire her to drop her stiffness and act. The hatpin, whose sexual equivalent is not hard to imagine, is a central symbol in the film. (When she walks out on him, she takes the hatpin with her, enshrining it in a jewelry box. Barrymore loses his power to make another star and remains in that condition until he finally retrieves Lombard– and the hatpin.) Barrymore first picks up the pin by pulling it from a corsage. Hawks presents this in a close-up insert, a key image in the film.

As the pin is pulled out, the flower falls from the frame. Flowers are associated in Hawks's work with idealized images of women, by way of symbolizing virgin purity. Thus, this shot constitutes a kind of schematic portrait of Barrymore's act of taking possession of Lombard, and he christens this star who bears his mark "Lily Garland." In *His Girl Friday*, Grant's decision to pursue Rosalind Russell until she remarries him is synchronized with his gesture of putting a flower in his lapel. *The Big Sleep* has its wonderful dialogue about the foulness of orchids. *Rio Bravo* has Angie Dickinson courting John Wayne by throwing a flowerpot through a window. *A Song Is Born* has the "nuptial hut bedecked with flowers" so enticingly described by Danny Kaye. And so on.

Birds. In *Bringing Up Baby*, Cary Grant is, in one of his biological transformations, covered with chicken feathers. Birds, of course, play a variety of roles in *Only Angels Have Wings*. Monroe and Russell are festooned with feathers at the opening of *Gentlemen Prefer Blondes*. There is *The Big Sky's* character "Teal-eye," *Rio Bravo's* "Feathers," and *Bringing Up Baby's* "Miss Swallow." *A Song Is Born* finds Virginia about to change her name by marriage from Swanson to Crow. And there is a central question posed by *Barbary Coast*: Is Miriam Hopkins a swan (Edward G. Robinson calls her "Swan") or a Siren? Lauren Bacall, in *The Big Sleep* and *To Have and Have Not*, very much invokes the figure of the Siren who lures sailors to doom on the rocks. Marilyn Monroe in *Gentlemen Prefer Blondes* is named "Lorelei"; in her opening song, she vows to send men to their doom over rocks. But "Lorelei" is also "Laurel-eye," a name comparable to *The Big Sky's* "Teal-eye" – she is a laurel to the eye and also has an eye for laurels, for diamond tiaras and such. In *Monkey Business*, after all, Monroe goes by the name of "Lois Laurel" or simply "Miss Laurel."

Water. The motif of water takes many forms in Hawks's work. For one thing, it relates to the recurring metaphors of the sailor and the ocean voyage, for example, in *A Girl in Every Port*. At sea, sailors live a form of life that denies their sexuality. Figuratively, they are surrounded by water, but do not plunge in. In *Twentieth Century*, Barrymore compares working together on a theatrical production with being shipmates on a long ocean voyage, a comparison complicated by the fact that he and "Lily Garland" share a bed shaped like a boat. *Only Angels Have Wings* has its airships, always filmed bouncing through water on takeoff and landing. In *Red River*, the cattle drive is repeatedly compared to an ocean voyage, a metaphor literalized by *The Big Sky*. There is the ocean voyage in *Gentlemen Prefer Blondes*, the trip by boat in *I Was a Male War Bride*, and the boat designed to carry the Pharaoh to his afterlife in *Land of the Pharaohs*. *The Thing* has again its arc/ark, a multifaceted symbol. An arc of electricity (a projector, too has its arc) destroys the Thing. But the war against the Thing is interwoven with the romance of the Captain and his woman. The setting at the North Pole reminds us that Earth itself is polar – sexual – as are the human beings opposed by the alien, asexual Thing, which has arrived in a spaceship/ark, which in turn brings us back to the ocean voyage.

A key to the further resonance of water in Hawks's films can be found in *A Girl in Every Port*. Louise Brooks plays a circus performer whose act consists of climbing a high ladder (framed by Hawks in some of the most erotic images in all his cinema) and then jumping into a tub of water.

She initiates her seduction of Spike by splashing him with water as she lands. It is only a couple of steps from this moment to the immersion of Grant and Hepburn in deep water in *Bringing Up Baby*. Only a step further is the spectacular musical number in *Gentlemen Prefer Blondes* in which Jane Russell, finding none of the members of the Olympic team, red corpuscles and all, in the mood for "love sweet love" ("Tennis anyone? Court's free!"), jumps into the swimming pool to "cool off." And then to *Man's Favorite Sport*?

The sexual dimension of the plunge into water is sustained with bitter, almost grotesque, irony in *Red River*. The river itself is the film's central symbol. Associated with sexuality and death, it relates to the rivers in, for example, *The Big Sky, Rio Bravo, El Dorado*, and *Rio Lobo*. The river is the place where John Wayne leaves his woman behind. When Wayne plunges into the river, he does so to kill an Indian, who turns out to be wearing the woman's bracelet. Their mortal struggle in the water cruelly mocks Wayne for the scene he did not allow to take place earlier. (It is appropriate that this river is named the Red River.) The Red River also marks the place where Wayne's bull is united with Matt's cow, giving birth to the Red River D herd. Years later, when the cattle drive approaches the Red River from the south, Wayne increasingly loses control of himself. His inability to sleep is attributable to the significance the river holds for him as a reminder that the birth of his herd is linked to his own sexual denial. If *Bringing Up Baby* had no Miss Swallow and Cary Grant had rejected Katharine Hepburn, and she had then gone on to collect a million dollars for Grant's museum and died in the process, this great herd of cattle would be the equivalent of Grant's brontosaurus. *Red River* is very close to the more or less explicitly Freudian films of the late forties, such as Fritz Lang's *The Secret Beyond the Door* and Hitchcock's *Spellbound*: Wayne's "voyage" is also a voyage into himself, in the course of which he comes to grips with a sexual trauma in his past. Wayne's specific provocations that lead his men to mutiny make sense in these allegorical terms. They include his insistence that the drive cross the river before nightfall, his refusal to allow the men to linger around good water, and his insistence on harsh punishment for the man whose sweet tooth caused the fatal stampede (regarding this last, remember that "Sugar Puss O'Shea" is Barbara Stanwyck's moniker in *Ball of Fire*).

Nor are we far from the idea of immersion in water as baptism. Thus, for example, the play on the idea of baptism in *Twentieth Century*, echoed in *Only Angels Have Wings* when Cary Grant pours a pitcher of cold water over Rita Hayworth's head.

Baptism may be by fire, of course. Hence we have, for example, the image of Tony's comical sidekick in *Scarface*, lead flying all around him, with hot water from a canister hit by gunfire pouring down in a parabola onto his thigh, as though he were pissing in his pants with fear.

Hands. In Hawks's films, the hand frequently serves as a substitute penis. This, too, occurs in *A Girl in Every Port*, with its outrageous close-up inserts of one hand pulling the fingers of another. Also, there are Bat's burned and bandaged hands in *Only Angels Have Wings,* Kirk Douglas's amputated finger in *The Big Sky*, and John Wayne's wounded hand in *Red River* and immobilized hand in *El Dorado*, not to mention Dean Martin's shaking hands in *Rio Bravo* – they shake so bad that he cannot roll his own cigarette (a nice example of a linkage of motifs). And consider the scene in *I Was a Male War Bride* in which Cary Grant, locked in the sleeping Ann Sheridan's room, but afraid to share her bed, tries to sleep in an easy chair, but cannot find a position that gives his hands anything satisfying to do.

Surely the most elaborate use of the motif of the hand is in *The Thing*. The Thing is asexual. As a source of disturbance (it disturbs radar, dogs, Geiger counter, the human community, radio communication) it is implicity compared in the film's dialogue to an attractive woman (although unlike, for example, Sugar Puss O'Shea or *A Song Is Born*'s Honey Swanson, it uses sweet syrup only as bait). The Thing is a mock man as well as a mock woman. This is reflected in the Thing's hand, which takes the form of, but really is not, a hand: it is a reproductive organ, a seedpod, in the shape of a hand. The Thing does not reproduce the way a real man does; it reproduces, in direct violation of the biblical injunction, by "scattering its seed." But, then again, if the Thing mocks the courtship between the Captain and his woman, that courtship equally mocks the Thing. He allows her to tie his hands behind his back, anticipating the Thing's later loss of its hand/seedpod. But the Captain does not really lose the use of his hand: He pretends he is securely bound, a game he plays as part of his courtship. The Thing, after all, is only a vegetable ("An intellectual carrot – the mind boggles!"), and the Captain destroys it by exploiting its impotence – he destroys it with an arc of electricity, a manifestation of the sexual principle it challenged.

I have already indicated some of the central symbols or principles of equivalence around which Hawks composes individual films. Let us consider several others.

For example, in *Gentlemen Prefer Blondes*, there is a key principle of substitution: For "diamond," read "penis" and also "breast." Innumerable images, lines, gestures, and situations in the film sustain this outrageous dual doubleness. for example, such lines as "Didn't you notice, his pocket was bulging," "That makes me feel all warm inside," "It can never be too big," "Looks like it ought to have a highball around it," and "I just love to find new places to wear diamonds" are among the most outrageous double entendres in all of Hawks's films. There are supplementary ones as well; for example, "She gets sick if she rides backwards," "He's the only four-letter man on the team," the magnificent "You're half sweet and half acid," and the line in the song " ... Time rolls on and youth is gone, and you can't straighten up when you bend." Then, too, the song that begins, "When love goes wrong, nothing goes right," reads like a recitation of the whole catalogue of Hawksian sexual motifs: "Man takes flight . . . , a match won't light . . . , bees won't buzz . . . , fish won't bite. . . . "

Land of the Pharaohs extends the central symbol of *Gentlemen Prefer Blondes*. Pyramids are the ultimate "rocks which don't lose their shape." The pyramid sustains the dual sexual readings of the diamond: a parody of Joan Collins's breasts, it parodies the way she uses them in attracting men. But it also sublimates/denies/parodies the Pharaoh's masculinity. His pyramid is like Cary Grant's brontosaurus.

The pyramid in *Land of the Pharaohs*, in fact, is Hawks's most elaborate symbol. If perhaps some Warner Brothers executive was sold on the project by the idea that for "land of the Pharaohs" one was to read "Russia" (the film closely followed Stalin's death), it is clear to me that Hawks was inspired by a different equivalence: For "land of the Pharaohs," read "land of the moguls," that is, Hollywood.

As the film's dialogue makes explicit, a pyramid is so designed as to be perfectly, paradigmatically unitary on its surface. After all, it must serve its exoteric religious function, must inspire the masses as an icon of simplicity and pureness. But that is the other side of its esoteric function. The state religion supports a system of slavery that enables an elite class, and at its apex one man, to amass wealth and power. The pyramid is both a monument to that man and his guarantee of being able to keep his wealth forever.

Underlying the pyramid's unitary form, it is designed as a series of traps, cunningly constructed to keep the Pharaoh's treasure chamber inviolate. The hero of *Land of the Pharaohs* is the architect who designs the perfect pyramid and supervises its construction, despite his skepticism about the Pharaoh's religion, his growing blindness, and his expectation of being buried in the pyramid, unsung, his secret dying with him, when the Pharaoh dies and the central chamber is sealed.

The architect is Hawks's fullest allegorical representation of himself as a filmmaker. And the pyramid serves as a perfect symbol for *Land of the Pharaohs* itself. (I only hope that in saying this, in opening up the film's secret chamber, I will be spared the mummy's curse.) The self-reflectiveness that I impute to *Land of the Pharaohs* is the extreme development of an aspect that can be found in Hawks's films from the beginning of his career.

A basic principle of *Scarface*, for example, surely is that for "war between old and new gangsters" we are to read "war between old and new styles of filmmaking." The film's opening, its one representation of the old gangster society, is filmed in what amounts to a parody of Germanic silent-film style, with expressionistic lighting, long camera movements, and virtual silence. The style shifts to Hawks's own – much faster, more violent, filled with talk, comparable perhaps to the machine gun, the technological base of the new gangsters' takeover – when Tony gains control. It is difficult to avoid the image of Hawks himself, young, ambitious, staking out his territory, making his mark. *To Have and Have Not* presents the war between the Free French and the Nazis as a war between old-style and new-style gangsters. *Scarface's* famous "X" reappears in this film: When the Nazis appear on the scene with their machine guns, a ceiling fan marks the ceiling with its huge X-shaped shadow. In the intervening decade, Hawks's identification has shifted from "new" to "old."

In some of his films, particularly those made for Samuel Goldwyn, one especially senses Hawks confronting a studio apparatus that denies him direct expression. But if, in viewing, say, *Barbary Coast*, we hit on the principle that for "Barbary Coast" we read "Hollywood," the whole film opens up. The clash between Joel McCrea (the would-be poet poised between idealism and cynicism, a master of the ironic use of language who always intends the underside of his words) and Edward G. Robinson (a mogul type who thinks he can run California with his tainted money, and who is notable for his conspicuous incompetence in the use and appreciation of language, his conspicuous Goldwynisms) takes on an aspect of Hawks's (and, to be sure, also Ben Hecht's) plight in working for Goldwyn. The film scores its points by subverting its narrative in order to become a cutting parody of accepted Hollywood wisdom as to what makes a good film. Some lines seem entirely gratuitous, with no conceivable motivation beside putting on the studio and pleasing whatever "hip" audience the film might find. I am thinking, in particular, of Robinson's line when he offers Hopkins a drink in his ill-fated attempt at seduction: "We call it a 'Prairie Oyster.'"

In *Bringing Up Baby*, there is a radical separation between the literal and the allegorical levels, in the sense that the characters are innocent of the doubleness of their words and acts. They are like children. *Monkey Business*, which returns Grant to his preadolescent state, is a virtual sequel to *Bringing Up Baby*. Childhood restored, Grant performs the backflip of his early show-business days, Ginger Rogers dances, and Hawks returns to the style of *Bringing Up Baby*. The comedy in *Bringing Up Baby* in part derives from our perception particularly of Grant's unawareness. (Of course, it also derives from the idea that it is *Cary Grant* who enacts himself as sexually uninitiated.)

In *His Girl Friday*, by contrast, Grant is aware of, and consciously exploits, such doubleness. He and Rosalind Russell share a language. Better, they share a knowledge of language that enables them to communicate by indirectness, sharing access to each other's veiled meanings and unspoken thoughts. Sharing such knowledge is what unites the famous Hawksian community of professionals. This emerges clearly from those Hawks films that feature scenes of language instruction or initiation, such as *Only Angels Have Wings* and *Rio Bravo*. Complementing these scenes of instruction, there are the tests of mastery of indirect discourse, typified by Walter Brennan's recurring question in *To Have and Have Not*: "Has you ever been stung by a dead bee?" In *Ball of Fire*, Barbara Stanwyck teaches Gary Cooper the language of slang – the language in which sexuality may be expressed. These lessons also operate as lessons to the viewer, literal explications of Hawks's own favorite double signs; hence the sensual musical number in which Gene Krupa uses matchsticks for drumming until, at the climax, they ignite. (I am reminded of the way *Spellbound* literally explicates the visual motif of parallel vertical lines that recurs in all of Hitchcock's films, or the way *Marnie* literally explicates his characteristic use of the color red.) I also see in *Ball of Fire*, in its willful insistence on making explicit what Hawks would prefer to leave open to the viewer's imagination, that note of contempt he always seems to strike in his work for Goldwyn.

For Hawks, Humphrey Bogart is the paradigm of the figure who understands that remarks and gestures have undersides that speakers mean whether they like it or not. Thus, Bogart's exchanges with Bacall are the diametrical opposite of the Grant–Hepburn exchanges in *Bringing Up Baby*. Bogart and Bacall both get the joke in "You know how to whistle, don't you, Steve? You just put your lips together and . . . blow" and in the maze of jokes in the famous exchange that features the lines "I like a horse that comes from behind" and "It depends on who's in the saddle."

In the Hawks films that center on characters who are masters of indirect discourse, there are possibilities and necessities that have no place in *Bringing Up Baby*. Rosalind Russell's efforts to extricate herself from Grant in

His Girl Friday parallel Grant's efforts to extricate himself from Hepburn in *Bringing Up Baby* – except that Hepburn does not deceive Grant the way Grant deceives Russell (or the way Barrymore deceives Lombard in *Twentieth Century*).

Deception takes on special importance in *The Big Sleep*. Bogart, a private eye, speaks and acts in order to provoke revealing scenes. But he has an enemy, Eddie Mars, who operates behind the scenes, weaving deceptive appearances. The conflict between Bogart and Mars is intimately implicated in Bogart's struggle to recognize Bacall's nature and pierce through to an authentic relationship with her. Mars has left his mark on Bacall, and Bogart needs to discern its meaning. The sexual fencing between Bogart and Bacall is the other side of Bogart's struggle to see through the system of deceptions by which Mars veils that meaning. In a sense, Bogart, in his capacity as investigator, is our stand-in: It is his task to perceive and interpret the signs of doubleness, chief among them that most perplexing of mysteries, Lauren Bacall. And Eddie Mars is the representative of Hawks: His work is that of projecting appearances that tempt us to take them straight, but that, if taken straight, deceive.

In *Bringing Up Baby*, perception is not the real issue, the possibility of deception does not arise, and the corollary Hawksian theme of blindness is sounded only comically. Grant's blindness is an aspect of the comic convention that deprives him of his powers of coordination the moment the "love interest" appears on the scene. (What Hepburn does to Grant, Marilyn Monroe does in spades to Tommy Noonan in *Gentlemen Prefer Blondes*: Her close proximity is enough to make him all but throw up.) Another central Hawks theme is likewise barely touched on in *Bringing Up Baby*: the power of the past to haunt the here and now. Grant, a virgin, has no past "domestic entailment of any kind" that he could confuse with his present entanglement with Hepburn (it is not possible even for him to mistake her for Miss Swallow). By contrast, Grant in *Only Angels Have Wings* does find his relationship with Jean Arthur haunted by his past affair with Rita Hayworth. This contrast is reflected in a fundamental difference in formal structure between the Hawks films that do and those that do not emphasize memory and the past. *Bringing Up Baby*, for example, hardly avails itself of the systematic repetition, and significant variation, of camera setups that figure so importantly in *Only Angels Have Wings*. In *The Big Sleep*, another film that relies heavily on a virtual theme-and-variation structure of camera setups, the repetition, for example, of a triangular composition with Eddie Mars's door as apex can be understood as a formal anticipation of the film's violent ending, and at the same time a formal acknowledgment of the presence of Mars, whose power Bogart has not yet recognized, which in turn is an expression of Hawks's role as author of the film.

Bringing Up Baby is a Hawks film whose characters do not use signs the way Hawks does. Between the film's literal and allegorical levels there is, as it were, a barrier of consciousness. The two levels are balanced but separated.

His Girl Friday is a different kind of Hawks film: Its allegory and its literal level are also of equal weight, but are intimately intertwined. Grant and Russell are engaged in a struggle to assert the dominating reading of that very struggle, which Hawks presents straight, yet also allegorizes in sexual terms.

The Big Sleep takes *His Girl Friday* further, raising its allegory to a level of self-reflection, but without destroying the balance between allegory and straight presentation.

Barbary Coast is a Hawks film in which the balance is destroyed. The allegorical level dominates and betrays (but with provocation!) the literal level. The film reflects on itself, not so much explicating as diagnosing its narrative. *Land of the Pharaohs* goes beyond *The Thing* and *Gentlemen Prefer Blondes* in extending this dominance of the allegorical. In *Land of the Pharaohs*, indeed, this domination has become absolute: Hawks has completely sealed himself off from the literal narrative, and the film proves inaccessible to its audience.

When working on *Land of the Pharaohs*, Hawks spoke of it as his most ambitious work, the film that was to synthesize all of his themes and techniques. My sense is that the total commercial failure of this film, which embarrassed Hawks to the end of his life, precipitated a crisis in his career. Hawks's later films, wonderful in their way, seem reduced in ambition, as if their author had lost his sense of his work as unique and important. Ironically, this occurred at precisely the moment of his critical discovery or rediscovery in France and subsequently (almost single-handedly because of the persistent efforts of Andrew Sarris) the United States. The interviews and public appearances that appear to confirm Hawks's lack of self-consciousness and ambition date from this period or later.

In his last films, it is as if Hawks became disillusioned about his own filmmaking enterprise, with which he had kept faith for almost fifty years, coming to regard it as only a "search for El Dorado."

Rio Lobo's allegorical reading denies the possibility of the film's meaningfulness. Its implication is that Hawks's filmmaking seemed important to him only because he was involved in a war. But now the war was over.

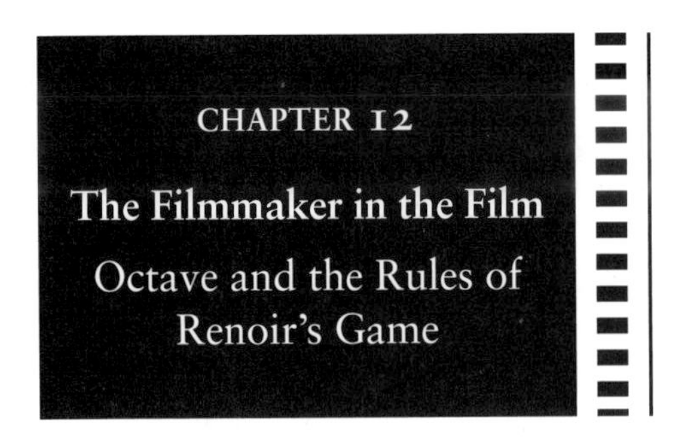

This chapter has two parts. First, it sketches a reading of *The Rules of the Game* that focuses on the figure of Octave. Then it examines the significance of *The Rules of the Game* within the context of Renoir's work. In brief, the claim of the first part is that Octave represents the film's author, serves as the filmmaker's surrogate in his intervention in the world of the film (the most direct possible point to Renoir's gesture of choosing to play the part of Octave himself). Octave's role constitutes a paradigm for the role Renoir conceives himself as playing as creator of films like *The Rules of the Game*. In this way, Renoir's conception of the creation of his art – a conception manifestly the subject of Renoir's late work (for example, the trilogy *The Golden Coach, French Can-Can*, and *Eléna et les Hommes*, and *The Little Theater of Jean Renoir*) – is inscribed within the *The Rules of the Game*. The film's delineation of Octave's role, its establishment of a certain relationship between the camera and the world it frames, and its story are integrally connected. *The Rules of the Game* is an acknowledgment by Renoir of the conditions of his own art.

The second part of this chapter argues that the way *The Rules of the Game* frames this acknowledgment is crucial to its significance in the context of Renoir's work. The claim is that *The Rules of the Game* brings to completion Renoir's filmmaking project to that date, and in turn determines the framework for the films that follow.

Octave's Role

When Octave gives his word that André will see Christine again ("If I don't see her again... I'll die," "You'll see her again.... I'll make it my

Reprinted: See "Notes on the Essays."

business"), he undertakes to bring together all the major characters of the film, setting off an as yet unspecified chain of events.

Much of the early part of the film is concerned with Octave's ingenious and persistent efforts to persuade Christine and Robert (but also the ever-skeptical Lisette, and even André, who at times falters) to allow him to accomplish this act of stage-setting. Indeed, at key moments in the film, a number of characters authorize Octave in his efforts (Christine: "Well, my friend, the rest is up to you.... I wash my hands of it"). The most general strategy employed by Octave in securing and acting on these authorizations is to instruct characters on the conditions of their roles. (Different characters accept Octave's tutoring for different reasons and in different spirits, however.) This makes it all the clearer that Octave's mediations, which he single-mindedly pursues, are intended to establish the conditions of a chain of events that constitutes a kind of production. He assumes a producer–director's responsibility for making a certain production take place. The relationship between the authorizations he secures and his assumption of responsibility is complex. After all, what gives these characters the power to grant Octave responsibility for this chain of events that ends in death? Their authorizations do not legitimate Octave's production, but rather implicate them all in its consequences.

The Rules of the Game, then, divides itself into (1) a backstage story of the mounting of a production and (2) the production itself (it could be called *The Sacrifice of André*) that opens with André's arrival at the chateau and closes with his death. When Octave enters Christine's bedroom, a bit anxiously followed by Robert, the camera suddenly tracks in through the frame of the doorway as Lisette raises a curtain, letting light stream in through the window. The sudden movement of the camera combines with the sound of the curtain to create an effect of violent disruption, appropriate to the occasion given the fact that the name "Schumacher" is about to be spoken for the first time. The curtain has risen on Octave's production.

It is hardly necessary to point out that *The Rules of the Game* incorporates many "productions": the hunt and the theatricals in celebration of the hunt, to name just two. That there is a bewildering array of productions helps give comic thrust to Corneille's response to Robert's plea that he do something to stop "this farce" ("Which one?" Corneille asks). It is part of my claim, though, that Octave's production, *The Sacrifice of André*, has a special status in the film.

Within this production, Octave plays a role that extends the one he plays in setting it up and initiating it. The necessity of playing this role is brought home to him at precisely the moment when he is poised to step out of character by thrusting into the spotlight to claim Christine in an erotic union. Lisette voices Octave's innermost doubt: "You're wrong, Monsieur Octave.... " Suddenly André appears on the scene, as if at the bidding of that doubt. Octave hands André Octave's own coat and sends André to Christine in his place, setting the stage for the production's climax and conclusion: André's violent death. As the film presents this moment, the camera pans from a close shot of Octave and Lisette (they face each other, but Octave's face is doubled in a mirror over her shoulder; Lisette is face-to-face with Octave, but he also stands apart, unseen by her) to a symmetrical, highly stylized image of André.

The gesture of sending André to Christine in his place doubles Octave's initial act of setting things up so that André can see Christine again. The earlier promise-making scene haunts this later moment. "If I don't see her again ... I'll die." Now Octave fails to "see to it," despite his best efforts, and André dies. By repeating within his production the act by which he had initiated the production, Octave becomes an agent of André's death. His gesture signals the end of the production and confirms his authorship of it.

Octave's two acts nevertheless cancel each other out. The one suspends André's death, for André had convinced Octave that he was sincere when he said that he would die if he did not see Christine. The other ironically brings it about, closing the prospect the first gesture had provisionally opened. In their motivation, they are enigmatic in exactly the same way. Why does Octave make that promise to André, and why does he send André to Christine in his own place? What does he think will be the outcome of the events set in motion by André's arrival at the chateau – what outcome does he desire? Does Octave act out of a wish grounded in pity to save his friend from death or the pain of his own unfulfilled desire? Out of a wish to keep faith with Christine's dead father, extricating her from a marriage built on a lie so that he might give her as a bride to the man who convinces him that he loves her? Out of a wish to possess Christine himself? To punish André for provoking him into denying his own desire – by assuming the author's role, instead of the hero's? From a wish to be completely absorbed in the author's role? We may ask such questions about the motivation for *both* acts.

The enigma of Octave's motivation turns on our difficulty in saying with certainty what Octave *knows*. Do we want to say that in a sense Octave knows from the outset how the events he authors will turn out or must turn out? (When Uncle Charles returns to his hometown in Hitchcock's *Shadow of a Doubt*, does he know that he is to die when he leaves it again? When Charles places a ring on young Charlie's finger, does he know that their "marriage" will be consummated only in her act of pushing him off the train to his death?)

We can say with confidence that the camera (the unseen presence the film invokes as responsible for its succession of views, thus the film's inscription of its own author, Jean Renoir) reveals that it "knows" all along that this production is to end with André's death. When Octave first makes his promise to André, they are shot in low angle, framed only against the sky.

This image of André-in-the-clouds, as though already dead but unable to rest, is linked ironically to the film's image of André's "real" death, which in turn has already been specifically imaged in the heart-breaking shot of a dying rabbit that weights the pivotal hunt sequence with its heaviest burden.

There are many small and large incidents of anticipation and/or echoing that invoke an author not dependent on the unfolding of the film for knowledge of events in the world of the film.

I want to say that upon completion of the events we have been calling "the production," Octave comes into unambiguous possession of knowledge that the film's author has possessed from the outset. For Octave, this knowledge is, at one level, of himself and the conditions of his role: knowledge that his world is complete without his bodily presence within it and that his dream of having a place in this world ends with a death. It is also knowledge of his place in this film and his identity with the film's author, Renoir. In a sense, the story of the film is the story of Octave's coming into this knowledge. This story, *The Education of Octave*, frames the production of *The Sacrifice of André*.

The crystallization of Octave's knowledge is registered, at his moment of doubt, in the pan from him to André.

The sudden transition from a frame whose subject is Octave to a frame from which he is absent constitutes a figure for the achievement of self-knowledge. When the world wells up in the person of Lisette to give voice to his innermost doubt, and when it fixes itself in a view of André, Octave can no longer fail to recognize himself.

That camera movement expresses Octave's subjective response at this moment in which the world closes itself off from him. But the expression itself is the camera's. The world's disclosure of itself to Octave cannot be separated from his own absence from the world. His gesture of sending André in his place, which authorizes the close of the production, comes about, then, when Octave realizes what the camera movement means. By formulating this expression of Octave's subjectivity, Renoir acknowledges that he and Octave are one.

This leaves one final act Octave must perform: He must banish himself irrevocably from the chateau. By withdrawing from the world of the film, Octave takes it upon himself to repeat the camera's exclusion of him from the frame by its pan to André. Octave thereby reclaims the camera's gesture as his own. He acknowledges his identity with the film's author by authorizing the film's ending, in particular its crucial expulsion of himself. Thus, finally the film completes its acknowledgments – at once Octave's and Renoir's – that Octave is Renoir and that Renoir is Octave.

But how can we identify Octave with the author of *The Rules of the Game* when part of what Octave comes to know in the course of the film is that the consequences of his actions are irremediably affected by forces beyond his control? Octave is powerless to banish Schumacher from the world of the film. Octave cannot change the course of the hunt, over which the gamekeeper presides, and which anticipates the death of André. So, too, the theatricals in celebration of the hunt are set up by Robert, not Octave – their liberation of nature's forces of death and desire is beyond Octave's control. Indeed, every major character in the film, though up to a point accepting Octave's direction of the production, also participates autonomously in determining its unfolding.

If Octave's intervention in the world of the film, his authoring of the production, was intended by him to keep André from death, still, as I have suggested, that intervention forms an integral part of the mechanism of André's death. In the world of *The Rules of the Game*, desire and death, forces of nature, are central and inexorable. When Octave assumes authorship of the production, he inevitably plays into death's hands. Octave cannot deny death; he is powerless to efface the signs of mortality everywhere in his world; he cannot even escape being the agent of death.

If the camera is engaged in instructing Octave within the world of *The Rules of the Game*, Octave is engaged in a struggle with the forces of nature. Octave cannot win his struggle to keep death from that world. But our conclusion from this is not that nature, and specifically death, is the true "author" in the world of the film, with Octave only death's puppet.

When the curtain falls on the theatricals, none of the performers is prepared to acknowledge the cries of "Author! Author!" that rise from the audience. Saint-Saëns's "Danse Macabre" begins to sound on the player piano, and the figure of Death (at least a man in a skeleton costume) appears in the auditorium and dances to this music played by no human hands. The apparition occurs at the moment it begins to dawn on Octave that the events of the production, though beyond his control, nonetheless bear an uncannily intimate relationship to him. Death's gesture of responding to the audience's call suggests that there is an authorship as yet unclaimed. Perhaps Octave's anxiety at the approach of self-knowledge finds expression in this entrance of Death into the theater. At another level, Octave's anxiety takes the form of feeling imprisoned in his own body. Octave discovers that the curtain is up and that he is being viewed. He cannot get out of his bear costume; he cannot "disappear down a hole," a wish he had expressed to Robert earlier in the film. But the camera can expose him, can entrap him in the frame.

This moment of helplessness was anticipated by an earlier moment, when Octave was unable to retrieve the field glass and see what Christine saw in it. The film's power to withhold views from Octave is the other face of the camera's power to view him against his will.

By contrast, at Octave's high points, he feels that his power is unlimited, as if even the camera must be subject to his will. We see this exhilaration, for example, in the scene where he dismisses Robert from Christine's bedroom so that he can talk to her alone. Octave allows a bit of small talk to take place before he grows impatient. At the moment he is ready to assume direction of the action once more, the camera "discovers" him on one of its trajectories. Here the camera all but acts as Octave's servant. Soon after, the moment it becomes absolutely clear that Christine will agree to invite André to the chateau, the camera assumes a slightly high-angle position. Now it reflects Octave's triumph, as though it quite naturally expressed Octave's feelings. (In fact, it is entirely exceptional for Renoir's camera to express a character's feelings in this way.)

As the film unfolds, Octave comes to recognize that his power, like that of any author, is real, but has limits. He learns that the camera must entrap him when he fails to acknowledge his bond with it, and he can subject the camera to his will only when the camera complies as a tactic in its instruction of him. The film implies that there is a necessary connection between the presence of death in its world and Renoir's incarnation in that world as a man who does not yet know himself. Death is an emblem of the bond between Octave and Renoir.

Death is not under Octave's control, and Octave is not death's puppet. Nonetheless, there are two fundamental links between death and Octave.

1. If Octave had no body, he could not be "discovered" by the camera, set to intervene in the world of the film. The fact that he is corporeal signifies his mortality. To acknowledge himself is to acknowledge that he must die. Octave's transition from a place within the frame to a place "behind the camera" is his death to the world of the film. This is part of the resonance of the film's final frame.

   It is a shot of the balustrade that Octave had used as a stage for reenacting his memory of Christine's father, at the same time enacting his own dream of contact with an audience. It is an image of an empty stage, complete with "footlights." It is also an image of a kind of bridge, a symbol of transition, all transitions connoting, for Renoir, the transition between dream and reality and from reality to dream; the transition, through death, from life to rebirth, and the transition, through life, from death to death.

   Of course, if Octave is corporeal and hence mortal, so must Renoir be mortal in order to incarnate him in the frame. Fixed by the camera, the film's author is exposed as only flesh and blood.
2. Octave's authorship is death-dealing within the world of *The Rules of the Game*. His production constitutes the machinery of André's death. Moreover, his final banishment of himself from the world of the film reveals that Octave is death-dealing in a larger sense. The film's ending presents Octave's death to his world and the death of that world to us. We might describe the camera's paradoxical perspective on the world of *The Rules of the Game* as belonging to the ghost of Octave. The camera haunts Octave, who sees its death mark everywhere and comes to recognize it as the sign of his own being. He frees himself from it by joining it "on the other side." Part of the force of the film's final image, engendered by Octave's self-exile, is that it shows us the death of a world

from the perspective of a figure who magically survives that death. It is important to note that if the film's opening presents itself as contingent (Octave's pledge to André is not the first of his interventions in the world; the film could have opened, say, with the camera's "discovering" Octave just before or just after Christine's father's death, or just before André's flight), its ending is definitive. There is no possible sequel, no *The Rules of the Game* II in which Octave plays the same role in the same world.

Corollary to Octave's death-dealing role is Renoir's insistence on the deadly efficacy of the camera's gaze, and the equally deadly results, potentially, of a character's failing to see what the camera sees. The camera's power of appropriating views makes it a kind of gun. This is most directly declared in the hunt sequence, and most specifically in the shot of the squirrel shivering in terror, trapped in the sight of the "innocent" field glass/camera, and in all of the shots of rabbits dying.

The particular image of the dying rabbit that is echoed in the presentation of André's death, indeed, unavoidably confronts us with the shocking knowledge that Renoir authorized the death of this creature for the sake of presenting this shot to us.

In making *The Rules of the Game*, Renoir exposes his mortality before us, and also he kills. However exhilarating our experience of it, this is a film made in grim earnest.

Renoir's Game

Why does Renoir tell this story of the filmmaker's intervention in the world of his film and his final withdrawal? Surely part of Renoir's motivation is personal. *The Rules of the Game* comes at a critical moment for him. In an uncanny way, it prophesies the coming turn in his life: his withdrawal from France at the Nazi conquest. Renoir's life in the world that was his home, and indeed that world itself insofar as he would call it home, is about to end. Renoir is on the brink of exile.

But I feel that *The Rules of the Game* addresses itself not only to an impending trauma in Renoir's life (and in the life of Europe), but also to a certain place Renoir had reached in his work. *The Rules of the Game* brings a series of films, Renoir's lifework up to that time, to completion. It is not that a certain project is arbitrarily broken off, but that *The Rules of the Game* constitutes the fulfillment of Renoir's original filmmaking project. It articulates the logic of development in the films that preceded it and, in turn, defines the challenges that are to occupy Renoir in his remaining films.

How does *The Rules of the Game* bring to completion the work of Renoir's French period? These films form a series of stories culminating in the story of *The Rules of the Game*. They present a series of characters summed up in the figure of Octave and a series of central symbols brought to an end in the symbol of the balustrade/stage/bridge in the film's closing sequence. Perhaps most important, they represent a series of formal developments that find their fullest extension in *The Rules of the Game* and are never really carried over to Renoir's later work.

In the classical cinematic narrative, the camera represents itself as "capturing" beings who thrust themselves into the world of the film. The camera's agency – constituted by its framings, by reframings through the camera's movements, and by cutting from shot to shot in ways that sustain an impression of continuity – establishes an analogue of a novel's narrator. The narrator of a novel is, at one level, an inscription of the author in his work, as if the novel were the address of the author, speaking in the narrator's voice, to the reader. The narrator is also a special kind of character (although novels in which the narrator is identified literally as a character in his own narration are, of course, not uncommon). A problem arises when we imagine a film whose camera is to be literally identified with a character visible on the screen. The camera's presence is manifest as a series of views. The classical film's analogue of a narrator is the unseen figure (ordinarily, he or she also has no voice) who authorizes those views. Given its prohibition against the camera's framing views of itself (for example, glimpses of itself in the mirror), the camera's absence from the frame is its sole mark on the frame. Thus, no being visible within the frame can be identified, in any simple way, with the figure represented by the camera. Even when the director of the film appears as an actor on the screen, the frame serves as a kind of formal barrier separating the figure who authorizes the framing from the figures framed, thus also from himself or herself.

How might a relationship of identity between a figure disclosed by the camera and the unseen figure who authorizes that disclosure be established and acknowledged in the succession of frames of a film? *The Rules of the Game* can be seen as Renoir's solution.

Why does this problem arise for Renoir at the moment of making *The Rules of the Game*? To answer this question, we must reflect on the nature of Renoir's formal innovations.

André Bazin was the first serious critic who attempted to describe the formal strategies that set Renoir's French films apart from other films of their time. He cited Renoir's tendency to dispense with the classical cutting style. Renoir replaced analytical editing (cutting for dramatic emphasis and to suggest point of view) by a certain characteristic practice of reframing. Thus, Bazin argues, Renoir respects the freedom of the filmed figures and the reality and integrity of their world. Viewed "objectively," without the classical "narrator's" mediation, these beings-in-a-world naturally reveal the inner truth about themselves.

My own sense is that the primary thrust of Renoir's formal innovations was not to dispense with narrative's process of mediation, but to give the camera/narrator a new stance: one that renders problematic, or exposes as already problematic, the camera's relationship to the world it frames and the human figures in that world.

Renoir's films up to and including *The Rules of the Game* create a role for the camera that breaks with its classical role. Renoir's camera denies the power of a character's interiority to motivate a framing or a cut, and it all but abandons the practice of responding to the drama of the scene enacted before it. Renoir can thereby create the impression that the figures in the frame have been freed from a stultifying mediation, as Bazin suggests – they are free to reveal their inner truth. Have we not all at some time thought, while viewing one of Renoir's great works of this period, that no one but Renoir has ever placed such movingly human beings within the frame of a film?

But Renoir's camera can create a different impression as well: not that it abandons the classical role to give the viewer unmediated access to human beings, but that it *disdains* to perform the classical gestures. Better, it plays the classical role *with disdain*. Renoir's camera can appear unresponsive, expressing indifference to the events unfolding within and around the frame. Even while his characters move us as though they were fellow human beings, we can see that they have all but lost a human dimension for the camera. [The idea that his films' characters are puppets with no true interiors, already implicit in *The Little Match Girl* (1928), in which Catherine Hessling moves with the jerkiness of a marionette, is explicitly articulated in *La Chienne* (1931).]

If Renoir's camera expresses slight concern for the human beings before it, what motivates its framings, reframings, and cuts?

Renoir's camera is most characteristic when it seems primarily concerned with establishing the contingency of its frame. By this I mean the impression that the world of the film extends beyond the boundaries of the frame, so that any particular placement of the camera is only contingently determined by the world of the film. Further, Renoir's camera frames and reframes in such a manner as to suggest that it reserves as much interest (and as little) for what is outside the frame as for what happens within it. Hitchcock's camera in a certain mood dogs its characters, attending to the interior struggles betrayed by their movements and gestures. Renoir reframes upon the movements of his characters in the manner of a cat following the dinner party into the living room. The cat's movement is couched in indifference, as if to claim that it is the merest coincidence that she has chosen to make this move at just the time the people moved.

The Renoir frame characteristically conveys the formal indifference to what it frames that the proscenium arch automatically has to the gestures performed by actors on the stage. It is not that Renoir's camera animates no "narrator," but that the authorial figure it animates through its special strategies of reframing is one that may well strike us as specifically inhuman: The camera stands unresponsive before its human subjects as though to it they are always merely acting. Their sufferings and joys move us, although the camera frames their world as though it were inhabited by puppets, not people.

The process of developing this camera stance and reflecting on its implications engaged Renoir in the films leading to *The Rules of the Game*. This evolution could be analyzed in detail, revealing that even in the extraordinary *Boudu Saved from Drowning* (1932), Renoir's camera is not yet fully itself. By *Toni* (1934), however, the characteristic stance of Renoir's camera has fully emerged.

The central symbol of *Toni* is a bridge. Toni arrives by train across the Spanish border. Every day, workers come on this train to start a new life. The camera tracks with these workers as they make their way, singing from the station to the town nearby. Gradually, the camera slows, so that it no longer keeps up with the immigrants, who file through the frame. When all the human figures have left the frame, the camera – still haunted by the singing of the workers now unseen – continues its slow movement until it composes a perfect picture of the bridge.

This bridge functions as one of the film's main settings, but only the ending of the film declares its significance as a symbol. Toni dies just past the end of the bridge. As the camera tilts up, we see a new train arrive, a whole new potential cast of characters filled with hope. The film ends on a final camera movement that exactly repeats the first, and again it concludes by framing the bridge, as if it is in this bridge, not in any of its human subjects, that the camera finds its own likeness – this despite the fact that in *Toni* the film has a protagonist whose passivity matches the camera's own apparent indifference to him, as if the film is intent on denying its bond with Toni.

Out of the process of developing this characteristic camera stance emerges a closely related task: to confront the "inhuman" camera, unmasking its apparent indifference and revealing it as representing a figure who is, after all, human – who is, indeed, Renoir himself. This is the task completed by *The Rules of the Game*, which breaks through the camera's displays of indifference, exposing them as a natural expression of Renoir's bond with the world of his films.

In *The Crime of M. Lange* (1935), *Toni*'s practice of reframing undergoes a further development pertinent to this project: The camera, while retaining and even exaggerating its attitude of indifference, is provoked to take sides for the community and against the monstrously charming Batala. Crucially here, the camera undertakes to sum up characters. It sums up the benevolent figure of Lange, for example, with a tour of his room early in the film. And it sums up the evil Batala in an incredible, perfect Renoir shot that sweeps full circle around the courtyard – the film's central symbol – passes an overflowing garbage can, and ends on the body of Batala. The camera completes its trajectory as though this juxtaposition is none of its concern; yet it makes the point – not less surely for appearing to all but throw it away – that Batala is garbage.

The Crime of M. Lange reveals that at least at an intellectual level, Renoir's camera is not indifferent – it is committed to its world. The full acknowledgment of the commitment motivating its apparent indifference is only completed in *The Rules of the Game.*

Before *The Rules of the Game*, Renoir had never attributed the camera's apparent indifference to a figure within a film. In *The Rules of the Game*, Renoir mobilizes the camera to sum up Octave and attributes its stance to him. When the camera frames the balustrade for its final image, it identifies itself symbolically with it, as Renoir's camera had identified itself with the bridge in *Toni* and the courtyard in *The Crime of M. Lange*. This final image presents, emblematically, the inhuman forces of the world of *The Rules of the Game*, but at the same time it is an image of and by Octave/Renoir. The integrity of Renoir's camera is sustained. His "inhuman narrator" is disclosed to be Octave, thus, in turn, the human author Renoir himself.

With the pan from Octave to André that crystallizes Octave's self-knowledge, and with *The Rules of the Game's* closing image, Renoir's project to that date – establishing a camera that appears enigmatic and inhuman, then unmasking the figure it invokes as, after all, the human author Renoir – is completed.

The Rules of the Game necessitates a new beginning for Renoir as author. Octave withdraws irrevocably, and the world of every subsequent Renoir film is one from which the author figure, who demands acknowledgment, has already withdrawn. There are no further Renoir protagonists like Toni, who does not know his bond with the camera, which in turn does not acknowledge that it sees itself reflected in him. Almost all subsequent Octave figures remain behind the camera, invisible to inhabitants of the film's world; if such an author figure does intervene in the world of the film, he now does so only on the condition that the camera reveals that he possesses from the outset knowledge of his role and his identity – knowledge that he has no possibility for permanent romantic union within the world of the film, knowledge of his bond with the camera.

The numbing depression of Renoir's American films suggests that these conditions precipitated a grave crisis in his filmmaking. In *Swamp Water* (1941), for example, the central symbol is the swamp to which the Octave figure, played by Walter Brennan, has withdrawn before the opening of the film. Unjustly accused of murder, he maintains within his swamp an exile's connection to the outside world. A young man (Dana Andrews) undertakes to clear Brennan's name and prepare the world for the return of the "dead man." The film ends with Brennan physically back in the world, but spiritually dead to it. From the outset, the camera openly identifies with the Brennan character, who in turn openly identifies himself with the swamp. For example, before we ever see Brennan in the frame, he is introduced by a shot from his point of view of a stranger penetrating the swamp. We know that this is a point-of-view shot, but when it appears, we know the bearer of that point of view only as a being linked to the swamp. The view is, as it were, the swamp's own, the view of a being who has been claimed by the swamp.

Swamp Water tests itself as a possible sequel to *The Rules of the Game*. It opens with the camera in the position it held there at the close. But if *Swamp Water* seems to follow Octave back into the world, its conclusion is that *The Rules of the Game* has no real sequel. Returned to the world, Brennan is only a ghost.

Swamp Water leaves Renoir still without a project; nor is one found in such films as *The Southerner* (1944), or in its despairing companion piece, Renoir's last American film, *The Woman on the Beach* (1947). All of Renoir's American films do, however, keep faith with *The Rules of the Game*. They meditate on the impossibility of their having the life of Renoir's great French films, and they have at their heart a deep sense of the loss of that life.

Rising out of despair, *The River* (1951) seems to mark the reanimation or rededication of Renoir's filmmaking. It inaugurates a series of films, in certain ways comparable with the series completed by *The Rules of the Game*, that *The Little Theater of Jean Renoir* (1969), his last film, concludes. The conditions of this rebirth are perhaps most explicitly articulated in the most perfectly realized of Renoir's late works: *The Golden Coach* (1953) and *French Cancan* (1955).

I shall conclude this chapter with a reading of the ending of *French Cancan*.

French Cancan is about the creation of a theater. This theater, the film's central symbol, is a kind of protocinema, indeed a prototype of Renoir's own cinema. Like its historical original, Danglard's Moulin Rouge takes the shape of a windmill, a machine to reap the wind, to harness the forces of nature. It breaks down the old barriers between performers and spectators while attaining freedom from the tyranny of time.

The protagonist, Danglard (Jean Gabin), is an artist–impresario whose lifework is fulfilled in this latest and consummate creation. Clearly, he is an Octave figure, but of course Octave had no such privileged place within which his production could be framed. Danglard intervenes in a world animated by his art, and he does so already knowing and accepting his role as an author. Not only does he know how to instruct others about their roles, as Octave did, but also he knows what his identity as author makes of him.

The film accepts Danglard as the authority on his own role. His understanding is most explicitly declared in an extraordinary speech near the end of the film. Nini, whom he has trained for the stage, is about to make her first entrance. By this entrance, she will burn all bridges to her old life. She hesitates, having just seen Danglard turning his amorous attention to his latest discovery, another girl/woman ripe for creation. In a memorable peroration, he declares that it is the condition of his role to pass from woman to woman, giving himself to each only until she breaks through into the life of the theater, always holding part of himself back. He knows that the performances within his theater are rites of spring and that he himself can have no partner, can enter into no marriage, can attain no permanent romantic union either within or outside his theater. He cannot even possess the contact with an audience that will be Nini's.

Danglard is set forth by the film as its author's spokesman. Indeed, when Danglard makes his speech, Renoir has Gabin appropriate the gesticulating manner we know and love as Octave's. Renoir so directs Gabin as to give us the uncanny feeling that it is not Gabin, but Renoir himself incarnate in the frame, making manifest, and perhaps thereby helping to exorcise, the figure who haunts Danglard throughout the film.

From the outset, there is an identification of the camera and Danglard. Early in the film, there is a scene of a Saturday night dance at a dance hall. Danglard discovers a dancer (Nini) and rediscovers a dance (the cancan). The dancing is viewed through Danglard's eyes. If at the opening of *The Rules of the Game* the most significant event is the camera's "discovery" of Octave, *French Cancan* opens with the camera identifying Danglard as the agent of its discoveries.

Like *The Rules of the Game, French Cancan* divides into a backstage story and a production, both in turn placed within the larger frame of the film. In mounting his production, Danglard openly plays the part that Octave plays more or less covertly. Like Octave, Danglard finds himself called upon to play a role within the production that mirrors his role in creating the production itself. Unlike Octave, though, Danglard knows all along how his production will end.

The construction of the theater has been completed. At the start of the opening-night performance, Danglard, backstage, attends to the show with the nervousness of an expectant father. As if overcome with tension, he sits in a chair, his back to the curtain. Renoir begins to cut back and forth between Danglard's face and the goings-on within the theater. This cross-cutting creates the impression that each view of Danglard shows his reaction to what we just saw (for example, to little flirtations in the audience inspired by the animating dancing on stage) and shows his cue signaling what we are about to see. He cannot see what we see; he knows all that happens within his theater without the need to gaze upon it. Nor does any performer in the theater need to see him. Finally, he closes his eyes in satisfaction, completely possessed of the life within his theater.

The world within his theater is a projection of Danglard's imagination; so he can possess it completely. "Reality" now has no hold on him; they die to each other. This moment at which he accepts his creation as born is also a moment of death. Its equivalent in *The Rules of the Game* is the pan to André that crystallizes Octave's self-knowledge.

Danglard's foot now begins to tap in time with the music, and we realize that he has fallen under the spell of his own creation, which has the same power over him that it has over all human beings. He finds himself drawn from backstage into the theater. At the moment he joins the others in the theater, his separation from the camera, already signaled by the transformation of Danglard/Gabin into Octave/Renoir, is achieved. Renoir exorcised, Danglard loses his special status in relationship to the camera, which, like the music and dancing, assumes its power over him. It places him alongside all of the film's characters within a montage that declares all to be equal even as it sums up and differentiates their individualities. This is a montage of couples, save for Nini (who is married to her audience), the old conductor (who is married to his music), and Danglard (who is married to his role as the creator of stars). Within this montage, we see Danglard, who is now shoulder-to-shoulder with the audience, eye the woman next to him (who bears more than a passing resemblance to Ingrid Bergman, star of Renoir's next film, *Eléna et les Hommes*), and begin yet again the process of creating a star.

Danglard's assumption of his role *within* the theater affirms the naturalness of authorship. Despite everything (the inhuman aspect of his role, for example), the author Danglard is a creature suited by nature to membership in the human community. Indeed, it is his role to assume responsibility for the creation or re-creation of that community, a community that retains the aspect of a dream – Renoir's dream.

Danglard's assumption of his place within his theater crystallizes his separation from the camera, from Renoir. This is reaffirmed in the film's final image. Renoir suddenly cuts away from the theater and frames it *from the outside*. An anonymous figure leaves the Moulin Rouge, staggers drunkenly to the foreground of the frame, and bows, as if acknowledging our applause for the film that is ending.

In a sense, *French Cancan* repeats but reverses, undoes, the story of *The Rules of the Game*. It is as if Octave is reclaimed by his world, which his art brings back to life, as if the part of Renoir that is Octave dies to him as he gives life to this film. When *French Cancan* ends with Danglard enclosed within a theater framed within its world, Renoir is once again alone.

It remains for *The Little Theater of Jean Renoir* to close out Renoir's lifework (as *The Rules of the Game* closed out the series of films it culminated). Renoir once more appears on the screen as an actor, in an Octave role. But now he explicitly identifies himself as the producer–director of the four short pieces that compose the film. He casts himself as the author of *The Little Theater of Jean Renoir*. (Indeed, these short pieces reprise moments from nearly every Renoir film. To be the author of this film is to be the author of Renoir's entire oeuvre. It is to be Jean Renoir.) Renoir does not intervene in the world of his last film. Standing alone before his creation, he speaks directly to us.

CHAPTER 13

Stagecoach and the Quest for Selfhood

Stagecoach (1939), in its day, was more often characterized as a melodrama than as a western. It is true that what we might call the salvation of a woman and the formation of a romantic couple are central to its narrative. Yet on the whole the roles of women in *Stagecoach*, and in John Ford's films in general, seem more conventional than in the Hollywood movies of the 1930s and 1940s that Stanley Cavell has dubbed "comedies of remarriage" and "melodramas of the unknown woman."[1] In the course of *Stagecoach*, not one but two women achieve a new perspective. However, neither Dallas nor Lucy has much in common with the heroines of such films as *The Philadelphia Story* or *Now, Voyager*, women who are passionately committed to their quests for selfhood. The leading "classical" genres embrace an Emersonian philosophical perspective. Ford's cinema, like Hitchcock's, stands in an uneasy relationship to that philosophy.

Stagecoach seems to have more to do with such matters as social class and prejudice. On those matters, the film judges American society – "civilization" – to be wanting. In the end, when Curly (allied with Doc) subverts the rule of Law he is sworn to uphold, Dallas and Ringo are free to settle down on his ranch – but only south of the border, in Mexico, a place outside "civilization," to which they will never be free to return.

[1] That classical Hollywood movies inherit the philosophical perspective of American transcendentalism – a tradition of thought that affirms the possibility and necessity of relying on one's own experience, and on the acknowledgment of others, to achieve selfhood – is an idea articulated by Cavell in his indispensable books *Pursuits of Happiness: The Hollywood Comedy of Remarriage* (Cambridge, MA: Harvard University Press, 1981) and *Contesting Tears: Hollywood Melodramas of the Unknown Woman* (Chicago: University of Chicago Press, 1996). Cavell demonstrates how the genres he studies work through the Emersonian problematic of self-reliance and conformity and thereby sustain serious conversations with their – our – culture on such matters as the human need for society and the equal need to escape it, the search for community, and the fate of the American dream.

What does Dallas want? She wants to be a mother, for one thing. And she wants Ringo. At first, she tries to get him to forgo revenge and head off to his ranch in Mexico, where she will join him – but only after she fulfills her duty to serve Lucy and her baby. Dallas is even a step ahead of Ringo. Anticipating that he will agree, she has his rifle ready for him. And for the moment he is willing.

If at that point Ringo had not been stopped – or, rather, stopped himself, when he saw the Apache smoke signals – from riding off to his ranch, as Dallas had suggested, to be joined by her once the stagecoach carried Lucy and her baby safely to Lordsburg, he would have failed to play his part in fighting off the marauding Apaches. Everyone's blood – including Dallas's – would then have been on his hands. So *Stagecoach* cannot be saying that Ringo should have run off to his ranch. Then is the film saying that it is wrong to run away – to avoid what is not to be avoided? And is this a principle that holds for women as well as men?

Once in Lordsburg, of course, Ringo could still forgo revenge and propose to Dallas that she wait until he gets out of prison. Or he could forgo revenge and escape to his ranch with Dallas. True, he has given his word to Curly, the U. S. Marshall, but to kill the Plummers, he has to break his promise, in any case ("I lied to you, Curly. I got three [bullets] left"). We accept – and, it seems, Curly accepts – that facing this moment of reckoning with the Plummers *is* something Ringo "has to do," given the reality that, although the Law has men as honorable as Curly to enforce it, the rule of Law has not yet been firmly established in such a place as Lordsburg. Once Ringo has successfully completed this task, turning himself in to Curly is the second thing he "has to do."

Dallas, too, "has to do" two things. One is to let Ringo know who she is in society's eyes – a prostitute – so that he has a fair chance to reject her once he knows the truth.

The second thing Dallas "has to do" is cater to Lucy and her newborn baby, putting their well-being ahead of her own, until the stagecoach reaches Lordsburg and others can relieve her of her duty. To contemporary sensibilities – mine, for one – it rankles that *Stagecoach* seems to be endorsing Dallas's notion that it is her "duty" to serve Lucy, as if it is natural, even noble, for one of society's outcasts to value a "respectable" woman's happiness more than her own. When Dallas momentarily succeeds in persuading Ringo to ride off to his ranch immediately, even though that means sacrificing his wish for vengeance, but then tells him that she will have to meet him later because continuing to cater to Lucy and the baby is something she "has to do," I think of her not as being noble but as chickening out, failing to rise to the occasion, like the aviator André, the "modern hero," in Renoir's *The Rules of the Game*, who tells Christine that he would like to run off with her now, but has to wait until he ties up some loose ends, because there are *rules* about such things.

In any case, to suggest that Dallas thinks of serving Lucy and her baby as her "duty " does not register an even more rankling element of her motivation. As Tag Gallagher notes, in his book on John Ford (a book that, with all its ecentricities, remains the most illuminating critical study of the director's work), it is an element highlighted in Dudley Nichols's script, for example in his description of the moment Dallas presents Lucy's newborn infant to the male passengers.

> The last trace of hardness has vanished from Dallas as she holds the infant in her arms, and there is a glow of wonder in her face. She stands for a moment in the doorway, a smile in her eyes.... Her experience of the last few hours has deeply affected her, taken all the defiance out of her face, and softened it into beauty.[2]

To be sure, Ford's realization of this moment considerably downplays the screenplay's claim that it represents a grand epiphany. As Gallagher observes, "Dallas has all along been eager to be pleasant; she does not abruptly shift attitudes; she is merely relieved momentarily from self-shame, which soon returns."[3] Nonetheless, Nichols's rather nauseating idea that witnessing the miracle of birth transforms hard-edged, defiant Dallas by bringing out in her the softness, the nurturing, maternal quality, that is the true essence – the beauty – of womanhood is so crucial to *Stagecoach*'s screenplay that vestiges of it inevitably remain in the completed film.

It is important to keep in mind, though, that, as Ford films it, there is a profound ambiguity to the moment Gallagher singles out. Smiling as she cradles Lucy's baby in her arms, Dallas happily and proudly presents the infant to the assembled men. But among those men is one who means the world to Dallas. The emotional heart of this passage is the exchange of looks between Ringo and Dallas that Ford registers in a pair of big close-ups.

[2] Quoted in Paul Jensen, "Dudley Nichols," in Richard Corliss, ed., *The Hollywood Screenwriters* (New York: Avon, 1972), p. 118.

[3] Gallagher, p. 150.

Ringo's trace of a smile registers his approval of Dallas. She is his kind of woman. But what kind of woman is she? What does he see in her face at this moment? What do we see? On Dallas's face, as we view it in this extraordinary close-up, there is a "glow of wonder," no doubt. But does this glow reveal the quality Nichols envisioned, the beauty of a woman who knows, and becomingly submits to, her subordinate place? Or is her glowing smile, as she frankly meets Ringo's unwavering gaze, smoldering with desire, like his?

In his useful monograph on *Stagecoach*, Edward Buscombe dwells at some length on the ensuing scene, in which Ringo observes Dallas going outside for some air and follows her. The scene "is no more than a bridge between the previous one, in which the passengers digest the news of the baby's birth, and the following one, in which Ringo will finally declare his feeling for Dallas."[4] In this scene, Buscombe notes, there is a "calm beauty...which is in excess of the demands of the narrative, but not superfluous to our satisfaction as an audience." It is a key to Ford's cinema, Buscombe argues, that every scene, every shot, is, like this one, "more than just functional to the narrative; there is always some added value" – some special beauty or pleasure, whether it results from "a particular felicity of framing, or the subtlety with which the actors are blocked, or an elegant camera movement."[5]

Gallagher makes a similar point when he argues that in *Stagecoach* "interest in the characters stems from their interaction, from subtle details of gesture, intonation, and staging, and from tension between the type and the individual inhabiting it."[6] However, Gallagher's formulation has the advantage over Buscombe's that it recognizes that Ford's cinematic style is not fruitfully thought of as "adding value" to narratives that are in principle separable from that style. Rather, Ford's stylistic choices are internal to his narratives, playing essential roles in making them – and in revealing them to be – the narratives they are. (The problem with Buscombe's formulation, it is worth noting, is one endemic to the field of film studies, which in the 1970s adopted an antinarrative bias it has not yet fully outgrown.)

In the scene in question, for example, the calm beauty of the passage, the satisfying mood created largely through framing and lighting, cannot really be said to be "in excess of the demands of the narrative." The satisfaction the scene provides suggests, rather that its specific mood, its calm beauty, is somehow *demanded* by the film's narrative. Or, at least, that this scene,

[4] Edward Buscombe, *Stagecoach* (London: BFI, 1992), p. 55.

[5] Ibid, p. 56. [6] Gallagher, p. 149.

as Ford presents it, is a satisfying response – perhaps not the only possible one – to the narrative's demands.

As Buscombe describes it, the scene begins with "Ringo, screen left, leaning against the wall, looking down a dark corridor, away from the camera. Dallas comes out of a doorway on the right and, without seeing Ringo, turns and walks off towards the door in long shot. As Ringo moves to follow her; the camera remains still, watching him walk away."[7]

Actually, Dallas is already in the corridor – already being watched by Ringo, in the foreground of the frame, and by us – as she walks away from the camera and toward the door in the background. And what is most visually noteworthy about this deep-focus shot, is not the darkness of the corridor, but the way that darkness emphasizes the luminous doorway, which is doubled by its bright reflection on the ground. The doorway frames Dallas's silhouetted figure – the light coming through the door is what casts her figure in silhouette – even as the doorway's reflection frames her shadow in a perfect frame-within-the-frame.[8]

The doubling of Dallas's image within this frame resonates with the film's repeated assertions that there is a split between her social role, who she is in the eyes of society, and who she is in Ringo's eyes – and ours. Beyond this, the deep-focus cinematography emphasizes both the three dimensionality of this space and the flatness of its projected image, both the reality and the unreality of the world on film. As Dallas walks, her figure diminishes in size, the exaggerated foreshortening creating the impression that when she reaches the end of this tunnel, she will cross the border into another world, the world from which this beautiful light is emanating. The effect is precisely

[7] Buscombe, p. 56.

[8] In *Shadow of a Doubt* (1943), when Uncle Charles, having just learned that the police were off his trail, stops on the stairs and turns to face the camera, Hitchcock cuts to a shot, from Charles's point of view, which I find strikingly reminiscent of this shot from *Stagecoach*. In Hitchcock's shot, young Charlie, centered in an almost symmetrical frame, is beautifully backlit by the doorway that frames her. Her figure is doubled by her shadow, which is perfectly framed by the doorway's reflection on the floor. In *Hitchcock – The Murderous Gaze*, I argue that this shot is an instance of a motif – I call it Hitchcock's "tunnel image" – that recurs in virtually every one of the director's films. See William Rothman, *Hitchcock – The Murderous Gaze* (Cambridge, MA: Harvard University Press, 1982), pp. 224, 236, 290, 361.

opposite to that of the moments, obligatory in a remarriage comedy, when the camera declares the flesh-and-blood identity of the leading actress. The woman who appears in this frame, by contrast, is an apparition – an emanation of that other world to which she finds herself drawn. What makes this passage dreamlike rather than nightmarish is Dallas's serene calmness as she walks toward the light, and the beauty of the light itself, which makes the frame seem to glow from within.

Ford elides Dallas's entrance into this charged space. Then, too, in the previous scene (in which Dallas presents Lucy's baby to the male passengers and secretly exchanges looks with Ringo), Ford downplays Dallas's exit from the room, rendering it almost invisible, and altogether refrains from showing Ringo's exit, which is separate from Dallas's (although presumably cued by it, whether consciously or not). In that scene, the mostly comical exchanges among the other men, which culminate in Doc's relieved "Whew," serve to distract us from attending to Dallas's and Ringo's almost simultaneous exits. This enhances our sense that when we next view Dallas and Ringo, in the corridor, they appear out of nowhere, as if magically transported to another dimension. And the corridor's charged space itself appears as if conjured by magic.

Again, when this shot begins, Dallas is already in the corridor, already walking toward the light at the end of the tunnel. We do not, as Buscombe claims, see Dallas come out of a doorway and, not seeing Ringo, turn and walk toward the door.[9] We have no idea whether she knows he is there, whether she is wordlessly inviting him to follow. Our sense is that she is so absorbed in her private thoughts as to be under a spell. Surely her "private thoughts" are about the baby she helped bring into the world, about the miracle of birth, about her own all-but-abandoned dream of being a mother. Surely, too, she is thinking sweet thoughts about Ringo. Even if she does not know he is there, surely she imagines his presence, wishes for it. And surely Ringo, himself under a spell, senses, or, at least, imagines, this.

Before Ringo performs the fateful gesture of following Dallas down the corridor, he looks back, almost directly at the camera.

[9] Buscombe, p. 56.

This gesture has a realistic motivation – presumably Ringo is checking to make sure that Curly is not watching. It also has an uncanny aspect. It reminds us that the *camera* is watching. *We* are watching. Like us, Ringo is outside the space of the corridor, looking in. When he looks back toward the camera and then follows Dallas into the depths of this space, it is as if, like Buster Keaton in *Sherlock, Jr.* (1924), he is breaching the barrier-that-is-no-real-barrier of the movie screen. It is as if he is entering, awake, the world of his dream.

The passage in question, in any case, is not really a bridge between the scene in which the male passengers digest the fact of the baby's birth and the following conversation in which Ringo finally declares his feelings to Dallas. It is a bridge, specifically, between the smoldering looks that pass between Ringo and Dallas, which are the emotional heart of the preceding scene, as I have said, and the ensuing conversation, which takes place outside when he catches up to her and, separated from her by a wooden fence, at once awakens and breaks her heart by proposing marriage. But to say that the scene is a bridge is not to deny its importance. In a metaphysical mood, *Stagecoach* is reminding us that all film scenes are bridges. The medium of film itself is a bridge (between past and present, between fantasy and reality, between filmmaker and viewer).

The moment Ringo begins following Dallas, Chris, the Mexican innkeeper, emerges from a side door, and Ford cuts, on this action, to a two-shot of Ringo and Chris. It is a beautifully lit shot in which Chris is in profile on the left of the screen, Ringo on the right with his back to the camera and his face, catching the light, half-turned toward Chris.

Within this framing, Chris – heretofore a stereotypical comical Mexican, Ford treats him here, gratifyingly, with respect – informs Ringo that all three Plummers are now in Lordsburg. Ringo then bends down to the lamp to light his cigarette, the smoke shining white as it drifts through the lamplight. He resumes walking down the corridor, watched by Chris and by the calm, steady camera, until he disappears from view through the door.

As is clear from the language of my description, Ford tries to film the exchange between Ringo and Chris, which serves an expository function, in such a way as to sustain the metaphysical mood, the air of unreality, of the previous shot. Ford does not want to break the spell because he wants it to infuse the ensuing conversation between Ringo and Dallas. But Ford, I find, is not entirely successful in this. Inevitably, Chris's intrusion to some degree dissipates the magical mood of the passage as a whole and does so to the detriment of the film. It is one of many points in *Stagecoach* at which Dudley Nichols's screenplay seems to me to be thwarting Ford's deeper instincts as a director. In all honesty, though, I must add that there are also points in the film at which Ford, himself, seems to disappoint me.

Gallagher is right in pointing out how frequent an occurrence it is for a Ford character to intimate a depth beyond what seems his or her familiar type. The "tight juxtaposing of so many archetypes in archetypal adventures" evident in *Stagecoach*, Gallagher writes,

> seems an extreme application of Ford's vignette techniques of characterization (whereby a hypertypical cameo immediately defines a character); yet vignetting is blended with extended character development, and the result becomes a sort of archetypal fireworks show of increasing brilliance, as Ford freely plays each situation to an extreme degree of stylization and composes vignette "magic moments."[10]

Throughout most of the film, for example, Buck mostly acts like a simpleton. But when the stagecoach reaches its destination, he looks Ringo squarely in the eye and says, simply, "Lordsburg." The gravity of his voice and demeanor reveals him to be a man who is capable, despite his apparent oafishness, of recognizing the fatefulness of this moment. Ford gives every character, except for the reprehensible Gatewood, at least one bit of business that reveals the character to have unsuspected depths.

In doing so, we might note, Ford repeatedly uses a motif that amounts to a stylistic signature. Literally dozens of times, Ford incorporates into a

[10] Gallagher, p. 149.

scene – most frequently, he ends the scene with it – a lingering reaction shot, which we might more accurately call a "reactionless shot," in which a character stares, more or less without expression, and more or less in the direction of the camera. For example, shortly after Ringo joins the motley group on their fateful stagecoach ride to Lordsburg, he mentions that his brother was murdered. This revelation is followed by a close-up detailing Dallas's reaction, then by a reaction shot of Peacock and Doc. The sequence concludes with a frontal "reactionless shot" of Ringo.

Such a shot does not specify *what* the character is thinking or feeling. It only asserts that he or she *is* thinking and feeling, that this is a human being who possesses a depth, an inner life, not reducible to the familiar features of a type. However, because *as* individuals the characters in *Stagecoach* remain all but completely undeveloped, I sometimes find myself feeling that Ford is using this device merely for effect, that he is trying to make us to feel for characters that his film has failed to invest with any real depth (whatever "real depth," in a movie character, may actually come to).

Then, too, if Dallas were played not by Claire Trevor but by Marlene Dietrich – Walter Wanger's original choice for the role – or, say, Barbara Stanwyck, or, for that matter, the Maureen O'Hara of Ford's own *How Green Was My Valley*, or if Ford had directed Trevor differently, *Stagecoach* would not give the impression it does that Dallas has so little sense of herself that she feels crushed by an unjust society's judgment upon her. A Dietrich, a Stanwyck, or an O'Hara would never whine with self-pity, as Ford has Trevor do almost every time she opens her mouth. When *Stagecoach* is viewed with the sound muted, Trevor is magnificent – a woman of strength and unfathomable inner resources. But when Ford has her speak the words the screenplay gives her to speak, her voice is almost always pitched at the edge of hysteria, and grates on the ears – at least, my ears – like chalk on a blackboard. Louise Platt, as Lucy, is likewise splendid – except when she speaks. She delivers all her lines, not hysterically, but in an impersonal, uninflected voice that would never pass the lips of a Katharine Hepburn, say [who, in *Mary of Scotland* (1936), successfully imprinted a sense of her strength and intelligence on a Ford film of the period].

In *Stagecoach*, in other words, Ford has both leading women speak their lines in voices terminally lacking in spunk. How striking a contrast is John Wayne's Ringo Kid! Viewers who know Wayne only from his later films might well be surprised by how youthful-looking – and beautiful – he was as a thirty-one-year-old. But his voice already possessed that magic that can turn the most basic of lines ("A man could live there... And a woman"; "I asked you to marry me, didn't I?"; "We ain't never gonna say goodbye"; "I gotta know where you live, don't I?"; "Wait here") into poetry – not the poetry of poetry, but the poetry of film speech, the poetry in the fact that just this human being is speaking just these words in just this way at just this moment.

To specify further both what I find wonderful and what I find disappointing in *Stagecoach* and to pursue further themes that have already made their appearance in the present essay, I conclude by examining in detail three passages that revolve around the relationship, or lack of a relationship, between Dallas and Lucy. The first is the initial encounter – or nonencounter – between the two women, when first Dallas and then Lucy board the stagecoach bound for Lordsburg. The second is the passage in which, as Gallagher puts it, "Dallas the whore [offends] propriety by sitting next to Lucy the lady, who, by the morals of the day, must register shock."[11] This is the sequence from *Stagecoach* that has received by far the most critical attention to date, having been the object of a highly influential analysis by Nick Browne that was, in turn, the object of an almost equally extended critique in Gallagher's book on Ford.[12] The third is the final encounter – or, again, nonencounter – between the two women when they disembark in Lordsburg and go their separate ways.

The Initial Encounter

As Buck calls out the names of the stagecoach's scheduled stops, Lucy, accompanied by two other "respectable" women, is in the middle of the frame walking toward the camera.

[11] Ibid, p. 153.

[12] Nick Browne, "The Spectator-in-the-Text: The Rhetoric of *Stagecoach*," *Film Quarterly*, Winter 1975: 26–38. Gallagher, pp. 153–60. Gilberto Perez, in an incisive footnote, convincingly takes both Browne and Gallagher to task. His analysis of the sequence nicely complements my own. See Gilberto Perez, *The Material Ghost: Films and their Medium* (Baltimore: Johns Hopkins University Press, 1998), pp. 425–6.

There is a cut to Dallas, with her chaperones from the "Law and Order League," also walking toward the camera, but not centered in the frame. Dallas exits the frame, as two men stare after her. Cut to a shot, more or less from their point of view, of Dallas raising her leg so as to board the coach. At the sound of a wolf whistle coming from off-screen, she looks toward the camera, and there is a cut back to the two men, viewed from the same angle, but closer. They wink suggestively. There is a cut back to Dallas, who does a little curtsy in mocking appreciation of their mocking appreciation of her. Then comes a medium shot of Dallas in the coach, framed in profile, breathing deeply, but otherwise showing no reaction. In this shot, the camera angle, hence the screen direction, is strangely reversed.

This is followed by a shot of the stagecoach that returns to the original angle – and frames Dallas through the frame-within-the-frame of the open door, looking almost at the camera – as Doc Boone clambers on board.

Then there is a cut to a shot of one of the "respectable" women, Mrs. Whitney, and Lucy. The fact that Lucy is in the middle of this frame, looking at something off-screen, has the effect of retroactively revealing the preceding shot to be – or turning it into – something like a shot from her point of view.

When a third woman enters the frame, saying "Mrs. Whitney, you're not going to let your friend travel with...," Lucy seems to be looking past this woman to the stagecoach (to Doc? to Dallas?). As the woman says these words, Lucy – only reluctantly taking her eyes off what she is looking at – looks momentarily at Mrs. Whitney, then back, turning the following shot – a reprise of the medium shot of Dallas in profile – into one that, although the angle is reversed, *feels* as if it is from Lucy's point of view. On the hurtful words "...that creature," Dallas turns, looking almost toward the camera, as she endures these hurtful words. Presumably, Dallas is hiding her eyes from the respectable women who so strongly disapprove of her. And yet, as Ford presents this view to us, it *feels* as if Dallas, as she endures Mrs. Whitney's "She's right, Lucy," is *meeting*, not avoiding, Lucy's gaze.

Not as candid about her social prejudices as the other woman, Mrs. Whitney adds, "Besides, you're not well enough to travel." When Lucy replies, in a matter-of-fact tone, "It's only a few hours, Nancy; I'm quite all right," she addresses Nancy's concern for her medical condition (we soon learn that Lucy is pregnant, the "blessed event" expected at any moment). And she avoids addressing the alleged impropriety of traveling in a coach with such a "creature" as Dallas. As Lucy says these words, she looks briefly at her friend, as politeness requires. But it is clear that Lucy only *reluctantly* pulls her eyes away, even for a moment, from the object of her fascination. Even before Lucy finishes speaking her lines, her gaze has already returned to Dallas.

As this description makes clear, what is most surprising – and remarkable – about this passage is its emphatic, repeated intimations that there is a mysterious bond, an unspoken mutual attraction, between Dallas and Lucy.

The Encounter at the Way Station

The second sequence begins approximately a third of the way into the film. The stagecoach has stopped at a way station. Geronimo is reported to be in the vicinity. The passengers are to vote to decide whether to return to Tonto or press on toward Lordsburg. They vote to go on. As the wife of Billy Pickett, the innkeeper, enters with a pot full of food, there is a cut to an "objective" view of the whole room, with Lucy, in the right foreground, sitting at the head of the table, then to a shot more or less from Lucy's point of view, as Dallas passes behind Ringo toward a chair by the wall. As Ringo says, "Sit down here, ma'am," their gazes meet.

In an "objective" shot, Gatewood, Doc, Pickett, Hatfield, and Lucy all turn their eyes to Ringo and Dallas. Then there is a cut to a shot – from Lucy's point of view? – of Ringo helping Dallas with her chair, the camera dollying in as Ringo takes a seat beside her. Dallas's eyes are downcast, averted from the camera (from Lucy?). When finally Dallas looks up, our impression is that she is glancing at someone – Lucy – out of the corner of her eye.

As we hear the offscreen sound of a plate being picked up, presumably by Ringo, there is a cut to an almost frontal medium close-up of Lucy. The fact that as this shot begins she is staring at someone, presumably Dallas, suggests that this shot is from Dallas's point of view. This suggestion is seconded when Lucy's gaze wavers, as if in reaction to Dallas's no longer merely glancing at her but decisively meeting her gaze. Then there is a medium close-up of Dallas, angled obliquely to register Lucy's point of view. At the head of this shot, Dallas is almost fiercely meeting Lucy's gaze. This confirms that the preceding shot of Lucy was, indeed, from Dallas's point of view. Because Dallas is meeting Lucy's gaze by staring at her out of the corner of her eye, of course Ford makes the shot of Lucy almost frontal, whereas he shoots Dallas from an oblique angle.

Within this frame, Dallas looks down, thinks for a moment, then lowers her gaze even more. Lost in thought, she seems on the verge of saying or doing something, or at least formulating some idea or judgment, when there is a cut to the "objective" shot. Gatewood takes a plate of food being passed (by Ringo, offscreen) and holds it out to Lucy. At the head of this shot, Lucy is still looking at Dallas. But then she, too, lowers her gaze, lost in thought.

All the while staring at Lucy, Hatfield takes the plate from Gatewood and holds it out to her, but she makes no move to take it from him. Then Hatfield puts the plate down and directs his gaze at Dallas and Ringo, evidently assuming that it is Dallas's proximity, forced on Lucy by Ringo's improper invitation for her to join him, that is keeping Lucy from eating. There is a cut to Dallas and Ringo, in almost the same framing as earlier, but now from Hatfield's point of view, not Lucy's; then a cut back to the "objective" shot. Hatfield says to Lucy, "May I find you another place, Mrs. Mallory? It's cooler by the window." Finally, Lucy emerges from her absorption with her private thoughts enough to look up, and there is a cut to Dallas (who is still looking down) and Ringo (who is looking at Hatfield and Lucy), then again back to the "objective" shot. Lucy turns her eyes toward Hatfield, then in the general direction of Dallas (but now looking "through," not at, her). As Hatfield pulls out her chair, Lucy says "thank you" in her usual impersonal, uninflected voice, and exits the frame, followed by Hatfield. Gatewood, too, begins to get up, and there is a cut to the establishing shot, from the head of the table, that opened the sequence.

Lucy, Hatfield, and Gatewood take new seats at the other end of the table as Ringo watches and Dallas stares ahead of her. There is a cut to a frontal medium two-shot of Dallas and Ringo. Ringo turns to Dallas, looks down, looks back at the others, and says, to his plate, "Looks like I got the plague, don't it?" Dallas looks briefly at Ringo, then down and away, saying, or whining, as quiet music begins, "No. No, it's not you." "Well, I guess you can't break out of prison and into society on the same morning," Ringo says, and gets up, angrily. She takes his arm to stop him. "Please." She looks into his eyes. "Please," she repeats, this time without a trace of a whine. Then she removes her hand, looks away, and passes him a bowl of chili. She is about to serve him, but, taking the ladle from her, he serves her. Then, as the music continues, there is a cut to a general shot of the whole room – almost a reprise of the shot that opened the entire sequence – as the camera dollies in.

As Nick Browne reads the sequence, we spectators share Lucy's gaze, but not Dallas's.[13] Experiencing the sequence as though it were narrated by Lucy, Browne claims, we find ourselves implicated when Lucy repudiates Dallas. Yet our emotional identification with Dallas is so strong that we are prompted to repudiate Lucy's claim to occupy a position of moral authority. Repudiating Lucy's gaze, we thus repudiate the position we ourselves have occupied. According to Browne, Ford "masks" his activity as narrator becomes "invisible," and uses Lucy as "a visible persona .... to constitute and make legible and continuous the depicted space, by referring shots on the screen alternately to the authority of her eye or the place of her body, [so that] the story seems to tell itself [and seems to deny] the existence of a narrator different from the character."[14]

[13] Browne, pp. 35–7. [14] Ibid.

Gallagher contests Browne's reading by arguing, shrewdly, that it mistakenly approaches Ford as though he were Hitchcock. Hitchcock allows his camera to assume one subjective point of view after another. Ford, however, exacts "empathetic distance," as Gallagher puts it, in every shot. He argues that we experience every Ford shot, even those that are from a character's literal point of view, *as* a Ford shot, an expression of Ford's narrating presence. Thus we are never, as Browne claims, so implicated in Lucy's repudiation of Dallas that we are provoked to repudiate our own position, as well as hers. We see *that* Lucy and the other intolerant characters view Dallas in a way that social custom decrees, a way that is "far less empathetic toward their victims" than is the way of seeing vouchsafed to us by Ford's narration. Ford makes this particularly clear, Gallagher argues, by showing Dallas from Lucy's perspective even before he shows Lucy staring at Dallas from that perspective. Importantly, Gallagher adds, although Ford shows Dallas from Lucy's perspective, he never shows Lucy from Dallas's perspective. If Ford were to show Lucy from Dallas's perspective, "[t]he conflict and the terror such a perspective would convey would detract from the greater, philosophic question." That question is, Gallagher claims, "*How can they act that way?*"[15]

But what way *does* Lucy act? Despite their disagreements, Gallagher is in accord with Browne on the crucial point that Ford does not balance the subjective shots from Lucy with matching subjective shots from Dallas, thereby emphasizing "Dallas's passive victimhood and Lucy's active aggression, and also Dallas's inferior position."[16] As is clear from our close reading of the passage, however, on this crucial point Browne and Gallagher are both in error. Ford *does* show Lucy from Dallas's perspective, just as he shows Dallas from Lucy's perspective.

Browne and Gallagher are likewise both in error when they characterize Dallas as the "passive victim" and Lucy the "active aggressor" in their exchange of glances. Hatfield simply assumes that Lucy disapproves of "impropriety" as strongly as he does, and chivalrously takes it upon himself to rescue her from her proximity to Dallas. Too much the southern gentleman to state his real reason, he invites Lucy to move with him to the far end of the table "where it's cooler." Thoughtful after her unsettling exchange of glances with Dallas, and in any case perplexed that she cannot quite place the familiar-looking southerner who is going out of his way to be so considerate to her, Lucy politely says "thank you," and follows Hatfield's lead. But at no point can Lucy really be said to be "repudiating" Dallas, or, for that matter, to be claiming for herself a position of moral authority.

[15] Gallagher, p. 160. [16] Ibid., pp. 153–4.

As in the first encounter between Dallas and Lucy, Ford's presentation here again intimates that these two women, although they do not know what to make of each other, nonetheless find themselves mysteriously drawn to each other.

The Final Encounter

When we arrive at the final encounter between Dallas and Lucy, we viewers hope – and therefore expect – that there will at last be a clear acknowledgment, each for the other, on the order of Dallas's last conversation with Mr. Peacock, in which he calls her "Miss Dallas" and invites her to visit his family some day.

"Respectable" women from the town – no doubt members of Lordsburg's "Law and Order League" – are welcoming Lucy to Lordsburg. One of these women, perhaps a nurse, says to Lucy, "Where's the baby, dear?" Without saying a word, Lucy looks screen right. There is a cut to Dallas, who is at this moment stepping down from the stagecoach, holding the baby. As Dallas walks toward the women, the camera pans left with her, until she meets up with the nurse (if she is a nurse), who takes the baby away from her and then exits the scene, accompanied by the other "respectable" women, who likewise say nothing to Dallas. As the woman are walking off, we hear Lucy – she is barely visible at the lower left of the frame – say "Dallas ..." There is a cut to a low-angle shot of Dallas, then to a high-angle shot of Lucy. "... If there's ever anything I can do for...."

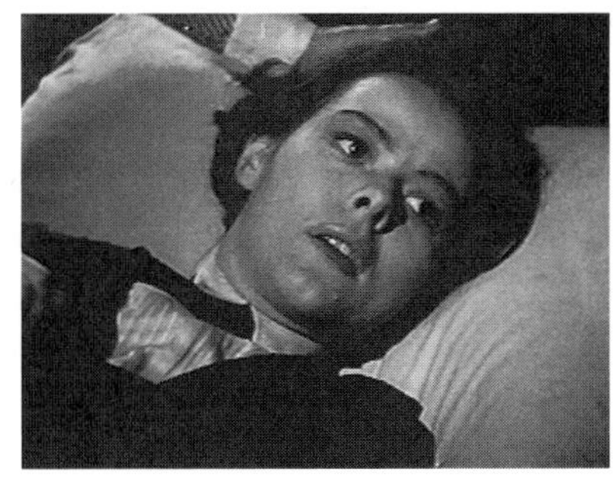

Lucy cuts herself off, stares, then lowers her gaze, swallowing hard. There is a cut back to Dallas, who says, with a rueful smile, "I know," then takes off her coat and hands it to someone out of the frame. There is a cut to a longer shot as Lucy pulls the coat over herself as she's carried away on her stretcher, her gaze locked with Dallas's.

Then Dallas steps back and turns away, the camera reframing with her as she picks up her bags, stares at them, then looks up. From her point of view, we see soldiers arrive.

Dallas has earned Lucy's respect, as well as her gratitude. We know that Lucy knows this. We know that Dallas knows that Lucy knows this. When Dallas steps down from the stagecoach, cradling the baby in her arms, it provides Lucy with a perfect opportunity to say in public what she privately knows to be true. Even when the baby is wordlessly taken away from Dallas, Lucy remains silent. Only when the other women have departed the scene does she speak – and then she finds herself saying something utterly impersonal. But then – this is one of the most mysterious moments of the film – Lucy stops herself. She is suddenly at a loss. Surely at this moment she recognizes – and recognizes that Dallas, too, recognizes – the inadequacy of what she was about to say, of anything she could now say, given her failure, just now, to put in a good word for Dallas when it might have counted for something.

Dallas's "I know" is spoken with no special hostility, but no real warmth, either. We hear in her voice only a trace of her usual self-pitying whine. But it is enough to register not only that Dallas is disappointed with Lucy, but also that Lucy's failure comes as no surprise to her.

Ford refrains from suggesting, in other words, that a redemptive communion takes place between these two women. They are ships that pass in the night. But why? Why cannot Ford bring himself to allow Dallas and Lucy the kind of mutual recognition that, say, Stella and Helen achieve in *Stella Dallas* (1937), when despite the unbridgeable barriers that separate them, they nonetheless share an unspoken understanding? Lucy is condemned to civilization, whereas Dallas is condemned to live outside it, or, as it will turn out, to escape from it. But neither woman embraces nor even accepts her own or the other woman's placement. Why not?

Dallas's whole existence, Gallagher writes in a fine passage,

> is a kind of dream; every moment, not just this one, has its glow or gloom, its warmth or chill; an accepting baby on one hand and a repelling propriety on the other dramatically define the boundaries of Dallas's affective consciousness, and thus exacerbate the vibrant oscillations twixt hope and despair with which Dallas

experiences Ringo's presence.... And it is this melodramatized representation of inner experience that Ford aims for.[17]

The fact that Ford aims for such a "melodramatized" representation of Dallas's – and, for that matter, Lucy's – inner experience means that he envisions them as irreparably split, as incapable of becoming whole. Little wonder that in these women Ford does not find the capacity for change, the hopefulness, the spunk, that enables the Emersonian heroines of remarriage comedies and melodramas of the unknown woman to embrace so wholeheartedly their heroic quest for selfhood.

Movingly, when Ringo learns that Dallas is a prostitute – I like to believe he always knew it – he does not disappoint her, as Lucy did. As they approach the red light district, the mood is dreamlike. Dallas tells Ringo not to follow her any further. But she knows he will. Saying "Wait here," he goes off to kill the Plummers before returning, so he thinks, to bid her *au revoir* until he finishes serving his jail time ("We ain't never gonna say goodbye," he has already promised her). When Curly, the U.S. Marshall, allied with Doc Boone, subverts the rule of Law he is sworn to uphold – why did the Hays Office allow this? – Ringo and Dallas are free to settle down on his ranch in Mexico.

We are enormously gratified when Curly and Doc dispatch Ringo and Dallas to cross the border into freedom. Yet the ending of *Stagecoach* is no more a conventional happy ending than are the endings of Ford's non-Western firms of the period, such as *Young Mr. Lincoln* (1939), *The Grapes of Wrath* (1940), or *How Green Was My Valley* (1941). For all the pleasure it provides us, it is an ending infused with a sense of loss, an ending that forsakes the optimism, the utopianism, of genres like the remarriage comedy and the melodrama of the unknown woman. Those genres judge America as it stands to be wanting, yet affirm the possibility – at least the hope – of transforming America into the kind of community we dream of. Ringo and Dallas escape from an America unworthy of them, an America their escape does nothing to change. The price of this couple's freedom is permanent exile. And their escape holds out no real hope for us. In reality, we cannot get to Ringo's ranch from here. If it is possible for us to cross that border, *Stagecoach* itself – the art of film as John Ford has mastered it – is the only bridge.

[17] Browne, pp. 150–1.

CHAPTER 14

To Have and Have Not Adapted a Film from a Novel

Ernest Hemingway and I were very good friends. ... I said to him, "I can make a picture out of your worst story." He said, "What's my worst story?" I said, "Why, that goddamned piece of junk called *To Have and Have Not* ...."

– Howard Hawks[1]

This chapter describes some of the ways in which Howard Hawks's *To Have and Have Not* (Warner Brothers, 1944) cannot, and some of the ways it can, be regarded as an adaptation of the Hemingway novel. It analyzes some important respects in which the film differs in perspective and position from the novel, indeed constitutes a critique of it. And it concludes with some general observations about Hawks's films.

Robin Wood asserts that Hawks cheated in his demonstration that he could make a film of Hemingway's worst story. "His movie is in no real sense a version of the novel. Only the first ten minutes – the scenes involving Mr. Johnson, the would-be big-game fisherman – have anything much to do with the original."[2] Although this assertion cannot ultimately be accepted, it is important to recognize its plausibility.

For one thing, the Bogart–Bacall romance at the heart of Hawks's *To Have and Have Not* departs drastically from the relationship of Harry Morgan and Marie Browning as Hemingway presents it. Physically, Hemingway's hefty, middle-aged ex-prostitute is poles apart from the young world-traveler Bogart insists on calling "Slim" (as she insists on calling him "Steve," although his name is Harry). In the novel, Harry and Marie are

[1] Howard Hawks (as told to Steven Fuller), "Hemingway, Faulkner, Gable, Duke and I," *Crawdaddy* (date unknown).

[2] Robin Wood, "To Have (Written) and Have Not (Directed)," *Film Comment*, 9(3):35 (May–June 1973).

Reprinted: See "Notes on the Essays."

married and have children, and the protection of their shared home is essential to Harry's motivation throughout. The film's basically lighthearted courtship (which provocatively mirrors the real courtship of Humphrey Bogart and Lauren Bacall, who fell in love during production) is not really taken from the novel at all. Hawks has suggested that the film tells the story of how the novel's Harry and Marie originally met and fell in love, but this seems facetious.[3]

Then, too, as Wood points out, the theme of commitment to antifascism, which the film interweaves intricately with its romance, is no doubt more influenced by the film's Warner Brothers genre predecessor *Casablanca* than by the Hemingway novel. For example, M. and Mme. de Bursac, the French patriots Bogart ferries to Martinique, and the heroic Resistance leader they hope to free from Devil's Island seem primarily derived from *Casablanca*. And nothing in the novel corresponds to Cricket (Hoagy Carmichael), whose role is clearly derivative of *Casablanca's* beloved Sam, although Cricket also has deep Hawksian roots.

Perhaps the most fundamental difference between novel and film, however, is that of emotional intensity and tone. *To Have and Have Not* is, after all, the Hemingway novel that led F. Scott Fitzgerald to invoke Dostoevsky in describing the undeflected intensity of the writing. Hawks's film is anything but tragic. Infused with the purest form of the Bogart–Bacall screen magnetism, it is one of Hawks's most easygoing, pleasurable films, despite its carefully worked-out dramatic structure. There could be no greater emotional contrast than that between Hawks's ending (Bacall's joyous departing hip-wiggle, Walter Brennan's shuffle, and the closing shot of the bopping musicians) and the widowed Marie's chorus of lamentation with which the novel closes.

On the other hand, there *are* many connections between the novel and the film, although some of these links reveal that the two stake out significantly different positions.

Neutral Traces of the Process of Adaptation

A viewer familiar with the novel will discover innumerable details derived by the film from its literary source. In many cases, these details seem to have no particular significance beyond serving as artifacts of the process of adaptation. For example, Harry's boat in novel and film is the *Queen Conch* out of Key West. When de Bursac is wounded in the film, he is shot in the

[3] Wood, op. cit., p. 35.

right arm, just as Harry himself is wounded in the right arm in the book. Lines of dialogue from the novel repeatedly pop up in the course of the film (for example, in the descriptions of Eddie as a "rummy"). M. Rénard, the Gestapo chief (memorably played by Dan Seymour), is once referred to as "Beelips," the name of an important minor character in the novel.

Action Lifted Bodily from Novel to Film

As Robin Wood implies, the whole opening reel of the film – the scenes involving the rich American businessman Mr. Johnson, who pays Bogart to take him out on the *Queen Conch* so that he can live out his fantasy of being a big-game fisherman – is remarkably faithful to the book. Hawks perfectly renders Hemingway's semidocumentary account of the process of deep-sea fishing. The sequence of events and the action correspond almost point-for-point to many whole pages of the novel, and the characterization of the insensitive, mean-spirited, piggish American businessman is retained.

It might be pointed out, however, that, although this whole first reel seems lifted bodily from the novel, the scene invites a level of reading in the film that is closed to the novel, for Hawks himself stood in a relationship to his studio bosses not altogether different from Bogart's relationship to Mr. Johnson, whereas Hemingway was rarely, if ever, dependent on the financial support of Johnson-like figures. I read the film's bitter depiction of Johnson as an expression of Hawks's alienation from the Hollywood in which he worked. (*To Have and Have Not*'s dark companion piece, *The Big Sleep*, is much more systematic in its indictment of Hollywood.)

The Character of Harry Morgan

The Bogart figure and Hemingway's Harry Morgan share an essential characteristic: a potential for shocking violence. The moment when Bogart's pent-up tension is released in the gesture of shooting his gun through his desk drawer, killing one of Rénard's men, is identical in effect with the moment in the novel when Hemingway's Morgan opens fire on the group of revolutionaries he is illegally carrying on board his boat. Bogart's sadistic tactic of alternately pistol-whipping Rénard and his lieutenant until one of them breaks down and assures him safe passage out of Martinique (with relish, Bogart points out that this will mean that one of them will have suffered a beating for nothing) recalls the strong streak of sadism in Hemingway's Harry Morgan that has caused consternation among the critics.

The moment at which Bogart slaps his "rummy" friend Eddie (Walter Brennan) is likewise shocking in its violence. (The novel's Morgan, afraid that he will lose his payday if Eddie talks, seriously contemplates killing his friend.)

To be sure, although the images of violence in novel and film are in a sense almost identical, their meanings are different. Bogart's violence confirms his commitment to love and justice, the commitment he comes to acknowledge in the course of the film. Thus, he unleashes violence on Nazi bullies, or affects violence so as to protect those he loves (he slaps Eddie hard so as to stop him from endangering himself by staying on board during the upcoming mission). But the violence that dominates the novel emotionally is much more problematic, particularly in its bearing on Harry Morgan's character. The critical literature is divided on the implications of Morgan's violence. Carlos Baker, for example, maintaining that Morgan, given his self-reliance, self-command, and self-knowledge, is Hemingway's first true hero, claims that his violent acts are morally justified by his human needs (he needs money to protect his family).[4] Gerry Brenner takes Morgan to be a divided man of real intelligence, a heroic figure tragically flawed by his violent streak.[5] But the prevailing opinion is that most pungently expressed by Edmond Wilson: Morgan is a combination of a wooden-headed Punch and Popeye the Sailor – a buccaneer, a vicious thug, whose terror we may feel, but whom we cannot pity.

The Romance

Although Hawks's suggestion that the Bogart-Bacall romance is simply an earlier stage of the novel's Harry–Marie relationship may be facetious, the two relationships have an affinity as at least limited triumphs of Eros. As Richard Hovey points out, "Marie and Harry are the only couple in all the Hemingway novels who find happiness in a marriage that works."[6] *To Have and Have Not* is Hawks's most joyous representation of an erotic relationship between a man and a woman. And Eros is represented in the novel with a positiveness unique in Hemingway, although even here the author seems to be suggesting that the love of man and woman is not

[4] Carlos Baker, *Hemingway: The Writer as Artist* (Princeton, NJ: Princeton University Press, 1963), pp. 197–222.

[5] Gerry Brenner, "*To Have and Have Not* as Classical Tragedy," in Richard Astro and Jackson Benson, editors, *Hemingway in Our Time* (Corvallis: Oregon State University Press, 1974), pp. 67–87.

[6] Richard Hovey, *Hemingway: The Inward Terrain* (Seattle: University of Washington Press, 1968), p. 139.

enough. (Again, *The Big Sleep* is much darker than Hawks's *To Have and Have Not,* in which no deceitful Eddie Mars has his mark on Bacall.)

Plot Design

As Hemingway was working on *To Have, and Have Not*, civil war broke out in Spain. Hemingway hastily completed the novel by adding to the two Harry Morgan stories he had already published a third, much longer, story that follows Harry's career to its tragic end. This third story incorporates a complex of subplots that, among other things, contrasts the fulfilled erotic relationship of Harry and Marie to the unfulfilled relationships of several other figures, most notably the failed author Richard Gordon and his wife. (This schematic subplot is as much as anything responsible for the low esteem in which the novel is generally held.) Whereas M. and Mme. de Bursac are clearly distinct from Mr. and Mrs. Gordon (and, as was suggested, betray the influence of *Casablanca*), they serve comparably as a contrast with the central couple of Bogart and Bacall by virtue of Madame's lack of perception and tact and Monsieur's ineptness and weakness. However, his weakness is not, like Richard Gordon's, absolute. Thus, he has the power to perceive and articulate a basic truth about Bogart's character: that "betrayal for a price" is not a possibility for him. By announcing this, he plays an important role in the process that brings Bogart to self-awareness, and wins Bogart's respect.

Theme

The rhetorical center of Hemingway's novel is the "message" that Harry Morgan utters as he is dying: A man alone stands no chance in this world. The film, too, can be seen to revolve rhetorically around an idea that could be expressed in similar words. Hawks's *To Have and Have Not* takes the form of what was known by Hollywood pros of his time as a "delayed-conversion story": Bogart comes to realize the need to break the bonds of isolation, and the film ends with a union of three characters ("Steve," "Slim," and Eddie) who acknowledge this principle and commit themselves to each other and to the fight against fascism.

The dying words of Hemingway's Harry Morgan, which sum up the consciousness toward which he was striving his whole life, form a nexus of critical debate. Do they reflect a convincing conversion? If so, what is the precise nature of that conversion? Does this message reflect a new social conscience awakened in Hemingway after years of criticism from the Left? Or does it reflect only a generalized consciousness of the importance of love?

In the film, as already suggested, the value of commitment is very clear and has both a romantic dimension and a political dimension. The idea that a man alone stands no chance is very much the premise of both the film's political plot and its romance. On both levels, the Bogart character, in the course of the film, is called upon to declare his commitment. He is a man who acts as if he were self-sufficient, but who ultimately comes to recognize the "strings" that tie him to a woman, to a man who is also a child, and to a cause. As the film is conceived, the patriots' undertaking of leading Bogart to a recognition and declaration of his commitment to their cause is systematically intertwined with the development of the Bogart–Bacall relationship. Frenchy (Marcel Dalio, beloved from *Grand Illusion* and *The Rules of the Game*), Bogart's closest friend in the Resistance, and Cricket – neither of whom derives from the novel – play complementary roles in this double process. Frenchy continually interrupts Bogart and Bacall to remind them of the urgent political situation. Cricket continually directs them toward their erotic union as he works on the song he is composing for Bacall to sing to Bogart, which he will call "How Little We Know." The union of Bogart and Bacall takes place only when it can be blessed by both Frenchy and Cricket: Music and the spirit of liberty, in secret alliance, conspire to teach Bogart a double lesson about himself.

In the novel, Harry Morgan's conversion comes too late. He has no chance to channel his hard-won understanding into meaningful action nor to communicate that understanding to his wife, who is left utterly bereft by his death. Indeed, his understanding comes to him in complete isolation, and he dies without communicating it to anyone; his dying words are mistaken for delirious ravings. Family or no family, Harry is a man alone, and his death confirms that, in truth, he had no chance at all in Hemingway's world. In the film, however, Bogart is not – no one really is – alone. His self-sufficient act is precisely an act, and he does not come to drop this act on his own, but is led to do so by the concerted efforts of a community within the society at large, friends who teach him who he really is.

Narrative Technique

To Have and Have Not is, perhaps more than any other Hemingway novel, an experiment in narrative voice. Part 1 is narrated by Harry Morgan. Part 2 is in the third person. In the long Part 3, the narrative point of view undergoes several shifts: first-person narration by a minor character; first-person narration by Harry; third person; third person mixed with Harry's stream of consciousness; narration by Richard Gordon's wife; third person; Marie Morgan's stream of consciousness.

If we keep in mind the foregoing discussion, we can appreciate that Hawks's film is in its own way as experimental in narrative technique as the novel. Hemingway's experiments derive primarily from a desire to give palpable substance to Morgan's stultifying aloneness. The film's experiments primarily derive from Hawks's endeavor of articulating the process by which Bogart's self-sufficient act is exposed and broken down.

One specific strategy Hawks employs to this end is his repeated gesture of concluding sequence after sequence with a reaction shot, in the course of which Bogart, unobserved by anyone within the world of film, reflects on the scene he has just witnessed, then breaks into a laugh or at least a smile, as if in self-satisfaction at his superior detachment from the world. For example, when Bacall leaves Bogart, promising to see him later at the hotel, and sidles over to a sailor, intending to fleece him for her evening's work, the sequence ends with such a shot of Bogart, momentarily reflecting on this scene, and finally laughing to himself at the fade-out; the next sequence ends with another such shot, within which Bogart reflects on the implication of Bacall's provocative line. "You know how to whistle, don't you, Steve? You just put your lips together and . . . blow." Even the moment at which Bogart violently slaps Eddie occurs within a sequence that ends with an image of the solitary Bogart laughing.

This strategy constitutes a real break with the Hollywood convention that accords to the "reaction shot" privileged access to a character's innermost subjectivity. The conventional reaction shot extracts the character from the social space within which he can be observed by others in the world of the film. Thus isolated, the character exposes his innermost thoughts and feelings, transparently and expressively, to the camera. But Hawks's implication throughout *To Have and Have Not* is that even when Bogart is placed within the sanctuary of the private space of a reaction shot, he continues to act, marshaling his theatricality in an attempt to deceive himself about his own nature.

Bogart's displays of bemused detachment when he is alone complement his visible impulse to act in the presence of others in a way calculated to make them "sore." In *The Big Sleep*, Bogart adopts provocative tacks in his dealings with others, but is motivated in doing so in part by professional considerations: The reactions he provokes contain revelations that he finds helpful to his detective work.

But what leads him to act this way with "Slim" in *To Have and Have Not?*

When Bacall tells Bogart the story of her life, Bogart ends by assuring her that she will have no trouble in getting the money to find her way home. In context, this remark implies that Bogart finds her to be acting at this moment; it is as an actress, a deceiver, that she is "good, really good" – she is "that kind of woman." But after she leaves his room, she figures out in private that this was not what he really meant at all: He meant that he was going to take the dangerous job so that he could give her the money to return home. She figures out, that is, that Bogart had revealed his feelings indirectly. She has come to understand a principle of Bogart's language that he himself does not yet consciously grasp. Her reading of him is confirmed at the crucial moment in the film when she sees the anguish on his face when he hears that the Gestapo is torturing Eddie.

Bacall's perception of Bogart – which complements the one M. de Bursac finally puts into words – takes precedence over Bogart's own view of himself. It accounts for Bogart's private laughter, which it interprets as theatrical. Again, it is Bogart *acting for himself* that the camera discloses in these recurring reaction shots.

By such strategies, Hawks presents Bogart as a figure who is led to acknowledge the inadequacy of his own conception of himself – this despite the fact that *To Have and Have Not* also breaks with Hollywood convention by the degree to which one figure (Bogart) dominates the shot-by-shot construction (Bogart is on screen in nearly every shot, and in most of the others his point of view is projected).

The terms in which Hawks's work is usually discussed relate directly to terms often invoked in describing Hemingway's writing. They are said to share a concern for "men without women" in life-and-death situations, facing death in conformity to a "code." The celebrated directness of Hemingway's prose seems analogous to the stripped-down "functional" camera style of Hawks, with its eschewal of fancy cutting and elaborate camera movements.

Comparison can seem strained, however, when one takes into account Hemingway's reputation as a major author and his manifest ambition. In Hemingway's writing, we see Hemingway himself, convinced of his own place near the center of modern man's aspirations. Hawks, by contrast, describes himself in interviews as an unpretentious story-teller and entertainer. Yet it would be a serious mistake to take this avowal, or disavowal, at face value. Surely part of the motivation of Hawks's film is to put Hemingway in his place.

At the risk of oversimplifying, we may generalize some of the foregoing conclusions by saying that, for Hemingway, man is ultimately alone – tragically and nobly alone. For Hawks, man is by nature social, and human society has erotic and political dimensions, intimately linked, although human society can all too readily be poisoned by those (fascists, for example) who are ultimately unwilling or unable to acknowledge their humanity. Hawks, unlike Hemingway, continually celebrates the positive value of human social relations. Hawks celebrates, specifically, music making, wit, sex, and making films that both celebrate and manifest such positivities. Hemingway believes in bull-fights, and his literary oeuvre embodies and champions a stoical individualism.

Hemingway accepts the ideal of the macho hero, and indeed all too clearly – and pathetically – modeled his own public (and, increasingly, his literary) persona on that role. If Hemingway in this persona were a character in a Hawks film, Hawks would treat him ironically, implicitly criticizing him, perhaps placing him within a community that cares enough about him to force him to drop his self-sufficient act and rediscover his capacity for spontaneity and commitment. After all, it is by similar treatment of Hemingway's hero, Harry Morgan, that Hawks made a film we can believe in out of a "goddamned piece of junk."

CHAPTER 15
Hollywood and the Rise of Suburbia

In "Hollywood Reconsidered," I pinpointed the late forties and early fifties as a decisive turning point in the history of American film:

> Hollywood's audience was fragmenting. The older generation, once the audience for classical Hollywood films, stayed home and watched television. Why the men and women of this generation abandoned movies, or were abandoned by movies, is no less a mystery than why they once demanded movies that spoke to them with the greatest seriousness. Surely, they could not have really believed that America in the fifties *fulfilled* the transcendental aspirations expressed by the movies they had taken to heart. Yet they opted for television's reassurance that what was happening *now* was not really passing them by, that they were plugged into a human community after all. At the same time, rock 'n' roll (with its seductive promise of breaking down barriers *now*), not film (in which a screen separates the audience from the world of its dreams), fired the imagination of the young. The fate of film in America, and the longing to become more fully human that it expressed, hung – and still hangs – in the balance.[1]

In the present essay, I wish to return – with a bit more sympathy – to this mysterious moment at which the generation that was Hollywood's American audience in the thirties bought into suburbia in the forties and opted to stay home and watch television.

The rise of suburbia in the period following the Second World War, and with this the transformation of the American metropolis into a ring of suburbs surrounding a decaying "inner city" with pockets of gentrification (that is, pockets of suburbia within the city), together with the simultaneous ascendancy of television and consumerism, is the central development in American society in the second half of the twentieth century. It is not difficult to understand how this development changed the patterns of American

[1] William Rothman, "Hollywood Reconsidered," *East–West Film Journal*, 1(1):40 (December 1986).

moviegoing, leading to the present situation in which the primary audience for films in America is under the age of twenty-five years and suburban, at least in outlook. What remains mysterious is why the generation that was Hollywood's American audience in the thirties bought into suburbia and its attendant consumerism, how it reconciled this with the utopian dreams of the films it had taken to heart. Surely part of the explanation is that suburbia was aggressively *sold*, that Americans were manipulated and exploited by forces (the automobile lobby, for example) that stood to profit – and are still profiting – from this wholesale transformation of the American landscape and social fabric. But to say that Americans were sold a bill of goods does not explain why they bought it.

One possible explanation is that Americans changed their minds, converted, gave up an old dream in favor of a new one – or in favor of no dream at all. I recognize the truth in this view but also the truth in the opposing explanation that Americans saw their investment in suburbia as not only consistent with the old dream but compelled by it, as if at the end of World War II America was seizing a world historical moment to undertake the heroic enterprise of making *real* the collective dream of its movies.

When film was first displayed in Paris and New York on the eve of the twentieth century, it was the latest technological marvel; that is, film was originally a creature of the city. In France, "the city" means Paris; in England, London; in Mexico, Mexico City; in Japan, Tokyo. What is "the city" to the United States? In our time, New York City has been and is a major world capital and a center of American cultural and intellectual life. It is not a question of whether Paris is un-French, London un-English, Tokyo un-Japanese, or Mexico City un-Mexican. Yet it is a question of whether New York City, to America, is American (as opposed, say, to un-American). Sophisticated Paris defines France, but sophisticated New York City does not define America. Indeed, what makes the American-ness of New York a question is precisely the fact that it is sophisticated, is a cosmopolitan center of culture and intellect or at least fashion, is perhaps less than fully committed to the break with Europe and its culture of sophistication that serious American thinkers have taken to be a condition of a specifically American society. For what is America if Americans rank Americans by their degree of cultivation?

As narrative became the dominant mode of film production in the first decade of the twentieth century, the new medium hooked up with the chains of vaudeville theaters that already blanketed the nation. By the time of the country's entrance into the First World War, the audience for film in America encompassed small town, medium-sized city, large city, and metropolis. In this period, it was D. W. Griffith whose ideas and attitudes were most in tune with this audience. And his ideas and attitudes about the city were, I believe, deep sources of his hold, and film's, on the American imagination.

Griffith grew up in Kentucky but dreamed of making his mark as author of the Great American Play. That means he dreamed of conquering the New York theater world. Yet he failed to receive New York's recognition as a major playwright, barely scraping by as an actor before he sank so low as to accept a job – under an assumed name – as an actor, then as a director, for the new medium of film. Through film, Griffith was destined to conquer New York after all. But the failure of the New York theater world to recognize him, combined with his self-reliance in refusing to lose faith in himself despite the pain of that rejection, taught Griffith to think of film as at war with "legitimate" theater and with New York's valuation of sophistication over native genius.

A crucial event in the history of American film was the shift of production in the mid-teens from New York to California, a development that coincided with the birth of film as a modern industry. Los Angeles was hardly a city at that time and to all intents and purposes, Hollywood did not even exist: The American film industry and Hollywood were each other's creations. As Hollywood became the center of film consciousness, Griffith's experience of the real city of New York lost its apparent relevance and authority. Such men as Cecil B. DeMille gained in prominence as Griffith's prestige and power receded. Yet despite its growing fascination with urbane "Jazz Age" values, the American silent cinema never unambiguously broke with Griffith's vision. The silent films Ernst Lubitsch directed in America are exceptions to this, but in their celebration of sophistication they remained expressions of a European, not an American, sensibility. Countering Lubitsch's European outlook was that of F. W. Murnau, another European whom Hollywood imported at the close of the silent era. *Sunrise*, Murnau's first film in America, made an enormous impression on Hollywood. *Sunrise* took a Griffith-like stand against the corrupting influence of city sophistication, although its cachet in Hollywood was inseparable from Murnau's reputation as an artist in the vanguard of sophisticated European ideas about the cinema. It was not until the simultaneous occurrence of the talkies and the Great Depression, I take it, that Hollywood formulated new ideas about the city, ideas that were specifically American, ideas that reconciled the opposition between Griffith and DeMille, between Murnau and Lubitsch.

Films like *Mr. Deeds Goes to Town* and *Mr. Smith Goes to Washington* may lead us to think that American films of the thirties were opposed to the city or at least suspicious of it. Yet it is important to keep in mind that for Capra the city, by virtue of its energy and the diversity of its people, also *represents* America, an America in crisis. After all, Mr. Deeds's ideas turn out not to be alien to the city, as they win over the judge and the cityfolk on the jury. The city as such is not un-American, in Capra's understanding; America's cities need spiritual renewal, to be sure, but so does all of America.

Many American films of the thirties seem to tip the balance toward the city, toward the judgment that city sophistication is superior, not inferior, to a small-town or rural outlook. Musicals of both the Busby Berkeley and the Astaire–Rogers persuasions celebrated the American city – they were America's version of Europe's "city symphonies." Fast-talking comedies like *The Awful Truth* and *His Girl Friday* took undisguised pleasure in sophisticated wit that often manifested itself in wisecracks – Ralph Bellamy always seemed to be their butt – that hilariously poked fun at such "square" places as Oklahoma City or Albany. The brilliance of Hollywood's wit resulted directly from a new infusion of New Yorkers, or at least Broadway theater people, into the film industry, and perhaps indirectly to the studios' going into receivership with Wall Street. Broadway and Wall Street, of course, are as mythical as Hollywood and not simply identifiable with the "real" New York. Yet there was a genuine cross-fertilization of New York and Hollywood sensibilities in the early years of talkies. In part from this cross-fertilization emerged a constellation of new movie genres and – unpredictably – an era of astonishing popularity and creative achievement.

The consciousness that emerged in the 1930s Hollywood was not Griffith's but it also was not DeMille's. Neither was it Murnau's or Lubitsch's (although Murnau had an enduring influence on young Hollywood directors such as Hawks, von Sternberg, Capra, and Ford, and Lubitsch, as director but even more as Paramount production chief, played a major role in the period immediately preceding 1934, the year *It Happened One Night* swept the Academy Awards and inaugurated a new era). The consciousness of post-1934 Hollywood was American, not European; and it was new, although recognizably an inheritor of an old tradition, the tradition of the American transcendentalism of Emerson and Thoreau. It is not an urban consciousness, but it is not opposed to urbanity either.

Just as Hollywood films of the thirties constitute a stage in the development of the consciousness of women, as Stanley Cavell argues in *Pursuits of Happiness*, a stage at which what is at issue is mutual acknowledgment of equality between men and women,[2] it also constitutes a stage in the development of the consciousness of the American city. This stage likewise can be characterized as a demand for mutual acknowledgment, for equality of consciousness, in this case between urban America and the America of small town and country. Hollywood films of the thirties are saying that America

[2] Stanley Cavell, *Pursuits of Happiness* (Cambridge, MA: Harvard University Press, 1981).

can fulfill the utopian social aspirations of its founders only if it overcomes the failures of communication between the city and the rest of America – not by denying their differences but by attaining a new perspective that acknowledges the equal claims of both sensibilities.

Cavell's book focuses specifically on what he calls the "Hollywood comedy of remarriage": By this he means such films as *It Happened One Night, The Awful Truth, Bringing Up Baby, His Girl Friday, The Philadelphia Story, The Lady Eve*, and *Adam's Rib*. As exemplified by this genre, Hollywood films of the thirties attempted to formulate the conditions of a radically new kind of marriage between a man and a woman, a marriage that acknowledges their equality without denying their difference. As envisioned by these films, such a marriage also "marries" the realities of the day and the dreams of the night; the realms of public and private; and the worlds of city and small town or country. This last point is registered in the films' insistence that, for the man and the woman to resolve the conflicts in their relationship, they must at a certain moment find themselves in a location conducive to the attainment of the new perspective. Shakespearean criticism calls such a place the "Green World," and it is typically located, like Thoreau's Walden, just outside a major city. As Cavell points out, Hollywood films usually call this place "Connecticut."

When America emerged from the Great Depression and the Second World War and undertook to create suburbia, it aspired to make this Hollywood dream real by making it possible for all Americans – not really for all Americans, but we will come back to this point – to own a house in the real Connecticut or its equivalent. This appears to interpret "Connecticut" as a real, not a mythical, place; to interpret America's lack of perspective, its need for revewal, as a material, not a spiritual, condition. Or was the post-World War II aspiration the transcendental one of *creating* the spiritual out of the material, *transforming* the real Connecticut into the mythical Connecticut, *making* the dream real?

The creation of suburbia heralds the ascendancy of consumerism in America, the ascendancy of materialism over transcendentalism, but it also expresses America's continuing wish for a spiritual renewal. In this sense it sustains the utopianism of Hollywood films of the thirties. Indeed, it precisely articulates an intuition crucial to these films, the intuition that happiness is not to be sought in some vague future, some "other" realm in which we might live "happily ever after," but is to be achieved in our lives here and now by our living every day and night in a festive spirit, a spirit of adventure. And suburbia goes the remarriage comedy one better. Even in *The Awful Truth*, after all, the thirties comedy that most emphatically insists that spiritual renewal calls for a transformed perspective on the everyday, Cary

Grant and Irene Dunne make the move only once to the film's equilvalent of Connecticut. If "Connecticut" means the perspective that discovers happiness in the everyday, how much truer to the spirit of thirties Hollywood to buy a house in the real Connecticut, like Cary Grant in *Mr. Blandings Builds His Dream House* (1948), and make the commute every day! That would be to participate in the creation of a new American form of life in which renewal was itself an everyday occurrence.

In pondering these matters, I think of *It's a Wonderful Life*, surely a profound expression of America's mood immediately after World War II. I am struck especially by the Jimmy Stewart character's devastating depression as he finds his dream of seeing the world, his dream of adventure, continually deferred. And by his rage and despair – to the point of madness and suicide – when he realizes that he is fated never to leave his home town of Bedford Falls, that he is condemned to a life divided between domesticity and work. Stewart's particular dream was not to live in a great city, exactly, but his dream could easily have taken the form of finding adventure in New York. When Stewart dies and is reborn into humanity like the heroine of a remarriage comedy, he comes to understand what his wife, played by Donna Reed, had always known: that his dream of adventure had come true without his ever realizing it.

When Stewart awakens to the fact that his everyday life was all the adventure of his dreams, a powerful resistance an American man might feel to settling in a suburb is overcome. (Moving to a suburb would have been less frightening to Stewart than staying in a town like Bedford Falls, because in a suburb a man is within commuting distance of the city, from which only half his life need be divorced.) After his conversion, the renewed Stewart rededicates his life to his Savings and Loan, to helping the town's "little people" buy their own little houses with yards, their own stake in suburbia. The film's most prophetic image – to me perhaps its most horrifying one – is the glimpse it offers of the new suburb with its with neat little streets of identical matchbox houses, a veritable miniature Levittown.

It's a Wonderful Life prophesies the creation of suburbia and envisions it as a utopian undertaking, the real fulfillment of Stewart's and America's romantic dream. Yet for the Stewart character himself, the man who dreams the Emersonian dream at the heart of Hollywood films of the thirties, choosing to live in Bedford Falls – and hardly in a matchbox – is the outcome of a terrible spiritual struggle. What is devastatingly honest in the film is its deep acknowledgment that, for the generation that was Hollywood's audience in the thirties – at least for the men of that generation – settling in suburbia felt like the loss of a dream, a trade-in of freedom and adventure for an unsatisfying life divided between career and family. What is devastatingly dishonest is the film's claim that Mr. Potter, the archetypal American capitalist, stands to lose rather than profit from the creation of suburbia; its assurance – or is this ironic? – that, if one is worthy enough, a "guardian angel" will see to it that one's dream will come true in the end, that one will pass safely through one's dark night of the soul and gain all that one risked – and more; its insistence that "little people," unlike Stewart, have everything to gain and nothing to lose by moving into matchboxes; and its portrayal of the Donna Reed character, a woman who never doubts for a moment that marrying the right man, being mother to his children, and raising them in the right house, will make her happy.

This unequal division between man and woman is not at all what the remarriage comedies had in mind, as we can be see by contrasting *It's a Wonderful Life* with a film contemporaneous to it, *Adam's Rib*, the latest of the definitive remarriage comedies and a film starkly isolated within late forties Hollywood production. In *Adam's Rib*, Katharine Hepburn and Spencer Tracy are both successful lawyers, and the film endorses the woman's demand that their equality be acknowledged privately, within the intimacy of their marriage, and also publicly, by society at large. In its depiction of Donna Reed as happy without such acknowledgment, *It's a Wonderful Life* betrays the spirit of Hollywood films of the thirties. On the other hand, Stewart's desperate wish to reconcile dream and reality, romance and everyday life, and the film's conviction that one never wins one's dream without taking the risk of losing it, remain faithful to that spirit. (The situation is complicated by the fact that Donna Reed's role in *It's a Wonderful Life* is like the man's role in remarriage comedy, whereas Stewart assumes the woman's role, a role that also puts him in the company of the heroines of melodramas like *Stella Dallas* and *Now, Voyager*, as Cavell has observed.[3] In *It's a Wonderful Life*, the woman knows and pursues her desire from the outset, while it is the man who is in desperate search of his identity, who is blessed with a Shakespearean father, who nonetheless suffers and has to die and be reborn before he can realize his dream.)

In any case, *It's a Wonderful Life* is saying to its audience that we have to risk change, America has to risk it, if Hollywood's dream of the thirties is not to be forsaken; and beyond this, that we must change *now* or our American dream, our dream of America, will be forever lost. *It's a Wonderful Life* entertains a vision of the death of the dream of thirties Hollywood only to proclaim – however problematically – the dream's rebirth. At precisely the same moment in the history of American film, however, film noir was

[3] Stanley Cavell, "What Becomes of Things on Film," *Themes Out of School* (San Francisco: North Point Press, 1984), p. 180.

claiming to unmask that dream and embracing its destruction. In a film noir like *The Postman Aways Rings Twice, Scarlet Street*, or *The Lady from Shanghai*, a man possessed by a romantic dream, the dream of Hollywood films of the thirties, undergoes disillusionment. He comes to recognize that his dream was an illusion, that he has been the victim of this dream and the cynical, greedy men and evil women who exploit it. If he is lucky, he lives to tell the tale and goes on to marry a nice girl and live a safe, normal life – ideally in Connecticut – stripped of illusions. In film noir's nightmare revision, suburbia is not the fulfillment of the Hollywood dream of the thirties. It is what is left standing of America after the destruction of that dream, a destruction the film welcomes.

What is striking is that both film noir, which deconstructs the thirties Hollywood dream, and *It's a Wonderful Life*, which reaffirms it, point their audience in the same direction: toward suburbia. On this point, there is a consensus. (At this moment Hollywood also all but stopped making "women's films," a genre that might have found it more difficult to endorse this consensus.) A subtler point is that both an unreconstructed utopian like the Jimmy Stewart character and the disillusioned protagonist of film noir share a characteristic prophetic of the fate of Hollywood's American audience of the thirties: Both men can readily be imagined as regular moviegoers before their metamorphosis, but after it, Hollywood movies – perhaps movies themselves – would seem no longer to have anything to offer them. On this point too, there is a consensus, which provokes me to observe that the concept of "consensus" is as useful in thinking about this period in American film as it is in thinking about this period in American politics. The late forties and early fifties constitute a period of transition in which consensus gains ascendancy over conversation in American culture. Consensus is both a condition and an effect, for example, of television's supplanting of film as the dominant American medium. *It's a Wonderful Life* gives way to the "Donna Reed Show," and the glorious conversation of thirties Hollywood film finally falls silent; or rather, it is reduced to "talk."

The reality of suburbia has proved to be a cunning instrument, not for marrying urban and small town or rural America, day and night, men and women, as Hollywood films of the thirties envisioned, but for dividing them. Rather than joining men and women in marriages that acknowledge their equality, suburbia locks women into the domestic realm while it accords men – but not women – a public identity. And the aspiration of Hollywood films of the thirties of envisioning a radically new kind of marriage, a marriage that would be of value in itself, decisively gives way in the fifties to the more traditional imperative of raising children in the "proper" environment, as if bringing up babies could be the only valid purpose of a marriage. Suburbia protects children from living in the city without depriving them of the city's "advantages," that is, its culture. In other words, suburbia also divorces culture from the domestic realm, as though civilization within a marriage, or within a family, could be taken for granted. In all these ways, and more, the reality of suburbia stands in opposition to the Hollywood dream of the thirties, which it precisely denies, that is, represses.

This repression of the Hollywood dream of the thirties is again both a condition and an effect of the triumph of consumerism. Consumerism was postwar America's solution, along with the Cold War, to the threat of sliding back into economic depression. However, in the thirties, consumerism was already the dark side of Hollywood's utopianism: American capitalism had begun to market products by exploiting the glamour of movie stars. By the forties, the American film industry was acutely conscious of the benefits of promoting films, especially "women's films," by linking them with product tie-ins. Manifestly, however, the primary product of Hollywood remained movies. What Hollywood sold was theater admissions, not consumer goods. The age of consumerism called for television, called for the repression of film. Specifically, it called for the repression of what I have been calling the dream of Hollywood films of the thirties, America's dream of fulfilling its utopian aspirations by attaining a new perspective that would allow Americans to acknowledge their equality without denying their differences, like the woman and the man in a remarriage comedy. In the fifties, Hollywood's once-profound conversations about marriage all too often degenerated into the belief that when one meets and marries Mr. or Ms. Right happiness will automatically follow; and the cognate belief that appearances count for everything (after all, if love is at first sight, one had better keep one's hair in fighting trim, one had better dress properly and have the correct things to say, to ensure that one makes the right impression). This pernicious ideology left the children of Hollywood's aging thirties audience bewitched, bothered, and bewildered, and with deep emotional scars. Then why were their parents unable or unwilling to protect them from stepping into this ideological trap?

Part of the explanation must be the sheer power of television at the service of forces that aggressively used the new technology to sell consumerism by exploiting the utopian dreams of Americans, as well as their narcissism and greed. But another part of the explanation must be internal to the Hollywood films of the thirties themselves, to the dream that underwrote their bond with their audience. The reality of suburbia failed to realize that dream, but the dream failed, too – it failed to acknowledge the new suburban reality.

Cavell puts his finger on one source of this failure, I believe, when he points out that the Hollywood remarriage comedies, when they envision marriages that are of value in themselves, always represent such marriages as being without children, and when he observes that fathers but not mothers play major roles in these comedies. Remarriage comedies avoid addressing motherhood, and in the "women's films" of the thirties and forties that do center on motherhood, a woman's fulfillment in marriage and her fulfillment in motherhood never turn out to be compatible. The creation of suburbia coincides, of course, with the celebrated "baby boom," that is, the moment at which the generation that was Hollywood's American audience in the thirties stopped putting off having children. A house in Connecticut is one thing for two professionals with no children like Spencer Tracy and Katharine Hepburn in *Adam's Rib*; it is another thing when the wife has no career and is stuck in the suburbs with the kids. Hollywood films of the thirties never envisioned combining children with a happy marriage. Hence the conversation of these films provided no inspiration or instruction for coping with the stultifying new situation in which their audience, and especially their audience of women, now found themselves.

So it was up to their children, with no help from conversation with their parents and no help from Hollywood movies (or from television, but that is another story) to create the next stage of feminism. In this stage, career and motherhood, not marriage, became the central issues for women. And it will be up to that new generation's children, the children of the children of Hollywood's American audience in the thirties, to achieve the next stage in the development of the American city. Their unenviable task will be to resolve the conflict between the suburbs and the "inner city," to attain a new perspective that will enable that conflict to be resolved. This would be to achieve a happy marriage of suburbia and the "other" America whose dispossession is the other face of suburbia's creation. This is an aspiration worthy of a renewal of American film, a renewal of the utopian spirit of Hollywood films of the thirties.

CHAPTER 16

Nobody's Perfect

Billy Wilder and the Postwar American Cinema

Film scholars often attribute differences between pre–World War I and post–World War II Hollywood films to the influx of exiles from strife-torn Europe. Film noir, in particular, is said to reflect themes, character types (the "*femme fatale*"), and stylistic devices (oppressive shadows) associated with the "expressionist" cinema of Weimar Germany. Billy Wilder, an East European Jew who came to America in the early 1930s and whose first noteworthy directorial effort was *Double Indemnity*, a prototypical film noir, is a critical case in assessing the European influence on post–WWII Hollywood.

The matter is complicated, however, for at least three reasons. First, because "expressionist" German silent cinema had already had a profound impact on Hollywood movies of the 1930s, above all in the impact of F. W. Murnau's *Sunrise* (1927) on directors like Capra, Hawks, von Sternberg, Cukor, and Ford. *Sunrise* was the ultimate achievement of the German silent cinema. It was also an *American* film, however. Made in America for the Fox studio, *Sunrise* uncannily anticipated the contours of the genres that were soon to crystallize in Hollywood – in particular, the genre Stanley Cavell calls the comedy of remarriage [*It Happened One Night* (1934), *The Philadelphia Story* (1941), *et al.*] and, a few years later, film noir. Second, because "expressionism" is at most a superficial feature of Wilder's films, which align themselves primarily with the comedies of Ernst Lubitsch, whose American films reflect a very different aspect of German silent cinema. There is a third reason as well. In the first edition of *The "I" of the Camera*, I sketched a view of the history of American film that envisions the shift from pre–WWII to post–WWII Hollywood movies less as a liberation from constricting generic formulas than as a failure to sustain the Emersonian philosophical perspective that, as Cavell has argued, allowed American movies of the 1930s their combination of extreme popularity and extreme seriousness. Because American transcendentalism was America's inheritance – and revision – of German idealism, it is no simple matter to separate what is European from what is American in post–WWII – or, for that matter, pre–WWII – American movies. Film noir, like *Citizen Kane*, is as American as apple strudel. Although within the 1930s American cinema the Lubitsch comedy represents an alternative to the remarriage genre, the close affinity between the two is fully manifest in Lubitsch's great *Shop Around the Corner* (1940) (scripted by Samson Raphaelson, the New York-born Jew who also wrote *The Jazz Singer*) and his almost-as-great *Ninotchka* (1939), whose screenplay Wilder coauthored.

Perceptively pinpointing some of Wilder's limitations as a director, Andrew Sarris relegated Wilder to his "Less than Meets the Eye" category in *The American Cinema* (a negative judgment Sarris, perhaps not so perceptively, has since amended). It is not quite accurate to charge, as Sarris did, that "visual and structural deficiencies" diminish all Wilder's films. The best of them, such as *Double Indemnity* and *The Apartment*, are brilliantly structured and not at all deficient visually. Cinematography and art direction combine to create worlds with distinctive and thematically and dramatically appropriate "looks." (Just think of our first views of the insurance company offices in *Double Indemnity* and *The Apartment*. The company office in *Double Indemnity* already sports rows of interchangeable desks, visually auguring the threat of conformism that was to become such a prominent theme for Wilder and others in post–WWII Hollywood movies, reaching a culmination in *The Apartment*'s baroque version of the company office.)

Yet Sarris has a point. Lubitsch, like Hitchcock, was famous for his "touch." Viewing a Lubitsch comedy, we are mindful of the role of the film's author – aware that the camera is the author's instrument. There is no "Wilder touch" the way there is a "Lubitsch touch." Reading Wilder's screenplays, I am struck by the fact that they indicate few, if any, framings or camera movements. Wilder liked to say that he used the camera only to tell stories, not to call attention to itself. But *what* stories can films tell when the camera's role is thus limited? Not the story of Hitchcock's

Vertigo, for example – or Lubitsch's *Trouble in Paradise*, for that matter. Lubitsch loved to use the camera to comment wittily on the action, elegantly highlight the humor, or even to make gags (à la Buster Keaton). Wilder's script for *Ninotchka* provides Lubitsch few opportunities to use the camera to express itself in the ways he usually favored. Nonetheless, Lubitsch's "touch" is evident in this film, even though it is limited to using the camera to read between the lines of a screenplay that incorporates few "parentheticals" to characterize gestures, expressions, or tones of voice, and restricts itself to describing characters' actions "objectively," without interpreting them psychologically. That *Ninotchka* "feels" like a Lubitsch film testifies to the director's faith in the camera's powers of revelation or transfiguration, which is also a faith in his stars' capacities for transformation. Lubitsch's comedies share this faith with remarriage comedies. Wilder's own view of film, and of human nature, is too cynical for him to keep this faith.

In *Some Like It Hot*, for example, Marilyn Monroe is physically beautiful, but never radiant, as she is in Howard Hawks's *Gentlemen Prefer Blondes*. In *The Apartment*, the camera does capture, enable us to see, the qualities Baxter (Jack Lemmon) adores about Fran (Shirley MacLaine). Even in this film, though, Wilder fails to tap fully into the camera's powers of revelation as exemplified by the best 1930s movies. *Sunset Boulevard* is fundamentally flawed by Wilder's failure to reveal one iota of the charm and strength of character that her silent performances revealed Gloria Swanson to possess. I am aware that most critics believe that in *Sunset Boulevard* Swanson – even with all her mugging and eye-popping – gives one of the greatest of all screen performances. All one has to do is watch Swanson in her silent films, though, to regret – no, resent – the way Wilder turns her into a grotesque monster. ("It's the pictures that have become small" indeed!) Think of how different *Sunset Boulevard* would be if Lubitsch were directing Garbo in the role of the aging screen goddess! Think, too, of Charles Laughton's contemporaneous *Night of the Hunter*, which reveals the indomitable will that was the bedrock of Lillian Gish's stardom.

When Billy Wilder died, more than one obituary praised him for having the mind of a cynic and the heart of a romantic. I think of him, less admiringly, as having the mind of a romantic but the heart of a cynic. Wilder lacked the abiding faith in the all-but-magical powers classical movies invested in the camera, or in that protean quality, that capacity for change, requisite for both the leading characters of classical Hollywood movies and the stars who incarnated them. Did Wilder *wish* to believe in the magic of movies, but was too much a realist to suspend disbelief? Or did he use his so-called realism, his European "sophistication," as a cover for his failure to match the achievements of the best pre–WWII American movies? It is this charge that Sarris levels, in effect, when he writes, "Billy Wilder is too cynical to believe even his own cynicism." Then again, as Joe E. Brown says in *Some Like It Hot* when Jack Lemmon insists they can't get married because he's a man, not a woman, nobody's perfect.

This matter, too, is complicated. In the subsections that follow. I sort out some of these complications by addressing scenes from *Double Indemnity, Sunset Boulevard, Some Like It Hot*, and *The Apartment*.

Double Indemnity

More than once in my writings I have found myself turning to a particular sequence in *Double Indemnity* to illustrate my sense that film noir, at least on one level, is regressive in its treatment of women. In the passage I have in mind, Phyllis (Barbara Stanwyck), in close-up, is staring fixedly ahead. When she gives the prearranged signal, Walter (Fred MacMurray), her lover and coconspirator, reaches over from the back seat to strangle her husband, who is sitting beside her, just out of the frame.

It is illuminating to compare this passage, as Wilder films and Stanwyck enacts it, with the published screenplay, which Wilder wrote in collaboration with Raymond Chandler. In the passage in question, the screenplay specifies "a look of tension in her eyes."[1] What I see in Stanwyck's eyes, rather, is *excitement*. To be more precise, tension gives way to excitement the moment she hears the "struggling noises" and the "stifled cries" the screenplay indicates. "Phyllis drives on and never turns her head," the screenplay continues. "She stares straight in front of her. Her teeth are clenched." The screenplay does *not* specify that her face and body react viscerally to the sounds that betoken the murder taking place beside her. She does not literally view the murder – she is driving and has to keep her eyes on the road. Then again, there is no *need* for her – or us – to view a scene that she – and we – can so vividly imagine. Nor does the screenplay specify that, as she "stares straight in front of her," she is to be framed frontally, so that Phyllis staring at the road translates, on film, into Barbara Stanwyck staring in the direction of the camera.

In the film, but not in the screenplay, the scene of murder is at once real and a projection of this woman's imagination (and ours). This scene arouses her, turns her on (as it arouses us, turns us on). Phyllis is no nervous

[1] Billy Wilder and Raymond Chandler, *Double Indemnity* (Berkeley/Los Angeles/London: University of California Press, 2000), p. 57.

Nelly too fearful to ride this streetcar to the end of the line (to invoke one of the film's recurring figures). When the victim's stifled cries give way to silence – a silence underscored by a crescendo in Miklos Rozsa's music – Stanwyck, as if entranced, stares at or past the camera with a look of dazed satisfaction. Her face relaxes, her mouth closing in an enigmatic smile – is she smiling at us? oblivious of being viewed? – as the scene slowly dissolves to the next. Is this a human being, a mortal creature of flesh and blood? Or is she an inhuman monster, an agent of absolute evil, the Devil incarnate?

Stanwyck's smile, as the passage ends, is reminiscent of that of Marion Crane (Janet Leigh) in *Psycho* as she drives through the night imagining how people will react when they discover the crime she has committed, or that of Norman Bates (Anthony Perkins) at the end of that film, when his mummified mother's grinning death's head is superimposed over his face. It is even more reminiscent of Tippi Hedren's look in *Marnie*, when Marnie is satisfied that her beloved horse, which she has just shot, is actually dead. *As filmed*, this passage of *Double Indemnity* is remarkably Hitchcock-like in its intimation that this woman's powers, and the camera's, are unfathomable – and unfathomably linked. As *written*, though, the passage, although effective, is devoid of such ambiguity, mystery, and depth. Sad to say, the screenplay, not the realized film, divines the path Wilder was to follow in his postwar films.

I do not know whether *Double Indemnity*'s departures from its screenplay here are to be attributed to Wilder or to Stanwyck, who may well have taken it upon herself to revise, and deepen, the screenplay's understanding of her character. In any case, the film gains significantly from them. For one thing, the passage as filmed – not as written – puts us in a position to identify the look we see on Stanwyck's face with the look her stepdaughter saw there just before her mother's death, the look that convinced her that her stepmother-to-be was an evil monster. For another, the passage as filmed resonates more deeply with the climactic confrontation between Phyllis and Walter, another passage in which the film departs significantly from the screenplay.

Planning to kill Phyllis, Walter goes to shut the window. Suddenly a gun goes off. *She* has shot and wounded *him*. "Can't you do better than that, baby?" He begins walking toward her and adds, "Maybe if I came a little closer." Here the writers include the screenplay's one and only camera direction: "CAMERA IS SHOOTING OVER HIS SHOULDER at Phyllis as she stands with the gun in her hand. Neff stops after he has taken a few steps."[2]

What this camera direction does not specify is that the shot begins as if it were from Walter's point of view. When Walter enters the frame from the lower right-hand corner, his back is to the camera. The effect is uncanny, as if he has entered the field of his own vision, or stepped, awake, into his own dream or daydream. The framing suggests that Walter is in the world on film, as Phyllis is, but also looking in from the outside, as we are. Again, it is hard to believe we are viewing a Billy Wilder film, not a Hitchcock thriller, which always finds ways to incorporate sequences that suggest that the camera, by its very nature, is capable of crossing some metaphysical barrier (as we might think of it). There will be no such Hitchcockian sequences in Wilder's postwar films.

The uncanny effect is sustained as Walter advances toward Phyllis, who is in the left background of the frame. The camera begins moving with him, advancing on Phyllis as he does. It stops when he stops, still a couple of steps away from her, his back still to the camera: "How's this? Think you can do it now?"

"Phyllis is silent," the screenplay goes on. "She doesn't shoot. Her expression is tortured."[3] However, Stanwyck does not look tortured; expressionless, she meets his gaze. In response to his question, she simply lowers the gun, still staring at him as if she were in a trance. Evidently something she sees in Walter's eyes enables her own eyes to open. Does she see the love of her life? Does she see herself, as in a mirror? Does she see the Angel of Death, come to claim her? Whatever it is that she sees in his eyes we are not in a position to say, if only because Walter's back is still to the camera, he still cuts an uncanny figure in the frame, as he moves closer to her, takes the gun from her unresisting hand and asks, tauntingly, "Why didn't you shoot, baby?"

[2] Ibid., p. 112. [3] Ibid., p. 113.

Why not, indeed? And what gives Walter so much as the *idea* that, if he walks up to her, she will be unwilling, or unable, to pull the trigger? The screenplay's answers are quickly forthcoming. "Phyllis puts her arms around him in complete surrender." It is a common melodramatic device in Hollywood movies – I think of *Red Dust, Only Angels Have Wings,* or *Casablanca* – for a woman to threaten a man with a gun, perhaps even wound him, in an attempt to force him to do what she wants. Typically, he calls her bluff, and she proves unequal to the task of finishing him off, because – as he knows – she loves him too much to kill him. This is the explanation that *Double Indemnity*'s screenplay offers as to what it conceives of as Phyllis's *surrender*. Cold-blooded killer or no cold-blooded killer, and whether or not she realizes it, Phyllis is a woman in love – so surrendering simply comes naturally to her.

As filmed, Phyllis does not put her arms around Walter. When she reaches her hands out to him, Wilder cuts on this action to a close two-shot. We see her hair, not her face, so whether her expression is one of "complete surrender" we again are in no position to judge. (To be honest, I'm not sure I would recognize such an expression if I saw one. I have never *seen* "complete surrender" in a woman's eyes. Has any man?)

Wilder cuts to the reverse angle. Coldly Walter says, "Don't tell me it's because you've been in love with me all this time." As she keeps staring at him, we see in her eyes not "complete surrender," as the screenplay would have it, but *wonder*. (Damn, Stanwyck is good!)

She says, speaking the truth, "No, I never loved you, Walter. Not you or anybody else. I'm rotten to the heart. I used you, just as you said. That's all you ever meant to me – until a minute ago. . . . " She looks away for a beat, turns inward, as if coming to a realization even as she is speaking: ". . . when I couldn't fire that second shot. I never thought that could happen to me." "I'm sorry baby. I'm not buying." "I'm not asking you to buy. Just hold me close."

The screenplay goes on: "Neff draws her close to him. She reaches up to his face and kisses him on the lips. As she comes out of the kiss there is realization in her eyes that this is the final moment."[4] *As filmed*, though, Walter does not "draw her close to him." He does not respond to Phyllis

[4] Ibid., p. 113.

at all. In response to his withholding of any response, she throws herself into his arms with real emotion. He continues to say and do nothing that suggests that he feels a shred of human compassion for her, much less love or even desire.

Nor does Phyllis fail to pull the trigger out of weakness, as the screenplay implies. When she realizes that she cannot bring herself to kill Walter, she discovers the courage, the strength of character, to close the book on her loveless life of killing, even if that means facing her own death. She does not try to sell Walter the idea that she really loves him or believes he loves her. She does not claim that the miracle of love has already happened, or might still happen, between them. Evidently, she does believe that they are kindred enough spirits that she can explain herself to him, that he speaks her language, as it were. She wants him to know what she now knows, that humanity is the only thing that really matters. That is why she throws herself into his arms.

Suddenly, she pulls up with a start. She searches his eyes and is dismayed at what she finds there. With finality, he says, coldly, "Goodbye, baby." As the screenplay states,

> Out of shot, the gun explodes once, twice. Phyllis quivers in his arms. Her eyes fill with tears. Her head falls limp against his shoulder. Slowly he lifts her and carries her to the davenport. He lays her down on it carefully, almost tenderly. The moonlight coming in at the French doors shines on the anklet. He looks at it for the last time and slowly turns away. As he does so, he puts his hand inside his coat and it comes out with blood on it. Only then is it apparent that Phyllis's shot actually did hit him. He looks at the blood on his fingers with a dazed expression and quickly goes out of the room the way he came.[5]

As filmed, Phyllis does not "quiver" in Walter's arms. Her eyes do not fill with tears. She *embraces* her death. And Walter does not carry Phyllis "slowly," or lay her down "almost tenderly." (Wilder does not, for example, give us a last lingering shot of Phyllis from Walter's point of view.) After laying her body down, Walter grabs his own arm, but we see no blood. In any case, we are already aware, from his reaction when she shot at him, that he is wounded. Kneeling to pick up the gun, he looks back at her, but only to make sure he's leaving the crime scene the way he wants the police to find it. His gaze does not dwell on Phyllis's anklet – although Wilder takes care to make it shine in the moonlight so that *we* will notice it, will remember the way this ill-fated affair began, and recognize that Walter is in no mood to be sentimental.

[5] Ibid., p. 114.

In his introduction to the published screenplay, Jeffrey Meyers writes, "Phyllis, completely evil and cold-blooded, has destroyed a once-decent man.... He really loved Phyllis – and killed to get her. He feels remorse and is compelled to confess his crimes."[6] The *screenplay* may support this interpretation, but not the *film*. Here, too, we will probably never know whether the film's departures from the screenplay were due to Wilder's own inspirations, or his actors', or both. Whatever their provenance, they reveal Phyllis to be human after all, not an evil monster like the conventional *femme fatale*. They also spare her the abject surrender, the quivering and the tears, that the screenplay inflicts on her, adding insult to injury. To the end, Phyllis is a strong (if tragically flawed) human being akin to the strong women Stanwyck incarnates in films such as *Stella Dallas* or *The Lady Eve*. In asserting the sincerity of her deathbed conversion, they underscore the miraculous quality of her awakening – tragically too late – to her own humanity. They also underscore Walter's surprising – even shocking – indifference to this woman's spiritual rebirth. Walter kills Phyllis in cold blood. There is no sign he still loves her, that he ever loved her, or that he feels remorse when he kills her. He not only kills her, as no doubt she knows in her heart he must; he withholds his humanity from her as she is dying in his arms.

The film's departures from the screenplay at the same time deepen Phyllis's character and bring Walter into much closer alignment with the heartless Mr. Sheldrake, the reprehensible character Fred MacMurray will incarnate sixteen years later in *The Apartment*. To borrow the fine Yiddish word that Baxter's neighbor, Dr. Dreyfus, uses in *The Apartment* to condemn what he takes to be his selfish way of life, Walter is no *mensch*. Wilder might say, in Walter's defense, "Nobody's perfect." I'm sorry, Billy, but I'm not buying.

Sunset Boulevard

Wilder frequently used the technique of incorporating a voice-over narration spoken by the film's protagonist, as he does in *Double Indemnity*. This device might seem to make it difficult for a film to distinguish its own narrative point of view, or its author's, from that of its narrator/protagonist. Yet in *Double Indemnity*, as we have seen, Wilder's camera manages to drive a wedge between the film's point of view and the protagonist's. (Or perhaps Barbara Stanwyck drives this wedge by undermining Wilder's conception of her character.)

[6] Ibid., p. xii.

Sunset Boulevard's play with point of view is more complex, if less satisfying. In his narration, Joe Gillis (William Holden), a screenwriter, speaks from beyond the grave. Speaking directly to us, the film's audience, he seems to speak for Wilder, never more so than when the cops, coming to arrest Norma, are followed by "the newsreel guys" with their cameras. The narrator comments, bitterly, "Here was an item everybody could have some fun with – the heartless so-and-so's." (The "heartless so-and-so's," presumably, are both the newsreel cameramen and the viewers who will be sitting in the dark and enjoying the pathetic scene these cameramen are recording.) A moment later, Norma descends the stairs. Seeing her old director Max (Erich von Stroheim) – a Wilder stand-in? – next to one of the newsreel cameras, she believes, in her madness, that she is starring as Salome under Cecil B. DeMille's direction. She asks the imaginary director whether she can make a little speech before shooting her close-up, then tells everyone present – and those wonderful people who one day will be sitting in the dark, viewing her – how happy she is to be making a movie after all these years. She's ready for her close-up now. With Max directing, or pretending to be directing, the newsreel camera begins to roll. At this moment, Wilder's own camera – for the sake of the story, the director would no doubt say – subsumes its view into the view framed by the newsreel camera.

With this gesture, I take it, Wilder's camera abdicates its autonomy in order to equate *Sunset Boulevard's* audience with the "heartless so-and-so's" who, in Joe's words, will "have some fun" with Norma's descent into madness. Within this shot, Norma (that is, Gloria Swanson), head arched back, eyes staring ahead, reaches out as if to touch the camera, or to hold it at bay. As she walks toward the camera to get into close-up range, she also goes out of focus. The film ends with an empty frame.

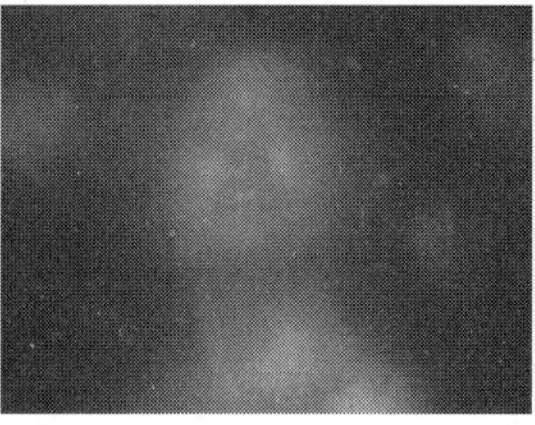

Wilder's handling of this sequence links it with an earlier passage in the film. The linkage underscores the deep bond between Wilder and Joe, the narrator/protagonist, and suggests that it is more than a merely clever device for this film's story to be narrated by a dead man.

The passage I have in mind begins after Norma shoots Joe and he staggers and falls into the swimming pool. Max rushes over to the pool and sees that Joe is dead. As Max is heading back toward the house, he spots Norma on the verandah. Wilder cuts to Norma, the low angle at first seeming to suggest that this is a shot from point of view. Norma says, to no one in particular (specifically *not* to Max's), "Stars are ageless, aren't they?" Speaking this line, she seems entirely oblivious of the fact that Max is watching her. The fact that she is looking *past* Wilder's camera, in a framing strikingly similar to the film's final shot, uncannily suggests that she is already imagining that she is on camera, performing in a movie, rather than living out her real existence, which has become a nightmare. This impression is enhanced when she goes out of focus, precisely as occurs in that shot, and her image blurs beyond recognition.

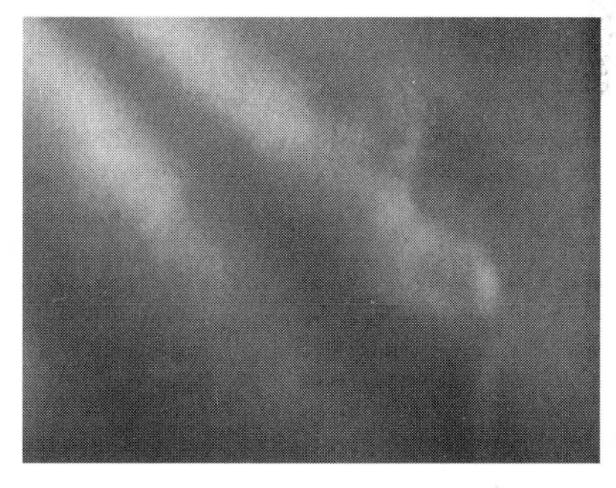

Gradually, a new image comes into focus. First we make out a bevy of news photographers, shot from below, snapping their cameras in the direction of Wilder's camera, which has assumed the perspective of whoever or whatever it is that they are shooting. Their popping flashbulbs momentarily blind us to the presence in the center of the frame of the object of their attention – Joe's lifeless body floating in the clear water of the pool, his arms spread as if nailed to a cross, his sightless eyes meeting the gaze of Wilder's camera.

It is precisely at this moment – the moment Wilder's camera brings home to us the terrible finality of death – that the narrator – the dead man – breaks his silence. "Well, this is where you came in," he reminds us in an amused tone of voice, "Back at that pool again."

In the film's final shot, Wilder rebukes the "heartless so-and-so's" in the audience – as Joe would no doubt have him do. As if taking pity on Norma, Wilder withholds, rather than presents, the pathetic close-up we imagine the newsreel camera to be "really" capturing. By thus distancing itself from the newsreel camera, Wilder's own camera might seem to be reclaiming its autonomy. On the other hand, Wilder also withholds, rather than presents, the glorious close-up Norma imagines the camera to be capturing – a transcendent close-up with the power to seal her immortality. In so doing, Wilder's camera is renouncing, or forgoing, its own powers of revelation. Unwilling or unable to reveal Norma Desmond – to reveal Gloria Swanson, the great star who incarnates Norma – as the camera revealed her in the silent era, Wilder instead uses his camera to obliterate her image. His camera shoots her dead, symbolically, and thereby seals its own fate. We might also say that this woman kills Wilder's camera, symbolically, or, at least, compels it to efface its own identity, enacting the death of the author, in effect.

In his subsequent films, Wilder's camera never fully reclaims its autonomy.

Some Like It Hot

Near the end of Wilder's celebrated farce, Joe (Tony Curtis) and Jerry (Jack Lemmon), masquerading as Josephine and Daphne, discover that the gangsters who want to kill them have tracked them down. Their would-be assassins are watching the roads, the railroad stations, and the airports – but not the yachts. So Joe orders Jerry – he's always bullying him – to call Osgood (Joe E. Brown) – the multimillionaire who has been courting "Daphne" – and tell him that "she" wants to elope with him this evening and that he should have his motorboat waiting.

As Jerry goes into a phone booth to make the call, Joe hears singing coming from downstairs. ". . . For I must have you or no one. . . . " It's Sugar (Marilyn Monroe), the woman Joe seduced by pretending to be Junior, the fabulously wealthy heir to the Shell oil fortune. "And so I'm through with love. . . . " Entranced by Sugar's singing, Joe starts walking down the grand staircase leading to the ballroom. Pausing, he gazes down at Sugar, and Wilder cuts to his point of view. Absorbed in the song, he descends a few more steps, then pauses again.

Then, as inconspicuously as possible, Joe goes down the remaining steps and scurries to the side of the stage. Half-hidden by a curtain, he can watch Sugar. Wilder cuts to a medium close-up of Monroe singing. She is not shot from Joe's point of view, as we might expect. Rather, she is framed frontally, as if she were singing for the camera as audience.

Monroe is singing in a real woman's voice, not the phony, breathless "blonde bimbo" voice Sugar sports in the rest of the film. From the heart, she is singing to the man who deceived her into believing he cared, that special man she despairs of having. She is confessing that she has "locked her heart," resolved to keep her feelings hidden, and has also "stocked" her heart with "frigid air" (to deaden her feelings? to preserve them, as if in a museum?).

Watching from backstage, Joe (still dressed as Josephine) appears deep in thought, his face in shadow, his mood dark.

Sugar has touched Joe. But how can he claim her? He has doubly deceived her (by pretending to be a woman who selflessly befriends her; by pretending to be the millionaire of her dreams, a man he impersonates by means of a rather miserable Cary Grant imitation), and she's in love with another man. That Joe *is* that other man only complicates his plight.

If this were a 1930s movie, Joe's challenge would be clear. To win Sugar, he would have to unlock her heart. But he would not be able to unlock her heart simply by revealing that *he* is Junior, the man she thinks she loves. For he would also have to prove that he is *not* Junior, who does not really care. Nor would it be sufficient for Joe simply to reveal that he is Josephine, Sugar's friend. For he would also have to prove that he is *not* Josephine, who wishes only to be Sugar's friend; not her lover. (If Josephine does wish to be her lover, she deceived Sugar, befriended her under false pretenses, and is no real friend at all.) And it would not be enough for Joe simply to reveal his true identity. Like Phyllis in *Double Indemnity*, he has been a "taker" all his life. He would have to prove that he is no longer "rotten to the heart," that Sugar's love has made a *mensch* out of him, that he has *changed*. But if he has changed, who is he, really? Is he Junior, Josephine, and Joe all rolled into one? Is he none of these characters? That human identity is not fixed is a bedrock principle of 1930s movies. Is it a bedrock principle of Billy Wilder's comedies, too?

When Sugar finishes her song, she bows her head and slumps down, lost in her private reverie. The spotlight is turned off, leaving her face in shadow, as the band closes out the song.

Purposefully, Joe leaves his hiding place, crosses the stage, kneels beside her, puts his hand under her chin, lifts her face, and, before she fully opens her eyes, kisses her.

That she returns this kiss reveals that she mistakes it for a continuation of a kiss she is already *imagining*. She senses no difference between the kisser in her fantasy – it can only be Junior – and the real kisser. As she gradually awakens to the inexplicable fact that what is happening in her fantasy is happening in reality as well, she pulls out of the kiss with a start. Opening her eyes, she recognizes, or thinks she recognizes, who her real partner is. Astonished, she cries out, in Sugar's "bimbo" voice, "Josephine?!"

Scandalized, the prudish bandleader lets out a shriek, alerting the gangsters, who are on the lookout for Joe, to look twice at the inter-loper. "Hey, that's no dame!" one cries out. Before all hell breaks loose, Joe takes a moment to wipe a tear from Sugar's eye, and says to her, in Josephine's voice, "None of that, Sugar. No guy is worth it."

Then, realizing his would-be assassins are clambering across the stage in his direction, he scampers away, leaving Sugar gaping. Doing a double take, she cries out again, "Josephine!!!" Although Marilyn Monroe's performance here leaves much to be desired, we understand from her altered tone of voice that it has just dawned on her that Josephine *is* her beloved Junior.

Joe does not *claim* Sugar, the way the man in a remarriage comedy claims the woman he loves in order to win her. Rather, he walks out on her. (To be sure, Joe has to leave in a hurry because he is pursued by goons who want to kill him. But he *meant* this to be a *goodbye* kiss.) He does not assert that he is – or that he is committed to becoming – worthy of her love. On the contrary, he leaves her with the thought that no man is. Yet he kisses her anyway. He is up to his old tricks, stealing a kiss without caring about its consequences. Nonetheless, when Sugar puts two and two together, she recognizes that this is the man for her and follows him to the dock where Osgood's motorboat is waiting.

When Joe sees that Sugar has followed him, he says in exasperation, "What are you doing here?" "I told you I'm not very bright," she replies. As the boat speeds toward the yacht moored in the harbor, and with a romantic moon shining on them, Joe insists he isn't worthy of her: "You don't want me, Sugar," he says in his own voice, taking off his wig, "I'm a liar and a phony. A saxophone player. One of those nogoodniks you keep running away from."

"I know," she replies gleefully. "Every time!"

"Sugar, do yourself a favor. Go to where the millionaires are. The sweet end of the lollipop, not the coleslaw in the face, the old socks, and the squeezed out tube of toothpaste."

"That's right, pour it on," she says with a big smile. "Talk me out of it."

Joe is about to bluster something in response when Sugar throws herself into his arms and shuts him up with a kiss. Their relationship ostensibly resolved, there is a cut to the other couple on board – Jerry (still dressed as Daphne) and Osgood. The stage is set for their celebrated final exchange, which ends with Jerry insisting they cannot get married because he's a man, not a woman, and Osgood responding, with Joe E. Brown's goofy sweetness, "Nobody's perfect."

Joe isn't perfect either. He's no millionaire. He's one of those saxophone players Sugar is always falling for. A nogoodnik. He's not worth the tears she will shed over him. By *confessing* that he is a liar and a phony, is he revealing that he has changed? But he is not *claiming* to have become a *mensch* or promising that he will never lie to her again. Sugar, too, is not claiming to have changed. Every time she falls for a saxophone player, she ends up in tears. Will this time be different? One difference is that she is no longer under the illusion that she really wants a millionaire, not a saxophone player. Another is that she is not running away from *this* sax player – at least, not yet; so far, he's done all the running. Are these distinctions without a difference? Be that as it may, she knows from their last kiss that she's his kind of woman and he's her kind of man. He does not want her to change. And she does not want him to be different. He can really blow that sax.

Whether the ending of *Some Like It Hot* satisfies us depends on how seriously in need of change we find its characters to be and how fully we find ourselves able to *believe* in them. Do I believe in Sugar and Joe and the love between them? No. She is Marilyn Monroe, after all, and he is, well, Tony Curtis. When the film asks us to believe that this woman buys this man's Cary Grant imitation, it is being unforgivably condescending toward Sugar, toward the troubled actress who plays her, and toward Cary Grant as well, as if Grant – star of so many of America's most glorious films – represents, on screen, nothing but a phony ideal deserving of being mocked by the likes of Tony Curtis. Do I believe that Sugar *should* love Joe, that he *deserves* to win her, that this makes for a happy ending? No. He acts in ways that are so crude, bossy and mean spirited, toward both Sugar and the hapless, incredibly irritating Jack Lemmon character, that Joe – like Walter in *Double Indemnity* – is only a small step removed from Sheldrake, the reprehensible Fred MacMurray character in *The Apartment*. The only thing that mitigates the offensive way *Some Like It Hot* winks at Joe's immorality is the fact that we don't really believe in him or his world at all. Still, I cannot help feeling that Wilder lets Joe off the hook far too easily.

Nobody's perfect.

The Apartment

Sarris observes that "Jack Lemmon keeps *The Apartment* from collapsing into the cellar of morbid psychology," while noting that "Wilder deserves full credit" for Lemmon's performance. Lemmon is quintessentially American (a fact Wilder shrewdly and comically exploits in *Irma la Douce* – in many ways a companion piece to *The Apartment* – by casting him as a Frenchman). Part of Lemmon's American-ness is his brashness, a quality he shares with Gene Kelly and Fred Astaire, for example. They, however, have a confidence in their ability to attract women that Lemmon lacks. If Baxter were played by Kelly or Astaire, Sheldrake – the uncharismatic Fred MacMurray – would not stand a chance with Fran. In doubting his ability to win a woman's love, Lemmon is akin to Charlie Chaplin. Baxter's doubt is fed by the fact that, although he is no Tramp, his social status is decidedly lower than his rival's; Baxter's doubt, like the Tramp's, also seems fed by the star's slight physical stature, a feature especially emphasized in *Irma la Douce*. As I have argued in the chapter "The Ending of *City Lights*" the Tramp's doubt of his ability to win a woman's love is complicated by a doubt that he is able to love (as opposed to his undoubtable ability, as an entertainer of unrivaled gifts, to manipulate people into feeling what he wants them to feel). Lemmon, afflicted with a most un-Emersonian concern with the impression he is making, an obsessive eagerness to avoid disappointing people, seems to lack that lust for power that made it a stroke of genius – and daring – for Chaplin to cast himself in *The Great Dictator* both as a lovable Tramp-like Jewish barber and that most unlovable tyrant, Hitler.

Why doesn't Baxter simply declare his feelings to Fran? One answer: She tells him that she is in love with another man. What right does he have to go against her wishes, to try to change her thinking? What reason does he have to believe he could succeed, even if he tried? Once he learns that the man she is in love with is his own boss, Sheldrake, he knows that he would treat her better than his rival does. This leaves Baxter torn. Again and again, he finds himself called upon – *by* his better nature, but also *against* his better nature – to plead Sheldrake's cause to Fran. (Ironically, Sheldrake reciprocates by repeatedly – if unwittingly – pushing Fran and Baxter into each other's arms – by giving Baxter two tickets to *The Music Man*, for example, and by giving Baxter no choice but to stand in for him in overseeing Fran's recovery from her suicide attempt.)

The morning after her suicide attempt, for example, Fran confides in Baxter that she is still in love with Sheldrake even though she knows that he is a liar who does not really care whether she lives or dies. Baxter lies through his teeth to try to convince her that Sheldrake really does love her. He does this both because he respects her in a way his predatory boss does not and because he is afraid that she will try again to take her own life – especially after she tells him that she thinks she is going to "give it all up." Soberly, Baxter asks what she means by this. She explains that she means giving up loving. (I think of Sugar, in *Some Like It Hot*, singing "For I must have you or no one, and so I'm through with love.") But to give up loving is to give up love. It is to give up the possibility of a life worth living.

In part to keep Fran from dwelling on her depressing situation, Baxter undertakes to entertain her. He takes out a deck of cards and they begin the game of gin rummy they are destined not to finish until after the film's final fade-out. By playing cards with her – and, later, by cooking spaghetti – he is, whether consciously or not, also courting her in his own way, by showing off his gifts as a clown. (Jack Lemmon's gifts as a clown may not equal Chaplin's, but they are formidable in their own right.) Baxter does everything he can imagine to make Fran fall for him – everything *except* declaring his love, or, what amounts to the same thing, revealing to her how adoringly he looks at her. This leaves *her* torn. Absent a clear signal from Baxter, how can Fran renounce Sheldrake for him? Baxter is so preoccupied with making a spectacle of his absorption in the card game that he withholds his adoring gaze from the woman he loves. He does not even notice when she closes her eyes and falls back into sleep.

In Baxter's case, as in the case of the Tramp, there arises, along with his doubt that he is lovable, a doubt – his? hers? ours? – that he is *able* to love, and hence is *worthy* of being loved. At times, Baxter comes close to rendering himself completely unlovable. This occurs, crucially, in the scene in his new office in which he brags to Fran about his promotion (without telling her, of course, how he "earned" his new position) and asks her opinion of the bowler hat he bought himself. Is it appropriate for his new position or does it make him look like an entertainer? There is a long pause before she tells him that she likes it. "Well, as long as you wouldn't be ashamed to be seen with me – how about the three of us going out this evening – you and me and the bowler – stroll down Fifth Avenue – sort of break it in...." She replies, "This is a bad day for me." Indeed it is: Unbeknownst to Baxter – who does not yet know she is having an affair with Sheldrake – Fran has just learned that she is only the latest in a long line of his mistresses and that he made to them the same phony promises he has been making to her. "I understand," he replies, not understanding at all. "Christmas – family and all that – "; she tells him that she should go back to her elevator so she won't be fired. "Oh, you don't have to worry about that. I have quite a bit of influence in Personnel. You know Mr. Sheldrake? He and I are like this."

We realize that he doesn't know that she is in pain and that his words are pouring salt on her wound. Still, we cringe to hear him speaking this way. It makes him sound too much like Sheldrake – as if he thinks Fran can be bribed into going out with him. We cringe even more when he shows her the Christmas card he received from "The Sheldrakes," and adds, "I thought maybe I could put in a word for you with Mr. Sheldrake – get you a little promotion."

Suddenly, Baxter becomes concerned that the bowler is tilted too much on his head. She hands him her compact so he can see in the mirror that he's wearing it the right way. Wilder cuts to a symbolically charged shot of Baxter, his back to the camera, staring at his reflection in the frame-within-the-frame of Fran's mirror – a reflection fractured because of the crack that runs the length of the glass. This echoes a shot a few moments earlier in which it was Sheldrake, not Baxter, whose reflection appeared in this mirror.

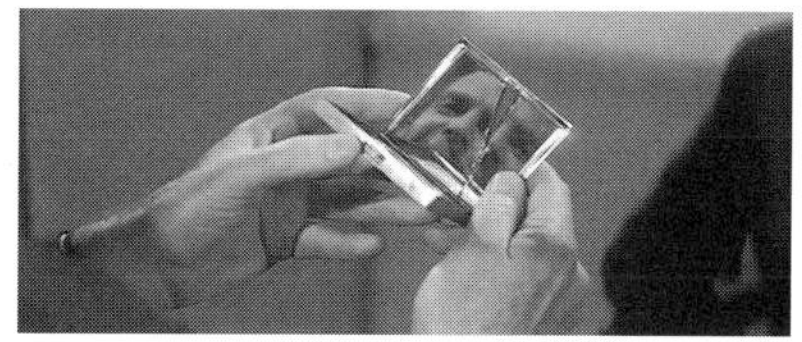

By pairing these two shots, Wilder makes sure we recognize, as Baxter does, that this is the mirror Sheldrake's lover left in the apartment. He also makes sure we understand that it is in the course of this shot that Baxter first realizes that Sheldrake's lover is none other than Fran. When Baxter closes the compact, Fran, sensing that his mood has darkened, asks what's wrong. He says, his voice now cold and impersonal, "It's broken." Her voice lacking its usual warmth, she replies, "I know. I like it that way. It makes me look the way I feel."

If Wilder links the two mirror shots to make sure that we read between the lines and follow what is happening at this moment, he is also making an authorial comment, as he rarely does in his later work. By putting Baxter in Sheldrake's position, in effect, Wilder underscores that Baxter is implicated, partly unwittingly but partly consciously, in the corrupt system that is victimizing Fran. Furthermore, at this moment Baxter is looking at *himself*, not at Fran. He is so absorbed in his own pain that he is oblivious of Fran's, even though, as we are to discover, she feels so alienated, and is in such pain that she feels she has no choice but to take her own life. The mirror shot underscores Baxter's failure to acknowledge the depth of this woman's despair. Yet at this moment Wilder's camera, too, focuses on Baxter, not Fran. Wilder is implicated in Baxter's failure to acknowledge her. Later, Baxter will make it up to Fran. Will Wilder?

It is instructive to compare Wilder's shot of Baxter viewing his reflection in Fran's cracked mirror with the strikingly similar shot Hitchcock presents in *The Wrong Man* (1956). It is the climax of the unsettling sequence in which Rose (Vera Miles) violently attacks her husband Manny (Henry Fonda), in the process cracking a mirror hanging on the wall.

Manny has been so wrapped up in the ordeal of his trial that he failed to notice his wife's deepening depression. Like Wilder, in other words, Hitchcock uses his mirror shot to indict his male protagonist for thinking only of his own pain, not that of the woman he loves. In Hitchcock's shot, though, the view in the mirror fills the screen (the way in *Psycho* the shower curtain fills the frame before it is violently pulled open and Marion finds herself face-to-face with her murderer). The effect is to identify the view in the mirror with the camera's view, the glass surface of the mirror with the camera's lens. And Manny, his image fractured by the cracked mirror/lens, is staring, transfixed, directly at the camera – as if the camera, not Rose's hairbrush, were the instrument – or the source – of the violent attack. That the role of film director has a murderous aspect, that the camera, like the saxophone, is an instrument best played by "heartless so-and-so's," are ideas that Hitchcock's films, but not Wilder's, seriously address.

In any case, we know that Baxter is not really the self-centered, unfeeling heel that Dr. Dreyfus, his neighbor (and Wilder stand-in?), believes him to be. Dreyfus challenges Baxter to become a *mensch*. To be a *mensch*, though, it is not enough for Baxter to *have* a heart. He has to *follow* his heart. He has to *claim* Fran. Until the very end, however, we doubt that he will ever do this. Like Joe in *Some Like It Hot*, Baxter is ready to walk out on the woman he loves rather than claim her, even after he breaks with Sheldrake by refusing to let him use the apartment to resume his affair with Fran. When Sheldrake informs her of this, she walks out on him. *She* then claims *Baxter*, it seems. But it would be truer to say that they claim each other.

Wilder handles this passage brilliantly. He cuts from a brief sequence in which Baxter is interrupted in his packing by Dr. Dreyfus, who invites him to his New Year's Eve party. This little scene establishes the champagne bottle that figures in what follows. Alone again, Baxter stares at the tennis racket he used as a spaghetti strainer when he was nursing Fran back to health – and courting her. He removes a strand of spaghetti and stares at it. Obviously thinking about that night, he twirls the noodle. Wilder dissolves to Fran at the Chinese restaurant that she and Sheldrake used to frequent. A New Year's Eve party is going on. Two glasses of champagne and a strand of confetti floating through the frame link this space with Baxter's apartment.

The visual linkage infuses the shot with Baxter's subjectivity, as if the camera is framing what he is also imagining. Baxter is thinking, dreaming, of being with Fran. And she is thinking, dreaming, of being with Baxter. Fran looks up, and Wilder cuts to a shot of Sheldrake making his way toward her table.

In the shot–reverse-shot dialogue sequence that ensues, Sheldrake informs Fran that he had to book them a room in Atlantic City because it's not possible to find a hotel in New York on New Year's Eve. She says, parroting his previous mistress, "Ring out the old, ring in the new, ring ding ding." MacLaine says this with her delicious, and inimitable, deadpan, offbeat, affectless delivery. Her expression is not *in* the lines she speaks, but must be read *between* the lines. Mistaking her bitter anger for mere annoyance, he explains that he did not plan it that way: "Actually, it's all Baxter." Betraying only the slightest excitement, she repeats, "Baxter?" Still bugged, he complains that Baxter wouldn't give him the key. "He wouldn't?" she says with a sweet smile that bespeaks – by not expressing – her joy at what she's hearing.

Sheldrake explains that Baxter just quit, throwing his "big fat job" right in his face. We see flickering across her face a fleeting impulse to laugh. Thinking better of it, she says, slyly suppressing a smile, "The nerve!" Oblivious to her sarcasm, he goes on, "He said I couldn't bring anyone to the apartment. Especially not Miss Kubelik." Again, she withholds all expression. We see her *think*.

When he asks, perplexed, "What does he have against you, anyway?" we know that she is flabbergasted that this nogoodnik can be so blind, so arrogant, that he believes it must be her fault, not his, that Baxter wouldn't give him the key. She affects exaggerated innocence. "I don't know. I guess that's the way it crumbles." Keeping a straight face, she meets his gaze, then looks slightly off – as if addressing the absent Baxter – and, with a secret smile, adds, "Cookie-wise." With this line, Fran is not only paying homage to Baxter's favorite locution, she is literally mimicking his response, the morning after her suicide attempt, to the rhetorical question she posed to him, "Why couldn't I ever fall in love with someone nice, like you?" By affectionately repeating Baxter's own words and imagining herself speaking them to him, Fran's signals her recognition that Baxter is a real man, not merely "someone nice," and that he's in love with her. She also recognizes, at this moment, in other words, that she *has* fallen in love with Baxter – and that she can't wait to tell him.

Sheldrake asks, "What are you talking about?" "I'd spell it out for you – only I can't spell." Obviously it's not that she can't spell; it's that he, unlike Baxter, lacks the imagination needed to read her. Then, losing interest in trying to follow her thinking, he takes another drink of champagne, sealing his fate. The band starts playing "Auld Lang Syne," and Wilder cuts to an establishing shot of the festive scene. (Surely Wilder has Chaplin's *The Gold Rush* in mind here.) The lights dim. Sheldrake gives Fran an impersonal kiss, then turns to look at the dancing couples. She gazes in his direction, framed in profile. There is a cut to her, lost in thought. As she is thinking – we know she's thinking of Baxter – she fingers her necklace and her face lights up in a radiant smile. Suddenly Fran's smile drops and she takes her hand from her necklace. She looks serious, as if it is just now dawning on her that the moment of decision has at last arrived.

Wilder cuts back to the establishing shot as the song ends, the cut masking Fran's exit from the restaurant. When the lights go on, Sheldrake turns back to Fran – but she is gone. There is a dissolve from her

empty chair to Fran running down the street in front of Baxter's brownstone.

As the screenplay puts it, "There is a happy, expectant look on her face. She hurries up the steps and through the front door." She bolts joyfully up the stairs – until what sounds like a gunshot comes from Baxter's apartment. No doubt remembering Baxter's story that he had once shot himself – in the knee, but nobody's perfect – over his unrequited love for his best friend's wife, she pounds frantically on his door. After a long moment, it opens. There stands Baxter, a just-uncorked bottle of champagne foaming over in his hand.

"Sagging with relief," as the screenplay puts it, Fran stares back at Baxter: "Are you all right?" She does not directly express her feelings. Nor does he. Rather than acting overjoyed, he is awestruck, as if he is witnessing a miracle. "I'm fine." "Are you sure? How's your knee?" (an allusion to his old suicide attempt). He replies, quizzically, "I'm fine all over." "Mind if I come in?" "Of course not."

Once inside, Fran sees his belongings packed in boxes. There's one empty champagne glass on the coffee table. Baxter takes another from a carton. Looking around, she asks, "Where are you going?" "Who knows? Another neighborhood – another town – another job – I'm on my own." "That's funny – so am I." Finding the deck of cards, she settles herself on the couch and starts to shuffle the cards. "What about Mr. Sheldrake?" According to the screenplay, she replies, "I'm going to send him a fruit cake every Christmas." Again, she alludes to Baxter's suicide attempt, this time by way of announcing to him that her affair with Sheldrake is now history (ever since he got over his infatuation with that woman, Baxter once told Fran, she sends him a fruitcake every Christmas). In the film, though, Fran seems to say, "We'll send him a fruitcake every Christmas." I say "seems to say" because the first word is muffled, as if the editor trimmed the beginning of the line in an attempt to cover up MacLaine's departure from the script. I like to think that the actress deliberately departed from Wilder's wording here in order to strengthen the screenplay's conception of her character. With "we" substituted for "I," the line not only announces that she is now available, and hence invites Baxter to claim her, it lets him know that in her eyes they are already a couple. That is, she is claiming him.

The significance of Fran's remark is not lost on Baxter. Staring adoringly at her, he sits on the couch beside her. She holds out the deck and says "Cut." He picks a card. Not looking at it, he keeps staring at her and says,

"I love you, Miss Kubelik." She doesn't say anything, but rather picks a card and hands back the deck. "Did you hear what I said, Miss Kubelik? I absolutely adore you." Meeting his gaze, she smiles adorably and says, "Shut up and deal," As he deals, not taking his eyes off her – he is long past pretending to be more interested in gin rummy than in Fran – she removes her jacket and arranges her cards, not taking her eyes off him. She is smiling even more adorably as the film ends.

Fran's words might seem to be denying that ending up with Baxter is a triumph of romantic love. But she is really saying, "I love you, too." And "Shut up and deal" doesn't just mean "Let's not talk about love; let's play cards." It also means "Let's make love, not just talk about it." This is made clear by the subtle seductiveness of MacLaine's gesture as she slips off her jacket [to get down to the serious business of cards? to the (more?) serious business of sex?]. Her fetching smile is infused with that ineffable quality – originally discovered by Hitchcock in *The Trouble with Harry* (1955) – that makes the young Shirley MacLaine so appealing – and sexy – on screen.

Fran is not squelching Baxter. She's saying, "With me, you don't have to worry about the impression you're making." She loves him not in spite of, but because of, that quality of his character or nature manifest in what he just said and the way he said it. By ordering him to shut up, she is declaring her commitment to their ongoing conversation. By *ordering* him, it might seem that she is claiming to be in charge. But she is ordering him to *deal*. Who's in charge is as exquisitely in question as in the ending of a remarriage comedy like *Adam's Rib*; or, rather, in both films the woman and the man in the end achieve a conversation of equals, a relationship in which neither can be said to be "in charge," in which their differences are freely acknowledged and they share power equitably.

When Sarris credits Jack Lemmon with keeping *The Apartment* from "collapsing into the cellar of morbid psychology," he is seconding Wilder's own view, I take it. Obviously, Sarris overstates the case when he asserts that "Wilder deserves full credit for Lemmon's performance" (auteurist though he may be, Sarris does not really think that Lemmon himself deserves no credit for his knockout performance). Yet by all accounts, Wilder devoted extraordinary attention to filming Lemmon, shooting take after take until the actor – who shared Baxter's obsessive eagerness to avoid disappointing people – was satisfied. The fact that Wilder regarded Lemmon's character as a privileged figure receives surprising confirmation in the way he and I.A.L. Diamond end the screenplay. "Shut up and deal," the last line of dialogue, is followed by this description: "[Baxter] begins to deal, never taking his eyes off her. Fran removes her coat, starts picking up her cards and arranging them. [Baxter], a look of pure joy on his face, deals – and deals – and keeps dealing." Then the screenplay adds, "And that's about it. Story-wise," emulating Baxter's favorite way of speaking, locution-wise.

In privileging Lemmon's role, however, Sarris uncharacteristically neglects to give Shirley MacLaine her due. In fact, she is the key, for it is Fran who keeps Baxter from "collapsing into the cellar of morbid psychology" the way the Lemmon character in *Some Like It Hot* surely does. To be sure, Baxter also keeps Fran from "collapsing" (both by nursing her back to health after her suicide attempt and by proving to her by his example, when he finally repudiates Sheldrake, that not everyone in her world is corrupt). And yet, although *The Apartment* begins with a narration spoken by Baxter, it is Fran, as incarnated by MacLaine, who has the moral or spiritual authority to speak for the film. MacLaine's performance invests Fran with a depth that goes beyond the screenplay's conception of her character. And I dare say that it is the star herself, not Wilder, who deserves the primary credit for her performance. In that sense, *The Apartment* is reminiscent of *Fargo*, in which, as George Toles points out, the cynical Coen brothers, despite themselves, create a character, incarnated by Frances McDormand, whose moral or spiritual authority, thanks to her performance, overcomes or transcends their own view.[7]

At every moment Fran appears on screen in *The Apartment*, it is obvious to us that she can tell the difference – and cares about the difference – between a *mensch* and a heartless so-and-so. If this character is such a sage, though, how can she be in love with Sheldrake, who seems obviously despicable every moment he appears on screen?

It requires no special explanation to believe that a man as powerful in the company as Sheldrake, a man who is a polished and unscrupulous salesman to boot, would be able to sell a bill of goods to a young woman as innocent – and as romantic – as Fran. In the corrupt world of *The Apartment*, the film makes abundantly clear, men hold all the cards. Baxter's male co-workers view Fran only as a "piece of ass" they would love to get into the sack. That's how Sheldrake views her, too. He "hits the jackpot" by pretending to be different, pretending to be "serious" about her. By the time Fran gives him a recording of "their song" as a Christmas gift and he slips her a hundred dollar bill in lieu of a real present, though, Fran knows that he has been deceiving her all along – and that she has been deceiving herself.

[7] George Toles, *A House Made of Light* (Detroit, MI: Wayne State University Press, 2001), pp. 259–83.

When Sheldrake leaves early to spend Christmas Eve with his wife, Fran stays behind in the apartment (to "fix her face," she says). For the only time in the film, the camera takes the opportunity to view her alone. She goes over to the phonograph and plays "their song." As the romantic music swells on the soundtrack, she roams restlessly around the room. We take it that she is reliving, one last time, the romantic dream that she now knows was only a dream – a dream that has ended. The music underscores her emotion, or, rather, provides us with our only access to it, as the camera frames her from a distance, with her face turned away.

With the romantic music still playing, she picks up her handbag and walks through the hallway to the bathroom – to "fix her face," we assume. As the music rises in a crescendo, she catches sight of something – her own image, presumably – in the shaving mirror prominently placed in the frame. Wilder's camera moves in, as if to lend dramatic weight to what is to follow.

What we expect to follow is a shot that presents Fran's view of herself in the mirror. Such a shot, of course, would echo the shot of Baxter's face framed in Fran's cracked mirror. In effect, it would present the view of Fran that Wilder withheld in that earlier sequence – a pathetic close-up that shows the way she sees herself. Or would it present an altogether different view of this woman, a transcendent view that reveals her to be not pathetic at all, but rather to possess the unfathomable depth, the mysterious powers of revelation or transfiguration, of the women of the best American films of the 1930s?

In the closing shot of *Sunset Boulevard*, as we have seen, Wilder withholds the pathetic close-up of Norma the newsreel camera is "really" capturing and withholds as well the transcendent close-up she imagines the camera is capturing. At this crucial moment in *The Apartment*, Wilder similarly withholds the view of Fran – whether pathetic or transcendent – that we have every reason – and every right – to expect. He cuts to a shot of the shaving mirror from her point of view. But what we see framed in the mirror is a bottle of sleeping pills, not Fran's face.

At this moment, this shot cleverly indicates to us that the thought of committing suicide has popped into Fran's head. But the shot withholds

the view of Fran – her view of herself – that might reveal what motivates this woman to think of killing herself, how and why such a thought emerges from her way of thinking. Is her suicide attempt an act of weakness, a surrender to forces she feels powerless to resist? Or is it an act of resistance or defiance that reveals her strength of character, her capacity to pass judgment on the world? The shot Wilder presents to us reveals nothing about this woman, allows her no say. Unwilling to picture his adorable heroine as pathetic and lacking the faith in his camera – and his star – required to make the depth of this woman's unknownness known to us, Wilder forgoes the camera's powers of revelation altogether. Instead, Wilder's camera *plants* the thought of suicide in Fran's head.

From the outset, Fran wishes to believe Sheldrake's lies. But why does she wish so desperately for their affair to be a true romance that when she becomes disillusioned with him she is so devastated that she feels she has no choice but to commit suicide? And why is she still in love with Sheldrake, why does she still feel powerless to resist him, when she recovers from her suicide attempt? To believe these things, we have to believe that Fran has what screenwriters call a "backstory" – we do not have to know what that story is – capable of explaining how it is that this brutal, unjust world has wounded her so deeply that she finds herself completely devoid of hope. Because she is incarnated by Shirley MacLaine, we do believe that Fran has such a story, a story only hinted at by the screenplay – a kind of intimate story about a woman's unknownness that Wilder does not tell in *The Apartment*, or, for that matter, in any of his films.

This is not the only passage in *The Apartment* that leaves me with the disturbing impression that Wilder is not only avoiding intimacy with Fran, but victimizing her, making her suffer in order to give himself an opportunity to show off his own cleverness. Perhaps the most striking example is the passage in which Fran mistakes the pop of a champagne cork for a gunshot and is desperately afraid that Baxter has killed himself. Fran does not need such a scare to realize that she loves Baxter. She is no heartless so-and-so. But that is what Wilder appears to be in this passage in which he inflicts pain on Fran so he can have a little fun with a naughty visual pun as his camera envisions Baxter's champagne bottle "ejaculating" when the woman he adores shows up at his door.

As I have suggested, the idea that a film director may be the moral equivalent of Sheldrake, that the camera, like the saxophone, may be an instrument best played by a heartless so-and-so, is one that Wilder's films never seriously address. Unlike Hitchcock, Wilder does not reflect, in his films, on the dark side of his role. Then again, nobody's perfect.

"Nobody's perfect" is one way of summing up the Emersonian lesson Katharine Hepburn learns in *The Philadelphia Story* on her way to becoming a real human being, as she puts it, or, as *The Apartment* puts it, a *mensch*. But "Nobody's perfect" means very different things in the two films. In *The Philadelphia Story*, the idea that nobody is perfect, combined with the idea that human identity is not fixed, underwrites the film's moral perfectionism. In remarriage comedies, American society as it stands lacks the moral authority to legitimize the couple's union. Hepburn and Grant are committed – as all remarriage comedies are, as the films wish everyone to be – to perfecting themselves and their world.

There is a bittersweet quality to the ending of *The Apartment* that results in part from these characters' realization that Baxter has quit his job, that Fran is about to be fired, and that they are without obvious prospects. Nothing in the film suggests that in America other corporate work places are better, morality-wise or otherwise-wise, than this insurance company that considers Sheldrake a model executive. Baxter's bags are packed, but we don't know whether the two will leave the big city together or will try to survive within its oppressive world. In truth, it feels as if they'll never leave this apartment. In this respect, the ending of *The Apartment* is reminiscent of the ending of John Ford's *Stagecoach*, in which Ringo and Dallas ride off to his ranch in Mexico to live "happily ever after" – on the condition that they never return to America. *The Apartment* despairs of an America hopelessly corrupted by corporate values, hopelessly out of touch with human values. Baxter and Fran find happiness in each other. But they forgo any hope of changing the world.

Wilder's comedies share with remarriage comedies the conviction that to pursue happiness we must chart our own path, follow our own inner compass rather than conform to society's conventions. At the end of *The Philadelphia Story*, the couple is unsponsored by society, just as Fran and Baxter are. Unlike Fran and Baxter, however, Hepburn and Grant are at home in the world, not just in an apartment. And *The Philadelphia Story* presents their marriage – and the story of their marriage, as the film tells it – as of national importance, as if this couple's "achievement of true marriage" might, in Cavell's words, "ratify something called America as a place in which to seek it."[8] Wilder does not share with remarriage comedies this faith that we have the power, or film has the power, to change society, to make the world better – better morally, that is.

[8] Stanley Cavell, *Themes Out of School: Effects and Causes* (San Francisco: North Point Press, 1984), p. 172.

In most Wilder films, indeed, characters do not even change, or wish to change, each other or themselves, as they do in remarriage comedies. At the end of *Some Like It Hot*, as we have seen, Sugar does not want Joe to be different. Nor does he want her to change. What does it matter if she's none too bright and he's a *nogoodnik*?

In *The Apartment*, Fran is bright enough to know and to teach Baxter – and perhaps even Billy Wilder himself, although the lesson did not permanently take – that in her book these things *do* matter. Unlike *Some Like It Hot, The Apartment* meets the remarriage comedy halfway, morality-wise. In my book, that matters, too. But it also matters that even here Wilder fails to go all the way, fails to achieve, or fully acknowledge, the Emersonian philosophical perspective that allows remarriage comedies, and other pre-World War II American movies, their combination of extreme popularity and extreme seriousness.

CHAPTER 17

The River

God dwells in the heart of all beings, Arjuna; thy God dwells in thy heart. And his power of wonder moves all things – puppets in a play of shadows – whirling them onwards in the stream of time.

– Krishna, in *The Bhagavad Gita* *

Hands lovingly paint intricate filigrees on the ground. A sitar plays the serene opening strains of a raga as the narrator, a mature English woman whose voice is wise and comforting, begins to speak: "In India, to honor guests on special occasions, women decorate the floors of their homes with rice flour and water. With this ... we welcome you to this motion picture, filmed entirely in India, in Bengal, where the story really happened."

Thus, *The River* (1951), the film that inaugurates the second great period of Jean Renoir's career, presents the first of its interpretations of itself, its own views, its creation, and its audience: The film is a beautiful design painted by loving hands to welcome us as honored guests on a special occasion. (It is a magical moment when, at the midpoint of the film, this opening image is reprised on the occasion of a wedding – a wedding that is the centerpiece of the film-within-the-film that represents a story told by the narrator's past self.)

The narrator goes on: "It is a story of my first love, about growing up on the banks of a wide river. First love must be the same any place ... but

* Juan Mascaró, translator, *The Bhagavad Gita* (New York: Viking Penguin, 1962), p. 120.

Reprinted: See "Notes on the Essays."

the flavor of my story would have been different in each, and the flavor of the people who live by the river would have been different."

It is the flavor of *The River*, what classical Sanskrit aesthetics would call the *rasa* of the film, that I wish above all to impart here, and to savor. The way I know best of doing this is by attending to the film's images, sounds, and words as they unfold, starting from the beginning. *The River* is an extraordinarily rich and complex work, and what follows is only a fragment of a reading, but I hope it is sufficient to convey something of the film's flavor.

An image of a singer in a boat, weaving a fishing net, fades in. A series of documentary – like images follows: shots of boats and oarsmen, a man washing, a boy rolling spices, a temple. "... It was one of the many holy rivers. Its waters came from the eternal snows of the Himalayas and emptied into the Bay of Bengal. ... The river had its own life. Fishes and porpoises, turtles and birds and people who were born and lived and died on it."

After several shots of a jute plant and its workers, the narrator introduces the first of the film's dramatic characters, creating the first of many bridges between documentary and drama; and in saying "My father was in charge of a jute plant ...," the narrator also intimates that *she* has a role to play in the story, has an incarnation within the film's world.

The father buys a kite at the bazaar, then walks across a bridge. "... The days followed one another in the even tenor of Bengal." She describes the Bengalis as "content in their traditions" as, on screen, we see her father give the just-bought kite to a child. This man, too, is sustained by *his* traditions, his Christian ways of giving. And *The River* itself is a gift.

There is a dissolve from the water buffalo outside the gate to a young boy. "... We were five children, all girls and my brother Bogey. ... " The camera tilts up and pulls out to frame a garden house, a group of children, and a kindly looking Indian woman with a twinkle in her eyes. "... Time slipped away unnoticed." On these words, chilling in retrospect (Bogey is going to die), there is a cut to the woman and a young boy. She commands him to come and learn his spelling. "I don't like spelling, I like turtle." But she points out that he *has* to learn to spell. "Imagine a man who couldn't read a newspaper." He replies, "I don't want to *be* any of those men," and there is a slow dissolve to Kanu, a dark-skinned Indian boy, climbing over the garden wall.

Bogey's "I like turtle" will be echoed in his fatal "I like cobra." Indeed, every appearance of Bogey in *The River* inscribes a premonition of his death. For example, when he says he does not want to be the kind of man who reads a newspaper, we might take the dissolve to Kanu as implying that this

is who Bogey wishes to be. But Kanu will be the sole witness to Bogey's death; hence, this dissolve suggests, darkly, that there is no kind of man Bogey wishes to be, as there is no kind of man he is fated to become – he will die without ever becoming a man.

This dissolve seals Bogey's fate, although the narrator passes over this declaration in silence. Yet we have the strong impression throughout *The River* (it grows with every new viewing) that the narrator's words and silences are attuned to all the camera's revelations. She speaks for the film's author, Renoir, as fully as *True Heart Susie*'s titles speak for Griffith. In *The Rules of the Game*, Renoir steps forward in person to play the role of Octave; in *The River*, he identifies himself completely with a woman who remains unviewed, although her past self is subject to the camera's gaze. Rhetorically, the narrator and the film's author are one. Yet Renoir is also one with every other major character in the film (except, perhaps, the beautiful, wealthy Valerie, whom the narrator speaks of as not being "one of us"): Bogey; Kanu; Ram Singh, the old Sikh gateman (an incarnation of von Rauffenstein, the Erich von Stroheim figure in *Grand Illusion*); Nan (the "bridge ... from dreams to reality, from reality to dreams"); the philosophical but secretly despairing Mr. John; the one-legged Captain John, made stranger to his own people (Renoir was wounded in World War I and suffered the rest of his life from the wound and the limp it caused); Melanie (who does not know why she was born and wishes to escape from the cycle of birth, death, and rebirth); Harriet (the young poetess who is the narrator's past self); Harriet's mother and father (who teach her, after Bogey's death, the painful necessity of "going on," of keeping up appearances, that is, living in the world); even Hoppity the rabbit. There is a bridge – unique in each case – between each of these characters and Renoir, a particular way of seeing each as an aspect of the film's author or, perhaps, of whatever *he* is an aspect of.

On the words "...all wrapped up in Hoppity her rabbit was little Victoria" there is a dissolve to a three-year-old holding a rabbit, followed by a cut to Victoria with an older girl, about thirteen, self-conscious and gangly, who has yet to be introduced. (They are framed against the sky in trademark Renoir fashion, like Octave and André in *The Rules of the Game* after their automobile accident.)

The older girl asks, "What are you doing to Hoppity?" Victoria answers, "Hoppity is my baby. He's just been born." "But you had him born last week." "Babies can be born again and again, can't they?" *The River* presents its story as involving real people in a real setting, yet at the same time as a fairy tale in which the dead come to life, a girl is transformed by a kiss, and ordinary human beings are incarnations of legendary men and women like Marc Antony and Cleopatra and of gods and goddesses like Krishna and Kali. A human life is lived once; it begins with birth and ends with death, but the present is always also past, and the past, future.

Victoria's remark prepares for the introduction of the beautiful, red-headed Valerie, viewed literally on her high horse in a slow dissolve to another trademark Renoir framing, a frame-within-the-frame that invokes the unreality of a painting, and even more a theater stage.

The narrator introduces her other sisters ("My sisters were much younger. The twins, Muffy and Mouse, and Elizabeth, the pianist"). The father cries out: "Good heavens, whose filthy little children are those?" There is a cut to the mother, calmly pouring tea: "Yours." The narrator introduces her simply: "Mother was beautiful. She loved music. . . . "

We dissolve to Ram Singh, the old Sikh gatekeeper, and the camera moves in on him. ". . . Before being our gateman, he had been a valiant soldier. . . . " Then there is a dissolve to Nan, the Indian woman we have already viewed, but who has not yet been introduced. ". . . Nan was the bridge to life, bringing us back from dreams to reality, from reality to dreams. . . . "

In long-shot, Nan shouts, "Harriet!" There is a cut to reverse field, with Bogey and the gangly thirteen-year-old in the background and Nan in the foreground, her back to the camera, presiding over the frame-within-the-frame.

Nan is unhappy that Harriet is barefoot. "Why can't you be obedient, like Elizabeth?" Harriet replies, "It's easy for her to be good, she *is* good." (What is Harriet's nature, her place in *The River*'s world?)

Nan suppresses a smile, which finally breaks through. ". . . Nan, always filling our heads with tales of romance, setting the stage for the arrival of love. . . . " Nan laughs out loud, and there is a cut to Harriet, her expression impenetrable. We do not know whether she takes Nan to be laughing at her or *with* her, whether or not Harriet finds the mystery of her nature to be a laughing matter. To this point in the film, we have viewed Harriet, but have not been introduced to her. Perhaps this girl's awkward self–consciousness in the face of the camera may lead us to suspect that she and the narrator are one. (Even her mother, when Harriet presses for an opinion whether or not she is beautiful, cannot honestly say more than "You have a nice interesting little face.")

On the words "... and I see myself, an ugly duckling determined to be a swan ... ," there is a dissolve from Harriet gazing inscrutably into the camera to Harriet lying on the grass with her book of poetry in front of her (this is where she will be much later in the film when she awakens to discover that Kanu is beckoning her to follow him, and he leads her to where Bogey lies dead, bitten by a cobra).

Harriet begins to recite a poem (reading from her book? writing in it?). This view of Harriet on the grass represents how the narrator sees herself *now* as she was *then*. It corresponds to the narrator's "inner vision" of the past, her remembrance. But this view also represents how Harriet envisioned herself *then* as she stared ahead and, inspired to or by poetry, contemplated the disturbing mystery of her nature. That is, the narrator's inner vision comes together with the private thoughts, the imagination, of Harriet, her past incarnation, to give birth to the mysterious views projected on the screen. And as the intimate view of Harriet reciting her poetry dissolves to a panorama of the river, the narrator's voice takes over from Harriet's: "... Then, as the river brought everything, it brought a young man on the weekly steamer."[1]

[1] At the end of the film, Harriet recites a poem, and the narrator for the last time takes over from her, but then the narrator *completes* the poem. The camera moves in on Harriet, but then its continuing motion excludes her from the frame (like the singers at the conclusion of *Toni*), and all we see in the end is the river, now explictly identified with the film itself.

There is a dissolve to Valerie and Harriet in the foreground and Nan in the background. Nan cries "He's come! Let's look at him!" and rushes from the depths of the frame (like Robert in *The Rules of the Game*, when André first appears at the chateau).

On the narrator's "... We knew very little about him ... ," there is a cut to Nan and the girls viewing, first framed within a frame-within-the-frame and then – in a composition that will be reprised at Bogey's funeral – framed looking over the garden wall. Again and again in *The River* (and to a large degree this is a new development in Renoir's work) "viewers" are placed within the frames-within-the-frame that ordinarily, in Renoir's films, invoke a theater stage. The implication is that viewing *is* theater, acting, performance; like actors on stage, viewers play roles, participate in the theatrical spectacle of the world.

The image fades out, then fades in on Valerie, breathless with the news that the new arrival, Captain John, has an artificial leg. But this, in Nan's imagination, makes him no less eligible for the role of romantic hero. Captain John is an American back from the war who is visiting Mr. John, their neighbor. Making part of Octave's role her own, Nan suggests that the girls invite him to their party celebrating the upcoming festival of Diwali.

Moved by the moment, Harriet, addressing the letter of invitation, recites the address out loud: "The little house. Our village. Bengal. India. The Eastern Hemisphere. The world." But when Valerie claims the right to deliver the letter, Harriet quickely slips out of her poetic mood: "It's *my* house and it's *my* party!" In the course of her transformation into the wise narrator, Harriet learns to transcend her possessiveness. (*The River* is, at one level, the story of Harriet's metamorphosis, or at least its first stages, which call for her to plunge into the river, to die, and to be reborn, and also to recognize that no one writes poetry without help.)

As Harriet climbs over the wall separating her garden from Mr. John's, the narrator speaks: "... Since the death of his wife, a beautiful Hindu woman, India had absorbed our neighbor completely...." There is a cut to reverse field, and Harriet walks into the background as Nan and Valerie remain in the foreground, viewing. (Both these framings will be reprised much later in the film, when, with Harriet now the viewer, Captain John follows Melanie into the grove, and he and Valerie kiss. "It was my first kiss," the narrator says, still smarting after all these years, "but received by another. I couldn't bear it.")

"... His house was full of Indian friends, Indian books and Indian music ... and he had a daughter a little older than I." A coach pulls into the frame, and there are excited shouts of "Melanie!"

There is a cut to a medium long-shot of Harriet and Melanie, the open doors of the coach forming a perfect frame-within-the-frame, the curtains of the doorway of the house enhancing the invocation of theater.

Suddenly the curtains part, and Mr. John makes his entrance, as Melanie cries "Father!"

Momentarily, Melanie makes her entrance, joining her father within the frame-within-the-frame, and they embrace.

Mr. John speaks the words "Oh Melanie Melanie Melanie Melanie" like an incantation. (It will be echoed by Harriet's terrible incantation "Bogey Bogey Bogey Bogey" when she first sees her brother's motionless body on the ground.) "... We've been starving for the sight of each other!"

Inside Mr. John's house, introductions are made. Harriet cannot take her eyes off Captain John as she hands him the invitation. Painfully awkward in her forwardness, she launches into an embarrassingly impassioned speech: "We always give a party for Diwali because that's the best time. Ram Singh has brought lamps and we light them before you come and we have ice cream and fireworks in the garden and we wear our new frocks and we dance and mother makes us gold and silver crowns. Will you come?"

Captain John replies noncommittally, "That's all very nice," then turns to ask Mr. John, not Harriet, what Diwali is. He replies: "The Hindu festival of lights." Then Harriet, unfazed, takes over: "Hundreds and thousands of little lamps burning everywhere ... " There is a disolve from Harriet, gazing ahead, spellbound, to a succession of documentary views of the festival. In these views, Harriet's poetic imagination and documentary "reality" are seamlessly joined.

Equally seamlessly, Harriet's voice segues into the narrator's "... I can still see the little oil lamps. Diwali means 'garland of lights' ... " The views that follow are *real*, but they are also what Harriet, in the face of the camera, is envisioning in her inner eye. And they are what, across the bridge of time, the narrator can "still see" even as she speaks. These views, which bridge past and present, reality and imagination, imagination and film, are views, as the narrator puts it, of lamps lit "in memory of a great war, the old eternal war between good and evil. For each life given in this war, a light is lit. ... " This is another of *The River*'s interpretations of itself: This film, too, is such a lamp. (Renoir's *The Little Match Girl* identifies itself symbolically with the sparkling, hallucinatory flame with which the Little Match Girl attempts to keep from freezing to death.)

The documentary views of Diwali conclude with the launching of a little boat, a burning lamp aboard, accompanied by the narrator's words: "For Hindus, all the universe is God, and since God is everywhere, it is only natural to worship a tree, a stone, a river. They all declare the presence of the one supreme."

The camera follows the boat as other small boats, likewise bearing lamps, cross its path. (This precise image will be echoed when Harriet launches her own boat into the river the night she sets out, after Bogey's death, to drown herself.)

There is a breathtaking dissolve to the girls, framed by curtains, watching as Captain John arrives at the party. "... At our house, we were all excited. Captain John had arrived.... Never before had Diwali seemed so wonderful."

From the father inviting Captain John to a tiger hunt, there is a cut to Ram Singh lighting a great pillar of sparks, then to a new angle on the spectacle, an empty swing conspicuously placed in the frame. (Whose swing is this? Who is absent from this scene?)

"... It was a fairy–tale come true...." (What is "wonderful" in *The River* is always a fairy tale come true.) There is a cut to Nan, laughing, then to the children. "... Even the little ones were caught in the spell...."

There is a magical cut to Harriet, curtsying against a black background, to Valerie, similarly framed, and then to Captain John, a grave, inscrutable smile on his face. "... Valerie and I pretended not to be aware of his presence, but we knew perfectly well that his eyes

were on us. . . . " (This passage is strikingly reminiscent of the equally eloquent scene at the opera house in Max Ophuls's *Letter from an Unknown Woman.*)

There is a cut to an extreme long–shot of the whole setting, dominated by the great tree and the spectacular pillar of sparks. Ram Singh runs to and fro, gesticulating frantically; this is one of Renoir's wittiest yet most poignant images of the act of *directing*. Then there is a dissolve to a procession of worshipers, which effects a transition to another documentary passage: ". . . Hindus believe in one god, but they worship different symbols, which they regard as the embodiments of virtues and qualities of the supreme being. . . . " There is a cut to a temple, framed to invoke a theater, an effigy of the goddess Kali "on stage," then a cut that isolates the idol in the frame.

". . . And among these symbols is Kali, goddess of eternal destruction and creation, creation being impossible without destruction. In our village, on that night, the great terrifying Kali held court in all her magnificence, and the villagers gathered to ask protection. For through the destruction of the elements of evil, good is born . . . " On these charged words, which reverberate throughout Renoir's authorship, there is a dissolve from Kali to Bogey, who is dancing with Elizabeth and carrying Hoppity in his arms.

For a long moment, the terrifying figure of Kali is superimposed over Bogey and Hoppity. Kali "holds court," as the narrator puts it, claims center stage, but she also posseses a gaze. Her gaze singles out this innocent rabbit that has already been born again and again – that is, has *died* again and again (to all viewers of *The Rules of the Game*, rabbits are a symbol of mortality as well as fertility) – and this little boy who is about to die. In *The River*, Bogey's death is the most shattering exemplification of the principle, incarnate in Kali, that creation is impossible without destruction.

Bogey and Victoria exit, Melanie asks her father to dance, and Harriet pulls Captain John to his feet. But his "I shall be honored, little kitten" stings Harriet with its condescension, and she angrily sits down. Then Mr. John asks Melanie to entertain Captain John, who rises when she enters the frame. The music stops and, ill at ease, Captain John and Melanie sit down. Elizabeth winds up the phonograph, and the music starts again, animating the scene (as music always does in Renoir's work).

A shadow appears in the frame; then Valerie enters in the flesh, eclipsing Melanie. (This expressive device, like so many others Renoir employs in *The River*, is also a staple of Hitchcock's technique.)

Saying "Captain John, you *must* dance," Valerie grabs his hand, and they join the other dancers. There is a cut to Melanie, Harriet, and Nan, who are watching, then back to the dance floor. The music stops. Valerie goes to "put it on again." Captain John, alone in the frame, gingerly flexes his artificial leg. Unwilling to endure again the painful and humiliating ordeal of dancing, he retreats to the verandah. Excited, Nan says, "Let's go!" Harriet follows her, but Melanie stays behind.

Captain John enters the verandah, viewed in extreme long-shot from Harriet's and Nan's point of view in yet another framing that invokes the stage. So, too, does the counter shot of Nan and Harriet viewing from within a frame-within-the-frame (one of the film's recurring visions of the theatricality of viewing itself).

Valerie joins Captain John in the extreme long-shot frame. There is a cut to a conventional "objective" medium two-shot that breaks with the longer perspective of Nan and Harriet, the two "viewers." As waltz music filters from inside, Captain John warns Valerie to be careful ("Because you're a little beautiful."). There is a cut to a new, closer shot of the two "viewers" – another "objective" view, no longer a frame-within-the-frame that invokes theater. (The camera passes effortlessly back and forth between the perspective remembered from the past and the perspective representing the narrator's inner vision. The medium of film bridges past and present, inner and outer, as it bridges acting and viewing.)

Harriet repeats in disbelief, "Beautiful!" There is a cut to Valerie, in close-up, stroking her hair. "Maybe I'm dreaming...," Captain John says, and there is a cut from the two "actors" to the two "viewers," then back again, as Captain John hands Valerie a cigarette. "She's smoking!" Harriet says in shock and dismay. "She's growing up!" Nan exclaims with a delighted smile.

At the moment Valerie's cigarette is lit, we are returned to the extreme long-shot that represents the point of view of the two "viewers" and places the "actors" on stage, then to the original view of Harriet and Nan, again framed within a theatrical frame-within-the-frame. The next cut – a reprise of the "objective" framing of Captain John and Valerie – further pulls the ground from under us. As Valerie takes her first daring puff, there is an even more disorienting cut (this is one of the most privileged moments in the film) to Melanie, framed in the window, viewing.

This is followed by the "objective" framing of Captain John and Valerie, who cannot keep from coughing, then by the two "viewers" who laugh at Valerie's discomfort, as we do, and then by a reprise of the mysterious vision of Melanie, accompanied by angry-sounding Indian music. Then Melanie slowly dissolves into the figure of Kali.

Melanie has not literally seen the exchange between Captain John and Valerie, but in her heart she knows what has taken place, I take it. This knowledge springs from the powers of imagination normal for a girl who feels rejected by the man she wishes to be her first lover, but it also has a supernatural aspect, as if it springs from the powers of the goddess Kali (as all knowledge does, perhaps). We may take this dissolve to identify the two figures, to declare that Melanie is an *incarnation* of Kali; but we also may take it rather as a declaration that Kali *possesses* Melanie, that Kali pulls Melanie's strings.

From Kali, there is a cut to an overall view of the temple, again framed as a theatrical space. Fire dancers are "on stage." Then there is a cut to the dancers' audience: a sea of inscrutable faces as impassive and impenetrable as the *commedia dell'arte's* audience of Incas in *The Golden Coach* (or as *The River*'s audience of Americans).

There is a cut to Kali, presiding over the scene, then a dissolve to a small boat bearing a clay effigy, which is being cast into the river.

The next day, at the setting of the sun, the symbols of Kali are taken to the water for the final ritual, made of clay taken from the river, carefully shaped and artfully painted. The goddess has accomplished her manifold tasks. Pious worship, sweet incense and generous offerings approach their end. On the river and on its banks, young and old, rich and poor pay their last homage to the goddess. . . .

There is a cut to Melanie and Mr. John, among the throngs viewing the ceremony from the riverbank, then to the boat as it glides silently into the water, then back to father and daughter. ". . . Arisen from the bed of the river, Kali returns to the river. Clay goes back to clay. . . . "

Mr. John casts his eyes toward Melanie, then looks away with a solemn expression, and the image fades out with exquisite slowness. The terrible wish inscribed in this look, passed over in silence by the narrator, yet poetically expressed in the engulfing of the frame by blackness, is that Melanie find release from the life her father unforgivably gave to her – that Melanie die, like her mother in the past, like Bogey in the future. It is also the wish that Mr. John's own dead love, the mother of Melanie, return to life.

When the image fades in, we view Mr. John reading a newspaper. Somber chords played on a sitar – these are like the tolling church bells in *Toni* – awaken him from the unreality of the newspaper stories. He looks up, and the camera pulls out, disclosing that Captain John is present with him in the room. The two men walk toward a curtain, and there is a cut to reverse field. Mr. John opens the curtain, and, from his point of view, we see the resplendent vision of Melanie dressed, for the first time, in a sari.

Mr. John says, "For a moment, I didn't recognize you!" Then he takes her hands and stares at her in wonderment, and she announces that she will wear a sari always.

When Melanie's own father fails to recognize her, who do we imagine that he thinks she is? Surely, one answer is his dead wife, Melanie's mother; another is Kali. The goddess Kali presides over all creations of life out of death, which are also creations of death out of life. This is yet another of *The River*'s interpretations of itself: The camera's gaze is the gaze of the goddess Kali, who incarnates the principle that creation is impossible without destruction.

As we have seen, *The River*, like Renoir's *Toni* and Griffith's *True Heart Susie* before it, begins with a claim that its story is literally true, that it really happened. But in *The River*'s meditation, as in classical Indian philosophy, what "really happens" cannot be separated from what is dreamed, fantasized, remembered, acted on stage, or, for that matter, projected on a movie screen. "Reality" itself is theater, a spectacle through which alone the truth reveals itself to human beings, a spectacle whose creator and audience are, ultimately, one, even as they are separated by a border.

The border between imagination and reality, like the border between India and the West, is itself a creation of the human imagination. Paradoxically, this means that nothing is or could be more real to human beings.

The River takes up and literalizes the fantasy (which goes back to the works of Griffith and Chaplin and to Renoir's own earlier work) that the movie screen is no barrier. And it broadens that fantasy into an all-encompassing metaphysical vision – a vision that is indigenous to India, but which has always been at the heart of Renoir's work. "Reality" is illusion, "illusion" is real, and to suppose otherwise is "the grand illusion." This idea is India's teaching; it is what *The River* takes from India. But it is also what Renoir brings to his encounter with India; it is Renoir's guiding intuition as well.

The River is Renoir's meditation on his oneness with India. It is also his meditation on what separates him from Indians, what makes him the particular human being he is. In meditating on India's teaching that diversity is the expression of oneness, Renoir discovers his own civilization, the civilization of the West, as his subject. Hence, *The River* is followed by the dazzling reflections on European culture of *The Golden Coach, French Cancan*, and *Eléna et les Hommes*.

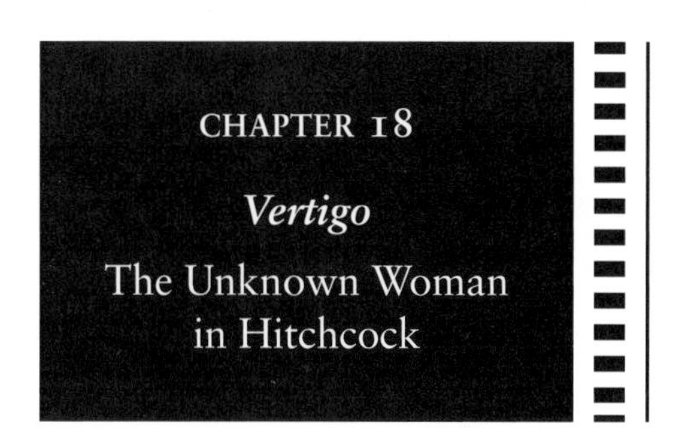

CHAPTER 18

Vertigo: The Unknown Woman in Hitchcock

In "A Closer Look at Scopophilia: Mulvey, Hitchcock and *Vertigo*," Marian Keane contests the view that in *Vertigo* the camera allies itself exclusively with the male position.[1] She argues that *Vertigo*, like all of Hitchcock's films, concerns a search for identity and what Stanley Cavell has called "the identifying and inhabitation of a feminine regoin of the self." If this is true, *Vertigo* has a close affinity to so-called women's films, in particular to the genre Cavell terms "the melodrama of the unknown woman."

At the end of *Vertigo*, Scottie (James Stewart), like the Louis Jourdan figure at the end of *Letter to an Unknown Woman*, awakens to the realization that he has failed to acknowledge the woman he loves. In both films, this realization comes poetically too late. Then are we to count *Vertigo* as a member of the unknown-woman genre? If not, what does its exclusion from the genre, or rejection of the genre, reveal about the unknown woman melodramas, about the Hitchcock thriller, about the concepts of genre and authorship as instruments of film criticism, about the conditions of being human (Cavell's deepest concern, and that of the films we both study)?

In the chapter that follows, I address such questions obliquely, letting my thoughts emerge out of detailed readings of two sequences in the film. In contemplating *Vertigo*'s relationship to the melodrama of the unknown woman, a personal motivation is my wish to reflect on the relationship between Cavell's writing about film, guided by and to the discovery of

[1] Marian Keane, "A Closer Look at Scopophilia: Mulvey, Hitchcock and *Vertigo*," in Marshall Deutelbaum and Leland Poague, eds., *A Hitchcock Reader* (Ames, IA: Iowa State University Press, 1986), pp. 231–49. Although there are significant points at which they diverge, my understanding of *Vertigo* and Ms. Keane's exemplary essay are in such close sympathy that I shall not attempt to note all the places where our readings are congruent.

Reprinted: See "Notes on the Essays."

film's major genres, and my own, drawn to meditate on film as a vehicle of authorship. Thus, I follow the method of *Hitchcock – The Murderous Gaze*,[2] in which I "read" five Hitchcock films from opening to closing.

The first sequence directly precedes the grueling passage in which Scottie, overcome by vertigo, fails to make it to the top of the bell tower and witnesses what he takes to be the death of Madeleine (Kim Novak). It opens on an extreme long-shot of Scottie in his apartment, lost in thought, perhaps dozing, on the sofa. At the sound of a buzzer, he looks up and goes to the door, the camera reframing with him. There is a cut to a shot in which Scottie, in shadow, is in the far left of a frame almost entirely occupied by the featureless expanse of the door. (This setup will be repeated, but reversed, when Scottie first visits Judy's hotel room in the second part of the film.)

His hand below the frame line, Scottie opens the door, creating what I call Hitchcock's "curtain-raising" effect and opening a bracket that will be closed at the conclusion of this sequence. (*Vertigo*'s most celebrated curtain-raising effect occurs when Scottie, trailing Madeleine down a dark alley, opens the door through which she disappeared – and a flower shop full of brilliant color fills the screen.)

As always in Hitchcock, when a curtain is raised, theater is invoked. Scottie is the audience – we are too, of course – for this theatrical entrance. But whose entrance is it? We see only a silhouette, a shadow among shadows.

In *Psycho*'s famous shower murder sequence, Hitchcock films the murderer's entrance in this way. However, Marion Crane is turned away when the shower curtain opens – she does not open it herself – so that we alone see the knife-wielding killer framed in silhouette Rhetorically, the *Psycho* sequence's identification of the shower curtain with the movie screen – that "safety curtain" we assume will separate us from the world of the

[2] William Rothman, *Hitchcock – The Murderous Gaze* (Cambridge, MA: Harvard University Press, 1982).

film – presents this silhouetted figure not as a denizen of a world safely cut off from our own but as *real*, as though we were face-to-face with our own murderer.[3]

The filming of the woman at Scottie's door in silhouette, by contrast, intimates that she is not fully, or not exactly, real, as though we are seeing not a woman of flesh and blood but a ghost. Indeed, this silhouette prefigures, among other moments, the ghostly apparition that rises into Judy's view at the climax of the film, precipitating her death. Hitchcock understands that in the face of the camera, the future as well as the past may haunt the present. And it is one of his abiding insights that there is an aspect of the supernatural, a ghostliness, in all human beings on film, all subjects of the camera.

Scottie believes, or desperately wishes to believe, that human beings create their own destinies: If ghosts are real, human beings are not free, and he is condemned to his vertigo. Throughout the ensuing dialogue, Scottie is intent on proving that Madeleine's possession by Carlotta manifests no supernatural agency. Hence, it is expressively appropriate that he immediately flips a light switch, causing the silhouette to be fleshed out: It is Madeleine (the eminently palpable Kim Novak).

For Scottie (at least, this is what he tells himself), Madeleine's mystery is only an enigma: How is Carlotta Valdes's hold over her to be explained and thereby overcome? In his role as investigator, but also as therapist, Scottie (the "hardheaded Scot," Gavin Elster calls him with veiled irony) undertakes to solve this riddle, to explain everything.

But Scottie makes a mistake: He falls in love. By a series of stages that Hitchcock precisely plots, Scottie's project in the first part of the film, which casts him at once as investigator/therapist and as romantic hero, becomes a calling – some would say an obsession – on which he stakes his entire being. By explaining everything, he will prove to Madeleine that she is free, will save and win this damsel in distress. But who is this woman to him? Scottie is intent on denying the Carlotta in Madeleine, but what if it is Madeleine's fatedness that really draws him, the doomed Carlotta with whom he has fallen in love? Is Scottie, untutored in the ways of the heart, embracing her mystery, not denying it?

[3] For an extended analysis of this sequence, see Rothman, *Hitchcock – The Murderous Gaze*, op. cit., pp. 288–312.

Scottie does not know, nor do we, seeing *Vertigo* for the first time, that the woman at the door is not Madeleine, Gavin Elster's wife, but Judy Barton from Salina, Kansas, who is acting the role of Madeleine – more precisely, acting the role of Madeleine possessed by Carlotta Valdes – in a piece of theater authored by the diabolical Gavin Elster. What Scottie *cannot* know, but Hitchcock calls upon us to acknowledge, is that Elster, despite his aspirations to authorship, is no less than Judy a creature of the *real* author, Hitchcock. Then, too, we know, as Scottie cannot, that Judy is Kim Novak acting the role of Judy. That is, Kim Novak is possessed by Judy, who is possessed by Madeleine, who is possessed by Carlotta Valdes, who is.... Then who is this woman we know as Kim Novak? Who is she in the face of Hitchcock's camera? And who is Hitchcock, that he, like Scottie, has fallen in love with her? Who are we, that we, too, have fallen?

"Madeleine!" Scottie says after switching on the light. "What's the matter?"

"... The dream came back again."

Scottie reassures her, a trace of a smile playing on his lips. "It's going to be all right.... You're awake.... "

She stares at him as he concludes. "You're all right now." His eyes narrow as he scrutinizes her closely, searching for a clue on which he might hang an explanation. "Now can you tell me?"

She turns away and walks across the room. The camera reframes with her as she begins to relate her dream of a tower in an old Spanish village. Then Hitchcock isolates Scottie and Madeleine in separate frames.

As Madeleine speaks, Scottie narrows his eyes, an explanation dawning. As she goes on, he moves left, the camera reframing with his gliding movement. Then he interrupts, gesturing in the inimitable James Stewart manner: " ... It's no dream. You've *been* there before. You've seen it."

She looks away and sits down. "No, never!" she says with all the petulance of disavowal.

"Madeleine, a hundred miles south of San Francisco there's an old Spanish mission. San Juan Bautista, it's called. It's been preserved exactly as it was a hundred years ago as a museum. Now think hard, darling. Think hard. You've been there before. You've *seen* it.... Now go on about your dream. What was it that frightened you so?"

To frame Madeleine telling the end of her dream, with its chilling anticipation of the nightmare that precipitates Scottie's breakdown, Hitchcock alternates a pair of close-ups, Scottie and Madeleine each framed almost in left profile, that are perfectly expressive of the intimacy and the separation of analyst and analysand.

"I stood alone on the green, searching for something. And I started to the church. Then the darkness closed in. I was alone in the dark being pulled into the darkness. I fought to wake up."

The camera moves with Scottie as he goes to Madeleine's side. On his words "You're going to be all right now, Madeleine," the lamp momentarily eclipses Scottie in the frame, a quintessentially Hitchcockian effect.

Finally framed with Madeleine in a normal two-shot, Scottie takes charge: "I'm going to take you down there to that mission this afternoon, and when you see it you'll remember when you saw it before and it'll finish your dream. It will destroy it. I *promise* you."

As Scottie speaks, Madeleine's eyes shift to the left, to the right, and then down.

Who is the figure of mystery on view in this frame? Are we viewing Judy acting in character as Madeleine – that is, playing Madeleine thinking about her dream, haunted by Carlotta's fate – or Judy stepping out of Madeleine's character to think about her own dream, her dream of happiness with Scottie (a dream that Scottie's plan, unwittingly crowning Gavin Elster's grand scheme, is indeed destined to "finish" and "destroy")?

Silently, Judy meets Scottie's gaze and then looks down, at which point Hitchcock cuts to a high-angle shot (cutting to a high-angle shot at the moment a human fate is sealed is another quintessential Hitchcock gesture). The camera glides with Scottie as he leads Madeleine to the door and announces, with an air of calm assurance, "You'll come back here around noon." [Scottie's manner brings to mind the penultimate sequence of *Notorious*. This is how Devlin (Cary Grant) leads Alicia (Ingrid Bergman) to safety.][4]

The cut to the high-angle shot is succeeded by yet another Hitchcockian declaration of the camera, actually a conjunction of Hitchcockian signature gestures. As Scottie opens the door and Madeleine passes through it, the door fills the frame, closing the bracket opened by Madeleine's entrance and creating a blinding white flash. (Another such white flash will occur within Hitchcock's presentation of Scottie's nightmare.)

There is a dissolve to an extreme long-shot of Scottie's car on a mountain road, then to the two in the car framed frontally. Scottie and Madeleine are looking at the road ahead, wrapped in their private thoughts. She turns to look out of the side window, which cues a shot from her point of view: trees hurtling by overhead, framed against the sky.

This is a significant moment. Hitchcock has presented us innumerable shots from Scottie's point of view, but except for the enigmatic view of flowers floating on the water that precedes her leap into San Francisco Bay, this is the first point-of-view shot granted to Madeleine, the camera's first direct acknowledgment that she possesses her own separate consciousness.

This shot, devoid of human countenances, represents Madeleine's view, what she literally sees, but it is also expressive and evocative, a *vision*: at once a terrifying vision of nothingness (Judy is hurtling blindly into the unknown) and a meditative vision of a higher, but inhuman, realm that "takes no notice" when human beings are born or die.

Scottie, *Vertigo's* protagonist, intent on denying the mystery that also draws him, is an object of study to Hitchcock's camera: Scottie's thoughts are perfectly legible to us. The camera's relationship to Kim Novak/Judy/Madeleine/Carlotta is more intimate and ambiguous: She is an object of desire to the camera, but they are also *attuned*. This point-of-view shot and Madeleine's reaction to it do not allow us to read this woman's thoughts; they reveal only that she is meditating, as Scottie is not, on the mystery – the mystery of birth and death and freedom and love and entrapment – that lies at the heart of Hitchcock's films.

[4] For a reading of *Notorious*, see William Rothman, "Alfred Hitchcock's *Notorious*," *The Georgia Review*, 29(4):95–120 (Winter 1975).

With a trace of a smile, Madeleine looks screen right toward Scottie, then left and down at the road going by, then *quickly* past the camera again, only then raising her eyes to look at Scottie. All this time she avoids, and *appears* to avoid, the camera's gaze. Sensing her eyes on him, Scottie looks with concern to Madeleine. When he sees the grave expression with which she meets his gaze, he returns his eyes to the road, a pleased smile coming over him (this is not a smile intended to be seen). We read Scottie – as does Madeleine – like an open book.

Looking away from Scottie, Madeleine breathes deeply and stares ahead. No longer avoiding the camera, she stares now directly into it, or through it, as if absorbed in a scene she is envisioning.

What follows is a series of hypnotically slow panning movements linked by equally slow dissolves, a series uncannily expressive of this woman's entrancement. But their effect goes beyond this: Coming in response to the shot of Madeleine staring into the camera, they affect us virtually as point-of-view shots, as if the views framed by the camera, our views, are projections of what she is imagining, as if what follows, perhaps all of *Vertigo*, represents Madeleine's meditation.[5]

The key shot in this series starts on a strikingly composed frame-within-a-frame. (Such compositions, which I take to be, at one level, invocations of the film frame, echo through *Vertigo* and indeed all of Hitchcock's films.) Slowly, the camera pans to the right until stone wall finally gives way to archway, and another curtain is raised, a curtain that will be lowered only in the final shot of the film.

The long duration of this movement combined with its elegiac slowness make this shot an *image* of the traversal of space and time, as if raising the question how human beings ever get from there – from

[5] For pointing out the uncanniness of this passage, I am indebted to James Shapiro, whose doctoral dissertation on the role of the artist in the films of Hitchcock (among other matters) is studded with such discoveries.

Madeleine staring into the camera as Scottie's car hurtles through the trees, for example – to here, and the question of where "here" is. How can human beings possibly exist in space and time? This movement echoes the camera's exquisitely slow traversal of Scottie's apartment that prefaces his first conversation with Madeleine and, before that, its traversal of Ernie's preceding Madeleine's entrance into the film. This latter shot is itself repeated in the second part of the film when Scottie returns to Ernie's, this time with Judy. And at the end of the present sequence, this movement will be reprised, and then echoed in the beautiful slow pan across the San Francisco skyline that effects the transition to the second part of the film.

Another slow dissolve takes us to the outside of the livery stable. The camera continues its movement until it frames the doorway in another perfect frame-within-the-frame. For a long moment, the camera holds this framing, through which the tiny, distant figures of Madeleine and Scottie are on view.

Finally there is a cut to the interior of the livery stable, as Scottie asks, "Madeleine – where are you now?" Madeleine replies, with a smile, "Here with you." Then where has she been, and where have we been, while the camera was "away"? And what commits the camera – what commits Hitchcock, what commits us – to return to these human subjects?

"It's all real," Scottie says, as if convinced that Madeleine will now come to her senses. But as he speaks, her eyes slowly turn toward the camera.

"*Think* of when you were here," he implores, taking her arm. As Madeleine begins, she stares into the camera, which moves in slowly toward her. "There were not so many carriages then. There were horses in the stalls. A bay, two black and a gray. It was our favorite place, but we were forbidden to play here, and Sister Teresa would scold us." Her words come ever more haltingly, as if it is an effort to keep from being engulfed by her memory.

Realizing that Madeleine is slipping away, Scottie impatiently looks all around him until he discovers a wooden horse: "Here's your gray horse. He may have a little trouble getting in and out of the stall without being pushed [the story of Scottie's own life], but even so.... See, there's an answer for everything."

Scottie's claim occasions a memorable Hitchcock brilliancy, as he cuts to a shot that sums up everything that Scottie has no answer for: Madeleine framed with her back to the camera in a charged frame-within-the-frame, within this world, yet viewing it from the outside, attuned to the mystery Scottie cannot explain.

Madeleine stares into the frame as if possessing it: She is the camera's subject, yet also its stand-in within the frame, its embodiment.

Dropping his pretense of being the detached investigator/therapist committed only to finding rational explanations, Scottie pleads with her, revealing his desire: "Madeleine, *try*. Try for *me.*"

Yet her eyes remain fixed on the camera even as she lets him pull her into his arms and kiss her. Then suddenly she closes her eyes and joins with him in the passion of this romantic, heartfelt kiss. But she is allowed, or allows herself, only the briefest moment of ecstasy. Her eyes drawn to something offscreen, she pulls out of the kiss just as Scottie at last declares himself: "I love you, Madeleine!"

Still looking off, she says, "Too late. Too late.... There's something I must do."

"No, there's nothing you must do," he says, trying to kiss her again. "No one possesses you. You're safe with me." But she pulls away and leaves the frame.

He runs after her, catching her on the green. Looking into his eyes, she says, "You *believe* that I love you?"

"Yes."

"And if you lose me then you'll know I ... I loved you and wanted to go on living with you?"

"No, I won't lose you."

"Let me go into the church. Alone."

She kisses him, and he lets her leave. When she pauses to look up at the tower, Hitchcock cuts to Scottie's view as he follows her gaze. Alarmed, he cries out "Madeleine!" and a chase begins. It is, of course, Scottie's vertigo that prevents him from making it to the top of the tower before Madeleine disappears behind a trapdoor and a body plummets to the roof of the church far below.

There is no denying the violence in Scottie's entire project, in the second part of the film, of making Judy over into the semblance of Madeleine. Yet before condemning Scottie, it is best to keep a number of points in mind.

First, Judy *is* Madeleine. Although Scottie cannot bring himself to touch Judy until she acknowledges the Madeleine in her, from the outset he glimpses the woman he loves in Judy ("No, Judy, there's something in *you....*"). When Judy writes the note she never sends to Scottie – and what a remarkable gesture it is for Hitchcock to let us in on Judy's secret, apparently breaking all the rules of the Hitchcock thriller – she contemplates staying and lying and making him love her "for herself" and thus "forget the other, forget the past." She may think that the Judy persona – Judy's way of dressing, making herself up, carrying herself, speaking – *is* her self, at least is her own creation. (But whose creation would she then be?) Yet "Judy" is unfinished, uncreated; surely it is her longing for creation that draws her into the role Elster creates for her. Once she is transfigured into Madeleine, there is no bringing Judy back. She may act the part of Judy, but only by repressing the Madeleine within her, only by theatricalizing herself. In any case, who is "she" at this point? Who is the agent of this repression? Who is acting? This line of thinking leads to the understanding that no matter how violently Scottie treats Judy and however little self-awareness he may possess, his goal is to liberate this woman's self, not suppress it. Furthermore, he is acting out of love for *this* woman. If Judy were some other woman who simply looked like Madeleine, would he treat her – and would she let him treat her – like this? I take it that Scottie knows in his heart – and in her heart Judy knows that he knows – that Judy and Madeleine are the same woman.

Second, Scottie promised Madeleine that he would not lose her, which means, in part, that he would not let her be lost, that he would keep her safe. His desperate project is undertaken not only for himself but also for Madeleine's sake, hence Judy's sake. Again, were Judy any other woman, it would be wrong – although psychologically understandable, in principle forgivable – for him to treat her only as a means to keeping a promise to Madeleine. But Judy is not another woman, she is who Madeleine is. *Vertigo* is the story not of the creation but of the re-creation of a woman.

Third, although we tend to think of Judy as an innocent victim, like Carlotta Valdes, of "the power and the freedom" of men, Judy is party to a murder (even if she tried to prevent it when it was too late) and to a diabolically cruel plot against Scottie. How can Judy make Scottie love her "for herself" if, even now, she lies to him, denying who she is? The deepest interpretation of Judy's motivation for "staying and lying" is that she *wishes* for Scottie to bring Madeleine back (which means that it is no accident when she puts on the incriminating necklace). Judy wishes for Scottie to lead her to the point at which she can reveal who she is – but without losing his love. As cruel as Scottie is in "changing" Judy, he would be crueler if he failed to fulfill the role Judy calls on him to play. Scottie himself desperately needs healing; yet he heeds Judy's plea and becomes her therapist.

Fourth, Scottie promises to love Judy if she lets him change her. And he keeps his promise, as James Stewart always does in his truest movie incarnations. This is a point at which Marian Keane's reading and my own diverge. Hitchcock indicts many of his ostensible heroes, such as Sir John in *Murder!*, but I do not believe that he indicts Scottie's project, although *Vertigo* insists on its monstrous, inhuman aspect and also insists that it cannot succeed. What gives rise to Scottie's monstrousness is his heroic refusal to let his love be lost and his equally heroic willingness to plunge into the unknown. His failure is a tragedy.

The second sequence I would like to examine is the film's ending, starting with the completion of Judy's "change." Within the frame of Scottie's point of view, Judy/Madeleine steps out of the bathroom, suffused in a green haze (ostensibly from the neon sign outside the window). Then she steps forward, desire in her eyes, and becomes "real."

Their kiss is rendered in a glorious 360-degree camera movement in the course of which, famously, the background changes to the livery stable. Scottie notices this and (like Buster Keaton in *Sherlock, Jr.*) is momentarily bewildered – this is an inspired touch – yet he lets himself be absorbed again by the kiss. There is a fade-out; presumably, they make love for the first time.

When the view again fades in, Scottie has undergone a transformation: This is a man blissfully in love, and the "real" James Stewart, boyish and chipper, has come to life. (This is like the moment in *Notorious* when, in peril down in the wine cellar, Devlin finally stops sulking and becomes the "real" Cary Grant.) But then Judy puts on Carlotta's necklace.

This occurs within a conversation about where they will go for dinner ("Ernie's?" "You have a thing about Ernie's, don't you?" "After all, it's our place.") that is interrupted for a digression that is studded with ironies ("C'mere." "Oh no, you'll muss me." "That's what I had in mind, now *c'mere.*" "Too late, I've got my face on."). Judy says, "I'm suddenly hungry." "Would you rather go somewhere else?" "No, no, Ernie's is fine. I'm gonna have – I'm gonna have one of those big beautiful steaks. Let me see, to start, I think I'll. . . . "

At this comical revelation of the enormity of Judy's appetite, she turns to him for help with her necklace. "How do you work this thing?" "Can't you see?" Finally he *does* see, and we cut to his view, the camera moving in on the necklace reflected in the mirror.

This provides an occasion for another of Hitchcock's virtuoso declarations of the camera. There is an "invisible" cut to the portrait of Carlotta, the camera continuing its movement in, then pulling out until it frames Madeleine in the museum, spellbound in front of the painting.

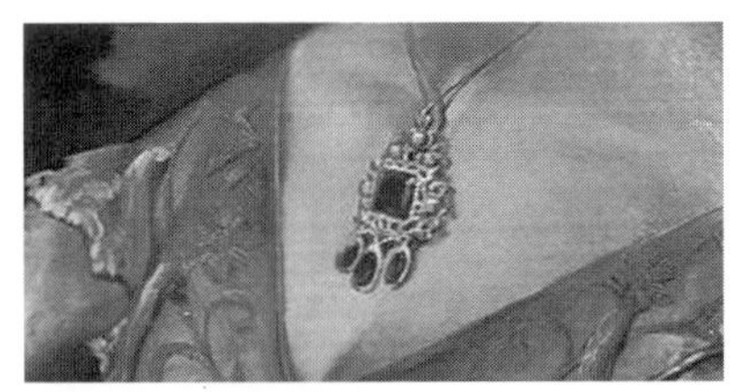

As the image slowly dissolves back to the present, the painting frames Scottie's eyes, a perfect Hitchcockian declaration of the camera.

Knowing now (But what does he know?), and without Judy knowing he knows, Scottie's manner changes ominously. Saying "First muss me a little," she puts her arms around him, but his lips will not meet hers. Less claiming possession than seeking reassurance, she asks, "Oh Scottie, I do have you now, don't I?" But he suggests they drive out of town for dinner, withholding his answer.

There is a dissolve to the car on the road. In this passage, Hitchcock repeats shots from the earlier drive to the mission, crucially including the shot of trees and sky from Madeleine's point of view. This makes us conscious of Judy's consciousness that what is happening is a repetition and renews our sense of her attunement to the camera.

Finally Judy asks, "Where are you going?" Scottie replies mockingly, "One final thing I have to do . . . ," and Hitchcock cuts to Judy's point of view: Scottie's face chillingly turned away in profile. (Using such a profile shot to signify withdrawal or withholding is yet another Hitchcockian signature.) ". . . And then I'll be free of the past."

There is a dissolve from Judy's troubled face to the car pulling onto the mission grounds. When she asks Scottie why they are here, he replies that he has "to go back into the past ... for the last time. Madeleine died here, Judy. I need you to be Madeleine for a while. And when it's done we'll both be free."

Judy is reluctant, to say the least, and makes several attempts to break away, but Scottie makes her go with him to the church, all the while relating what happened the fatal day Madeleine ran into the tower. (Throughout this passage, and in the grueling ascent of the tower, Hitchcock repeats shots from the earlier sequence.)

At the base of the tower, Scottie says, "One doesn't often get a second chance. I want to stop being haunted. You're my second chance, Judy. You're my second chance. You look like Madeleine now. Go up the stairs!"

"No!"

He pushes her. "Go up the stairs!"

As Scottie follows Judy up the stairs, waves of vertigo assault him. Hitchcock again reprises shots from the earlier sequence, including Scottie's famous views down the stairwell that vertiginously combine zoom and pan, creating the illusion of a space at once receding and unmoving. *What* recedes in Scottie's vision is the bottom of the stairwell, which forms another emblematic frame-within-the-frame, another invocation of the film frame.

The shots that express Scottie's vertigo are also Hitchcockian declarations of the camera: Scottie's vertigo is his intimation that he is condemned to the gaze of Hitchcock's camera.

Finally Scottie reaches the point at which, the first time, his vertigo made him stop. "This was as far as I could get." He looks at her. "But you went on."

She stares at him in alarm.

" ... The necklace, Madeleine.... I remembered the necklace."

"Let me go!"

"No, we're going up the tower, Madeleine!"

"You can't, you're afraid!"

"Now we'll see. We'll see. This is my second chance. . . . "

"No, please!"

"But you knew that day that I wouldn't be able to follow you, didn't you? Who was up there when you got there? Elster and his wife?"

"Yes."

"Yes, and she was the one who died. The real one, not you. You were the copy, you were the counterfeit, weren't you?"

Scottie's hands on Judy's throat, he is in a terrifying fury. "Was she dead or alive?"

"Dead. He had broken her neck."

"He had broken her neck. He wasn't taking any chances, was he?" He drags her bodily up the stairs.

The power of *Vertigo*'s climax turns on our conviction that Scottie really has it within him to strangle Judy, to break her neck, to throw her off the tower. And James Stewart's enactment of rage and Kim Novak's enactment of terror are so compelling that I have found myself fantasizing that at this point in the filming, Stewart lost control, that what the camera then recorded was no longer acting, and hence that Hitchcock, himself carried away, continued shooting anyway. (Or had he anticipated Stewart's breakdown?) This fantasy brings out a crucial feature of *Vertigo*'s climax: Once Scottie drags Judy to the top of the tower, no human being on earth can know what he will do. (Frank Capra's *It's a Wonderful Life* first plumbed Stewart's capacity for rage, the dark side of his unequaled willingness to stake his entire being on a wish.)

"So when you got up there he pushed her off the tower. But it was you that screamed. Why did you scream?"

"I wanted to stop it, Scottie. I ran up to stop it. I. . . . "

"You wanted to stop it. Why did you scream? Since you'd tricked me so well up to then? You played the wife very well, Judy. He made you over, didn't he?"

"Yes."

"He made you over just like *I* made you over. Only better. . . . And you *jumped* into the bay, didn't you? I'll bet you're a wonderful swimmer, aren't you? Aren't you?"

Her "Yes" is barely audible.

"*Aren't* you?"

"Yes."

"And *then* what did he do? Did he train you? Did he rehearse you? Did he tell you exactly what to do, what to say?"

She nods.

"You were a very apt pupil, too, weren't you? You were a very apt pupil.

Well why did you pick on *me? Why me*? I was the setup, wasn't I? I was the setup. I was the made-to-order witness. I was. . . . "

Suddenly realizing that he has reached the trap door to the top, Scottie becomes strangely calm. "I made it. I made it."

"What are you going to do?"

"We're going up and look at the scene of the crime. C'mon, Judy."

When finally Scottie pulls Judy to the platform on top of the tower, he flings her to the far end. (They are framed in a charged setup that repeats the key shot of the flashback sequence.)

"So this is where it happened. And the two of you hid back there and waited for it to clear, and then you sneaked down and drove into town, is that it? And then – you were his girl, huh? Well what happened to you? What happened to you? Did he ditch you? Aw, Judy, with all of his wife's money and all that freedom and that power. . . . "

Scottie moves toward Judy, the camera following him to the left. Recoiling from him, she desperately presses herself against the wall.

"And he ditched you. What a shame. But he knew he was safe. He knew you couldn't talk. Did he give you anything?"

"Some money."

"And the necklace. Carlotta's necklace. There was where you made your mistake, Judy. You shouldn't keep souvenirs of a killing. You shouldn't have been. . . . " Almost overcome with the memory of his love, Scottie takes a deep breath, choking back sobs. " . . . You shouldn't have been that *sentimental.*" He rears his head back, rolls his eyes, takes another deep breath, and pours all of James Stewart's longing into his next words. "I loved you so, Madeleine!"

"Scottie – I was safe when you found me. There was nothing that you could prove. When I saw you again, I. . . I couldn't run away, I loved you so. I *walked* into danger and let you change me because I *loved* you and I wanted you." She inches forward. "Oh, Scottie . . . Oh Scottie, please. . . . You love me now. Love me. . . . "

Hitchcock has filmed this part of the dialogue as an alternation of shots that isolate Judy and Scottie in separate frames. Still coming forward, she enters the frame of "his" shot and throws her arms around him: "Keep me safe!"

"Too late, it's too late," Scottie says, echoing Madeleine's words. "There's no bringing her back. . . . "

"Please!"

Scottie looks at Judy, stares at her, and then... *kisses* her passionately as he had in the hotel room, and before that in the livery stable. He does not ask for proof of Judy's love; he *believes* her, as he had the first time. Whatever the woman in his arms has done and whoever she is, he loves and forgives her. As far as *he* is concerned, their kiss is forever. He has overcome his vertigo and fulfilled his quest. But Scottie, worthy romantic hero though he may be, exists within the frame of a Hitchcock film. He does not have the power or the freedom to keep Judy safe.

As at the stable, Judy pulls out of the kiss, her eyes drawn to something offscreen. This time Hitchcock cuts to her point of view. Judy sees a frame devoid of human figures, like the repeated point-of-view shot of trees and sky. Then within this haunting vision of nothingness, a silhouette appears, barely discernible in the shadows.

Judy's eyes widen in horror, but Scottie, not granted her vision, is unaware that anything is wrong, until, crying "Oh no, no!" she slips screen left out of the frame. Then Scottie turns and, moving toward the camera so that his face is magnified in the frame, looks screen right as a woman's off-screen voice speaks the words "I heard voices." There is a chilling scream, and Scottie wheels around with a look of horror and dread.

The scream still reverberating, the silhouetted figure steps into the light. It is a nun, and she is looking straight into the camera. Crossing herself, the nun intones "God have mercy" and begins tugging on the bell rope.

As the great bell tolls, the camera pulls out and twists counterclockwise so that the white wall of the tower fills the frame, creating yet another of Hitchcock's blinding white flashes and at the same time imaging the lowering of a curtain. The nun, pulling on the rope, rings down the final curtain, signifying the end of the performance. Yet Hitchcock's final virtuoso turn remains to be completed.

The movement continues, now revealing the camera to be – all along to have been – outside the tower chamber, occupying a position inaccessible to any human being on Earth.

The camera keeps pulling out until it frames Scottie, looking down, his hands at his sides in mute anguish and supplication, as the bell continues to toll. It is with this declaration of the camera that Hitchcock ends his film.

What vision impels Judy to plunge to her death? Who or what gives rise to this vision that Scottie does not, and perhaps cannot, share? And whose vision is it?

Surely, Judy thinks she sees a ghost. But whose ghost will not rest until Judy takes her own life? And why would any ghostly apparition have such power over her? Is it the ghost of the real Madeleine, Gavin Elster's wife, seeking to avenge her murder? The ghost of Carlotta Valdes, passing on her curse to Judy, calling upon her to take her life? Or is this Judy's own ghost, her vision of herself as already dead? (Here in Scottie's arms, Marian Keane suggests, the arms of the man she loves, Judy is forever condemned to be the ghost he loves.)

This ghostly apparition is "really" a stern mother superior. Perhaps Judy also sees this figure as exactly who she is: agent of God's law and representative of the world of women. In the nun's religion, Judy is a sinner who has not earned the happiness that seems within her grasp. But if Scottie can forgive Judy, why can't she forgive herself? Why should the nun's religion have such a hold over her? Or is it to the mad Carlotta Valdes's eyes that this vision is given? Is it Carlotta, possessing Judy, who sees the shadow and jumps to her death?

Or is it the specter of Gavin Elster that Judy sees?

To this characteristically Hitchcockian thicket of ambiguities and paradoxes another complication must be added: In Judy's vision, the author also steps forward – *Hitchcock* is the ghost, *Hitchcock* the God whose law has been transgressed, *Hitchcock* the stern mother superior, *Hitchcock* the diabolical Gavin Elster.

In plunging to her death, Judy acknowledges the conditions of her existence, the conditions of any being condemned to the gaze of Hitchcock's camera. Scottie has banished his vertigo, shaken off his intimations of the truth that stares Judy in the face. Kissing Judy, he genuinely believes that happiness is within their grasp – and Judy loves him for his innocence. But

Scottie has no access to Judy's vision, no idea of what haunts and ultimately claims her. *Vertigo*'s author is as diabolical, as murderous, as Gavin Elster and as much a victim, as much unacknowledged, as much a woman, as Judy.

Vertigo is not a melodrama of the unknown woman, although an "unknown woman" in precisely Cavell's sense – a woman who apprehends her condition more deeply than the men in her world, who possesses deeper vision, intelligence, and depth of feeling – plays an essential role in the film and in the Hitchcock thriller generally.

Judy's and Carlotta's stories are the very stuff of the unknown woman melodramas; yet they can seem to lack connection: Why should Judy be haunted by Carlotta's tragedy? It helps to think of Judy's bond as being not only with Carlotta Valdes, the mother whose daughter was taken from her, but also with Carlotta's daughter, the little girl whose mother failed to keep her from becoming lost.[6] This provides a key to Judy's psychology – she keeps a photograph of herself with her mother, who, after her first husband's death, married a man her daughter did not like, precipitating Judy's move to the big city in search of a man who would love her for herself, followed by her ensnarement by Elster. Much critical attention has been given to the relationships between mothers and sons in Hitchcock's films, but none to the tragedy that befalls women when the love between mother and daughter is thwarted, although this is a central theme in *The Birds* and *Marnie*, Hitchcock's last masterpieces, and is a thread that runs through the films that precede them. I am thinking, for example, of an extraordinarily suggestive line in *Stage Fright*. After her guilt is exposed, Charlotte (Marlene Dietrich) tries to tell the respectful detective Mellish how it is with her, to describe the feeling that gives rise to murder: "When you give all your love and get nothing but betrayal in return, it's as if your mother had slapped you in the face."

At one level, it is the figure of Gavin Elster – the man who gets to Judy first and, with her participation, first changes her into Madeleine – that separates *Vertigo* from the unknown-woman melodramas. Of course, Judy's past with Elster, which haunts her, is also her guilty secret. The woman's guilt is another aspect of what separates *Vertigo* from Cavell's genre. If it were not for Judy's guilty past with Elster, *Vertigo* would be very much like *Letter from an Unknown Woman* or *Random Harvest*: a melodrama about a woman in love with a man who fails to recognize her. Then nothing – except, perhaps, Scottie's self-aborption – would keep the film from ending happily.

[6] Charles Warren helped me to appreciate the significance of this point and offered a number of helpful suggestions on an earlier version of this chapter.

But without Elster and Judy's attendant guilt, *Vertigo* would not be a Hitchcock thriller. Part of what this means is that the film would not call for the declarations of the camera through which, as we have seen, Hitchcock claims his authorship, for in a sense it is the Gavin Elster in Hitchcock who declares himself in these signature gestures.

In the genres Cavell studies, the camera is a machine that transfigures human subjects independently of human intentions. In the Hitchcock thriller, as *Psycho* explicitly declares, the camera is an instrument of taxidermy, not transfiguration: The camera does violence to its subjects, fixes them, and breathes back only the illusion of life into these ghosts. (The camera is an instrument of enlightenment as well for Hitchcock, although its truths are also blinding.) It is this murderous camera, mysteriously attuned to the unknownness of women, that is the instrument of authorship in the Hitchcock thriller, the truest expression of who Hitchcock is.

Thus, it is also the whole panoply of Hitchcockian signatures – the curtain raisings, eclipses, white flashes, frames-within-frames, profile shots, symbolically charged objects, and so on, that mark every Hitchcock sequence – that excludes *Vertigo*, or by which *Vertigo* excludes itself, from the melodrama of the unknown woman. Hitchcock's signatures are expressions of his unwillingness or inability ever to forsake his mark, ever to absorb himself unconditionally in the destinies of his characters, ever to leave his own story untold.

Yet these gestures, as we have also seen, at the same time reveal Hitchcock's affinity, his *identification*, with the unknown woman desperately longing for existence. Hitchcock never gets beyond his own case, his own longing for acknowledgment. Hitchcock *is* the unknown woman, and this, too, separates *Vertigo* from Cavell's genre.

To be sure, *Letter from an Unknown Woman* metaphorically identifies itself with the letter that brings about the man's awakening, hence identifies its author with the unknown woman who wrote the letter. But *Letter* is such a dazzling spectacle that Ophuls's gesture of identifying himself with the woman who wrote the letter appears only rhetorical, only ironic, as if he had nothing on his mind but the creation of a perfect aesthetic object. (To be sure, Ophuls's distanced stance may itself be ironic, a mask for the unfathomable depth of his identification with – perhaps his indifference to – the unknown woman in the film.) By contrast, *Vertigo*, for all its irony, nakedly opens Hitchcock to be read.

Cavell, in his readings of the melodrama of the unknown woman and remarriage comedies alike, aspires to put into his own words what these films say to their audience. Speaking in his own philosophical voice and out of his own experience of these films, he declares himself to be, despite everything, a representative member of that audience. These American films' Emersonian aspiration of creating a more perfect human community, shared by their audience, is Cavell's as well. I find that reading a Hitchcock thriller, reading *Hitchcock*, with his ambiguous relationship to America, is a very different proposition. I find myself continually called on to make discoveries, to see things that viewers do not ordinarily see, or to see familiar things in an unfamiliar light, to discover unsuspected connections. The *Vertigo* that emerges, at least in fragments, in this essay is not the film as viewers ordinarily view it (although my reading is meant to account for the common experience, which it interprets as the experience that fails to acknowledge Hitchcock and hence misses his meaning).

To read a Hitchcock film is to understand that Hitchcock is the most unknown as well as the most popular of filmmakers. His films are meditations on unknowness, emerging from and addressed to a condition of unknownness. *Vertigo* envisions no transcendence, no ideal community or marriage or fulfilled human existence on earth; within every salvation there is a damnation; Hitchcock himself is damned, not saved. Hitchcock's films are also demonstrations that human beings *can* be known. Yet to receive Hitchcock's instruction, to know Hitchcock through his films, is to be condemned to unknownness, not to transcend it.

To investigate the relationship of the Hitchcock thriller to the melodrama of the unknown woman and the remarriage comedy, it is necessary to articulate the central role played by the figure of the author in a film like *Vertigo*. Do films like *Vertigo* that tell an author's story constitute a genre adjacent to those Cavell studies, or perhaps a constellation of genres (perhaps every authentic authorship discovers its own story)? Or are they inaccessible by the concept of genre, beyond its reach as a critical tool?

CHAPTER 19

North by Northwest

Hitchcock's Monument to the Hitchcock Film

Made in 1959, *North by Northwest* comes at the end of the period during which Hitchcock's popularity was at its height. It follows *Vertigo*, considered by many his greatest film, and is followed by *Psycho*, which throws the Hitchcock film, and with it the whole Hollywood tradition, into a state of crisis. *Psycho* prophesies the death of the world of movies, but *North by Northwest* is joyfully possessed by the spirit that animated *The Thirty-nine Steps*, the film that twenty-five years earlier first won the whole world as Hitchcock's audience and triumphantly established the "Hitchcock thriller" as a genre. *North by Northwest* perfectly recaptures the earlier film's exhilarating mood, building to a climax that leaves most audiences, even today, cheering on their feet. It is the definitive Hitchcock thriller, providing a bounty of matchless pleasures. Indeed, it goes beyond *The Thirty-nine Steps* by attaining an ending that is *perfectly* happy.

In *The Thirty-nine Steps*, the poignant death of Mr. Memory gives the union of Hannay and Pamela a melancholy aspect that compromises its joyfulness. The film is further haunted by the tragic fate of Margaret, the crofter's wife, the woman who gives Hannay the overcoat that stops the bullet aimed at his heart. Margaret is a woman of intelligence, passion, and spiritual depth, haunted by the knowledge that suffering is her lot; she is an ancestor of the tragic heroines of *The Wrong Man* and *Vertigo*. Margaret grants Hannay her blessing, as does the dying Mr. Memory, but she is barred from happiness. Her private tragedy is forced into the background; yet her anguish is a condition on which the lovers' union depends.

In the creation of the single complex figure of Eve Kendall, *North by Northwest* fuses the witty Pamela in *The Thirty-nine Steps*, the woman destined for union with Hannay, with the tragic Margaret, who blesses that union and resigns herself to forgoing happiness, and also with Annabella

---

Reprinted: See "Notes on the Essays."

Smith, the mysterious adventuress whose death plunges Hannay into his struggle with the villainous Professor. Or it might be said that the creation of such a woman was essentially completed by *Vertigo*, and in *North by Northwest* Hitchcock finds a way to bless this creation with happiness. What better way than to give her away, as a bride, to Cary Grant? But in *Suspicion, Notorious*, and *To Catch a Thief*, Hitchcock had raised disturbing questions about this star of some of the greatest American romantic comedies. To prove Cary Grant worthy of Eve Kendall, these doubts must be resolved to Hitchcock's, and our, satisfaction. Grant must be redeemed.

Part of what makes *North by Northwest* so satisfying is that it rethinks the conditions of the Hitchcock thriller in terms that acknowledge the roots of *The Thirty-nine Steps* in the earliest Hitchcock films. In what might be termed the "original" Hitchcock film (films like *The Lodger, Easy Virtue, Blackmail*, and *Murder!*), women like Margaret played central roles. *North by Northwest* declares its continuity with *The Thirty-nine Steps* and the thrillers that derive from it, and also with those yet earlier Hitchcock films that typically tell the story of a woman tragically consigned to unfulfillment by a man's world unwilling or unable to acknowledge her. All of Hitchcock's work thus stands behind, and is celebrated by, this film. *North by Northwest* is Hitchcock's monument to the Hitchcock film and to the "art of pure cinema" it serves. It is also Hitchcock's monument to film's power (or the camera's power) to create a new woman, to Cary Grant, and to America.

In *Saboteur*, made in 1942, Hitchcock satirized an America that cluttered its landscape with billboards. In the new America of *North by Northwest*, advertising is everywhere. America has become a place, the film continually reminds us, where human beings and works of art alike are reduced to objects bought and sold. Eve is treated as a piece of sculpture, and statues also are denied their souls. Yet *North by Northwest*, even as it extends and updates *Saboteur's* satire on America, also transcends it. The earlier thriller viewed America from the outside, through the eyes of a recent settler amused by his new home. *North by Northwest* acknowledges the awful truth that Hitchcock has become an American. And he has discovered his love for the America of which he remains an uncompromising critic. Part of what the comedy of *North by Northwest* declares is that, despite everything, the mythical America of Hollywood films of the thirties in which happiness can be imagined, and imagined to be fulfilled in the love between a man and a woman, indeed in a marriage, is still real to us. Of course, that we can still imagine happiness and that we still pursue it do not mean that even its possibility can be taken for granted, but that is the burden of *Psycho, The Birds*, and *Marnie*, not *North by Northwest*. In all these late films,

Hitchcock's meditation on his own authorship, his meditation on art (in particular, the art of film), his meditation on love, his meditation on human identity, and his meditation on America are seamlessly joined.

My remarks here attempt primarily to illuminate the medium of Hitchcock's meditations. They barely penetrate the surface of this film, although I hope they convey some sense of the kind of viewing a film like *North by Northwest* calls for if it is to be fully acknowledged.

First I discuss some aspects of Cary Grant's relationship to Hitchcock's camera, focusing on a passage that helps clarify what I mean by saying that *North by Northwest* undertakes to redeem him. Then I illustrate some of the ways Hitchcock's camera participates in creating the woman known to her world as "Eve Kendall." In conclusion, a brief word about the film's villains.

Cary Grant

In *North by Northwest*, Cary Grant plays Roger Thornhill, an advertising executive whom Phillip Vandamm (James Mason) and his ring of spies persistently mistake for "George Kaplan," whom they take to be a government agent on their trail, but who turns out not to exist. One joke in Roger Thornhill's being mistaken for a fictional character is that, as the film makes clear, Thornhill's form of life as an ad man pegs his identity on a role, or set of roles, he plays: Roger Thornhill is *already* a man whose every move is plotted (by his clients, secretary, ex-wives, and mother). But a further joke is in the idea that Cary Grant could ever be mistaken for any "Roger Thornhill" in the first place. Roger Thornhill is only a fictional character, created by Hitchcock and subject to his authorship – no more real than the non-existent decoy George Kaplan. Hitchcock's real agent is . . . Cary Grant.

Grant's complete visibility in the world of *North by Northwest* is an acknowledgment of his familiar way of inhabiting the screen. He is the screen's consummate performer. On camera, Grant is virtually always in public – on stage, as it were. In a sense, the camera *is* his public, the audience for whom he turns on his powers as a performer, which might also be called his charm.

As I have suggested, in his previous films with Grant, Hitchcock raised fundamental doubts about his character, perhaps most pointedly in *Suspicion*, when Grant looks right into the camera to join with Hitchcock in compelling our acknowledgment that we do not really know him, that for all we know he could be a murderer. Yet it is only in *North by Northwest* that Hitchcock definitively resolves these doubts. The moment when Grant proves himself capable and worthy of love is the first moment he is no longer performing. It comes shortly after the famous art auction sequence, in which Grant gives his most exhilarating performance, escaping Vandamm's trap by reducing the staid proceedings to bedlam and casting Vandamm's suspicion on Eve, the woman who lured Grant to his doom on the Twentieth-Century Limited.

The moment I have in mind comes when the Professor (Leo G. Carroll), the CIA mastermind who created the fictional George Kaplan and plotted his every move in order to divert suspicion from his real agent, tells Grant who Eve Kendall really is. At this moment, the camera moves in to isolate Grant in the frame. His face freezes, turns to stone. By this I do not mean to suggest that we have no access to what he is thinking or feeling. On the contrary, we can read him like an open book. We know his joy in realizing that it is possible that Eve loves him after all, his anguish at the thought of her suffering, and his terrible feeling of guilt. Unless he acts, Eve's blood will be on his hands; he will be responsible for the death of the woman he loves. We know, and know that he knows, the depth of his feeling and his desire.

Suspicion's question about Grant's capacity for murder is answered at once in the affirmative and the negative. He *has* acted vengefully, murderously. In his face, devoid now of all animation, we recognize a capacity for inhumanity. But we also recognize him as a man capable of self-knowledge and capable, and worthy, of love. From this view of Grant's face transfigured by love, we know him inside and out, heart, mind, and soul. His "charm" may be what allows Grant to make those who do not know him fall in love with him, as Eve charged; but no "charm" is at work now, when he is redeemed in our eyes. At this moment, Hitchcock lights the frame harshly, as if by a searchlight. What this lighting underscores is the monumentality of Grant's face. This shot is Hitchcock's monument to Cary Grant.

That Grant is an authentic American hero is, I take it, part of what is proclaimed by the extraordinary gesture Hitchcock now performs, as he effects a slow dissolve from Grant's face to the Mount Rushmore monument.

Of course, for Roger Thornhill – that is, for Cary Grant within the world of the film – this moment at which, under the camera's scrutiny, he recognizes his own capacity for murderousness is a moment of unbearable pain. The harsh light that almost blinds him – within the fiction, it is cast by an airplane as it taxis into position – is a metaphor for the pain of enlightenment. Hitchcock's filming also suggests that Grant's pain is *caused* by being subjected to the camera's pitiless gaze. Hitchcock is responsible for Grant's anguish, which is a condition of his enlightenment. Unless the author does whatever is in his power to secure Grant's happiness, Hitchcock will be exposed as inhuman. What is revealed about Grant in this frame not only frees Hitchcock to give Grant his blessing but also mandates that he *must* do so or be condemned in our eyes. Then, too, when the Professor tells Grant who Eve is, it is also Hitchcock's revelation that he has withheld the truth from us. Can we forgive Hitchcock for deceiving us, as Grant forgives Eve but eventually refuses to forgive the Professor? Has Hitchcock made a film that blesses us or one that curses us?

When the camera now starts moving in on Mount Rushmore, an irís mask appears to frame our view within the film frame, as though we were viewing these monumental faces through a lens. Of course, all the views that constitute the film are viewed through a lens – the lens of Hitchcock's camera. This mask is an ironic reminder that we are viewing a film. This gesture acknowledges, I take it, that the view that resolves our doubts about the Grant character awakens, and does not still, a doubt that, from the outset of his career, Hitchcock has repeatedly raised about himself, a doubt that may be articulated in the form of a question about the camera: Does the camera represent an agency that is human or inhuman, loving or murderous?

The following shot identifies this masked view as Grant's. Yet Hitchcock frames Grant, looking through the telescope, in profile rather than more or less full face as would be the case in a conventional reaction shot. Grant remains more an object of view than viewer (hence his joke that he does not like the way Teddy Roosevelt is looking at him). In the next shot, a long-shot with Grant at the left of the frame and the Professor at the right, Mount Rushmore looks like the backdrop of a stage set. In the ensuing dialogue, Grant once again finds himself performing and being called upon to perform in a world in which the boundary between theater and reality is difficult or impossible to survey. The extraordinary mode of direct address between author and viewer has been abruptly suspended. The film will return to this mode of discourse, however, and complete its statement on the central issue it has raised about the nature of the camera.

Eve Kendall

Eve Kendall is primarily the creation of Hitchcock's camera, or at least the camera's intimate *pas de deux* with Eva Marie Saint. Eve is not the creation of Saint's performance alone, impeccable though it is, and who Eve is has little to do with who this actress has been in other films.

That Eve has a special relationship with the camera is declared in Hitchcock's presentation of her first entrance, one of the most remarkable passages in the film.

From the hustle and bustle of Grand Central Station, a single cut plunges us into another world. The camera tracks with Grant as he walks to board and then disappears from view onto the train. (A "Watch Your Step" sign, visible through the open door, is a typical Hitchcock touch.) Then there is a cut to a frame void of human figures that, tonally and compositionally, breaks sharply with those that preceded it.

Framed symmetrically, the corridor tunnels into the depths of the space. This framing, which I call Hitchcock's "tunnel shot," occurs in every Hitchcock film and always announces a space of dream or nightmare, a space that is not quite or not exactly real. Grant enters this frame from its depths, makes his way quickly to the foreground, looks through the window, and runs back into the depths.

Hitchcock cuts to a frame likewise devoid of human subjects, but as emblematically flat as Grant's space is deep. Eve enters, gloved hand and handbag first, and only then "in the flesh."

Her entrance is precisely synchronized with Grant's entrance, creating a singular effect, as though this woman were his mirror reflection. As they try to pass each other, they go into a little lockstep dance, sustaining this effect, which is further underscored when Eve's open eye, looking right into the camera, is framed by Grant's shoulder (a framing that will be repeated later in the passage, and in Eve's Chicago hotel room much later in the film).

Hitchcock presents this routine by cutting back and forth between a two-shot that favors Eve and a two-shot that favors Grant.

In the latter setup, we do not view Grant over Eve's shoulder, as would be conventional. She stands, back to the camera, her blond hair the object of the camera's gaze. Eve is an object of desire for the camera, as for Grant.

Yet in this framing she also appears to preside over this space, possessing it with her gaze, as though hers were more than a merely human power of vision. This framing, which defines Eve as an object of desire, also links her with the divinity that holds sway over this world; it is repeated throughout the film.

Ordinarily, in cutting from two-shot to two-shot in a Hollywood film, screen direction is maintained: If Grant is to the left of Eve in one setup, he will be to the left of Eve in the other. But as Hitchcock composes this present sequence, Grant and Eve alternate places in the frame. Rather, Eve remains centered in the frame throughout, viewed alternately front and back, while Grant's figure jumps from side to side on the screen. Emblematically, Eve is doubled, is projected with opposing aspects. She will be doubled again and again as the film unfolds, most notably in the art auction, when, in another shot/reverse-shot alternation, she will appear both in Grant's frame and in Vandamm's, showing two faces to the camera.

Other symbolically charged ways of framing Eve recur throughout the film. For example, she is repeatedly the object of what I call Hitchcock's "profile shot." In the present passage, a shot from Eve's point of view reveals that she sees the policemen who have entered the car. In a silent and intense exchange of glances, she alerts Grant to the threat and ducks into an empty compartment. Hitchcock then perfectly frames Eve in profile within the frame of the closed compartment door.

Again and again in *North by Northwest*, Eve's image will be contained in a frame. This is one of the film's strategies for developing the theme of Eve's reduction to the status of a commodity bought and sold and the theme of the debasement of art by a world interested only in commerce. But Eve's framing in profile also declares an aspect of her relationship to the camera. In such a frame, she is turned away, indifferent, absorbed in her private world, inaccessible, mysterious.

On a number of occasions, however, the camera *does* penetrate Eve's inner life. For example, during their first embrace on the train – before Grant or the viewer knows of Eve's bond with Vandamm or her role as double agent – Eve and Grant never stop trading wisecracks, and there is no unambiguous sign that Grant is gripped by real feeling or passion. In an interval between jokes, however, we see Eve close her eyes in ecstasy. At this moment, surely, she is imagining herself in the arms of her dream lover. Of course, we do not know what her dream is. Grant jokes that for all she knows, he could be a murderer. Then is Eve ecstatically imagining herself in a murderer's embrace? We know that Grant is innocent of the crime for which he is being pursued, and we later learn that Eve, too, has known all along that he is not a murderer. Then is Eve imagining herself in the arms of an innocent man? Yet when Grant presses her to say what she knows about him, she reels off a telling list of indictments: He is an advertising man who makes words do anything he wants for him, sells people things they do not need, and makes women who do not know him fall in love with him. Has Eve fallen for his "charm" as she once fell for Vandamm's? Or is she immune to his charm, seeing this man who does not believe in marriage and is not honest with honest women as really no different from Vandamm? Does she take pleasure in seducing him, even in condemning him to death, as vengeance on one of the Vandamms of this world? Or does she see in Grant a hero come to rescue her? To send such an innocent to his destruction would mean to preside over the death of her own romantic dream.

When Grant and Eve once more embrace, we assume that she is again in ecstasy. Shockingly, however, like Judy/Madeleine in Scottie's arms at the climax of *Vertigo*, she opens her eyes and looks toward the camera as in her first entrance into the film.

At this moment, Hitchcock calls upon us to acknowledge that we do not really know her, that we have no access to her thoughts and feelings. Momentarily, she averts her eyes as though looking at something offscreen. As if cued by her gaze, Hitchcock cuts to the train corridor, where a porter hands a message to Vandamm. A major movement of the film comes to an end with this stunning revelation that Eve is in league with Vandamm. This is also a revelation that Hitchcock has been deceiving us.

Nowhere is Eve's bond with Hitchcock's camera clearer than in the exquisite passage in which Eve and Grant say good-bye at the train station. Here we witness the first clear sign that Grant is capable of feeling, although it is significant that the camera must look elsewhere than his face for this sign. As he says, "But how will I *find* you ... Please ...," there is a cut to Grant's hand, tenderly grasping Eve's arm, then a cut to Eve, struggling to find words to express her feelings or to avoid saying what she feels she has no right to say. She is locked in what Norman Bates will call a "private trap," from which she is powerless to free herself. At this charged moment, Hitchcock cuts to a shot from Eve's point of view, as she says, in voice-over, "They're coming!"

In this frame, we see no one coming. This view is also a *vision*: Eve's vision of emptiness, solitude, imprisonment, madness. This haunting vision, to which Grant, of course, has no access, crystallizes Eve's understanding that there is no way out.

The poignance of this moment is sustained in the eloquent transition to the following sequence, a slow dissolve from Eve's beautiful face to the flat, featureless prairie, metaphor for her desolate inner landscape. And it is also inscribed in the transition with which the scene of leave-taking is initiated. Cary Grant's riotously funny performance as he attempts to shave his face with Eve's monumentally small razor ends in a tableau: Grant peering at himself in the mirror, contemplating his own performance, as the man at the next sink returns to the serious business of shaving.

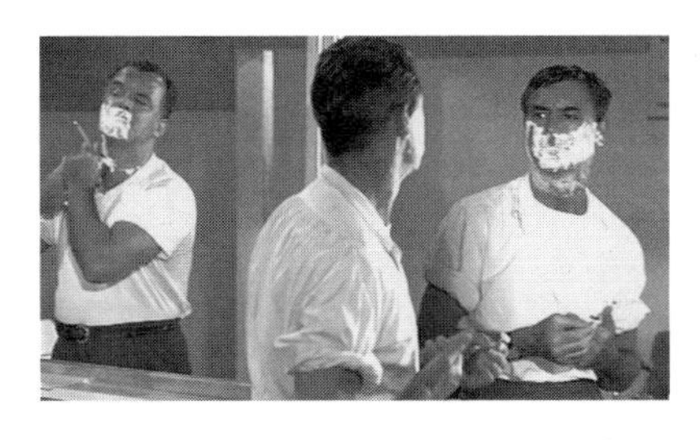

From this image, Hitchcock cuts to Eve framed in the window of a phone booth.

As so often with Hitchcock, the cut is treated as a dissolve, as though the two frames were really superimposed and that superimposition were a medium of significance. In this composite picture, Eve is imprisoned in her own frame, while Grant looks away, fascinated by his own reflection, oblivious equally of Eve's anguish and the precariousness of her survival in this world.

Hitchcock cuts to a frontal shot of Eve, and the camera moves on its own to reveal the sinister Leonard in one of the adjacent phone booths. This movement is just like those in which the camera excludes Grant and sets out on its own to frame someone whose presence is completely unsuspected by him (for example, at the Plaza Hotel when Hitchcock cuts away from Grant and the camera moves on its own to frame the two assassins, and at the General Assembly building when Grant looks away and the camera reframes on its own to disclose the knife-thrower). To invoke these movements in the scene at the train station is to underscore our sense that Eve has a bond with the camera – an attunement, an affinity – that Grant does not possess.

The scene in Eve's Chicago hotel room also manifests this bond. When Grant surprises her by appearing at her door, we are privileged to witness the look of happiness – unseen by Grant – in her eyes. She buries her face in his shoulder, not wanting him to see her emotion. His hands are poised as if undecided between caress and attack, or as if he were afraid of soiling them.

This frozen pose echoes their earlier embrace on the train and manifests Grant's resolution to withhold his humanity, and even his charm, from Eve – perhaps out of fear of being seduced again, perhaps out of horror at the murderousness in his own hands.

Having witnessed Eve's happiness at seeing Grant, we know that she is only acting when she now asks him to leave and claims that this request is motivated by a merely ordinary wish to avoid becoming involved. Eve's real feeling is expressed by the lamps and mirrors that are haunting presences on the screen, by the inclusion in shot after shot of the double bed that invokes her fallenness and longing for marriage, by the wallpaper over the bed, with its images of nature stilled, by the flowers and the paired oriental statuettes beside the television screen, and by the repeated framings of Eve in profile or with her back to the camera.

Perhaps more than any other in the film, this passage invokes the mood of *Vertigo* and declares Eve's power to haunt and be haunted by the camera. Its every framing is attuned to Eve's spiritual desolation, her despair, her renunciation. In this setting, Grant's refusal even to consider forgiving her is deeply disquieting.

The art auction sequence that follows is one of the film's great comic set pieces, providing the perfect music-hall stage for Cary Grant and the perfect occasion for Hitchcock to unveil the full magnitude of his own charm. Yet it is also the scene in which Eve feels most desperately alone. Indeed, it is by turning vengefully against Eve that Grant first gains the upper hand on Vandamm. Hitchcock's camera, however, never loses sight of Eve's silent presence, which makes Grant's turning away from her appear a betrayal. Thus, this passage sets up the scene at the airport, for it plays a crucial role in formulating the question about Grant's character that is answered when the Professor tells him who Eve Kendall is and the camera moves in to frame his face.

The Villains

At the climax of *North by Northwest*, Cary Grant – one hand grasping the ledge for dear life, the other clasping Eve's hand, keeping her from falling to her death – pleads to Leonard – Iago to Vandamm's Othello – for help. After keeping Grant and us in suspense for a long drawn-out moment, Leonard responds by grinding Grant's hand with the toe of his boot. I like to think that Vandamm, were he in Leonard's shoes (or perhaps I should say "shoe"), would relent, however reluctantly. Vandamm is, after all, enough of a sport to accept his final defeat with good cheer, the way Ray Milland does at the end of *Dial "M" for Murder.* But Leonard unmasks himself as an inhuman monster. His death, like that of the Nazi at the end of *Lifeboat*, is cause for celebration. Even Vandamm must be happy to be rid of this serpent.

When Leonard reveals to Vandamm that Eve is a double agent and Vandamm punches him in the jaw, he means to acknowledge Leonard's power, yet deny him his soul. Hitchcock, at this moment, calls upon us to recognize a fundamental difference between the two villains. Yet Vandamm is not endorsed by the film, sympathetic though any character played by James Mason must necessarily be. In Hitchcock's eyes, Vandamm stands guilty of using the powers unjustly given him in a man's world to claim Eve as a possession, although he only charmed her and never won her love. Vandamm attempts to create a world of his own, one he can control without ever having to acknowledge another human being. Hitchcock always pits his powers as author against such hubris. Nonetheless, Hitchcock's sympathies are more with Vandamm than with Leonard. Vandamm denies love out of his longing for love, a longing he is unable to satisfy if only for the unjust accident of fate that brought him into this world as James Mason and not Cary Grant. Leonard, by contrast, stands for the denial of all love, of all human dreams. In this, he is like the Professor, for whom human relationships, like international relationships, are only games.

Spiritually or morally, there is little to choose between Leonard and the Professor. Poetic justice demands a violent death for Leonard, whereas Hitchcock devises a very different punishment for the Professor. The Professor's punishment is to be forced to authorize the shot that kills Leonard. With this shot, the Professor sacrifices the plot he had so laboriously scripted. His elegant plan lies shattered, like the little statue with the microfilm that falls out of its belly. From this wreckage, the marriage of Eve and

Grant, the ending of Hitchcock's film, is born. Hitchcock turns the Professor's own lie ironically against him. The Professor had promised that once Vandamm was out of the country, Grant and Eve would have his blessing. The shot that kills Leonard and ends the Profesor's game is the means by which Hitchcock declares his authority and confers his blessing on this couple. The Professor proves to be only an unwitting agent of the film's author, the decoy of the real "Professor," Hitchcock.

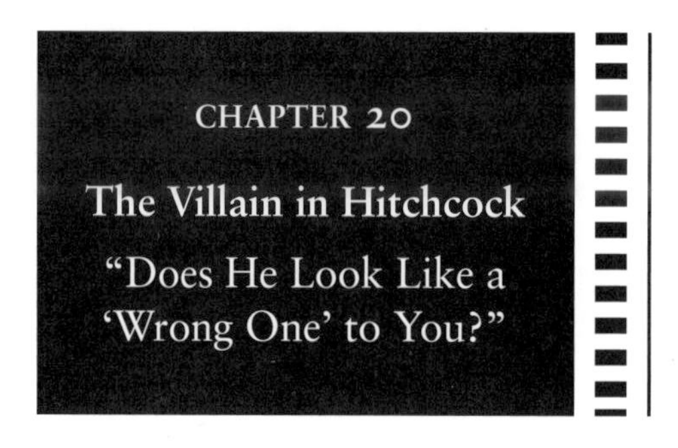

CHAPTER 20

The Villain in Hitchcock

"Does He Look Like a 'Wrong One' to You?"

Within Hitchcock's film, the villain represents a particular character type, or set of types, like the girl-on-the-threshold-of-womanhood (as I call her in *Hitchcock – The Murderous Gaze*) or the policeman who uses his official powers for his own private ends. As I argue in this chapter, the Hitchcock villain, master of the art of murder, is also an allegorical stand-in for Hitchcock himself, the master of "the art of pure cinema."

Numerous observers have noted that Hitchcock's villains are often the most interesting characters in their films – the most charming, and, strangely, even the most sympathetic. Hitchcock often seems to *identify* – however exactly we understand this term – at least as much with his villains as with his protagonists. (As I argue in the chapter "*Vertigo*: The Unknown Woman in Hitchcock," his identification with his female characters is equally strong.)

Most often, Hitchcock's villains possess the *sang-froid* of the gamesman, who treats matters of life and death as merely aesthetic matters. Just think of the moment in *The Thirty-nine Steps* (1935) when the Professor (Geoffrey Tearle), with a grin that invites an appreciative grin in return, holds up his hand, which is missing the top joint of its little finger, to disclose to Richard Hannay (Robert Donat) that he is the diabolical mastermind Hannay has been warned to be on the lookout for.

Villains are not the only Hitchcock characters who cultivate the style of a gamesman/aesthete, however. When at the end of *Frenzy* (1972) the inspector (Alec McCowen) catches the murderer with his pants down, as it were, he speaks the wonderful line, "Mr. Rusk, you're not wearing your tie," with exactly the same understated relish that we hear in James Mason's voice, at the end of *North By Northwest*, when Vandamm, now in custody, says to the Professor (Leo G. Carroll), who has just had a marksman shoot Vandamm's lieutenant, Leonard (Martin Landau), "Not very sporting, using real bullets."

With his Cockney upbringing, Hitchcock no doubt found satisfaction in embracing the honorable, time-honored tradition of associating villainy with the manners of the English upper class. (But compare *Frenzy*, with its unapologetically working-class villain.) The *effeteness* projected by this style also gives many Hitchcock villains a hint of homosexuality. This enhances our sense in a number of Hitchcock films, most notably *Strangers on a Train* (1951), that the bond between protagonist and villain is more passionate than the relationship either one has, or desires, with whatever woman whose affections are ostensibly at issue.

There are other Hitchcock films, however, in which the villain loves a woman, or at least passionately desires her. We see this in *Notorious* (1946), for example; hence Hitchcock's remark to Truffaut that Sebastian (Claude Rains) loves Alicia (Ingrid Bergman) more deeply than Devlin (Cary Grant) does. We see it in *North by Northwest* as well. When Leonard informs Vandamm that Eve Kendall (Eva Marie Saint) has betrayed him, Vandamm loses his composure and slugs Leonard. In *Murder!* (1930), Handel Fane (Esme Percy) momentarily loses control when Sir John (Herbert Marshall) has him audition for the killer's role in his new play. This moment reveals beyond a shadow of a doubt that, despite his disciplined efforts to keep his feelings hidden, this villain is tormented by seething, violent emotions that he struggles to control and mask. Having in mind the evocative question the state trooper asks the used-car dealer in *Psycho* ("Did she look like a wrong one to you?"), I call Hitchcock's tormented villains "Wrong Ones." Other examples that come to mind are the Avenger in *The Lodger* (1926); the "bloke what twitches" (the real murderer whom the falsely accused protagonist tries to track down) in *Young and Innocent* (1937); Uncle Charles (Joseph Cotten) in *Shadow of a Doubt* (1943); Bruno (Robert Walker) in *Strangers on a Train*; and, most famously, Norman Bates (Anthony Perkins) in *Psycho* (1960).

In *The Thirty-nine Steps*, we never see a crack in the villain's gamesman/aesthete facade that is wide enough to reveal what inner turmoil, if any, lies beneath. The only time the Professor drops his facade at all, and

then only for an instant, occurs when there is a knock on the door at just the moment he is waiting to see how Hannay will react to his theatrical masterstroke of unmasking himself by showing his hand. As the villainous Professor goes to unlock the door, he stops grinning and casts Hannay a look of frustration, as if he expects his intended victim to share his impatience with this untimely interruption.

It is the Professor's wife (Helen Haye), who tersely reminds him that lunch is ready. Her air of disapproval underscores our sense that the Professor resents her intrusion and expects Hannay to share his attitude. The look he casts Hannay invites him to acknowledge that he and the Professor are members of an exclusive club, as it were – a club that excludes this woman, perhaps all women. By presenting this look, is Hitchcock inviting us to imagine that the Professor's work as a spy is his one area of self-assertion in a sexless marriage, as if his traitorous schemes were displacements of a wish to murder his wife, perhaps a wish to do violence to all women. Such an interpretation, which would make him a descendant of the Avenger in *The Lodger*, remains speculative at best, however, precisely because we never see the Professor's *sang-froid* decisively break down. Rather, Hitchcock chooses to leave unresolved whether the Professor is really a "Wrong One" tormented by emotions he struggles to control or mask, or a heartless monster like the shipwrecked Nazi (Walter Slezak) in *Lifeboat* (1944) or Eric Mathis (Ivan Triesault), the most murderous of the Nazi conspirators in *Notorious*, who quite simply have no feelings to hurt.

Hitchcock's villains – whether they are tormented "Wrong Ones" or heartless Nazi types – are not the only characters in his films who perform acts of cruelty, of course. No one could be crueler than the detectives who interrogate Manny (Henry Fonda) early in *The Wrong Man* (1956). (When one of the detectives says to Manny, "This looks bad for you, Manny, it really looks bad for you," he is being so cruel, and his cruelty is so gratuitous, that in a perverse way I have always found this line to be one of the most hilarious in all of Hitchcock.) When the surviving Americans in *Lifeboat* realize that they have let the villainous Nazi outsmart them, they exact cruel vengeance, brutally beating the German before tossing him overboard to his death. Even Hitchcock's "heroes" can be as cruel as villains. In *Rear Window* (1954), for example, there is an unmistakable element of cruelty in the relentless efforts of Jeff (James Stewart) to prove that Lars Thorwald

(Raymond Burr) murdered his wife. (Jeff seems to feel no human sympathy for the dead woman or for the desperation that may have driven Thorwald to commit the crime.) In *Notorious*, Cary Grant is crueler to Ingrid Bergman than Claude Rains, the villain, ever dreams of being, and Grant is no less cruel to Eva Marie Saint in *North By Northwest*, especially in the celebrated art auction sequence. In *Vertigo*, Scottie is as cruel to Midge (Barbara Bel Geddes) as he is to Judy ("It can't matter to you," indeed!).

It is not a capacity for cruelty, then, that distinguishes Hitchcock's villains from his other characters – or from Hitchcock himself. In *Sabotage* (1936), Hitchcock cruelly traps Sylvia Sidney, the film's protagonist, in a marriage as frightful as Margaret's in *The Thirty-nine Steps*. Equally cruelly, he calls upon her to affirm her innocence by killing her husband, the film's villain, and plays for suspense – for kicks we might say – the violent death of her likable young brother, not to mention his cute puppy. *Sabotage* compels us to recognize that Hitchcock's capacity for cruelty – to his characters, to us – equals that of his villains.

When the Professor holds up his hand and Hitchcock cuts to a close shot from Hannay's point of view, the Professor presents to Hannay a view meant to shock and rivet him. At the same time, Hitchcock presents to us a view meant to shock and rivet us.

When describing what happens in a film, I wrote in *The Murderous Gaze* (1982, p. 144), "we frequently find ourselves identifying with the camera, saying, for example, 'Now we see. . . .' But the agency that presents us with *this* view cannot be thought of as "we." The view imposes itself on us, disrupting and compelling our attention. It is Hitchcock, as it were, showing us his hand." That Hitchcock's art has a murderous aspect is a – or the – quintessential Hitchcockian idea. *Sabotage* suggests specifically that Hitchcock's art is the murderous work of a saboteur – in today's parlance, a terrorist. Is Hitchcock, then, in our President's immortal phrase, an *evil doer*?

In *The Birds* (1963), a mother (Doreen Lang) accuses Melanie (Tippi Hedren) of causing the bird attacks. In a shot from Hedren's perspective, the hysterical woman screams right into the camera (symbolically, right at us, right at Hitchcock), "I think you're *evil*!"

I stand to be corrected, but this is the only occasion I can think of when a Hitchcock character utters the word "evil." One reason the moment is so

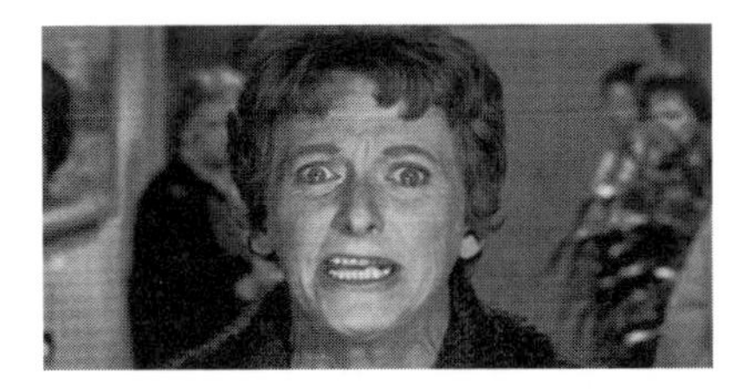

startling is that evil is a concept that seems alien to the Hitchcock worldview. In nineteenth-century theatrical melodramas, Peter Brooks[1] argues in his seminal work *The Melodramatic Imagination,* villains are exemplars of pure evil, understood as an occult, supernatural force in eternal opposition to Good (likewise an occult, supernatural force). In effect, Brooks argues, the villain in a nineteenth-century theatrical melodrama is an agent of the Devil. By contrast, the villain in a Hitchcock film is an agent of the film's author, a stand-in for Hitchcock himself. Hence it is an ironic moment when, in *Blackmail* (1929), the Artist (Cyril Ritchard), having lured Anny Ondra up to his atelier, waits for her to finish dressing, and Hitchcock contrives for there to be a shadow on Ritchard's face that momentarily makes him appear to have the curlicue mustache of a stock stage villain.

Vertigo demonstrates with exceptional clarity that the Hitchcock villain is an agent of the film's author, not an agent of the Devil, like the villain in a nineteenth-century theatrical melodrama. Gavin Elster is one of Hitchcock's least memorable villains. Hitchcock has little interest in him as a *character*. Yet the film's entire plot hinges on Elster's plot, which diabolically inflicts on Scottie the suffering of Job by cruelly transforming his darkest nightmare into reality. What motivates Elster? Profit? A wish to carry out a perfect murder, like the John Dall character in *Rope* (1948)? I cannot avoid the sense that Elster's motivation cannot completely be accounted for in such ways, as if he exists for no purpose other than to enable Hitchcock's masterpiece to be created.

In theatrical melodramas of the nineteenth-century, as Brooks understands them, the nightmare struggle for the liberation of virtue is won when goodness is publicly recognized in a "movement of astonishment," and evil – with its own lesser power to astonish – is driven out. They are dramas of recognition in which acts that Brooks calls "self-nomination"

[1] Peter Brooks, *The Melodramatic Imagination: Balzac, Henry James, Melodrama and the Mode of Excess* (New Haven, CT: Yale University Press, 1976).

play an essential role. "The villain at some point always bursts forth in a statement of his evil nature and intentions" (Brooks, 1976, p. 37), just as the heroine announces her moral purity. In films, however, characters do not have the authority to "nominate" themselves, to declare their moral identity, for they are always also the camera's subjects. As such, they are human beings, mortal creatures of flesh and blood, not agents of occult, supernatural forces. They do not, and cannot, know themselves the way the camera enables us to know them.

When Professor Jordan holds up his hand in *The Thirty-nine Steps*, the view Hitchcock presents to us matches the view the Professor presents to Hannay. The shot of Jordan's hand, viewed from Hannay's perspective, links Hitchcock with the villain (both are authors of views). It also links us with the villain's intended victim (Hannay is a viewer, just as we are). Hitchcock has set a diabolical trap for us, just as the Professor has set a trap for Hannay. And at the same moment Jordan unmasks himself to Hannay, Hitchcock unmasks himself to us. Indeed, Hitchcock's gesture not only declares its affinity with Jordan's, it trumps it. Through the gesture of showing his hand, Jordan opens Hannay's eyes to the fact that he has been the Professor's unwitting pawn. However, by presenting us with a view that *contains* the view Jordan presents to Hannay, Hitchcock opens our eyes to the fact that Jordan is *his* unwitting pawn, as surely as Hannay is. Jordan, too, is subject to Hitchcock's camera. Professor Jordan claims authorship of this moment, but like Hannay he is trapped within a world whose real author is Hitchcock.

In passages such as this, Hitchcock asserts an affinity between the villain's gesture and a gesture of the camera. In other passages, he has the camera assume the villain's point of view, or frames the villain staring into the depths of the frame in a way that makes of him a veritable stand-in for the camera. In these cases, the camera's passive aspect, not its agency, is associated with villainy. Hence they are akin to the Hitchcock passages that portray guilty acts of viewing. When Norman Bates views Marion Crane (Janet Leigh) through his secret peephole, this is not an example of a villain's self-nomination, as in theatrical melodramas. Unbeknownst to him, this villain is "nominated" by the camera, which links his villainy to his – and our – act of viewing.

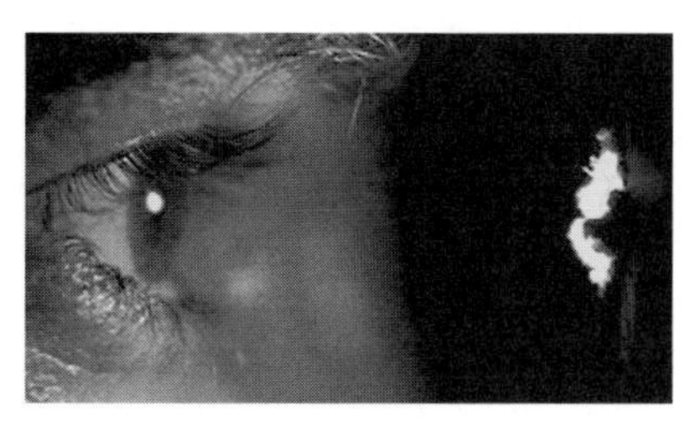

Another strategy Hitchcock uses to declare the camera's villainous aspect is exemplified by the ending of *Psycho*. When Norman Bates (Anthony

Perkins) raises his gaze directly to the camera and grins, he presents himself to be viewed.

Like the Professor when he shows his hand, he authors a view. But the view whose authorship Norman is claiming is a view *of him*. And it is presented *to us*. That is, it is a view framed by Hitchcock's camera. Presenting this view is at once a gesture performed by the camera and a gesture performed by the camera's subject. Their gestures are not only linked; they are one and the same. At this moment, Hitchcock and Norman Bates – or should we say "Hitchcock and Anthony Perkins"? – appear to be conspirators of such intimate complicity that a distinction can hardly be drawn between them. In effect, the film's author has become one with his camera's subject. As I put it in the chapter "Virtue and Villainy in the Face of the Camera," "Norman/Perkins has become a mask for Hitchcock, one of Hitchcock's stuffed birds. In turn, the grinning Norman/Perkins has been impressed indelibly on our idea of who Hitchcock is."

I would like to consider one last strategy Hitchcock uses to declare the camera's murderous aspect. It is exemplified by the passage late in *The Lodger* in which the lodger (Ivor Novello) looks directly at the camera as if he were a villain in complicity with it. The next shot, from his point of view, retroactively places him in the audience at Daisy's fashion show.

For a moment, we are relieved. This man no longer seems to be a villain, but only an innocent spectator who takes pleasure in viewing Daisy, exactly as we take pleasure in viewing her (and in viewing him viewing her). Then it strikes us that perhaps this viewer is not innocent after all. Perhaps no viewer is.

This sequence initially seems to unmask the lodger as a villain. Then it seems to assert his innocence. Ultimately it turns out to be ambiguous. The camera does not reveal him to be guilty. Nor does it reveal him to be innocent. Rather, we are compelled to recognize that we do not know whether his intentions are villainous. For all we know, Hitchcock is saying, this subject of the camera – any subject of the camera? – may have murderous intentions. In the face of the camera, the lodger is a flesh-and-blood human being, as we are, not an agent of an occult, supernatural force. But to be human is to be capable of villainy.

The grueling sequence in *Frenzy* (1972) in which Rusk (Barry Foster) rapes and murders Brenda Blaney (Barbara Leigh-Hunt), the protagonist's ex-wife, is in a sense the inverse of the *Lodger* passage. When Rusk visits Brenda in her office – she runs a matrimonial agency – she coldly informs him, on the basis of the information in his file, that her agency cannot, or will not, service a man with his repulsive sexual appetites. Finally he discloses to her that he does not want her to fix him up with someone. He wants *her*. She is "his type of woman." Repelled by him, she becomes more and more frightened as he seems increasingly to lose control. Soon he begins to rape her. When he comes too quickly, he seems so possessed by frustration and rage that his voice becomes strangely slurred, as if he were in the grip of an epileptic fit, and (to borrow a phrase from Norman Bates) he is gradually transformed into a "raving thing." At a certain point, Brenda knows that he is going to strangle her. But she believes that her killer is a pathetic, sick man driven mad by his sexual impotence. We believe this, too, until Rusk goes over to the dead woman's desk and stands there for a moment with his back to the camera. Still turned away from the camera, he picks up a half-eaten apple and takes a hearty bite. Then he puts the remainder in his pocket and, with a jaunty bounce to his step, walks coolly out of the office. From the moment he bites the apple, he no longer seems like a tormented "Wrong One." Now he has the insouciant air of one of those heartless Hitchcock villains who has no regard for human frailties – not an Adam, but a Serpent. Which is his true face, then? Which is a mask? We cannot know the answer to this question because Hitchcock's camera never unmasks Rusk. At the moment he bites into the apple, his face is hidden from the camera, or, rather, the camera hides his face from us.

By contrast, when Norman Bates – or Anthony Perkins – fixes the camera in his gaze (even as he is fixed in the camera's gaze, as the camera's subjects always are), a heartless villain appears to be unmasking himself, with the camera's complicity. But then "mother's" mummified face is momentarily superimposed over (surfaces from within?) this man's living face. Whom or

what do we take the figure in this frame to be? Male or female? Alive or dead? Son or mother? Murderer or victim? Character or actor? Creation or creator?

In *Hitchcock – The Murderous Gaze* (1982, p. 341). I interpret this composite figure, at once alive and possessed by death, as emblematic of the condition of all human beings on film:

> The camera fixes its human subjects, possesses their life. They are reborn on the screen, creatures of the film's author and of ourselves. But life is not fully breathed back into them. They are immortal but they are always already dead. The beings projected on the screen are condemned to a condition of death-in-life that may be a dream of triumphing over death, holding death forever at bay. But... the world of a film is not a private island where we may escape the conditions of our existence. At the heart of every film is a truth we already know: we have been born into the world and we are fated to die.

Because villains in theatrical melodramas are exemplars of pure evil, their moral identities are fixed. That is why they are capable of knowing, and "nominating," themselves. Human beings in the world do not possess such powers. Because we are always in the process of becoming, our moral identities are never fixed. Creatures of flesh and blood, we never fully know ourselves. The subjects of the camera are human beings in the world. They are mysteries to themselves, as we are. (It is no accident that film and psychoanalysis grew up together.) That is why villains in films cannot nominate themselves. The ending of *Psycho* is the exception that proves this rule. Only the camera can nominate a villain, and it cannot do so without nominating itself. When human beings perform villainous acts in films, as they often do, the camera is implicated – the film's author is implicated, we are implicated – in their villainy. No filmmaker has had a deeper understanding than Hitchcock of these conditions of the medium of film. His cinema is a sustained, profound meditation on their implications.

CHAPTER 21

Thoughts on Hitchcock's Authorship

When I was asked to contribute an essay to an event celebrating the centennial of Alfred Hitchcock's birth, I expected, and wished, to write something in a celebratory mood. The fact that we continue to recognize Hitchcock's achievements as a filmmaker a hundred years after his birth is itself something to celebrate. The present piece has turned out to be a somber one. For this, I blame Gus Van Sant, who in any case deserves all the blame anyone might heap on him for making his dreadful version of *Psycho*. Van Sant's actors seem to be going through the motions, to be following a bad script, to be reading lines that do not even seem to have been written for them. An apologist for the postmodern might praise Van Sant for undermining the "realism" of the original. But aren't we all tired of listening to such nonsense? Hitchcock proudly regarded *Psycho* as his most powerful demonstration of "the art of pure cinema," his gift (as he put it to Truffaut) to the filmmakers among his viewers. How could a director, especially one not devoid of talent, make a virtual shot-by-shot copy of *Psycho* that is interesting only for being so utterly uninteresting? In *Hitchcock – The Murderous Gaze*, I suggested that *Psycho* declared the death of the art of film as Hitchcock knew it and prophesied the emergence of different, perhaps freer, forms of cinema. The more I dwell on Van Sant's *Psycho*, the more it can seem that cinema itself has run its course, that the art of film is declaring bankruptcy.

Van Sant's film reminds us – as if we needed reminding – that we are to take with a grain of salt Hitchcock's remarks to the effect that his creative work was finished before filming began and his remarks to the effect that actors are cattle. It turns out – as if anyone could really have doubted it – that it makes all the difference in the world whether Marion Crane is Janet Leigh or Anne Heche, whether Norman Bates is Anthony Perkins or Vince Vaughn. But it already made a great difference to Hitchcock, when he was storyboarding his scripts, composing his films shot by shot, imagining the world on film before production began, who were to be the inhabitants of that world.

In *Hitchcock – The Murderous Gaze* I wrote somewhat unappreciatively of Janet Leigh as being in Hitchcock's eyes (and mine) an "ordinary bourgeoise."[1] Viewing the hapless Anne Heche in Janet Leigh's place, dressed like a clueless nitwit and flailing away in herky-jerky, birdlike movements, helps me to appreciate an important quality Janet Leigh possesses in *Psycho*, a calmness or poise that we might think of as a kind of passivity. This unanxious quality comes out strongly in the shots of her, wide-eyed, driving through the gathering darkness and the rain before arriving at the Bates Motel. Janet Leigh's calm, measured movements manifest themselves as an attunement to, or affinity with, Hitchcock's camera. For they match the camera's equally calm, measured movements (for example, when it patiently tracks Marion's every move as she approaches her fateful decision to steal the money). (In *The Wrong Man*, perhaps more than any other Hitchcock film, the camera's movements, as well as the cuts from shot to shot, consistently manifest this unanxious quality. More and more, it might be noted, I have come to regard *The Wrong Man* as one of Hitchcock's greatest achievements.) Marion's calmness, her passivity, is perhaps what makes Norman, with whom the camera identifies in a very different way, feel so superior to her. But perhaps it is also what makes her so threatening to him, as if he could already imagine that she would "look well, stuffed."

Vince Vaughn's nervous giggles give away from the outset that he is missing a screw or two. Combined with the fact that he is so hulking and physically imposing, his obvious weirdness makes it inconceivable that any woman worth caring about would willingly accept his invitation to dine with him. These qualities also make it impossible for us to view him, in retrospect, as a mastermind who may be capable of framing his own mother for the perfect murder he has himself committed. Vaughn lacks Tony Perkins's trademark boy-next-door quality, so we are precluded from imagining, as we view him, that behind the mask of the familiar, the ordinary, there is a being who is not what he seems, one of Hitchcock's sportsmen/artists, a stand-in for Hitchcock himself.

In Hitchcock's films, the figure of the author is an important – perhaps the most important – character. One cannot even accurately relate the story of a Hitchcock film without taking into account the author, or his instrument, the camera. With a few pointless exceptions (Van Sant's Arbogast is reduced to saying "If it doesn't jell, it isn't Jell-O," rather than the immortal line – it's in the pantheon with Emma's "It's the paprika makes it pink" in *Shadow of a Doubt* – "If it doesn't jell, it isn't aspic"; the state trooper's ominously

[1] William Rothman, *Hitchcock – The Murderous Gaze* (Cambridge, MA: Harvard University Press, 1982), p. 253.

Hitchcockian line "Did she look like a wrong one to you?" is reduced to the bland "Did she look like a bad one to you?") Van Sant's characters speak the same lines as the characters in Hitchcock's film. Often they mimic their expressions and gestures, too, although there are moments at which they interpolate mannerisms of their own (Vince Vaughn's nervous giggles and screen-shaking masturbating, Anne Heche's herky-jerky movements). Most of the gestures of Hitchcock's camera, however, Van Sant copies without alteration. Or does he? What counts as the *same* gesture of the camera? Indeed, what makes a movement of the camera, or a cut from shot to shot, something that counts as a gesture at all? For a shot cannot be defined purely in terms of formal elements such as lighting or composition or camera angle or camera distance. Indeed, a shot's "form" cannot be separated from its "content," the particular things and people, each with distinctive features and qualities, contained within its frame.

It is a central claim of *Hitchcock – The Murderous Gaze* that Hitchcock's films have a *philosophical* dimension. "Within the world of a Hitchcock film, the nature and relationships of love, murder, sexuality, marriage, and theater are at issue; these are among Hitchcock's constant themes. His treatment of these themes, however, and his understanding of the reasons film keeps returning to them, cannot be separated form his constant concern with the nature of the camera, the act of viewing a film, and filmmaking as a calling."[2] In demonstrating something about the "art of pure cinema," as Hitchcock liked to call it, Hitchcock's films are asserting, *declaring*, something about themselves, something about their medium.

In Hitchcock's films the camera performs gestures that have the force of claims, demonstrations, arguments. What a given gesture declares, I argue in *Hitchcock – The Murderous Gaze*, is not an unambiguous answer to the question of what film is. For at the heart of Hitchcock's artistic vision is a sense of film's possessing what seem to be incompatible aspects, irreconcilable tensions, or conflicts, that crystallize, or crystallize in, an awesome sense of mystery. Understanding, in Hitchcock's films, means acknowledging the limits of understanding, understanding that there is something all-important – something wonderful? something frightful? – that we cannot understand. Rose, in *The Wrong Man*, understands, when she suddenly breaks into uncontrollable laughter, that Manny, thinking he understands, doesn't really get it at all. And Hitchcock reserves some of his most virtuoso camera gestures for summing up reality's unfathomability, to which, in his view, the medium of film bears a special affinity.

I am thinking, for example, of the unforgettable moment in *Vertigo* in which the Kim Novak character (Judy? Madeleine? Carlotta?) says, "Can't

[2] Ibid., p. 7.

you see," and Stewart finally *does* see. This moment at which he overcomes his blindness is summed up in an extraordinary gesture of the camera, a slow dissolve that marks the man looking as himself framed, even as the woman he is viewing frames a woman in her view, a woman who is already framed in a portrait, a woman who is and is not the woman who is looking.

We can turn to an equally profound and moving moment in *The Wrong Man* and find a closely related gesture, as Hitchcock cuts from Manny's mother, praying, to Manny, who seems to be praying, too, then to a shot in which, as the camera moves in, Manny is a shadow in the left foreground, and a painting of Jesus is in the right background.

This charged framing/camera movement is followed by the virtuoso passage in which Hitchcock effects an elegiacally slow dissolve from a frontal shot of Manny's face to the real robber, who walks toward the camera until the two faces are perfectly superimposed.

We find a comparable gesture as far back in Hitchcock's work as *The Lodger*.

We can find such gestures in *Psycho*, too. First, in the framing of Norman Bates, just before he moves the painting to disclose the fatal peephole.

We find it again in the slow dissolve between the mummified Mrs. Bates's face, with its chilling grin of recognition, and the facade of the courthouse.

The dissolve momentarily superimposes Mrs. Bates's empty eye sockets over pillars that present a perfect instance of what in *Hitchcock – The Murderous Gaze* I identify as Hitchcock's "////" motif, one of a set of motifs or signs or symbols – they include what I call "curtain raisings"; "eclipses"; "tunnel shots"; white flashes; frames-within-frames; profile shots; symbolically charged objects (e.g., lamps, staircases, birds); symbolically charged colors (red, white, blue-green, brown) – that recur, at critical moments, in every Hitchcock film.

As I demonstrate in *Hitchcock – The Murderous Gaze*, the "////" sign functions, at one level, as an invocation of prison bars, reminding us that the creatures who dwell in the world on film are, within their world, imprisoned. But they are also imprisoned in another sense, unable to cross the barrier that separates them from us, trapped within the world of the film, a world presided over by the author, Hitchcock. We, too, are barred from crossing that barrier; there are limits to our access to the film's world. Hence the "////" sign also invokes the screen on which all that we view is projected, the barrier-that-is-not-really-a barrier that is the film frame.

Van Sant includes this dissolve in his version. Or does he? Is it the "same" dissolve as Hitchcock's? For one thing, in recreating Hitchcock's Mrs. Bates, Van Sant gives her wild long hair, like an unkempt hippie's, rather than the "original" hair style, in which the mummy's hair is curled in a tight bun with the spiraling twist she shares, uncannily, with Madeleine and Carlotta in *Vertigo*. The spirits of those ghostly Hitchcock women do not possess Van Sant's mummy, so his dissolve is from the outset devoid of the mystery Hitchcock invests in his. And the new courthouse lacks the old one's columns, hence there is no "////" in Van Sant's second shot. The superimposition of one shot stripped of its original significance over another shot likewise devoid of significance turns Hitchcock's complex and profound gesture not

into a gesture of Van Sant's own, however altered or diminished in meaning and expressiveness that gesture may be: Rather, Van Sant's dissolve is not meaningful or expressive, it does not have the force of a gesture at all.

What is missing at this moment is missing from every moment of Van Sant's film. Behind the surface of Hitchcock's films, or, rather, on the surface but "hidden" by being in plain view, are those motifs or signs or symbols, of which the "////" sign is one, whose presence participates crucially in the films's philosophical meditations. At another level, each sign, when it appears in a Hitchcock film, echoes other appearances of the sign in Hitchcock's work. At that level, these Hitchcockian signs, taken together, simply signify that these are Hitchcock films. They function as Hitchcock's signatures, like his name in the credits or his cameo walk-ons.

Any director can make a cameo appearance in his or her films, of course, but only in a Hitchcock film can it be Hitchcock who appears in such a cameo. Only in a Hitchcock film can the cameo serve as Hitchcock's signature. And any director can incorporate any of Hitchcock's signature motifs and use it for its metaphorical or symbolic meaning. I think of a shot in *The Thirty-nine Steps*, for example, in which Hitchcock frames Hannay, the suspicious crofter, and Margaret, the crofter's wife, through the slats of a chair at just the moment at which Hannay's fate seems to be sealed, and what seems a very similar shot in John Stahl's *Imitation of Life*, which frames Louise Beavers through the vertical bars of a staircase, suggesting that to be a black woman in America is to be imprisoned.

The shot in *Imitation of Life* does not – cannot – mean all that the Hitchcock shot means. It does not – cannot – signify Hitchcock's authorship. Thus the entire panoply of Hitchcockian signatures marks a private, or personal, dimension to Hitchcock's films, declaring that they are his creations, not anyone else's.

"Part of *Psycho*'s myth," I wrote in *Hitchcock – The Murderous Gaze*, "is that there is no world outside its own, that we are fated to be born, live our alienated lives, and die in the very world in which Norman Bates also dwells."[3] Hitchcock's famous shower murder sequence, for example, envisions the breaching of the movie screen barrier. When (through the simultaneous movement of Marian and the camera) the frame-within-the-frame of the featureless, translucent shower curtain comes to engulf the frame, it is as if nothing separates this curtain from the screen on which this view is projected.

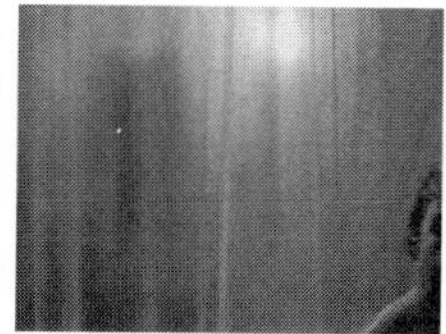
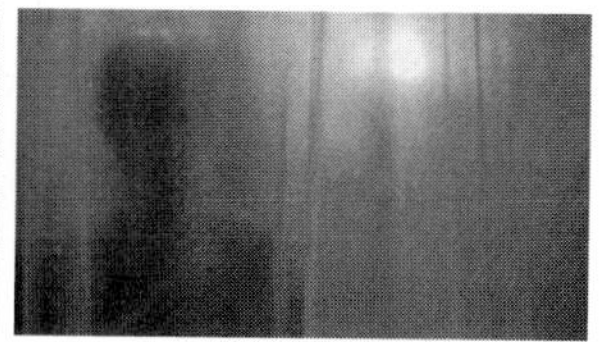

In this shower curtain, the camera's gesture declares, our world and the world of *Psycho* magically come together. Or this gesture declares that there has never been a real barrier separating them. Thus when Marion Crane's killer theatrically pulls the shower curtain open, it is as if the torn curtain reveals that we, like Marion, are confronting the imminent prospect of our own murder.

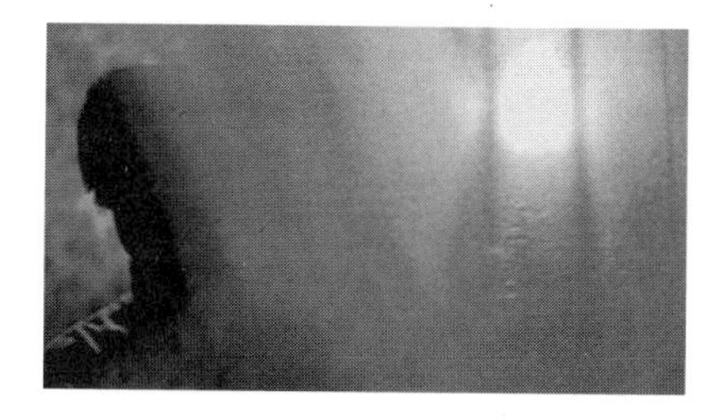

Again, Van Sant blows it. Unwilling to leave well enough alone, he provides a patterned shower curtain, not a featureless one, so he misses

[3] Ibid., p. 255.

Hitchcock's gesture of effectively merging the shower curtain with the movie screen.

To view the world on film as a "private island" (to use Marion's term) wherein we can escape the real conditions of our existence is to make the world on film a self-contained universe. This is to make the real world–the world into which we have been born, the world in which we are fated to die – only an image, not the real world at all. It is to be condemned to a condition of death-in-life, as if we, too, were shadows on a screen, not human beings of flesh and blood. *Psycho* is an allegory about the death of the art of film as Hitchcock has known and mastered it – the art of creating self-contained universes on film, private islands, to which viewers can imagine themselves escaping from the real conditions of their existence. "Marion Crane's dead eye and Norman/mother's final grin prophesy the end of the era of film whose achievement *Psycho* also sums up, and the death of the Hitchcock film," I wrote in *Hitchcock – The Murderous Gaze*. "In *Psycho*, Hitchcock's camera singles out a human subject *as if for the last time*, then presides over her murder. Marion Crane's death in the shower, mythically, is also our death – the death of the movie viewer – and Hitchcock's death."[4] In *Psycho*, Hitchcock envisions, in the medium of film, that the movie screen has magically been breached. Like Norman Bates, Hitchcock envisions no possibility of liberation. In *Psycho*, the breaching of the movie screen barrier does not mean freedom. It means death. That is, it changes nothing, for we are already fated to die. In Hitchcock's dark vision, we *are* condemned to a condition of death-in-life. We are born and die in our "private traps," as Norman puts it. We scratch and claw but never budge an inch.

Already when I was writing *Hitchcock – The Murderous Gaze*, and increasingly in the years since its publication in 1982, it was the dominant view within film study – as within academic criticism in general – that the concept of authorship had been discredited on theoretical grounds. No writing on Hitchcock goes as far as *Hitchcock – The Murderous Gaze* in keeping faith with the idea that he is an "*auteur.*" – Yet I still believe in the book, and would scarcely change a word of it if I were publishing it for the first time today.

[4] Ibid.

Hitchcock – The Murderous Gaze is an "auteurist" study. But it is also a study of the *conditions* of authorship in the medium of film. Hence it is a study as well of the ontology of film. A premise and conclusion of my book is that Hitchcock's films have a philosophical dimension, as I have suggested. They are thinking seriously about their medium, thinking seriously about themselves, thinking seriously about such matters as the nature and relationships of love, murder, sexuality, marriage, and theater. Thus the book rejects and contests the view, which has long held the status of a dogma within the field of film study but that I am proud to say I have always held in contempt, that some theory or other enables us to rest assured that films *cannot possibly* be thinking, that we know films to be in the repressive grip of ideology, a grip only theory can break.

That Hitchcock's films are philosophically serious is a view I share with Slavoj Zizek, for example, who recognizes in them an affinity with the Lacanian theoretical framework his own writing embraces.[5] Zizek views Hitchcock, in effect, *as* a Lacanian. There are Derrideans, too, who have found that Hitchcock's films see eye to eye with them, philosophically. The theory and practice of philosophy that *Hitchcock – The Murderous Gaze* aligns itself with is worked out most fully in the writings of Stanley Cavell. The American movie genres Cavell champions in his indispensable books *Pursuits of Happiness* and *Contesting Tears*, the genres he calls "the remarriage comedy" and "the melodrama of the unknown woman," reveal the "classical" Hollywood cinema to be committed to an Emersonian philosophical project that affirms the reality of human freedom, affirms the possibility, and the necessity, of radical change.[6] Cavell, too, is committed to this project, and in this he understands himself to be representative of the films' audience. However, the despairing Hitchcock who emerges in the pages of *Hitchcock–The Murderous Gaze*, it seems, is anything but an Emersonian.

Hitchcock was a master – some would say *the* master – of the "art of pure cinema." However, the film medium also mastered him, subjected him to an isolation so extreme as to partake of madness, allowed him no escape. One aspect of Hitchcock's work is its declaration of conditions that must be satisfied by anyone who would master this medium. Another is its confession that Hitchcock personally embraced those conditions when he dedicated his life to the films that bear his signatures, the films in which he

[5] Slavoj Zizek, *Everything You Always Wanted to Know About Lacan (But Were Afraid to Ask Hitchcock)* (London and New York: Verso, 1992).

[6] Stanley Cavell, *Pursuits of Happiness: The Hollywood Comedy of Remarriage* (Cambridge, MA: Harvard University Press, 1981); *Contesting Tears: The Hollywood Melodrama of the Unknown Woman* (Chicago and London: University of Chicago Press, 1996).

found his voice. His life's blood is on every frame of his films, as I rather melodramatically put it in *Hitchcock – The Murderous Gaze*.

In Hitchcock's dark vision, our world offers no real possibility of transcendence. Only in art – the art of cinema, perhaps the art of murder – can purity be glimpsed. At one level, Hitchcock's films expose the monstrous perversity of the artist's quest for a purity or perfection that human beings are incapable of living in the world. (*Rear Window* may be a near-perfect work of art, but in its purity it is also "cold and lonely," like the perfect emerald Uncle Charles gives Charlie in *Shadow of a Doubt*.) But Hitchcock's films are also products of such a quest. Insofar as they aspire to an inhuman perfection, they perversely go against the grain of the American genres Cavell studies. And they perversely go against the grain of film itself, as Cavell characterizes it in *The World Viewed*. (If the world is impure, how can a film, whose views are of the world, be pure?)

Unlike such American genres as the remarriage comedy or the melodrama of the unknown woman, I argue in "*Vertigo*: The Unknown Woman in Hitchcock" that the "Hitchcock thriller," as we might call it, is a genre whose features cannot be defined, whose underlying myth cannot even be characterized, apart from relating the role the figure of the author plays within it.[7] Without the villainous Gavin Elster, hence without a Judy implicated in his evil design, *Vertigo* might have been an "unknown-woman" melodrama, not a Hitchcock thriller. For in a sense, it is the Gavin Elster in Hitchcock who declares himself in the signature gestures of the camera through which Hitchcock claims his authorship:

> In the genres Cavell studies, the camera is a machine that transfigures human subjects independently of human intentions. In the Hitchcock thriller, as *Psycho* explicitly declares, the camera is an instrument of taxidermy, not transfiguration: The camera does violence to its subjects, fixes them, and breathes back only the illusion of life into these ghosts. (The camera is an instrument of enlightenment as well for Hitchcock, although its truths are also blinding.) It is this murderous camera, mysteriously attuned to the unknownness of women, that is the instrument of authorship in the Hitchcock thriller, the truest expression of who Hitchcock is.[8]

All the Hitchcockian signatures that *Hitchcock – The Murderous Gaze* identifies – the curtain raisings, eclipses, white flashes, frames-within-frames, profile shots, symbolically charged objects, and so on – that mark

[7] William Rothman, "*Vertigo*: The Unknown Woman in Hitchcock," in *Images in Our Souls: Cavell, Psychoanalysis and Cinema*, Joseph H. Smith and William Kerrigan, eds. (Forum for Psychiatry and the Humanities, Volume 10 (Baltimore: Johns Hopkins University Press, 1987) and in William Rothman, *The "I" of the Camera: Essays in Film Criticism, History and Aesthetics* (New York and Cambridge, England: Cambridge University Press, 1989), pp. 152–73.

[8] *The "I" of the Camera*, p. 172.

The Lodger and every Hitchcock film to follow thus also exclude *Vertigo* from the melodrama of the unknown woman. Hitchcock's signature gestures declare his unwillingness or inability ever to forsake his mark, to absorb himself unconditionally in his characters, to leave his own story untold. But they also reveal Hitchcock's affinity, his *identification*, with the unknown woman in *Vertigo* who desperately longs for existence. As I put it in "*Vertigo*: The Unknown Woman in Hitchcock," "Hitchcock never gets beyond his own case, his own longing for acknowledgment. Hitchcock *is* the unknown woman, and this, too, separates *Vertigo* from Cavell's genre."[9]

From a Cavellian perspective, remarriage comedies and melodramas of the unknown woman, which insist on the finiteness of people and things in the world (even as they insist on the unity of the world as a whole, on the fact that the world *is* a whole), affirm truths about the world, and about film, that Hitchcock's art would deny. Yet it is Hitchcock's wish to turn film against its own nature, as Cavell might put it, combined with the medium's stubborn resistance, that creates the tension specific to his films, a tension that enables them to push his view of the medium to its limits. Then perhaps it is my wish, in finding my own philosophical voice by writing about Hitchcock's films, to turn my philosophical way of thinking, aligned with Cavell's, against its own nature, combined with philosophy's stubborn resistance, that creates the tension specific to *Hitchcock – The Murderous Gaze*, a tension that enables me to push my view of Hitchcock, and my view of film criticism, to its limits.

Such limits are reached, for example, in the Postscript I wrote when Hitchcock died just as I was completing the body of the book. At his death, I felt moved to write, Hitchcock possessed a secret comparable to Uncles Charles's in *Shadow of a Doubt*:

> Part of what he knew is that America never really understood his films. Society's "tributes" were denials of the meaning of his work. Surely, the spectacle of America playing tribute to itself on the occasion of his death is a Hitchcockian one. I call it that because it would make a chilling, poignant and funny scene in a Hitchcock film, and because his work can teach us to recognize Hitchcock as its secret author. When Hitchcock authorized the language of his public tributes, and in general appeared to endorse the official view of who he was, in effect he scripted his own obituary, assuring that it would be silent on the meaning of his films. All Hitchcock's public speeches and gestures were also silences. I have no wish to attempt to reconcile the official Hitchcock and the knowing figure who emerges in my book, but to convey how the former may be viewed as the latter's creation, as a perfectly Hitchcockian figure, a projection of Hitchcock's authorship.[10]

[9] Ibid. [10] *Hitchcock – The Murderous Gaze*, p. 343.

In *Hitchcock – The Murderous Gaze*, as I acknowledge in the Postscript, I cast myself as the figure who steps forward to answer Hitchcock's call for acknowledgment. I knew full well that by assuming this role I was taking the risk of appearing mad or arrogant or merely foolish. In *Film Quarterly*, Brian Henderson (perhaps not quite sure which of these adjectives best fits the case) called the Postscript the single most pretentious piece of film criticism he had ever read (and he had been around.) But, as I put it in the Postscript, "I would not have written this book" – I would not have cast myself in this role – "if I did not believe that I had penetrated some of the secret places in Hitchcock's art."[11]

In following Hitchcock's films with an unprecedented degree and kind of attention, I knew I was also taking the risk of appearing too self-effacing, as if I were subordinating my own voice to Hitchcock's. In a remark notable for its obtuseness (or, perhaps, its disingenuousness) as well as its mean-spiritedness, Tania Modleski contemptuously dismissed me – but not before appropriating a number of the central claims of my book – as the ultimate male masochist for bowing so obsequiously to Hitchcock-the-Master.[12] But to say that is altogether to miss the thrust of the Postscript, its suggestion that a life-and-death struggle for authorship is waged, symbolically, in the readings that comprise the book. This suggestion culminates in the following passage:

> Charlie knows that her uncle secretly authored his own eulogy; she also knows that he arranged for the way she is fated to remember him. When I say that my writing aspires to answer Hitchcock's calls for acknowledgment, I also mean that Hitchcock's films call for writing such as this, even call it forth. If Hitchcock is secret author of his own obituary, my readings are equally projections of his authorship; only they are authorized not by his words but by his silences. The Hitchcock who emerges in these readings could well have written them himself. Yet the Hitchcock for whom I speak, who calls forth my words, is also my creation. I am his character and he is mine; the boundary between my identity and his is unfathomable, like that between Norman Bates and "mother." That the voice speaking for Hitchcock's films here is also possessed by them is what is most deeply Hitchcockian about the book, what Hitchcock would have appreciated, I believe, what might have moved him beyond words.[13]

In his invaluable recent book *Hearing Things: Voice and Method in the Writing of Stanley Cavell* (a book that ought to be required reading for

[11] Ibid., p. 346.
[12] Tania Modleski, *The Women Who Knew Too Much: Hitchcock and Feminist Theory* (New York and London: Methuen, 1988), pp. 118–20.
[13] *Hitchcock – The Murderous Gaze*, p. 346.

every film studies student), Timothy Gould appreciates the fact that in my critical work on Hitchcock I make use of my own philosophical sensibility to convert insights gained from Cavell's work into insights of my own. But he feels that in doing so I find myself in troubled waters, philosophically. He cites the following passage from "*Vertigo*: The Unknown Woman in Hitchcock" as revealing what he takes to be a conflict between my critical practice, which views itself as underwritten by Cavell's philosophical writings, and Cavell's own philosophical method:

> Cavell, in his readings of the melodrama of the unknown woman and remarriage comedies alike, aspires to put into his own words what films say to their audience. Speaking in his own philosophical voice and out of his own experience ... he declares himself to be, despite everything, a representative member of that audience.... [R]eading a Hitchcock thriller ... I find myself continually called on to make discoveries, to see things that viewers do not ordinarily see, or to see familiar things in an unfamiliar light, to discover unsuspected connections. The *Vertigo* that emerges ... in this essay is not the film as viewers ordinarily view it (although my reading is meant to account for the common experience, which it interprets as the experience that fails to acknowledge Hitchcock and hence misses his meaning).[14]

According to Gould, I take Cavell's philosophical method "to be one of putting common experiences – experiences that Cavell shares with an ordinary audience – into Cavell's own words," and I equate this "putting into his own words" with speaking "in his own philosophical voice," which "is evidently taken to be the method by which Cavell manages to evince his own uniqueness and to declare his 'representative' membership in a film's audience."[15]

However, in the passage Gould quotes, I do not equate Cavell's procedures *in general* with his putting common experiences into his own words. What I do say is that this is Cavell's approach in writing about these American comedies and melodramas. If he did not view these particular movies as philosophical, as sustaining a serious philosophical conversation with their – our – culture, he would have written differently about them (or not written about them at all). Nor am I claiming that, for Cavell, putting one's experiences into one's own words is equivalent *in general* to speaking in one's own philosophical voice. What I say is that in *Pursuits of Happiness* and *Contesting Tears* Cavell puts into his own words what these films are saying to their audience; that he does so by putting his experiences of these

[14] *The "I" of the Camera*, p. 173.

[15] Timothy Gould, *Hearing Things: Voice and Method in the Writing of Stanley Cavell* (Chicago and London: University of Chicago Press, 1998), p. 73.

films into his own words, and that in so doing he does find himself speaking in his own philosophical voice. Again, if these movies were different, if he (and we) experienced them differently, Cavell would have written differently about them. How Cavell feels these films call upon him to write about them, how they motivate him to speak in his own philosophical voice, is revelatory of what these films are. (Cavell has always embraced the Wittgensteinian philosophical principle that the kinds of things that are said, the kinds of things that can be said, about something provide evidence for understanding the kind of thing that "something" is.)

These facts are also revelatory of who Cavell is. Cavell is a philosopher. He personally has claimed a voice within philosophy, and it is within philosophy, above all, that he has found his voice. Not on every occasion in which he speaks in his own voice does he speak in his philosophical voice. But whenever he speaks in his philosophical voice, he speaks in his own voice, his "empirical voice," as Gould calls it. Gould allows that Cavell's empirical voice is expressive of his unique existence, but he faults me for believing that Cavell's philosophical voice expresses his unique existence, too. "This uniqueness of the individual voice is taken [by Rothman] to constitute the uniqueness of Cavell's contribution to philosophy," Gould suggests, formulating my view in terms I can recognize. But I cannot accept his assertion that, given such a view, "It seems at best an accident that Cavell – or Cavell's philosophizing–could ever speak for anyone else."[16] For if Cavell found himself unable to speak for others when speaking in his own philosophical voice, as philosophers must find ways to do, he could not have found his voice *within philosophy*.

When I suggest that in *Pursuits of Happiness* and *Contesting Tears* Cavell "declares himself to be, despite everything," a representative member of these films' audience, I do not mean that Cavell declares his representativeness *in spite of* the uniqueness of his voice. My "despite everything" alludes only to what I take to be Cavell's sense that some might suppose that his status as a philosopher excludes him from being representative. Cavell does not take himself to be unrepresentative for having a unique voice, for having a unique philosophical voice, for being who he is and not another person. Every human existence, hence every human voice, is unique. For Cavell, as for the American comedies and melodramas he studies, to be unique is to be exemplary of humanity, to be representative. To be representative is to be unique.

Thus in Cavell's account, he, the films, and the films's audiences all see eye to eye, philosophically. At times, to be sure, he claims to see things

[16] Ibid.

others have not managed to see in these films, or says what others have not said. But he does not believe that this forfeits his claim to representativeness. He does not take the members of the films's audiences, however average or typical, to be for the most part missing the films's meaning. In no way do I contest or reject Cavell's accounts of the films his books study, or his way of writing about those films. To be sure, I write differently about Hitchcock's films. But, as I have said, Hitchcock's films, too, are different.

For one thing, Hitchcock's films give prominence to the idea – it is typically expressed by Hitchcock's gamesman/artist figures, such as Uncle Charles in *Shadow of a Doubt* – that only exceptional people are capable of opening their eyes. Such people, Charles tells young Charlie in an effort to get her to overcome her blindness, are so different from the mass of "ordinary" people doomed to sleepwalk through life that it is as if they belong to a higher species. However, the idea also figures in Hitchcock's films that people like Manny in *The Wrong Man*, who are utterly incapable of opening their eyes, are the truly exceptional ones. When Rose suddenly laughs hysterically and accuses Manny of still not recognizing that their fates are in the hands of a malignant deity, part of the cruel joke, in her eyes, is that she finds herself married to a man who will never see what she sees, who will never get the joke.

To open one's eyes takes only a spiritual change, but it is a transformation so profound as to be tantamount to death and rebirth – the kind of spiritual change that is central to the comedies and melodramas Cavell studies, in which such metamorphoses, at least in principle, are open to all who have the will to change. In *Notorious* and *North by Northwest*, Cary Grant (who is not coincidentally the quintessential male lead of comedies of remarriage) undergoes such a change just in time to allow a "happy ending." In *Vertigo*, the man's transformation – poetically, tragically – comes just too late. In Hitchcock's films, what is required is not only the will to change, and not only an acknowledgment that one's control has limits, but also submission to a "higher power." In Hitchcock films, the "higher power" capable of making such miracles happen cannot be separated from the figure of the author, from Hitchcock himself.

"When Rothman accounts for the experience of the audience of a Hitchcock film," Gould writes, "he is not accounting for an error or an obscurity that he might himself have shared. He is accounting for a state of blindness toward Hitchcock's words that he himself has been delivered from."[17] Of course, if I have been delivered from the state of blindness of most of

[17] Ibid., pp. 72–3.

Hitchcock's viewers, that must be a state I once shared with them; were it not for my miraculous deliverance, I, too, would still be blind.

"It is a state of mind that cannot be alleviated by any ordinary act of viewing," Gould goes on,

> nor by anything that Rothman would be willing to call "representative." The viewing of the ordinary American moviegoer is blinded by the most intimate workings of American culture. It is blind from birth – doomed in advance, like one of Hitchcock's "wrong men." In Rothman's critical vision, we either give in to the commonplace viewing of a film, or we rise above what is (merely) representative in our viewing and achieve a state in which we are capable of acknowledging Hitchcock's authorship.[18]

However, if we have the ability to "rise above what is (merely) representative in our viewing," if we can "achieve a state in which we are capable of acknowledging Hitchcock's authorship," we cannot be doomed to blindness. Hitchcock's films call upon their viewers to open their eyes; *Hitchcock – The Murderous Gaze* argues, in the face of Hitchcock's conviction that most, perhaps all, will not heed this call. Who, then, has the ability to acknowledge Hitchcock's authorship? In *Hitchcock – The Murderous Gaze*, I declare that I do. But does that make me unrepresentative of Hitchcock's viewers? What of my readers? If I believed that readers were doomed not to see what I see in Hitchcock's films, I would not have written or published my book, which aspires to express in my own words what I see, and what I think and feel about what I see, as clearly as is humanly possible.

In the writing of *Hitchcock – The Murderous Gaze*, I declare in the Postscript, I step forward, single myself out from the ranks of Hitchcock's audience members, to play a particular role. In principle, any member of Hitchcock's audience could have assumed this role, as any viewer could in principle have discovered the genres Cavell discovers. But no one who was not a representative member of Hitchcock's audience, no one who was not once blind, could have felt called upon to deliver my book's message. What it might be about my "empirical existence" that provoked and prepared me to find or create my own voice in the writing of *Hitchcock – The Murderous Gaze* is not my book's concern. Its concern is to demonstrate a method that might enable my readers, who are members of Hitchcock's audience, to achieve the "state necessary to acknowledge Hitchcock's authorship."

Hitchcock – The Murderous Gaze offers practical instruction in viewing Hitchcock's films, thinking about Hitchcock's films, in ways that acknowledge Hitchcock's authorship. The method the book proposes is simply to

[18] Ibid., p. 74.

follow the "texts" of the films and one's own experience of the films with the degree and kind of attention required to follow one's own thinking. And it undertakes to demonstrate the efficacy of this method simply by "reading" five representative Hitchcock films.

My readings do not instruct readers how they might make *these* discoveries about Hitchcock's films, of course. They stake my claim to critical insights that are my intuitions, not anyone else's. But these readings do undertake to pay the full tuition for these intuitions, as Emerson might put it, by finding words from our common language, words I can believe in, to account so clearly for my own experiences that readers might turn from these words (accompanied by the frame enlargements I chose to accompany them) to the films and find themselves seeing what I see in them (whether or not they then find themselves willing or able to accept my interpretations of what I see). It was my hope that by reading this book, by following its thinking, readers might learn something useful about making discoveries of their own (about these films, about other Hitchcock films, about films not stamped by Hitchcock's authorship, about works of art in other media). As I put it in the Postscript, I wrote *Hitchcock – The Murderous Gaze* for Hitchcock's audience, which "stands in need of instruction in viewing his films." It was not to claim them for myself that I undertook to speak for Hitchcock's films. It was to free these films from me, to free myself from them, to claim my writing for my own.[19]

Nonetheless, Gould writes, in a stinging passage,

> [Rothman's] acknowledgments of Hitchcock's meaningfulness and unknownness are presented as exclusively the effects of Rothman's critical insight and, indeed, as exclusively Rothman's. They are not acknowledgments that might allow others to hearken to the same voice, or follow the same path of self-illumination, but are acts of private devotion to a greatness that is at once public and hidden. Rothman takes himself, perhaps rightly, to be going public with such acknowledgments at the risk of sharing Hitchcock's destiny of unknownness.[20]

Although my "acknowledgments of Hitchcock's meaningfulness and unknownness" are based on my own insights or intuitions, I do not present them as "exclusively the effects" of my "critical insight." By demonstrating that what I claim to see in the films is there to be seen, I make my intuitions, I make my self, intelligible to the reader. On what grounds can Gould claim to know, then, that my writing does not allow readers to "hearken to the same voice" or to follow their own "paths of self-illumination"?

[19] *Hitchcock – The Murderous Gaze*, p. 347.
[20] *Hearing Things*, p. 74.

The greatness of Hitchcock's work *is* at once public and hidden. This was true when I was writing *Hitchcock – The Murderous Gaze*, and it is no less true today. But the writing of *Hitchcock – The Murderous Gaze* was not an act of private devotion. I wrote the book, and published it, in the hope and expectation that it would be read. That is, I refused to accept that unknownness (however much it had been his fate, however much he had sought it) *was* Hitchcock's "destiny." To be sure, in undertaking to help the unknown in Hitchcock become known in all its unknownness, I took the risk that my writing, too, would remain unknown. What writer does not take that risk? What writer does not find that risk worth taking?

CHAPTER 22

Eternal Vérités

Cinema-Vérité and Classical Cinema

1960 was a watershed year in the history of film in America. I think of the release of *Psycho* in 1960 as marking the definitive end of the classical era of American movies. 1960 was the year the French "New Wave" broke on American shores. Perhaps not entirely coincidentally, 1960 also marks the emergence of what has been called "cinema-vérité." (This term is hopelessly inadequate, of course, yet I persist in the habit of using it. I find alternatives such as "direct cinema" no less inadequate and far more misleading. These days one is far less likely to fall into the error of supposing that cinema-vérité films are guaranteed to be truthful than the error of taking them to be "direct," that is, unmediated.)

Cinema vérité, of course, is a form of documentary film, or a method of making documentary films, in which a small crew (often a cameraperson and sound recordist, sometimes only a solitary filmmaker) goes out into the "real world" with portable synch-sound equipment and films people going about their lives, not acting.

Jean Rouch, collaborating with the sociologist Edgar Morin and taking instruction from the great French Canadian cameraman Michel Brault, made *Chronicle of a Summer* in France simultaneously with the earliest cinema-vérité films in America, such as the Drew Associates productions, of which *Primary* is perhaps the most famous. Nonetheless, for a number of reasons, I think of cinema-vérité as an essentially American phenomenon, not a European one. It is in America that the grandest hopes for cinema-vérité have been harbored. Over the ensuing decades, American filmmakers working within the cinema-vérité tradition have created a remarkably impressive body of work. And cinema-vérité has been, in important ways, perhaps the fullest inheritor of the concerns of America's "classical" cinema, the popular movies associated with the name "Hollywood."

Rouch's approach to cinema-vérité was highly sophisticated. He anticipated, and quite shrewdly addressed, the problems and paradoxes – epistemological, aesthetic, moral – that, as subsequent practitioners were to discover, inevitably attend this new, apparently more direct way of filming. Rouch understood that however "invisible" the man-with-the-movie-camera might make himself and however unself-conscious the camera's subjects might appear, filming is a real act performed in the real world with real consequences. He understood as well that sometimes a filmmaker has to foresake the passivity of a place behind the camera to provoke "reality" into revealing its deepest truths. For Rouch, already a veteran of over a decade of ethnographic filmmaking among the Songhay and Dogon peoples in West Africa, the new lightweight synch-sound equipment became an indispensable tool, an instrument, of a lifelong cinematic enterprise poised between science and art, between anthropological research and a personal need to give poetic expression to his conviction that so-called "primitive" societies possess knowledge that modern science must find ways to acknowledge, not deny.

For a maker of very American films like Richard Leacock, who was Robert Flaherty's cameraman on *Louisiana Story*, cinema-vérité was what film itself was to Griffith a half century earlier: It promised a radically new way of revealing the truth about humanity. This truth was to be found, not in Flaherty's romanticized vision of a person's struggle against the elemental forces of nature, but in the everyday struggles of ordinary men and women to retain their humanity in a hypocritical America of sex, lies, and exploitation. The human truth was to be found in the coarseness and ugliness of that America, but also in the flashes of beauty, tenderness, and compassion revealed to Leacock's camera.

To Leacock, the beauty fleetingly glimpsed by cinema-vérité offered the promise of redeeming America. Because it seems that promise was not fated to be kept, cinema-vérité also meant, for Leacock, a threat of disillusionment and despair. But he has remained faithful in his filming to the strict cinema-vérité discipline, as have Robert Gardner, John Marshall, and Frederick Wiseman, to name several of the great masters of cinema-vérité whose work I deeply admire and who happen to be based in the Boston area where I was able to become acquainted with them personally during the years I was teaching film at Harvard.

David Hume withdrew from his ordinary life into his study, shutting out the world in order to contemplate whether it was possible that the world does not exist. The author of *Walden* withdrew from society and spent two years at Walden Pond in order to gain a new perspective on the world and to learn how he might live in it. To film the world, the cinema-vérité filmmaker, too, withdraws from the world. To effect this withdrawal, he needs only to assume a place behind the camera. His philosopher's study, his Walden, so to speak, is the camera itself. This is a Walden one can bear on one's shoulder.

Behind the camera, practitioners of the cinema-vérité discipline foresake their ordinary lives to become observers who wait selflessly for the human beings they are filming to reveal themselves in their own good time and on their own terms. Or *are* cinema-vérité filmmakers selfless? What are the fantasies that animate their hours of silent watching? Writing about Alfred Hitchcock's neglected early masterpiece *Murder!*, and hence in a rather dark mood, I argued that the role of cinema-vérité filmmaker has an inhuman, murderous aspect:

> The cinema-vérité filmmaker withholds himself from the world in order to film it. Stepping behind the camera may appear an act of perfect innocence and purity. But it expresses, it does not overcome, the fantasy of power and murderousness that *Murder!* declares to be an inalienable constituent of authoring a film. The cinema-vérité filmmaker's fantasy of virginity and impotence has as its secret other face the fantasy of being author to the world, commanding it to unmask itself. Claiming exemption from responsibility for forging community within the world he is filming, he trains the camera's eye on that world, wreaking vengeance on it. These twin fantasies of impotence and omnipotence come together in cinema-vérité's underlying vision of a world condemned to a lack of human community by virtue of the act of filming.[1]

Led by Edward Pincus and his students at the MIT Film Section – for years, Pincus was co-director with Leacock of this unique cinema-vérité training ground – a new generation of filmmakers attempted to break away from the inhuman aspect of the cinema-vérité filmmaker's role while remaining faithful to the spirit of cinema-vérité. Their aspiration was to reconcile the conflicting demands of filming and living by learning to film the world without withdrawing from it. Inevitably the filmmaker's life and the demands of the filmmaker's role became increasingly explicit subjects of films by Pincus, Steve Ascher, Ross McElwee, Jeff Kreines, Joel DeMott, Mark Rance, Ann Schaetzel, Robb Moss, and other students and teachers at the Film Section. Their explorations culminated in two extraordinary epics, Pincus's *Diaries 1971–76* and McElwee's *Sherman's March*.

Within *Diaries*, a conflict emerges, seemingly inevitably, between the filmmaker's experiment of filming his life, a project only he can call his own, and the claims made upon him by his wife, children, parents, lovers, and friends who call upon him to acknowledge them as human beings separate from him – and from his film. The filming of *Diaries*, which has the aspect of a romantic quest, threatens to seal the filmmaker's isolation rather than free him to live freely within a human community, to turn him into a hero not of

[1] William Rothman, *Hitchcock – The Murderous Gaze* (Cambridge, MA: Harvard University Press, 1982), p. 105.

romance but of tragedy. This conflict between the romantic and the ordinary, between filming and living, emerges in *Diaries*, at least on the surface, as the primary obstacle to the filmmaker's goal of becoming fully human.

In the more ironic *Sherman's March*, the conflict between filming one's life and living it in a fully human way is as central as it is in *Diaries*. In McElwee's film, too, the filmmaker takes his project to be a romantic quest. But *Sherman's March*, made a full decade after *Diaries*, presents its filmmaker as a comical character on whom it asserts an ironic perspective. As viewed from that perspective, *of course* the filmmaker's attempt to become more human by filming his life is a foolish one doomed to failure. One might say that *Diaries* tells its story with a gravity akin to that of tragedy. A decade later, *Sherman's March* tells this story again, this time as farce. As surely as *Diaries*, though, *Sherman's March* demonstrates that there is an irreducible aspect of withdrawal and isolation, and of violence, in the cinema-vérité filmmaker's role, even if the people being filmed directly address the filmmaker behind the camera; even if others are allowed to turn the camera on the filmmaker, rendering him or her a visible, not invisible, presence in the film; and even if the filmmaker breaks his or her silence and enters into conversations with the film's other characters.

Reflecting on a history of cinema that is still far from perspicuous, we may find it quite remarkable that, despite film's long and illustrious documentary tradition, cinema-vérité emerged as late as 1960. There were isolated experiments, such as Flaherty's celebrated *Nanook of the North*, a film made forty years earlier but still of extraordinary power and interest. But most documentary filmmakers – even Dziga Vertov, so often claimed by cinema-vérité as a precursor – had little inclination to follow *Nanook's* example. Influenced in part by Marxist ideas about the necessity of transcending the individual protagonist, they veered in a different direction. In the films made in England by the talented filmmakers gathered around John Grierson, in the avowedly leftist films of Joris Ivens, and in the work of Pare Lorentz, Willard Van Dyke, and others in America, a dominant form of documentary emerged in the 1930s whose influence remains strong to this day. These documentaries composed their views of people lyrically or expressionistically and used them rhetorically in advancing a social thesis, usually explicitly stated by a (typically male) narrator's authoritative voice.

In postwar Italy, the neorealist movement championed the use of nonprofessional actors and "real" locations and strove to discover dramatic subjects in the realm of the everyday. However, the neorealists never took the decisive step of dispensing with scripts altogether and venturing into the world to film "reality itself." Nor did André Bazin, France's great theorist of cinematic realism, advocate this step.

In the 1930s and 1940s and even the early 1950s, the technology for portable synch-sound shooting was unavailable. Yet filmmakers could have made silent films that followed the lead of *Nanook of the North* or they could have shot their films silent and postdubbed them in the studio as the Italian neorealists did. For whatever reasons, however, filmmakers were not interested in filming "reality" this way.

Most American cinema-vérité films could not but be in synch-sound, could not but feature people who speak, speak spontaneously and in their own voices. When and why and how people speak, the powers and limits of language in our human form of life, were and remain central concerns of American cinema-vérité. (Perhaps it is no accident that cinema-vérité's emergence was simultaneous with the impact of so-called ordinary language philosophy.) This concern is manifest even in cinema-vérité's refusal to use "authoritarian" voice-over narration. In cinema-vérité, no voice is to derive authority apart from the person speaking, the words being spoken, and the particulars of the occasion.

In the 1960s, when the "classical" tradition had broken down and Hollywood's audience had become fragmented, cinema-vérité promised a new way to make movies that might seem as vivid and "real" as Hollywood films of the 1930s and 1940s had been, in their day, to their audience of all Americans (and to their audiences worldwide). By the 1960s, the classical conventions seemed to have lost most of their vitality and relevance, and America had all but lost even the memory of the wonderful conversation its movies had once sustained with their culture. Thus it was possible for filmmakers and audiences to be convinced that cinema-vérité owed nothing to classical movies, to think of "Hollywood" as its sworn enemy. Yet, in truth, cinema-vérité owes far more to popular Hollywood movies than it does to most earlier documentary films. In the 1960s, cinema-vérité represented a new way of making films that inherited the concerns of popular genres such as the "comedy of remarriage" and the "melodrama of the unknown woman" (as Stanley Cavell has named them) that had crystallized in Hollywood in the 1930s and 1940s. And cinema-vérité derived from classical cinema its picture of human being-in-the-world as an expression of a dialectical opposition between the theatrical and the nontheatrical. In "Virtue and Villainy in the Face of the Camera," I characterize classical cinema's picture of, and way of picturing, the human form of life:

> Film's opposition between the theatrical and the non-theatrical is grounded in, and grounds, its conventions for presenting human beings in the world. Typically, the

camera alternately frames its human subjects within public and private spaces. The frame of an 'objective' shot is a stage on which human beings perform, subject to view by others in their world. Within the frame of a reaction shot, a subject views the spectacle of the world, reacts privately to it, and prepares the next venture into the public world. Point-of-view and reaction shots together combine to effect the camera's penetration of the privacy of its human subject, who alternates tensely and hesitantly between acting and viewing as he or she prepares an entrance onto the world's stage, performs, and withdraws again into a privacy to which only the camera has access.[2]

As we shall see, cinema-vérité did not follow classical cinema in its use of point-of-view shots as a technique for distinguishing between the theatrical and the candid. Nonetheless, cinema-vérité inherited classical cinema's great stake in the realm of privacy and in the realm of the everyday, the ordinary. Cinema-vérité also inherited classical cinema's understanding that, within these realms, the noncandid – the unspontaneous, the manipulated and the manipulative, the theatrical – is everywhere to be found. It also inherited classical cinema's conviction that our happiness as individuals – and America's as a nation – turns on our ability to reconcile our private and public selves.

In thinking historically about the emergence of cinema-vérité in America, it is important to keep in mind that early cinema-vérité films such as *Primary* or *Crisis* were not made for movie theaters with their dwindling audience, but for network television, newly crowned as America's dominant medium. In the context of television programming, these films' identities were divided. Like "real movies," or like television dramas or even soap operas, they appealed to human emotions. Yet, as documentaries, they were "public affairs" shows, news.

Typically, news is presented on television by newscasters who address the camera directly. When news footage is shown, it is accompanied by a newscaster's voice-over that tells us how we are to understand what we are viewing. The newscaster on camera or speaking into a microphone is always "on." Television provides no system for distinguishing the person of the newscaster from the newscaster's role she or he is performing – no system for acknowledging, for investigating, or even for exploiting, the dialectic between theatricality and nontheatricality that is at the heart of cinema-vérité as well as classical movies.

Over the years, the format of television news has evolved to convey the impression that we know the private person behind the newscaster mask. Think of the way Walter Cronkite ended each broadcast. It was always a

[2] William Rothman, *The "I" of the Camera* (New York: Cambridge University Press, 1988), pp. 69–70.

privileged moment when he looked the camera directly in the eye with an expression that told us he was taking us into his confidence. Man-to-man, he acknowledged that he was no impersonal newscaster; he was a human being who had in some particular way been moved, just as we had been, by the story he chose to close the show. He had taken the story to heart, like a *mensch*. Then, with an authority to be understood as grounded in this display of emotion, he summed up his philosophy of life, always with the same words but every evening with a new inflection, one tailored to match the prevailing mood. His words were, of course, "And that's the way it is." This whole ritual, performed every evening, put Uncle Walter's personal stamp on the role of newscaster, and thereby revised that role, paving the way for others who have gone further – indeed, much too far, as witness the nauseating, shameless conviviality of local "news teams" – in incorporating displays of "personality" into a once rigidly impersonal role. The point is that the newscaster's role, however revised, however "personalized," nonetheless remains a role, a mask, no less so when the newscaster appears to be dropping his mask. The format of television news still provides no system for acknowledging even the possibility of such theatricality.

In classical cinema, we view "stars" continually putting on masks and taking them off. In most forms of television programming today, the mask is never dropped, unless beneath it another mask is already firmly in place. When television was primarily "live," to be sure, masks often slipped, or cracked, or were inadvertently put on crooked. Already by 1960, though, when cinema-vérité first appeared on network television, the nature of television was changing from a primarily "live" medium to one in which no discernible sign distinguishes what is "live" from what is, shall we say, canned. The result is not to make the canned seem live, but to make even the live seem unspontaneous, canned. (This effect, it might be said, is a denial of the uncanny.)

Thus when it first appeared on television in America, cinema-vérité represented, at one level, a rearguard assault from within against television's deadening denial of the distinction between theatricality and candor that has been the basis of American movies. By letting the audience view, say, John Kennedy when he was not performing in public (or at least by purporting to reveal the "private" man), *Primary* (and to a lesser degree *Crisis*) granted Americans a new perspective on Kennedy the public figure. (Of course, Kennedy's mask was hardly dropped completely. The camera was not granted access, for example, to his boudoir, to his private life as a stud.) All in all (and surely Kennedy himself anticipated this), these films served to reinforce his public image, which was that of a man who "had it all together," who was enviably successful in his career and enviably lucky in his marriage, and whose public and private selves were, even more enviably, a harmonious match.

What I am suggesting is that cinema-vérité was meant to undermine television's practice of packaging public figures as exploitable "images." Ironically, cinema-vérité itself quickly became a favorite tool of image-packagers who have learned to fabricate tolerable imitations of the look of spontaneity and candor. (The famous Nixon–Kennedy debates helped Kennedy and hurt Nixon, I take it, because both men, forced to be at least a little spontaneous, revealed something of their "true" characters to a camera that neither man was in a position to control, hence that took on something of the penetrating power of the camera in cinema-vérité. When Nixon was in a position to control the television camera, he was free to perform his "sincere act" without the threat that its theatricality might be exposed. Then television served Nixon well, as it did when he saved his political neck by staging his infamous "Checkers" speech.)

Many of the earliest cinema-vérité films in America revolved around celebrities and portraits of celebrities – political figures, sports heroes, movie stars, singers, and musicians – remain a staple of cinema-vérité. No political convention or major sporting event is complete without minidocumentaries that make public figures private by presenting them, in ABC's immortal phrase, "up close and personal." Cinema-vérité brings celebrities down to earth by filming them the same way it films ordinary people (which, of course, celebrities also are). The filmmaker's task in filming any human subject is to create a compelling figure on the screen, to make that figure as known to us, and as unknown, as James Stewart, Cary Grant, Katharine Hepburn, or any other star of classical cinema. Cinema-vérité transforms an ordinary person into a star, or reveals, as it were, the "star within" – at least if that person happens to "have what it takes." But that is precisely what classical cinema has always done. Classical cinema has always made its stars out of ordinary people who happen to "have what it takes."

Classical cinema instituted a system of production in which, first, a screenplay is authored; then that screenplay is realized by a process of filming in which the director plays a central role; finally, the film is edited in a process that reconciles the screenplay with what might be called the accidents of filming. In a cinema-vérité film, there is, at least in theory, no directing of actors, and the camera's gestures, too, are improvised, not directed; and, of course, there is no screenplay.

D. W. Griffith did not write or work from screenplays as such, although his films were hardly unscripted like cinema-vérité films. Griffith was able to envision the film he wanted to make and to realize his vision in the act of filming without first putting into writing what he saw in his mind's eye. However, as the Hollywood system of production became rationalized, Griffith's method was superseded. Written texts, screenplays, assumed a central function as blueprints for filming and editing, no doubt partly because studios wished to limit the risky (and potentially expensive) unpredictability inherent in the filming process. By the 1930s, the screenplay in America assumed essentially its current form.

In the voluminous writings about adaptations of literature to film, the screenplay has received virtually no attention. Perhaps the most surprising formal feature of the classical screenplay is that it uses no pictures or diagrams to help guide the reader in visualizing the film to be made. The screenplay is made up of nothing but words.

In the classical system of production, the function of the screenplay is to serve as an envisioning-in-advance, an imagining, of the film. One might think that yoking films to screenplays in this way subordinates cinema to writing. Yet the development of this mode of writing designed to be at the selfless service of film can also be thought of as an affirmation of cinema's authority over the written word. Screenplays demonstrate and declare film's powers, which are also writing's limits. For film has the power to make real, or to reveal to be real, what the words of a screenplay can never more than envision. To read a good screenplay and then to see the film made from it – if it is well made – unfailingly restores one's wonder at the power of cinema.

By enforcing the discipline that films were to be "realized" only after first being envisioned in advance through the medium of the written word, the classical system also acknowledged the power of writing, of course. This acknowledgment immeasurably strengthened the affirmation of film's authority. For film possesses precisely the power to reveal writing's limits, as I have suggested: Writing is not film. In turn, writing possesses precisely the power to challenge film to declare itself: Film is not writing. (In Griffith's hands, film comparably declared its authority over theater, and hence revealed the limits of theater even as it affirmed theater's power: Theater is not film, and film is not theater.)

Nonetheless, within the classical system, no film is made without a screenplay. In this system, film may appear to lord it over writing, but it is dependent upon it. Cinema-vérité constitutes an alternative system, one in which filming proceeds by improvisatory encounters with the world, by chance and whim (the filmmaker's whim, and the world's).

When cinema-vérité dispensed with the screenplay, it was a declaration of film's independence from writing. Yet by issuing this declaration, cinema-vérité was also following (or paralleling or leading) a literary trend, joining ranks with the self-conscious nonfiction novel (Truman Capote's *In Cold Blood* is the most famous example) that is cinema-vérité's exact contemporary. This suggests that cinema-vérité was not breaking with the written word, but with the discipline of composing the film in advance, the yoking of filming to envisioning or imagining.

To say that a screenplay envisions or imagines a film in advance implies that filming is a process of realization, or interpretation, of the text of the screenplay, in the sense that a performance of a musical composition is an interpretation of the written score. In realizing a screenplay, the director directs the actors in interpreting their roles as written, as in theater (the casting of a particular actor in a role is already an act of interpretation). The director also directs the camera, interprets the camera's role as written. Part of the actor's role, to be interpreted by the actor under the director's direction, is to present himself or herself to the camera in particular ways, ways that may encompass an interpretation of the way the camera views that actor. In turn, the camera – also directed by the director – addresses the actor – self-presentations (and interpretations of the camera) and all – as a subject in his or her own right.

No text has one and only one possible interpretation. If a classical film is an interpretation of its screenplay, this implies that other interpretations of the screenplay are also possible. Thus a screenplay can determine a film only up to a point, and can never fully determine a film in its concrete actuality, as we might put it. No moment of any film can be completely envisioned, imagined, in advance. That is not surprising: The actual filming transforms the screenplay in ways that are not perfectly predictable (and to be "not perfectly predictable" is to be unpredictable).

Film is photographic; there is an irreducible element of automatism in the way it reproduces the world. Nonetheless, screenplays bind classical film to the realm of interpretation, and to words. (Or do they reflect the fact that film is so bound by its nature?) Indeed, classical film is doubly bound to interpretation and to words because it is always possible, in the face of a realized classical film, to write in screenplay form what might be called a "transcription." Such a transcription is not an envisioning of the film in advance; nor is it an interpretation of the screenplay realized by the film. Rather, it is an interpretation of the film itself.

In transcribing moments of a classical film as one views or experiences them, one must find words that objectively characterize particular gestures, say, or intonations, glances, facial expressions, or movements of the camera. But these are things one cannot objectively characterize apart from characterizing, interpreting, one's subjective experience of them. Screenplays, too, routinely characterize such things as gestures, intonations, glances, facial expressions and camera movements – things one cannot describe without interpreting one's own experience. In a screenplay, as in a transcription of a realized film, "objective" description and interpretation cannot logically be separated.

That directing a film from a screenplay is a discipline that can be mastered, that masters of this discipline are capable of creating compelling, expressive, endlessly exhilarating and moving films by interpreting screenplays that are made up of nothing but words, is an inherently unpredictable fact about words, and about film. Writing a transcription of a realized film is also a discipline that can be mastered. Every masterfully written transcription, as I put it in the Preface to this volume,

> . . . is a study in the limits of what can be said. It is also a study in the limits of what goes without saying. What the possibility of such mastery reveals is that the limits of language and the limits of film coincide. That is, there is a boundary between them.

The screenplay of which a classical film is an interpretation and the transcription that is an interpretation of that film cannot be expected to coincide word-for-word. In principle, such coincidence is not impossible; it requires only a miracle. Some films (and hence their transcriptions) fail to acknowledge or realize the screenplay's own perspective on the world it envisions. Other films "go beyond" their screenplays in the sense of acknowledging and revising the screenplay's own interpretations (I am thinking, for example, of the ending of *Now, Voyager*. The screenplay takes the woman still be in love with the man, still to be putty in his hands, while the realized film understands her to have attained a transcendental perspective.) When a film does revise and deepen its screenplay, this revision could always in principle have been anticipated and incorporated into the screenplay. After all, in writing a screenplay, one continually revises and (one hopes) deepens one's imagining and one's understanding of what one is imagining.

This suggests that, although a classical screenplay is an "imagining" of the realized film that constitutes an interpretation of it (and that can, in turn, be interpreted by a transcription), the original screenplay, too, can be thought of as an interpretation, indeed a transcription. The screenplay cannot be a transcription of the "real" film that interprets it, because this film did not exist when the screenplay was written. Rather, one might wish to say that a screenplay is a transcription of a film that exists only in the screenwriter's imagination. [One might wish to speak, further, not only of a film that exists only in the screenwriter's imagination but also of a (different?) film that exists in the imagination of each reader of the screenplay (a different imaginary film for each reader?), and, crucially, in the imagination of one particular reader, the director (who may or may not also be the screenwriter) whose task it is to interpret the screenplay in the act of filming.]

Of course, it is not necessarily the case that a screenwriter first sees a film in his or her mind's eye, as it were, and then subsequently transcribes it. The writing of the screenplay may also serve as an instrument of this imagining. Perhaps it is better to think of "the film envisioned by the screenplay" as having no prior existence apart from the specific words and literary form of the screenplay itself. (As I become more and more deeply mired in such distinctions, I find myself homesick for the field of philosophy.) In any case, what is imagined in this imagining? What is this "film that exists only in the screenwriter's imagination"? Isn't it misleading to call it a film at all? (If it isn't a film, what is it?)

It obviously would be misleading to speak of a novel, say, as a transcription of a "novel that exists only in the novelist's imagination." This is because a novel, like a screenplay, is made up only of words, whereas presumably the novelist "imagines" not words but a world – a world that it is part of the discipline of the novelist to render in words. But how do we imagine a world? What is the medium of our imagining?

The way we imagine a world, the world, is akin to the way we dream, I take it. It is often said that we dream in images, but it seems more accurate to say – speaking at least of the visual aspect of the dream – that we dream in views. It is of the nature of a view that it is from a particular perspective or vantage. When a novelist imagines the world of a novel, the novelist is also imagining viewing that world, which entails occupying a vantage on it, or a succession of vantages.

The material basis of film, Stanley Cavell argues in *The World Viewed*, is a succession of automatic world projections. Film is the medium in which the world leaves its impression in the form of a succession of views; to imagine the world viewed, is, in effect, to imagine a film. This is precisely where film's uniqueness lies: We have no other way of imagining the world than by imagining viewing the world, that is, by imagining a film.

When a screenwriter envisions a film, however, isn't she or he imagining the world present in all its substantial reality, rather than imagining the shadowy projections of a world already past that constitute a film? Doesn't the screenwriter imagine not a film but a world as it presents itself to be filmed? Doesn't the screenwriter imagine what the field of film study calls "profilmic reality," not views of reality? But what is it to imagine reality (at least in its visual aspect) if not to conjure views of reality in one's imagination? The imagination itself is a faculty of projection. Nothing we can imagine is more real to us than views.

Views are the "medium" of imagining the world; imagining the world (in its visual aspect) is always imagining viewing the world; what one imagines are always views. Yet it cannot be denied that there is a difference between imagining and viewing. In viewing, the world makes its impression on me, although for an impression to be effected, my imagination must meet the world halfway. By contrast, in imagining, I create views, conjure them from within. Having conjured these views, I have no need actually to view them, any more than I have a need, when I am dreaming, actually to view the views that constitute my dream; I need do nothing with the views in my dream beyond dreaming them. And the screenwriter envisioning a film imagines the world viewed, imagines views of the world, but these views need only be imagined to be rendered in words; they do not need also to be viewed.

When a screenwriter imagines the film that is to be transcribed in the screenplay he or she is writing, the screenwriter does not imagine it as a film that has to be scripted and then realized by filming. To exist in the screenwriter's imagination, this film only has to be imagined. As it exists in the screenwriter's imagination, it is not a product of the classical system of production; to imagine the film he or she is writing, the screenwriter must only imagine viewing, only imagine views, only imagine that these views are impressions left by encounters with the world in which the world only needed to be met halfway. (This is not to deny, of course, that the films a screenwriter is willing or able to imagine may be inspired, or constrained, by the classically produced films that screenwriter has viewed.)

Paradoxically, then, a classical film is "authored" by first being envisioned as a film that has no author, envisioned as a film that comes into being through spontaneous encounters with unscripted, undirected "reality." Thus it is tolerably close to the truth to say that, in the imagination of the screenwriter (and in the imagination of the director whose task it is to interpret the screenplay) a classical film *is* a cinema-vérité film.

A cinema-vérité film is not envisioned in advance, and hence does not have a screenplay. However, insofar as it allows for transcription in screenplay form, it remains bound to the realms of interpretation and words. But *is* it possible to transcribe a cinema-vérité film, the way it is possible to transcribe a classical film?

The question of whether a cinema-vérité film allows for a transcription is akin to the vexing question of whether jazz can be transcribed. In the case of cinema-vérité, I take it, there is no special problem in transcribing the gestures and expressions of the camera's human subjects. What poses special problems for transcription, or challenges, are the movements and vicissitudes of the camera itself.

Screenwriters are habitually advised to write as few camera directions as possible, the ostensible reason being that directors are said not to like it when writers encroach on their prerogative. Yet one cannot envision actions in the world in concrete detail without at the same time envisioning particular vantages on those actions, which correspond, in film, to positionings and movements of the camera. Shrewd screenwriters specify framings or camera movements only when they are surprising or especially significant, and most often leave the camera to the director's imagination. They know full well, however, that the conventions of classical cinema all but dictate that the director imagines, say, a long shot here, a medium shot there, and so on.

In classical cinema, there are conventional categories of shots, and conventions for their use, although, to be sure, framings or camera movements may be called for that are so idiosyncratic that they require individualized descriptions. When an occasion does arise for specifying particular framings or camera movements, the screenwriter thus has at hand a repertory of conventional categories (close-up, two-shot, point-of-view shot, and so on), screenwriters' terms that evolved hand-in-hand with the evolution of conventions of cinematography. Even in the 1940s, when the long-take style flourished as an alternative to "analytical" editing, the "long takes" tended to take the form of stable framings – each virtually a separate shot, conventional in format – linked by reframings instead of cuts.

Typically, cinema-vérité is shot as close to "real time" as possible and by one handheld camera. Thus the cinema-vérité frame is rarely stable or fixed. Rather, there is continual reframing, and also zooming in and out (the zooms have the consequence that image size does not necessarily correspond to spatial distance). The camera is never completely still, but most of its movements have little or no particular significance apart from their status as indicators of two related conditions, which are linked. First, the incessant movement of the camera indicates that the camera *is* handheld, that it is an extension of the filmmaker's bodily presence, his or her hand (and eye). Second, in their characteristic hesitations, indecisions, incessant revisions of focus and framing, these movements are also indicators that this is not a scripted film, that the filmmaker is only a human being, not an omniscient "author."

It is not just for technical reasons that cinema-vérité films tend to approach as nearly as possible to the condition of complete continuity, I take it. This style also offers formal testimony to the method of filming – as if any cut would threaten the viewer's assurance of the filmmaker's dedication to the cinema-vérité discipline. Every cut could be a splicing together of shots taken at different times or different places. In terms of cinema-vérité discipline, every cut could be an instance of "cheating."

A corollary of this avoidance of cuts that break up continuity is that, as I have already pointed out, cinema-vérité abandons the point-of-view technique that is a stable of classical cinema. Point-of-view technique requires cutting back and forth between viewer and viewed, instantaneous shifts of perspective not possible for a filmmaker shooting with one camera in "real time." In cinema-vérité films, point-of-view shots can only be simulated, faked. The motivation for dispensing with this technique, too, is not just technical, however: Because the cinema-vérité camera is perceived as an extension of the filmmaker's body, the camera's presence is identified first and foremost with the person of the filmmaker. This means that there is a limit, in cinema-vérité, to the camera's ability to establish an identification with its (other) human subjects. Point-of-view shots would risk transgressing that limit; hence they are to be relinquished. In avoiding point-of-view shots, and in the motivation for this avoidance, cinema-vérité surprisingly reverts to Griffith, who never allowed the camera's gaze to stand in for the perspective of a character. Griffith's camera was always to be identified, first and foremost, with his own perspective, the perspective of the invisible author of the film.

The camera's "normal" state of incessant motion in cinema-vérité contrasts strikingly with the classical camera's "normal" state of motionlessness. In classical films, the camera's stillness is punctuated only by specific, composed gestures of the camera. Not moving the camera may itself constitute a gesture of this kind, and such privileged moments of stillness might be specified in the screenplay. Ordinarily, though, the classical camera's fixity of position, like the incessant motion of the cinema-vérité camera, has no particular significance apart from marking the camera's presence. The incessant motion of the cinema-vérité camera binds it to the bodily presence of a human filmmaker, whose hand and eye are continually revealed by this motion whether or not the filmmaker intends to reveal herself or himself. By contrast, the camera in classical cinema breaks its stillness to declare itself in specific, self-possessed gestures that call for acknowledgment.

Interestingly, when the camera is referred to in a classical screenplay, it is referred to as if it were a character, except that, by convention, references to characters are capitalized only when they are introduced the first time they appear in the film, whereas references to the camera are capitalized throughout. It is as if every time we are called upon to take note of the camera in a classical film, which means every time the camera declares itself, an introduction is performed, as though we had forgotten ever having encountered the camera before. The camera has been present all along, of course, but only on such occasions does it call for acknowledgment. Part of what is then to be acknowledged is that the camera has already, has always, been present. The significant point here is that the vantage of the camera is always open to being specified because, at every moment of every film, the camera frames the view, and it always does so from some particular vantage: This is a fact about what a film is.

A transcription of a cinema-vérité film could not be expected to register every movement of a camera that is constantly in motion. Yet some movements of the camera would have to be noted and interpreted – perhaps because they are deliberate gestures, statements, on the part of the filmmaker, perhaps because they are spontaneous expressions in which the self of the filmmaker is especially tellingly revealed.

For example, in the climactic passage of Richard Leacock's and Joyce Chopra's *A Happy Mother's Day* (1963), an early cinema-vérité film, a South Dakota woman who has given birth to quintuplets is stoically enduring a luncheon in her honor. As an amateur soprano sings with a perkiness she takes for sophisticated sauciness, Leacock's camera dwells on Mrs. Fischer, the mother for whom this luncheon is supposed to be, as one town booster puts it, "her own fun time." The camera remains on her so long that we may well begin to wonder what, if anything, it can possibly hope to discover in her plain face. As if suddenly sensing that the camera has been attending to her, she steals a glance at it. Her suspicion confirmed, she furtively shifts her gaze away. But then, no longer willing or able to continue the pretense that she is uninterested in its interest in her, she deliberately meets the camera's gaze with her own. At this moment, we feel that anything can happen, and everything is at stake. What does happen next, miraculously, is that, in recognition of the camera's capacity to acknowledge her, a trace of a smile appears on Mrs. Fischer's face.

At the same moment, as if authorized by Mrs. Fischer and in secret conspiracy with her, Leacock's camera begins to pan from person to person in the hall, finding obliviousness in the eyes of all the people gathered to honor this woman they do not really know: Unless a transcription notes these gestures of Leacock's camera, and interprets them in some such terms, the power and meaning of this wondrous passage is lost.

Within limits, then, a cinema-vérité film does allow for a transcription in screenplay form. In principle, such a transcription could have been written before the filming and could have functioned as an envisioning of the film and as a blueprint for filming, the way a screenplay functions in classical cinema. A cinema-vérité film can always be imagined to be a classical film. But can we imagine the reverse? Is it possible to imagine that a given classical film was really unscripted, was really made by the cinema-vérité method?

There are special cases, of course, in which this can readily be imagined: films designed to simulate the appearance of cinema-vérité, such as Mitchell Block's *No Lies* (1975), or specialized classical films like those of John Cassavetes in which the actors engage so extensively in improvisation that the camera, too, must improvise, giving rise to a cinematic style virtually indistinguishable, formally, from that of cinema-vérité. But what of classical films that are not "special cases"? What would we say if someone claimed that *Casablanca*, say, was really a cinema-vérité film, or *The Philadelphia Story*, or *Gaslight*, or *Psycho*?

Our first response would probably be to say that this is impossible, if only because, with the available technology, no cinema-vérité filmmaker could have shot, say, *Psycho*'s "shower murder" sequence, with its instantaneous shifts of camera vantage. The same is true, if on a less dramatic scale, for any classical sequence that uses "analytical" editing.

Apart from this problem, which is in a sense only a technical one, the camera in a classical film always seems to know exactly where to be to frame every action, and often seems to know this in advance, before the action takes place. The filmmaker would have to possess godlike powers always to be in the right place at the right time. Or else the filmmaker would have to be the beneficiary of an incredible succession of implausible coincidences. Such a run of luck is not impossible. Nor is it unimaginable. It, too, takes only a miracle. After all, it cannot be unimaginable for any given classical film to be a cinema-vérité film, because, as I have argued, every classical film is, in fact, first imagined this way, first envisioned as a creation of chance and whim, first envisioned as a cinema-vérité film.

It would take a miracle for a classical film, so self-possessed and composed, really to be unscripted and undirected. Yet every masterful cinema-vérité film, too, has a miraculous aspect. In every great cinema-vérité moment, the filmmaker happens on a situation so sublimely poignant, or so sublimely absurd, that we can hardly believe the stroke of fortune that reveals the world's astonishing genius for improvisation. Indeed, we never would believe it, if it were not on film.

That the cinema-vérité method, too, is capable of creating compelling, expressive, endlessly exhilarating and moving films is another inherently unpredictable fact about the world, and about film. In the face of their unexpectedly felicitous marriage, how can we not believe in miracles?

CHAPTER 23
Visconti's *Death in Venice*

Writing in 1928, Thomas Mann mockingly dismissed films as too "primitive" to be art. Instead of dwelling in art's cold, intellectual realm, films "present two young people of great beauty, in a real garden with flowers stirring in the wind, who bid each other farewell 'forever' to a saccharine musical accompaniment." Of course, in the silent era, some of these lovers on the silver screen had the stature of the great Lillian Gish, or Richard Barthelmess, or John Barrymore, or Charlie Chaplin, or Greta Garbo; in the early years of the "talkie," they included the likes of Marlene Dietrich, or Gary Cooper, or Greta Garbo (again), or Katharine Hepburn, or Cary Grant, or Ingrid Bergman. And film music was not always saccharine.

In any case, Mann's mocking tone strikes me as more than a little self-satisfied, or, perhaps more precisely, more than a little defensive. But there is an ambiguity in Mann's disdain for film: Is the problem the fact that movies happened to be made by and for people who must have appeared vulgar to a European of Mann's cultured sensibility, or does the problem lie in the nature of cinematic representation itself – the fact, or alleged fact, that film traffics in the realm of the concrete, the sensory, the individuated, not art's realm of ideas and ideals?

I suspect that Mann would not have mocked Luchino Visconti's aspirations or achievements as an artist. Who could doubt that Visconti's adaptation of *Death in Venice* does aspire to what Mann calls art's "world of inspiration, of style, of individual writings, inimitable form"? But how is it possible for what Mann would call art to be made out of the "primitive stuff" of cinematic representation?

One might be inclined to answer that just as Mann transcends the limitations of words by using them masterfully yet ironically, Visconti acknowledges and thus transcends the limitations of cinematic representation by at once mastering the film medium and using it ironically. For example, in Mann's novella, Tadzio is like Apollo, at least in Aschenbach's eyes. In Visconti's film, Tadzio is not a beautiful god; he is only a boy whose beauty is not, cannot be, ideal. Is that Visconti's point, then, that Visconti's Tadzio lacks the beauty of Mann's Tadzio, but that this is not a failure of the film, but rather an inevitable consequence of the limits of cinematic representation as such?

Yet I am convinced that Visconti *intends* his Tadzio to be as definitive an exemplar of beauty as Mann's Tadzio. I find this intention to be most explicitly declared in the early sequence in which Aschenbach views Tadzio in the hotel dining room, and Visconti conjoins shots of "viewer" and "viewed" with Aschenbach's stream of consciousness, which takes the form of an "interior dialogue" – it cannot be a literal flashback – between Aschenbach's own voice and that of Alfried, his friend, alter ego and philosophical interlocutor.

From Aschenbach's view of Tadzio, Visconti cuts to Aschenbach, the secret viewer, who is, presumably, contemplating the boy's astonishing beauty until his reverie is interrupted by a waiter bearing a bowl of soup.

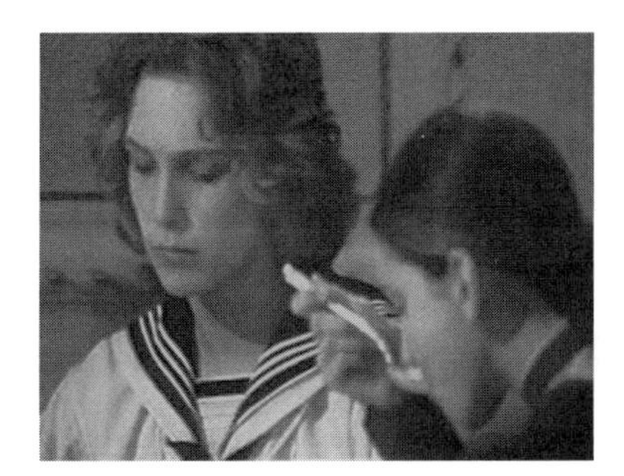

As Aschenbach lifts his spoon to his mouth, we suddenly hear Alfried's mocking voice: "Beauty? You mean *your* spiritual conception of beauty!"

Aschenbach's own voice replies (on-screen, his lips are not moving; his, too, is an "inner voice"): "But do you deny the ability of the artist to create from the spirit?"

As Aschenbach looks up to view Tadzio again, we hear Alfried's answer: "Yes, that is precisely what I deny."

At this moment, Visconti cuts to Aschenbach's view of Tadzio, then back to the secret viewer, who rubs his lip thoughtfully. "And so then, according to you, our labor as artists is. . . . "

"Labor. Exactly. . . . "

As Aschenbach raises his eyes, at once looking at Tadzio and mulling over Alfried's point, Alfried taunts him: "Do you really believe that beauty is the product of labor?"

So absorbed in this imagined dialogue that he visibly nods his head, Aschenbach answers, "Yes. Yes I do." Then he looks up yet again at Tadzio, and there is once more a cut to his point of view. Within this privileged frame, the boy's eyes momentarily *almost* meet the camera's gaze. At precisely this moment, Alfried says, astonishingly, "*That's* how beauty is born. Like *that. Spontaneously.*"

This remarkable moment decisively confirms that Visconti's film is, indeed, about cinematic representation. Alfried is making a claim about how beauty emerges in the world, or in perception, or in art. But Visconti is also making a claim, or at least posing a question, about how beauty emerges *in film*. This dialogue makes no sense unless this frame, or what is on view within it, is meant to have the status of a paradigm of film's capacity to capture or create beauty. After all, Alfried in no way denies that Tadzio *is* an exemplar of beauty; he only disagrees with Aschenbach as to what beauty is and what the example of Tadzio proves about art and life. Unfortunately, in my experiences of viewing this passage, it has everything it needs to sustain a philosophically serious meditation on film's ability to capture or create beauty except for the one essential thing – the beauty.

But *can* beauty like that possessed by the novella's Tadzio be conveyed by film? In pondering this question, it is important to keep in mind that Mann's narrator makes it clear that what Aschenbach finds divinely beautiful about Tadzio cannot be separated from the boy's humanity, which is stamped on him, as it were – the fact that Tadzio is not a god but, like Aschenbach himself, has been born into the world and is fated to die.

The narrator also makes it clear that Aschenbach's views of Tadzio do not *idealize* the boy. His beauty is not an abstraction, it is manifest concretely in all of his gestures, his specific, individuated ways of being-in-the-world, which in turn bear the aspect, to a viewer, of visible expressions of a harmonious and spontaneous inner life.

The boy Visconti casts as Tadzio is certainly quite handsome, but as Visconti directs him – and directs the camera that subjects him to its gaze – he appears wooden, manipulated, puppetlike. On screen, he projects no semblance of Tadzio's inner life, no spontaneity, no grace. In short, he completely lacks on screen what Mann's Aschenbach – or Mann's narrator, or Mann himself, or Visconti – would call "beauty."

However, isn't this lack precisely Visconti's point? I am open to the possibility that the sequence is to be "read" as siding with Alfried in opposing Aschenbach's – and Mann's – position that beauty is the union of the spiritual and the sensual or physical. All I am arguing here is that we cannot account for Tadzio's lack in this film of what Mann would call "beauty" by attributing it to the limits of cinematic representation as such. If that is what Visconti intended to demonstrate by this sequence, which I do not believe, he was misguided.

A human being on film is always also an individual, never purely an idealization or abstraction. It does not follow from this, however, that beauty such as is possessed by the novella's Tadzio is beyond the capacity of cinematic representation to convey. This would follow only if real human beings could never possess such beauty, or, should there be a human being who is beautiful in this way, if that person's beauty, for some reason, could never be captured on film.

Mann's narrator meditates on Socrates's question of whether the beauty of a beautiful boy is really "in" the boy or in the beholder. Aschenbach might not have recognized, or worshipped, Tadzio's beauty if he did not have an artist's eye, the product of a lifetime of dedication to art's strict discipline. Yet Mann's reader is not to doubt that Tadzio really *is* as beautiful as Achenbach thinks he is. This beauty is no illusion. It may fully emerge only in Aschenbach's views, but it is not the product of an artist's labor, like the beauty of Mann's burnished prose. Being who he is, all Aschenbach has to do is *view* Tadzio; the beauty emerges, as it were, automatically, the way the world emerges in a photograph. If others could view Tadzio from Aschenbach's perspective, they, too, would behold the boy's beauty, whether or not they were prepared to acknowledge it. With all their irony, Aschenbach never doubts this, nor does Mann's narrator, nor, I trust, does Mann himself.

It is the premise of the novella, its starting point, that there are human beings in the world, hence subject to be being viewed, who are capable of exemplifying beauty to those who view them. Furthermore, it *is* the case that the beauty of such human beings can be conveyed by film, although this could not have been predicted a priori.

When I suggested that the boy in Visconti's film completely lacks the beauty of the novella's Tadzio, I could equally have made my point by saying that the kind of beauty he lacks is that possessed by, say, Lillian Gish (or, for that matter, Richard Barthelmess) in *Broken Blossoms*, Marlene Dietrich in *Blonde Venus*, Greta Garbo in *Camille*, Katharine Hepburn or Cary Grant in *The Philadelphia Story*, or Kim Novak in *Vertigo*, to pick just a few examples from films whose concerns are intimately related to those of Mann's novella, films that are also profound meditations on the conditions of film's capacity to capture or create human beauty, as Visconti's *Death in Venice* aspires to be. I could also have invoked examples from Visconti's own work: Alain Delon in *Rocco and His Brothers*, say; or Burt Lancaster in *The Leopard* and *Conversation Piece*; or even Sylvana Mangano, who plays Tadzio's mother, in *Death in Venice* itself.

The crucial point is that film *is* capable of capturing or creating the kind of beauty that is the central subject of Mann's novella. Few filmmakers have known this, felt this, more fully than Visconti, which is what makes Tadzio's lack of beauty in the film so strange, so disturbing, so much in need of an account. Indeed, film is not only capable but is *uniquely* capable of conveying beauty like that of the novella's Tadzio, capable of conveying it directly, as it were, freed from the mediation of words.

Mann's narrator makes the point quite explicitly that he is aware that his words are inadequate to convey the concreteness, the particularity, with which Tadzio's beauty is manifest to Aschenbach in his views of the boy. The narrator laments that he has to resort to rhapsodic invocations of Apollo and other pitifully inadequate literary devices because his medium, words, cannot directly *show* Tadzio in the world. Yet the narrator never explicitly points out that there is now a new medium, film, which possesses precisely this power that words lack.

I suspect that Mann did not consciously make this connection when he was writing *Death in Venice*. The year of its publication, 1911, was the exact moment in the history of cinema in which the individual human figures we call "stars" were first emerging as the central focus of movies.

Death in Venice marks a major junction in the history of Mann's ideas about art, aestheticism, and modern life. It is a junction at which the histories of literature and philosophy meet. I would add that the history of film, too, passes through this crossroads.

The philosophical concerns of Mann's masterwork were to become central and abiding concerns of film. By 1911, though, no one could have predicted this. No film had as yet been made that definitively demonstrated what viewers and filmmakers, Griffith preeminent among them in this period, were on the threshold of discovering, that film is the ideal medium for capturing, or creating, or *transfiguring*, the beauty attainable, ideally, by individual human beings in the world.

CHAPTER 24

Alfred Guzzetti's *Family Portrait Sittings*

In the early 1960s, what might be called the classical period of cinéma-vérité, there was something like agreement among filmmakers in America on what a documentary was and how one was to be made. This consensus was at one level an agreement on the need to break with a tradition of American documentary, strongly influenced by British and European models, which in the late 1930s commanded *its* consensus, including such filmmakers as Pare Lorentz and Willard Van Dyke.

The older kind of documentary composed its views of people lyrically or expressionistically and used them rhetorically in illustration of some social theme. The ambition of cinéma-vérité, by contrast, was to capture the spontaneity of the human subject by recording people's behavior and interactions in their "natural" setting. The goal of filmmakers like Richard Leacock and D. A. Pennebaker was a film with no sign of direction or directedness to an audience, the screen transparently revealing human beings simply going about their lives. Increasingly flexible synch-sound technology was developed (often by the filmmakers themselves) along with increasingly effective strategies for filming people without making them appear manipulated or self-conscious.

What is projected on the screen in cinéma-vérité claims to be a recording of something that really happened, and the method by which the film was made – which defines a role for the filmmaker in filming the scene as it unfolds – seems to ensure the authenticity of the scene. Indeed, the film *formally* testifies to the method by which it was made by its camera style, which approaches as nearly as possible the condition of complete continuity – as if any cut would threaten the viewer's assurance that the filmmaker really followed cinéma-vérité method in making the film. This formal corroboration of the film's claim to be an authentic document is complemented by the

Reprinted: See "Notes on the Essays."

continuous look of unself-consciousness on the part of the filmed subjects, who appear, as it were, to *unknowingly* reveal themselves to the camera.

Part of the revelation of cinéma-vérité is that the *noncandid* – the nonspontaneous, the manipulated and the manipulative, the theatrical – is everywhere to be found in the real world. Cinéma-vérité is all but obsessed with the look of people being less than candid with themselves and each other while being unknowingly candid with the camera. In cinema-vérité films, there is another look that the camera accords a privileged status: the look of bewildered isolation of people alienated from the noncandidness in their world. People in cinéma-vérité film who appear fully human, or appear as though they know they are human, also appear alienated. Their human openness isolates them, even as it strikes us as the possible ground of a human community that does not exist within the world as framed by the film.

Cinema-vérité film affirms, then, the intelligibility of the idea of a human community, and what it "documents" is the nonexistence of such a community in one particular region of the real world. But this testimony is deeply problematic, for reasons that challenge the whole status of documentary film.

At one level, cinéma-vérité's claim to truth rests on a particular understanding of the look of unself-consciousness of the camera's human subjects. Cinéma-vérité claims that this look implies that everything within the film's frame is authentic. But this look can suggest something further, the possibility of which "classical" cinéma-vérité does not acknowledge. We cannot take for granted the authenticity of what is in the frame, because our means of access to it may be deeply implicated in its appearance. For example, the look of nondirectness-to-the-camera may itself be directed to the camera (with the filmmaker taken in by that look or in secret complicity with it). If that look of candor is authentic, the camera may nonetheless be implicated in it: The candid expression of human isolation may be seen as a mark of the presence of the filmmaker, whose role calls for him to withhold his humanity from the people he takes as his subjects. Cinéma-vérité stakes its authority on the reality of the act of filming, but it pictures the world as if this act has no tangible effect.

There is today no consensus on how to make a film that seriously claims the authority of a documentary. (There is agreement among serious filmmakers that it is part of the legacy of cinéma-vérité, and of the earlier style of documentary to which cinéma-vérité, was in part a response, that the making of documentaries constitutes a problem.) Recognizing that they cannot simply take for granted that there is a general method that ensures that the camera will reveal truths about its human subjects, some filmmakers have begun to confront the issues raised by that look of candor that cinéma-vérité took as resolving all doubts. Part of their problem is finding ways of acknowledging *within a film* the real status of the act of making the film for both filmmaker and subject, and the ways both parties have of comprehending that act. How may an investigation of the relationship of filmmaker and filmed subject be incorporated into the frame of a documentary film? How may that relationship be transformed so as to resolve the conflicts between the filmmaker's assumption of authorship of the film and the subject's right to participate in the authorization of public revelations about him or her?

Several recent types of documentary testify to this concern: for example, the autobiographical film and film diary (which make the filmmaker the explicit subject of the film) and the portrait film, with its subcategory the family portrait film.

There are several works in these genres that merit serious critical consideration, although they have received virtually none. (Then again, what area of contemporary filmmaking has engendered a humane critical literature confident of its ability to see through rhetoric and cant?) In my judgment, it is Alfred Guzzetti's *Family Portrait Sittings* (1976) that first took absolutely seriously the concerns underlying these genres and provided a compelling demonstration of one particular solution to the problem of making a documentary. (One no longer expects a general solution, the way filmmakers in the late 1930s and again in the early 1960s thought they possessed a general formula for making documentaries.) The appearance of this major work, which found a perfectly appropriate and adequate form and method, constituted an event whose importance still has not been widely recognized.[1]

The sound track of *Family Portrait Sittings* incorporates tapes of the voices of members of the filmmaker's family, reminiscing and reflecting on their lives. The characters whose narrations are thus included in the film are his mother and father, Susan and Felix; Susan's mother and her Uncle Domenick, the bachelor patriarch of the Verlangia family in America since the death of the filmmaker's grandfather; and relatives on the Guzzetti side of the family who still live in Abruzzo, Italy, and speak no English (their words are translated with subtitles).

This taped material, taken from a small number of sittings, is sometimes employed in synch-sound sequences in which the speaker is also shown. Often the taped voices are accompanied by other kinds of imagery, as discussed later.

[1] Alfred Guzzetti is Professor of Visual and Environmental Studies at Harvard University. Inquires about rental of *Family Portrait Sittings* should be addressed to Professor Alfred Guzzetti, Department of Visual and Environmental Studies, 19 Prescott Street, Cambridge MA 02138.

The voices recorded in these sittings speak narrations that thread through the entire film. The sittings also represent a clear *present* that sets off the pastness of the narrated events.

At one level, this narrative material is arranged simply chronologically. The film is divided into three parts (corresponding to its three 16-mm reels). Part 1 deals primarily with events leading up to the marriage of Susan Verlangia and Felix Guzzetti. Part 2 takes the story up to the filmmaker's early childhood. Part 3 deals with more recent events and presents as well a kind of reflective overview.

In these three parts of the film, then, the voices together tell the story of the two sides of the filmmaker's family in America, from the prehistory before the emigration up to the present. Their composite chronicle deals with such events as the coming to America of the Verlangias and the Guzzettis; the marriages of the filmmaker's sets of grandparents; the death of Dolores, the filmmaker's mother's little sister; the courtship and wedding of the filmmaker's parents; Alfred's own birth and later the birth of his sister Paula; the vicissitudes of the careers of the uncle (tailor), the mother (schoolteacher), and the father (coal business; then work on the side in candid black-and-white wedding photos; work at the Navy Yard during World War II; finally salesman in a camera shop); the move from South Philadelphia to the present semisuburban setting; Uncle Domenick's decision to remain a bachelor; Domenick's assumption of the role of head of the Verlangia family; the children's growing up.

If the spoken material is at one level organized as a complex sequential narrative, it is also arranged thematically. The film informally divides itself not just into chronological periods but also into sections devoted to different themes. Part 1 primarily concerns emigration and marriage; Part 2, childbirth and death; Part 3, work and politics.

This organization by themes, in turn, helps the film chart the concepts or categories through which the family members think of themselves, their relationships, and their world. To this end, the film's complex narrative structure complements its organization by themes. The film's story is told alternately by several narrators, each of whom is a figure in his or her own narration and also a character in the story as told by the other narrators. The terms in which each of these narrations is conceived harbor contradictions, and there are both discords and harmonies from narration to narration.

If this is a family portrait film, it is one that is seriously concerned with the place of its family within a larger historical context. Events such as the large-scale migration of southern Europeans to America around the turn of the century, the Depression, and World War II play crucial roles in the narrations of the family members. At one level, the film clearly apprehends its characters as living artifacts of a historical America. In a sense, the family portrait format is used to illustrate a particular view of history. The film, at one level, depicts the historicity of this family, as it were, from the outside, implying that an individual's form of life is determined by historical and economic forces and that an individual's form of life and consciousness are dialectically related. An individual's consciousness, reflected in the way he tells his own story, is threaded with contradictions, which in turn are bound to the conflicts and tensions integral to the fabric of his social life, very much including his life within his family.

In presenting its family as, at one level, a "case," the film establishes an "objective" authorial perspective that appears radically separate from that family's historical situation. Yet, at another level, the film constitutes the filmmaker's own acknowledgement that, despite everything, he is himself a member of this family, and dedicated to it. That is, the filmmaker's act of making this film is posited by the film as a moment *within* the family's history, although it also appears to assert a perspective separate from that history. Hence, the author implied by the film has a problematic duality. He is the analytical investigator, armed with a Marxist interpretation of history, presenting this family as a case. But he is also Alfred, son of Susan and Felix, wife of Deborah, and father of Benjamin: a major character in the film's story, an audible voice and a visible presence. Indeed, the filmmaker *as a character* shares many of the attributes the film's other characters display. He is determined, like his mother, and possessed of his father's rebelliousness and passive–agressive streak.

The filmmaker is a character in the film, but he is the only one who has this double role. As a character, he is disclosed by the camera; yet he alone, as filmmaker, has the power to direct such disclosures. But then again, part of what the film discloses of the filmmaker is that his authorial stance threatens to mask his identity as a member of his family. At one level, the film unmasks its author: This man with the movie camera is *this* son, *this* husband, *this* father.

As a member of this family, Alfred's perspective is limited, as are the perspectives of all his relatives. Then from what derives this film's *authority* – what I take to be, and accept as, its ambitious claims to speak about, and in the name of, family and filmmaking? (It would be a mistake to accept at face value the film's suggestions – for example, in its unprepossessing title – that its aims are really modest.) How can Alfred Guzzetti, from his place within his family, create a film that speaks with authority on issues such as these: What does it mean to be a member of a family? What does it mean to make a documentary film? Or even this: What does it mean to know a person? (I personally was what might be called a close acquaintance of the filmmaker when I first saw this film, the viewing and study of which leave me wanting to say two things: "Now I really know Alfred Guzzetti." "I have never known, and will never really know, Alfred Guzzetti.") The fact that whoever he or she may be, a filmmaker remains a stranger to a viewer has something to do with this film's claim that in the act of making a film, something fundamental about belonging to a family can be revealed. Part of this film's authority derives from its form, which enables its authorial perspective to emerge from the family and to be authorized by the family itself. But how can the filmmaker's family authorize his work without at the same time denying his authorship of it? This is a problem close to those we all face as we grow up and attempt to find ways of honoring our families without allowing them to dominate us.

The sound track primarily consists of taped sittings with family members. The images comprise a much wider variety of material.

1. The film opens with a series of shots taken through the front windshield of a car being driven down a typical and rather dreary Philadelphia street. Our impression is of endlessness – our penetration gets us nowhere. This series of shots comes to an end only when a traffic light signals a stop.

This series of shots suggests the arbitrariness of any entrance point into any history – and thus the arbitrariness of any way of opening this film. Perhaps it further suggests the arbitrariness of any entrance point, through birth, into life.

2. We pass to a close shot of a hand stitching a collar. It is a key to Uncle Domenick's privileged role in the film that this shot reappears much later, placed in a context that enables us to recognize that it is his hand, skilled and assured, performing this painstaking work. The film's titles appear over this shot. The last title dedicates the film to Benjamin, the filmmaker's son.

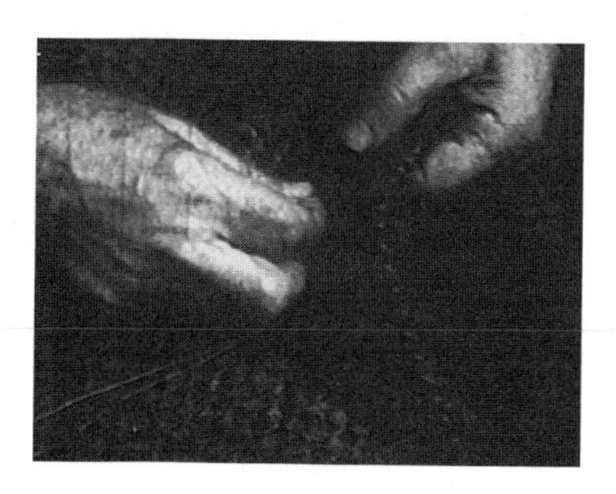

We also hear the filmmaker's voice, initiating a sitting, saying "I don't know where to start.... (As we shall see, it is only deep into the film that the status of the bearer of this voice is brought into question.)

We cut to Abruzzo, Italy, and another series of shots, closely related to the series of penetrations of space that opened the film. The family in Abruzzo is never shown, as if to acknowledge the filmmaker's own distance from them. In contrast to the overfamiliar, dreary images of Philadelphia, Abruzzo looks exotic, ancient, mysterious.

In general, the passage of the film's narrative to the present is formally marked by a succession of introductions of new, ever more "present" kinds of visual material. The shot of the uncle's hand stitching is displaced in terms of this progression; hence the need for it to return, correctly placed later in the film.

3. Footage from still photographs makes up a sizable portion of the film's image track. These photographs are manipulated in various ways. The camera rarely rests on them, but pans, tilts, pulls focus, moves out. Sometimes a shot of a photograph begins with the film's frame completely filled with white or black, so that it is only when the camera starts to move that we apprehend the object or person shown in the photograph. (Indeed, such a shot may play on a significant ambiguity. Initially, we may not even be able to tell whether we are looking at a photograph or a piece of "live" reality.) Sometimes such photograph shots are placed in series, invoking the series of shots that opens the film.

This photographic material has great beauty and poignancy. One shot in particular, beginning as a close-up of Alfred's grandfather's face and then moving out to encompass the whole photograph of grandfather and grandmother nestled on a cardboard crescent moon, magically sums up the innocence of this family's first embrace of the American dream. The manipulations of these photographs are in turn carefully intergrated into the overall composition of the film.

The most characteristic movement is one of pulling back. For example, a region of a photograph first appears in isolation, and then the cemera pulls back to disclose, if only partially, the social and historical context revealed in this wider view. Thus, a face first seen in isolation becomes a man surrounded by family and friends on the occasion of a wedding in the America of a particular era.

The expression of the face, at first seemingly entirely composed and self-contained, is revealed as well to be a reflection of a form of social life, itself embedded in a historical situation. Through such a pulling back, it is also forcibly brought home to us that this vital image was captured by a camera at a particular moment now long past, a moment irreversibly reduced by its fixation in a photograph. This realization sucks the life from the image, filling us with a sense of loss. This image does not enable us to know these people, and, in any case, the life crystallized in this image is long since gone.

4. Another kind of visual material makes its first entrance in the figure of the grandmother. This is the synch-sound footage in which we see and hear a family member speak to the camera during a formal sitting.

The film establishes its freedom to cut at any point to such "live" footage in which the present of the shooting manifests itself directly. The synch-signals on the film are not cut out, so each transition is signaled by a glaring flash of light and a loud, harsh buzzing like the ringing of an alarm clock (as if to express the shock of wresting such a present, or perhaps any present, from reminiscence of a past).

The uncle speaking in his great easy chair is the next figure presented in this way, and then the parents on their living-room sofa. These shots are composed with great care. For example, the setup showing the uncle speaking is so composed as to make most fully expressive his isolation within his easy chair – an isolation that at times suggests the authority of a patriarch, at times merely the loneliness of a bachelor.

Most brilliant, and most central to the film, is the composition of the setup showing the two parents on their sofa. For one thing, the rather long-shot places them, visually, squarely in the center of their living room. Like all the film's interiors, this room discloses its Americanness by its artifacts and their placement. Most conspicuous of these artifacts is the mirror that covers the whole wall behind the long sofa. In addition to serving throughout the film as a metaphor for the process of reflection, the mirror continually calls attention to the fact that something has clearly been excluded – or is at least not simply accidentally missing – from this frame. The mirror prevents us from merely taking for granted the absence from the frame of the filmmaker and his camera. This setup makes that absence strike the viewer as a manifestation of the filmmaker's *presence.*

As the film repeatedly cuts to this setup (with the accompanying synch-signal/alarm), we cannot help but observe the shifts in the poses and placement of the characters. The father is always seated screen right and the mother screen left, but at times they are very close to each other, at times at a middle distance, and at times as far apart as possible, as if the only limit were the (considerable) length of the sofa.

This specific composition indeed is perfectly designed to disclose the subtle interactions of the two figures as first one then the other speaks. As the one talks, we notice whether the other is attentive or fidgeting, supporting or undermining the other's narration. All of these little bits of behavior contribute to the establishment of an analytical perspective on the speeches themselves. From this detached perspective, the act of narration appears from the outside as a form of social behavior. We become interested in the relationships among the narration, the terms in which the narration is articulated, and what can be observed of the present behavior of the narrator and his or her temporarily silent partner.

5. Another kind of visual material is more elusive: the single-shot long-take portrait of a space, in the course of which the camera makes some circuit or partial circuit (for example, a 360° or near-360° pan that takes in a whole room; or a tilt down from white sky – in itself indistinguishable from the white of a photograph – passing down the whole height of the monument marking the grave of Dolores, the mother's younger sister, finally coming to rest and holding on the inscription on the base of

the monument). These "portraits" – sometimes deliberately overexposed or underexposed – are breathtaking in their beauty, possessing a quality of gravity, a gravity that at times masks an antic wit and/or an editorial comment. For example, at one point in the film, the uncle presents his views on the subject of religion, which are surprising (the two books he cites in the course of his sitting Marx's are *Capital* and Tolstoy's *Resurrection*). As he speaks, the camera makes a slow, grave circuit of a room. As he gropes to find a word for the power that holds sway over life, the camera for a moment places at the center of its frame a mirror in which we see, perfectly framed in reflection, a neartly made double bed.

It is as if the filmmaker's camera undertakes to identify a force that may or may not be identical with the divinity that Uncle Domenick has in mind. It is a force that is deeply problematic to this man whose bachelorhood is one of the central facts of his life. At one point, the camera continues shooting after the uncle completes an utterance about his bachelorhood and its presumed consequence that, after all his struggles, he will leave no one when he dies. At this moment, we can clearly see the patriarchal aspect drop away, and a look of disappointment and even bitterness rise to the surface, aspects ordinarily hidden in the makeup of his resignation.

6. The next kind of visual material that makes its entrance takes the form of home movies that turn out to have been shot by the filmmaker's father. The first of this movie footage pictures events associated with the marriage of Susan and Felix.

The filmmaker's own visual entrance into the film is effected through the emergence of home-movie footage in color (the evocative color of old home movies). The effect of this display of color nearly an hour into a film that has given all signs of being entirely in black and white is quite startling. All of this color home-movie material has a quality of unreality about it. It is also the material that most nakedly exposes the child

Alfred. Much of this footage is almost unbearably painful to watch, as if it contained private images of one's own unguarded childhood. Shots that especially have this painful private quality include the following: Alfred more or less tenderly kissing his newborn sister Paula; alfred being tucked into bed, but managing – with a lightning move – to insert his teddy bear under the advancing covers; Alfred playing ball by himself, the shot that opens Part 3 of the film; Alfred rummaging through his drawerful of books – like so many of the objects in the film, revealing artifacts of American life – selecting the cowboy book of his choice.

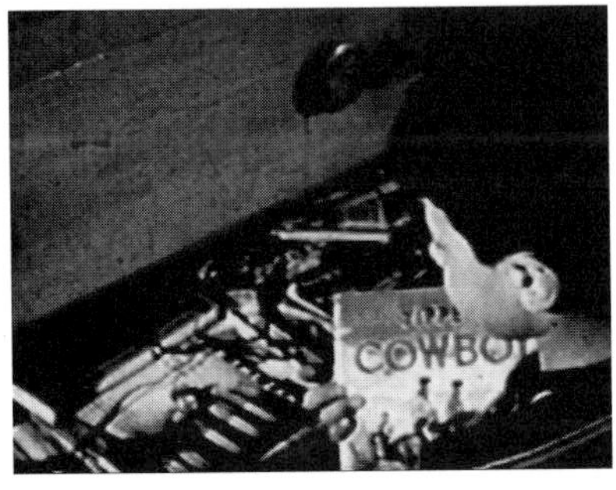

7. This leaves one last kind of visual meterial: candid cinema-vérité footage shot in the present.

We are given shots of mother, father, and uncle at work. The mother is in her classroom, with its all-too-familiar row of model script letters posted over the blackboard, and the father is selling film in the store. The uncle, tailoring, looks conspicuously less alienated, despite his own insistence that tailoring in a capitalist society is a form of slavery. This last image is the reprise of the shot of the stitching hand that was part of the credit sequence, here in its rightful place.

We are also given brief glimpses of the family gathered together socially: the family (including the filmmaker, his wife Deborah – who is never formally introduced within the film, although we hear her voice and occasionally glimpse her – and their son Benjamin) at dinner in the home of the filmmaker's grandmother, at Benjamin's birthday party, and joined by cousins, aunts, and uncles on the banks of the Schuykill in Philadelphia.

The earlier use of the color home-movie footage shot by the filmmaker's father adds to the resonance of these candid sequences, for now the filmmaker films his father filming him filming. He intercuts his own balck-and-white footage with the father's color footage, creating a sequence that incorporates images of father and son filmed by each other, disclosing both engaged in what is and is not the same activity. It is the son's film that accords the father's footage an audience beyond the family, but within this film, father's footage and son's footage are equal. The continuity between the two finds perfect expression in the attainment of a perfect matched action cut between color and black-and-white within the sequence.

Family Portrait Sittings is uncompromising in exposing tensions and conflicts that, it implies, have made, and continue to make, a struggle out of the loving relationship between Alfred's mother and father.

There are, for example, conflicts between their accounts of the history of their relationship. Each on occasion corrects the other. These contradictions often have an edge. For example, the father corrects the mother's account of a moment of reconciliation in their courtship by reminding her that his mother "never talked Italian" – a sore point in light of her family's belief that the Verlangias were higher in class than the Guzzettis (the idea is that the Guzzettis may have had more money, but the Verlangias had more respect for education).

Visible tensions reflect conflicts that run through the whole history of their relationship as they see it. Indeed, each on occasion gives the impression of wanting to go on record in declaring an area of friction in their past. Much of this friction involves ways in which they perceive their personalities as clashing. We get the impression that among their many pictures of their marriage – perhaps most of them visions of affection, respect, and love – mother and father privately harbor a few dreadful ones, which they subtly invoke in their tensest interactions, but without explicitly acknowledging them. The film is designed to enable us to read between the lines of the narrations to apprehend, for example, her picture of her husband as a failure (with the corollary that she failed to make something of him and thereby failed to redeem her marriage in her own eyes as a Verlangia). This picture is associated with her often expressed perception of his passivity. On his part, there is a picture of his wife as unbecomingly aggressive (with the corollary image of himself resenting and rebelliously, if futilely, fighting all of her efforts to dominate him).

Tensions between mother and father manifest themselves in part as a visible competition for narrative authority. Each has routines designed to undermine the other. The mother's articulateness and the father's reserved wit seem at times pitched against the other as the mortal enemy. The father's weapons include a barely perceptible rise of a skeptical eyebrow, a slight smile, and, when absolutely necessary, a flourish of nose-blowing. (He had a cold during filming and made good use of it.) By such means does he distance himself from his wife's poetic, yet sometimes barbed, embellishments to assert the superiority of his own easygoing style. For her part, the mother uses both fidgeting and a kind of fixed stare to express disapproval of certain elements in her husband's narration.

All of this, of course, is not to suggest that the film presents the relationship of the filmmaker's parents as nothing but conflict, or even as primarily tense, or that the filmmaker regards the tensions that exist between them as anything but ordinary. But the film does expose the intimate connections between the harmony within an ordinary American marriage and the conflicts integral to its history.

Among the most satisfying moments in the film are those in which harmony and discord are simultaneous. Part 1 ends with a discussion by mother and father about the era of their wedding. As their account draws to a close, we can sense a jockeying between the two speakers to get in the last word, to be the one to sum up what has been said about that period. As it happens, this competition ends in a dead heat. Closing summaries are spoken at the same time. It is a harmonious unison, except that they say different things. She: "You were doing things together." He: "You had a lot of fun." The close mesh between their two styles is apparent here, but so is the potential for friction between their narrative lines. And who can say whether at this moment in the film's present mother and father are together or apart?

Where they are in clear agreement is on the crucial subject of children. The father jokes about his wife's desire to have "a lot of animals" running around the house, but the two join in reverence of all aspects of the miracle of childbirth. This reminds us of an idea that is articulated more than once within the film: that the role of children is to fulfill the unrealized dreams of the parents. This, in turn, reminds us that these parents' competition for narrative authority is enacted before an audience. Here we come to a crucial point. The implied audience of this film, identified with the camera, is a double one. When a display of alienation from one parent's narration is directed by the other parent to the camera, the camera represents both us (strangers with no history of relationship to the characters, witnesses who are to accord the narrations the status of a document) and their son Alfred, for whose present attention they compete. The shots that expose the parents' competition for narrative authority expose as well the theatricality of their routines, reveal them to be performances directed to a present audience. Their attempts to set the record straight are also performances of old routines directed, now as always, to their son.

We return to the framing the filmmaker selects for the shots of his parents on the sofa. The fixed, frontal alignment suggests that what is enacted within this frame is a piece of theater. At one level, the framing invokes a history of performance directed by these parents to their child. But this invocation by the filmmaker/son confirms a transformation in their relationship. Alfred, as his parents' child, perhaps once felt compelled to respond with strict attention to the solicitations, commands, and so on, called forth by the magical performances directed to him. But the camera now establishes a perspective that is freed from such theatrical seductions; these performers have no power to compel *our* attention with their performances – their theatrical tricks and subterfuges are too transparent. This framing manifests the power of the child-turned-man to see through the strategies that once had helped bind him to the role of silent spectator. But a corollary of this is that this film can fully acknowledge the motivations of what its camera discloses only if the filmmaker finds a way of declaring the power of his presence behind the camera. Indeed, as the film unfolds, this power is progressively declared, until its limits are reached.

Except for his few words near the beginning of the film ("I don't know where to begin. . . . ") – which, as I have suggested, are placed outside their logical place in the film's order – we do not, until late in the film, hear the filmmaker asking any of the questions that trigger the spoken narrations. It is as if he is waiting for the right moment to speak, to assert his right to his own voice.

Before we hear the filmmaker address any formal questions, we overhear him muttering a little joke in response to his mother's claim that there was never any sense of competition between Alfred and his sister Paula. It is as if the filmmaker cannot resist dissociating himself from this claim, but is not yet ready to forsake the silence of his position behind the camera; so he gives his presence away, as it were, inadvertently.

This "slip" is followed shortly by the first of his questions that he leaves on the sound track. Alfred asks his parents why they decided to move from South Philadelphia.

This question has an edge to it. We sense a long-standing conviction that this move was a mistake – a mistake that caused the filmmaker untold grief. The new neighborhood is introduced in the film by a slow tilt down from white sky past factory chimneys to the dreary view from the back of the house. This shot in its movement and tone strikingly recalls the film's other slow downward tilt: the shot of the monument marking the grave of Dolores. (This is an example of the filmmaker's use of a "portrait" shot to make a witty, yet serious, editorial comment.)

The second question audibly posed by the filmmaker has a similar edge. He asks his parents why they decided to send him to parochial school. The answer is that the arrival of Paula precipitated this decision. With a second child in the house, Alfred had to be sent to the nearest school. Again, the film alludes to the possibility of conflicts between Alfred and Paula. The privacy of the relationship between the two is, however, faithfully respected throughout the film, opening one of the film's great mysteries. A discourse by the uncle about the inevitability of death closes with the words "Dust. . . . I don't know . . . ," conspicuously synchronized with a cut to Paula. The first time I saw *Family Portrait Sittings,* this moment and others made me think that Paula was no longer alive and that the filmmaker was preparing the viewer for a forthcoming account of her death. It is as if, through such melodramatic means, the filmmaker is expressing an ancient wish, grounded in the natural resentment of a first child for the second, to have his sister out of the way. If this was his wish, history has made it come true, only not by melodrama but by its ordinary way of separating people who once felt the daily pulse of each other's lives. The gentle lament for the distance that opened up between Alfred and Paula as their paths diverged is one of the obscurest, but also one of the most moving, strains in the film.

In part, through the filmmaker's questions, *Family Portrait Sittings* declares that the figure behind the camera who frames and places its images and sounds is Alfred, *this* son and father, possessed of *this* voice and body and life history. By relinquishing the sanctuary of his silence behind the camera, the filmmaker acknowledges that he is deeply implicated in the displays of tension and conflict that just seem to happen in the face of the camera. The camera's analytical, apparently disinterested stance reveals Alfred's power to motivate conflicts between his parents – a power bound up with a history of theatrical performances directed to him. He acknowledges his power in the film, and in the family, as an *agent,* one who acts, as filmmakers do – but then again, as grown children do, as parents do – by indirection.

The filmmaker's questions lead to one of the tensest passages in the film. Through most of its length, *Family Portrait Sittings* appears rigorously neutral in its presentation of the struggle between mother and father. The camera's analytical perspective – not as yet declared to represent the son for whom the parents within the frame are performing – does not seem to leave scope for taking sides. It is not yet clear what might turn on small or large victories in the competition for narrative authority. But shortly after the filmmaker declares his presence through his questions, a shift occurs. Perhaps my own experience of this part of the film has something to do with a sense of the poignancy of the filmmaker's humility in so understating the claim, implied in his questions, that his parents have passed over his desires. My experience hinges on suddenly getting the impression that the father has taken enough. When will he defend himself against his wife's unrelenting verbal assault? It is with real satisfaction that I witness him beginning to put his wife down. But then a corrective perception emerges. He has been playing to this desire that he assert himself, playing to an audience whose rooting interest he assumes. Has he, then, turned the camera into his accomplice, conspiring in a presentation of the mother's manner as unbecoming? Can the filmmaker be unaware of, or indifferent to, this conspiracy, or apparent conspiracy, with one parent at the price of betrayal of the other? That such secret conspiracies are part of any family's history I have no doubt.

But I feel that this film's claims to authority now call for some gesture of acknowledgment *by the filmmaker* of his compromised role. For in his act of making this film, must he not assume responsibility for his relationship with his family, even where this calls for a break with the history of his role in the family?

It is in this context that I understand the film's turning now to Uncle Domenick. It is as if to right the injustice of Alfred's treatment of his mother that her uncle characterizes her as possessing depth and a feeling for poetry. The filmmaker then presents to us the mother's voice speaking a haunting meditation on the swift and silent passage of the last twenty years of her life. Attuned to the mood evoked by her poetic voice, the film illustrates this meditation with shots of the backyard intercut with old color movie footage showing the same spot twenty years earlier. She brings her meditation to a close by remarking that her recent reawakening to the passage of time has led her to think about "generations." At this moment, we are given what we take to be a reprise of home-movie footage of the child Alfred playing with his electric trains – an image that consummates the intimacy of the sequence. But then the camera, *the father's camera,* in the present, tilts up to reveal Alfred, for the first time seen as an adult. Benjamin is the child we have just seen playing with Alfred's old trains.

Thus effected, Benjamin's entrance into the film is the moment of the filmmaker's deepest expression of commitment to both of his parents. The gesture that completes his expression of intimacy with his mother at the same time declares that he is his father's son.

This, the film's most celebratory passage, thus emerges out of one of its darkest sequences. From it, in turn, emerges another sequence of great tension.

Alfred asks his father why he never opened a photographic studio of his own. This is a tender subject. We are reminded again that before the engagement, Susan promised her family that she would "make something out of Felix." (Felix's announcement to her father was greeted with the shrug with which, apparently, he greeted all news.)

The question provokes the filmmaker's father to give an account of himself posed in an attitude of resignation that the mother clearly regards as in bad faith, and resents. Her stony silence seems to drive her husband to ever more extreme expressions of the hated resignation. Finally, he offers to the camera an indifferent shrug that uncannily recalls his description of her father's most characteristic gesture. At this moment, the whole history of their relationship unravels, momentarily exposing wounds unhealed after all these years of marriage, which at this moment looks to be a false union of beings bound to two separate families, two children.

The passage ends in a kind of tableau in which mother and father are united in a mortal appeal for help.

But their pose can also be seen as their joint expression of awareness that, singly or together, there is nothing they can now call upon their son to do, and nothing he can now call upon them to do. Perhaps it is at this moment of understanding that mother and father authorize their son's filming of them, an act of filming whose condition is that the filmmaker is neither to give nor to receive direction. The filmmaker is once again mute before these two loved figures trapped in history. But his is now the bondage of the adult who knows that there are moments when silence is the only possible mode of acknowledgment.

The film once again turns to Uncle Domenick. It is at this point that he speaks about the class struggle and tells the story of his own assumption of the role of head of the family. It is at this point, too, that the film once more presents its images of work, reclaiming the shot of the uncle's hands stitching – reclaiming, that is, the film's sole metaphor for the filmmaker's own work in creating *Family Portrait Sittings*.

Its narrations completed, its work authorized, and an image of its work reclaimed, the film is not quite ready to end. First, Uncle Domenick directly addresses Alfred behind the camera, asking the only question anyone directs to him within the film: Has the family ever asked more of him than that he allow it to witness him living a life that does honor to it? In a sense, the whole film constitutes the filmmaker's response to this question, which charges *Family Portrait Sittings* with a specific responsibility. Alfred cannot redeem his parents' dreams of themselves, as no child can. But this film, dedicated to *his* child, honors his parents even as it confronts their darkest secrets. At the same time, the act of making the film calls for the filmmaker to assume a role that places him both within and above his family, like a patriarch. When Uncle Domenick died about a year after the completion of the film, he may have thought he left no one to oversee the family. *Family Portrait Sittings* testifies otherwise. We viewers bear witness to the filmmaker's testimony.

CHAPTER 25

A Taste for Beauty

Eric Rohmer's Writings on Film

My films, you say, are literary: the things I say could be said in a novel. Yes, but what do I say? My characters' discourse is not necessarily my film's discourse.... What I 'say,' I do not say with words. I do not say it with images either, all due respect to the partisans of pure cinema, which would 'speak' with images like a deaf-mute with his hands. After all, I do not say, I show. I show people who move and speak. That is all I know how to do; but that is my true subject.

– Eric Rohmer[1]

In recent years, the advent of what is called "theory" in academic film study has led the field to turn away from the study of authorship in film, both from critical studies of individual authorships and from reflection on the implications of the fact of authorship in film, on the conditions that make authorship in this singular medium possible. Historically, this turning away occurred at the precise moment rigorous practices of film criticism, responsible to the films and to the critic's experience, were being instituted in the university, and film study was claiming – and beginning to earn – its rightful place in the university's intellectual life.

When the field turned away from "author criticism," it turned away from other modes of criticism as well. Instead of critical acts grounded in experience, it turned to a succession of "isms" that shared a common understanding of the role of theory: Theory was to be primary, and was to be applied to films from the outside, seeking neither inspiration nor evidence from the films themselves or from the theorist's experience of them. Predictably, these theorists discovered in the films only what the theories they were applying had already determined a priori to be there. As a consequence, the achievements of the masters of the art of film – that is, the films themselves and the achievements of those critics who defied fashion and never abandoned criticism – remain substantially unacknowledged by

[1] Eric Rohmer, "Letter to a Critic: Concerning my *Contes Moraux*," in *The Taste for Beauty* (New York and Cambridge, England: Cambridge University Press, 1989), p. 80.

a field that nonetheless possesses the means to acknowledge them. In other words, this "turning away" was – and is – also a repression.

For film study to undo this repression, to come to itself in the wilderness of theory, it must attain a new perspective on itself – on its own history; on its subject, film; and on film's history. I view the publication in English of this collection of Eric Rohmer's essays on film written between 1948 and 1979 as an important step toward this goal.

Love them or hate them – and all film lovers seem to fall into one or another of these camps – no one would deny that Eric Rohmer's films bear his personal signature. Rohmer has his own unique style, method, and thematic concerns and his own unique vision of the power and limits of the film medium. Rohmer is an *auteur* if ever there was one. And as the essays in this volume abundantly demonstrate, when it comes to film criticism, too, Rohmer is an author who must be taken seriously.

"I don't believe there is one good critic who isn't inspired by an idea, either of art, of man, or of society," Rohmer writes.[2] It is clear that Rohmer is indeed inspired by such an idea, around which all his critical writing revolves: It is Bazin's seminal insight that the key to film lies not in the realm of language but in the realm of ontology, in film's unique, unprecedented relationship to reality, a relationship that is radically different from that of literature, theater, or painting:

> Up until film, one had to either paint a painting or describe something. Being able to photograph, to film, brings us a fundamentally different knowledge of the world, a knowledge that causes an upheaval of values.[3]

Film does not say, it shows. For Rohmer, this principle has fundamental implications on the nature of the art of film:

> Painting, poetry, music, and so forth try to translate truth by the intermediary of beauty, which is their kingdom, and with which they cannot break without ceasing to exist. The cinema, on the contrary, uses techniques which are instruments of reproduction or, one might say, of knowledge. It possesses the truth right from the beginning, in a sense, and aims to make beauty its supreme end. A beauty, then, and this is the essential point, which is not its own, but that of nature. A beauty which it has the mission, not of inventing, but of discovering, of capturing like a prey, almost of abstracting from things.... But while it is true that the cinema manufactures nothing, it doesn't deliver things to us in a neat package either: it arouses this beauty, gives birth to it.... If it gave us nothing but things which were known in advance, in principle if not in detail, all it would capture would be the picturesque.[4]

[2] Ibid., p. 64. [3] Ibid., p. 11. [4] Ibid., p. 75.

In turn, what film is has fundamental implications for the direction the history of the art of film has taken:

Ever since the cinema attained the dignity of an art, I see only one great theme which it proposed to develop: the opposition of two orders, one natural, the other human; one material, the other spiritual; one mechanical, the other free; one of the appetite, the other of heroism or of grace; a classical opposition, but of which our art is privileged to be able to give such a direct translation that the intermediary of the sign is replaced by immediate evidence. A universe of relationships therefore appeared which the other arts may have illuminated or designated but could not show: the relationship between man and nature and between man and objects – directly perceptible relationships, which are quite beautiful – but also, since the age of the talkies, the less visible relationship between the individual and society.[5]

I have quoted these passages at length because they are so characteristic. Reading the essays in this volume, so profoundly insightful, so cogently and eloquently expressed, I am continually struck that Rohmer is very much a figure from a bygone age, an age these pages bring vividly to life, the postwar age when the best minds of a generation (at least in France) fervently believed in cinema, believed that making films, and also viewing and thinking about them, was a heroic enterprise. It was the age of André Bazin's pioneering investigations of the ontology of film, the age of the founding of *Cahiers du cinéma*, the age of the triumphant emergence of the "*Nouvelle Vague*." And it was also the age that immediately preceded film study's turning away from criticism. It is no accident that it was the thinking of this postwar age, and specifically thinking like Rohmer's, that film study repressed above all when the field turned away from criticism.

Nor is it an accident that the essays in this volume, which speak to us from a bygone age, are nonetheless so stunningly contemporary. I do not mean by this that they resemble current writing about film, which of course they do not. Rather, Rohmer's questions and ideas are fresh and alive today precisely because they have been repressed, not addressed, by film study. The vibrant life in Rohmer's writing gives it the power of making most of today's academic writing about film seem obviously repressed and repressive, dead from the neck up and the neck down, and specifically dated – dated because it is clearly past time for such denial of life to end.

As a filmmaker, Rohmer is not only still active but at the peak of his powers, continuing to make films that are at once classical and astonishingly modern. In his films as in his critical writing, Rohmer strikes me as a figure from a bygone age. Yet his films, old and new, also have the power of making most other films seem dated. These films about contemporary life, pulsing

[5] Ibid., p. 64.

with life themselves, are decisive demonstrations of the undiminished power of the ideas that are worked out in this volume – the ideas about humanity, freedom, history, space, time, language, art, beauty, and, of course, about the medium, the art, and the history of film.

The ideas that stand behind Rohmer's films are also the ideas that stand behind his critical writing, enabling it to penetrate to the heart of the films made by the masters he most admires, such as Renoir, Murnau, Hitchcock, Hawks, and Rossellini. Rohmer's own films cry out for criticism that is equally penetrating, honest, responsible and philosophical. I hope that the publication of this volume will help spur the field to undertake to acknowledge Rohmer's exemplary authorship. That is a challenge fit to awaken film study from its dogmatic slumbers.

CHAPTER 26

Tale of Winter

Philosophical Thought in the Films of Eric Rohmer

In his long career as a filmmaker, Eric Rohmer has made over thirty films that consistently evidence an interest in philosophy, as exemplified by his 1991 masterpiece *Tale of Winter*. My modest goal in this essay is to collect a few thoughts about *Tale of Winter*, all of them exploratory, that relate directly or indirectly to the topic "Philosophical Thought in the Films of Eric Rohmer."

There was a time when I confessed my taste for Rohmer films only with embarrassment. This was not only because so many of my friends found them boring. (Dwight McDonald once said that viewing a film by Antonioni was like watching paint dry. Some would say this of a Rohmer film, too.) There was also a sense that Rohmer films were ideologically suspect. Rohmer's characters talk a lot, and much of what they say irritated people, or, at least, my friends. Even critics who have cared enough to write about Rohmer's films have found themselves adopting a patronizing tone. And yet it now seems to me a fair wager that history will judge Rohmer, along with Jean-Luc Godard, to be the greatest of the "New Wave" directors.

Before he began making films, Rohmer, a founding editor of *Cahiers du cinéma*, was a formidable film critic and theorist, very close in his views to those of André Bazin. Rohmer's writings, like Bazin's, continually return to the fact or intuition that film's basis in photography makes it a medium in which reality plays a special role. In Rohmer's view, as in Bazin's, film transforms or transfigures reality, but it is reality itself – reality in all its beauty and mystery, life and not its mere semblance – that appears before us, transformed or transfigured in, or by, the medium of film.

Just saying this much brings to mind the wonderful passage in *Tale of Winter* in which Loic takes Félicie to a performance of *The Winter's Tale*. (Rohmer has said that a performance of Shakespeare's play inspired him to make *Tale of Winter* – his own tale about recovering what seems irretrievably lost – and, indeed, the entire series he calls "Tales of the Four Seasons.")

When Leontes expresses astonishment, and alarm, at an art capable of instilling in a lifeless statue the very breath of life, who can doubt that in this late work Shakespeare is reflecting on his own art of theater, an art that "brings words to life, or vice versa," as Stanley Cavell characterizes it in "Recounting Gains, Showing Losses (A Reading of *The Winter's Tale*)"?[1] And who can doubt that Rohmer, in his late work, is thinking of his own art of film, an art that brings not words but *the world* to life, or vice versa.

Already in D. W. Griffith's 1909 short film *The Drunkard's Reformation*, intercutting between actors performing a play on stage and members of the play's audience enabled a filmmaker to assert film's separation from theater by demonstrating the singular powers of the new medium. When Paulina brings the statue of Hermione to life, her art miraculously weds the real and the fantastic, the natural and the supernatural. "If this be magic," Leontes says, "Let it be an art as lawful as eating." (To the French, of course, to say such a thing is to speak a mouthful.)

For Shakespeare's moment to have its full effect, the play's audience must be mindful of what it would be like for anyone to behold a statue brought to life, and what it must be like, in particular, for Leontes, for Perdita, for Hermione herself, for Paulina, and for us. For Rohmer's moment to have its full effect, the film's viewers must be mindful of what Shakespeare's moment would be like to any audience member, and what it must be like, in particular, for Félicie, the film's protagonist, played so vividly by Charlotte Véry, and for us.

Shakespeare's moment speaks so particularly to Félicie because it mocks her own situation. She has left one man for another, whom she has in turn just now left for a lover lost so long there seems little chance of his ever returning. Like Anna Karina in Godard's *Vivre sa vie*, who weeps as she views Carl Dreyer's *The Passion of Joan of Arc*, Félicie weeps as she beholds the statue come to life. Are they tears of joy? Has this moment of theater awakened her hope? If faith, and art, can return Hermione from the dead, can it bring her lover Charles back to Félicie, too? Is Félicie capable of such a faith? Is Rohmer capable of such an art?

It is true, as Leontes says, that "no fine chisel could ever yet cut breath." But for a woman on film to breathe, to move, to speak, is only natural. What, then, makes Rohmer's moment almost as astonishing, and beautiful, as Shakespeare's?

Of all the gin joints in the world, Ingrid Bergman walks into Rick's. Of all the plays in the world, it is *The Winter's Tale* that Loic and Félicie have

[1] Stanley Cavell, "Recounting Gains, Showing Losses," in *In Quest of the Ordinary: Lines of Skepticism and Romanticism* (Chicago: University of Chicago Press, 1988), p. 97.

tickets for. In Griffith's *The Drunkard's Reformation*, it is no coincidence that it is a temperance play called *A Drunkard's Reformation* that the alcoholic father takes his little girl to see, for his wife, who stays at home, prays that he will recognize himself in the play's doomed protagonist and that the art of theater will move him to change his ways. But it *is* a coincidence that Loic takes Félicie to the one play that Shakespeare could have written especially for her. Loic, who has always found *The Winter's Tale* implausible and is unmoved by the performance, had no idea she would take it so much to heart. Then again, philosopher though he may be, Loic does not understand what Shakespeare's play is about.

Félicie is struck by how directly *The Winter's Tale* speaks to her, and we are struck by the astonishing coincidence between Shakespeare's tale and Rohmer's. We take this as a sign that, however "naturally" the events in *Tale of Winter* seem to unfold, however an author's hand seems absent, within this world there are no accidents. It is not only implausible, it is *fantastic* that Félicie finds herself attending *The Winter's Tale*, of all plays. However fantastic, though, we know it is *possible* for we see it with our own eyes. We know now, if we had not known before, that in the world of this film even that most implausible of all coincidences – call it a miracle – for which Félicie hopes against hope, the return of her lost lover, can – perhaps will – happen.

The point is that coincidences that would be astonishingly implausible in reality take place all the time in films. In the world on film, as Cavell observes in *The World Viewed*, anything is possible. So we are still left with our question, What makes Rohmer's moment almost as astonishing, and beautiful, as Shakespeare's?

When Leontes' faith has been awakened, and Paulina is satisfied that it is time to bring the statue to life, she says, "Music, awaken her! Begin!" and exits the frame. Throughout this sequence, it is worth noting, Rohmer is very particular as to who is inside, and who outside, each frame. In the rest of the film, Rohmer follows the so-called "180-degree" rule, the convention that a sequence may be made up of shots taken from a wide range of angles so long as the camera in every one of those shots occupies a position on the same side of an imaginary line. Shooting *The Winter's Tale* performance, though, Rohmer reverts to Griffith's way of shooting, long archaic. He allows the camera to vary the angle within a scene by pivoting on its tripod, and allows for cuts to close-ups, medium shots, and long shots to make the size of the image reflect greater or lesser intimacy or intensity of attention. But the camera remains fixed at one, and only one, point in space, as if to identify the world of the film with a play performed on a stage, and the camera's perspective, and ours, with the point of view of a member of the play's audience.

The moment Paulina exits our view, a flutist enters and raises her flute to her lips, the camera moving with her so as to bring first the curtain, and then the "statue," into the frame.

The flutist begins to play, not taking her eyes off the "statue," which raises first one hand and then the other as if she were animated by the spirit of the music.

Attributing life-giving power to music and by extension to film reveals what I think of as the Jean Renoir in Rohmer. But in this passage, what is crucial is not only the spirit of music, but this particular piece of music, which we recognize, and the fact that we recognize it. And this reveals the Alfred Hitchcock in Rohmer. (Think of the return of Mr. Memory, and his theme song, at the end of *The Thirty-nine Steps*.) Uncannily, the flutist plays the very tune we remember from the film's idyllic prologue. Within the prologue, that tune, repeated incessantly, expressed at once the carefree joy of lovers unaware fate is about to part them and a bittersweet awareness of the transience of all beauty. The duality of the prologue's music – in time, yet timeless – invites us to identify with the lovers, yet places us at an aesthetic distance – it is also an ironic distance – from them.

As the flutist repeats the tune, Rohmer cuts to Félicie, so moved she squeezes Loic's hand, then back to the stage, reprising the framing of the flute player and the "statue," which begins walking forward as Paulina's voice, offscreen, intones the words, "'Tis time. . . . "

The music that accompanies the prologue is virtually the only "movie music" in the film. We take it to have no existence within the world of the film, hence to go unheard by the lovers. When the flutist plays this tune, we can recognize it, but it is not possible for Félicie to do so. Her experience of this moment and ours thus diverge. Recognizing this tune, remembering the prologue, we feel that the film is revealing a sign to us, but not to her.

And yet Félicie feels that a sign is being revealed to her, too – a sign that repeats, and confirms, the earlier "premonition," as she calls it, that she experienced in the Nevers Cathedral. If, at this moment in the theater, we did not feel a sign was being given to us, how could we have so much as an idea of how Félicie is experiencing this moment, what, in particular, it means to her? At this moment, Rohmer's art, which separates us from this woman, also joins us with her. She is moved by Paulina's art, and Shakespeare's, to experience a premonition. We are moved by Rohmer's art to experience our own premonition, an uncanny sense that the future is being revealed in the present. And our premonition, like Félicie's, also coincides with remembering an earlier moment – the moment of her first premonition, and ours, in the cathedral. At that earlier moment, too, knowledge of the present, revelation of the future, and recollection of the past, coincided.

That passage begins with little Elise dragging her mother into the cathedral to see what the English subtitles call "the Nativity."

Abruptly cutting from the two outside the cathedral to the two now inside – Rohmer does not bother with conventional connecting shots; for all his alleged artistic conservatism, he remains, stylistically, a New Wave director – Rohmer cuts again to a close shot of the Nativity, which we can take to be from the point of view of Félicie, or Elise, or perhaps both.

In this shot, both the people and animals, represented by crude statuettes, are beholding a little figure in a straw bed. Félicie's voice says, over this shot, "See the little Jesus?"

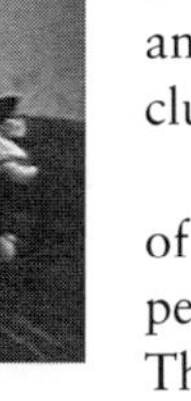

As if to answer Félicie's question – that is, as if the camera is claiming or acknowledging a special bond with little Elise – Rohmer cuts to a yet closer view, in which only "Jesus" and a lamb beholding him are included in the frame.

Over this haunting shot, its sense of silence enhanced by her whisper, Félicie says, "Recognize him?" Then, not as an answer to her question, this time, but in lieu of an answer, as if the camera has lost, or for its own purposes is deliberately suspending, its attunement with Elise, Rohmer cuts back to the longer, more matter-of-fact framing. Félicie tells her daughter to "Come along." But Elise wants to stay.

Félicie does not much care whether Elise recognizes Jesus, I take it. But she does want Elise to recognize Charles as her own father should he ever return. The effect of Rohmer's precise synchronizing of Félicie's questions with these particular cuts, though, is to identify Elise, beholding the Nativity as if it were a scene in a film, with the watchful little lamb within that scene, and to identify innocent child and lamb, both viewers, with us. It is as if Rohmer is here acknowledging how much he values, even as he questions, *our* capacity for recognition.

These shots recall an earlier passage that hinges on Elise's own paintings. Elise, the viewer, is also an artist. In their ways, Félicie and Maxence, both "beauticians," and Charles, a chef (if all the food he prepares is "lawful," that might help him earn a Michelin star), are artists, too. But it is Elise's art that the film presents as exemplary. (For whom does she paint her paintings, Elise is asked. Her answer: "They're for everybody.")

Early in the film, as Elise is telling Félicie about her day, she says "I played with Anna," and Rohmer cuts to a painting, taped to the wall, that we recognize, or try to recognize, as representing "Anna" in the little girl's creative imagination. Elise says "We played Daddy and Mommy" and "We played Yellow Mouse, Pink Mouse and Green Mouse," and Rohmer cuts to another, then yet another, of Elise's paintings. "We played the Mailman didn't come, and the Thief," Elise goes on, and Rohmer, wittily, cuts to no painting at all.

 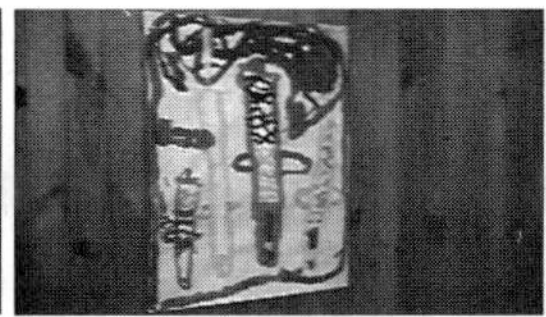 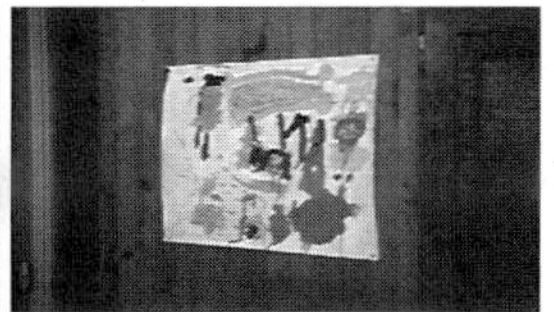

As Félicie moves away from the crib, holding Elise's latest painting in her hand, the camera's movement, paired with hers, effects at once Félicie's exit from the frame and the entrance first of a curtain – see Rohmer's filming of the moment the "statue" comes to life – then of a photograph of her lost lover, with a doll looking out at the camera from behind the photograph's frame, as if this were a shot from a von Sternberg–Dietrich film.

Félicie reenters the frame, eclipsing the photo, then exits, her movement and the camera's combining to make the photo, larger than ever, fill the frame as the image fades out.

 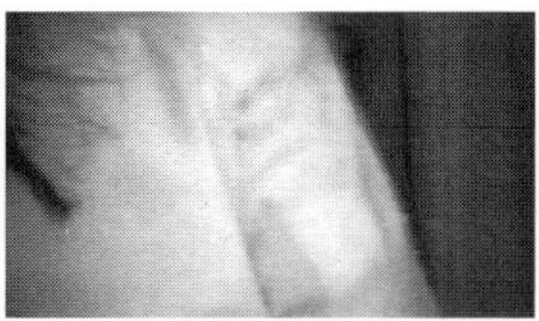 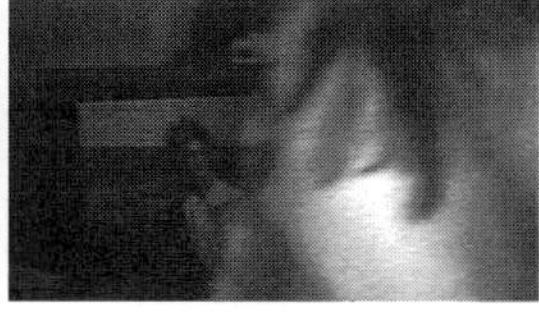

Later, in the climactic scene on the bus, Rohmer will marry the movements of Félicie and the camera to similar effect, revealing to us – but not yet to Félicie – that she is now face to face not with a mere photograph of the longlost Charles, but with Charles himself.

But back to the cathedral.

Saying "You can look, but don't touch," Félicie begins strolling screen right, the camera following her, so that Elise, continuing to look at the little Jesus, is made to exit the frame. Now alone on screen, Félicie continues walking along the edge of the stagelike platform, and then sits. On her motion, Rohmer cuts to a nearly symmetrical, airy shot, then to a medium close-up of Félicie, sitting alone amidst a sea of empty chairs.

This shot, one of the great glories of the film, lasts almost a full half-minute. As it commences, Félicie's eyes are looking ahead and up, as if she were still beholding the striking view that a moment ago had been ours. She looks down, looks a bit up, then, as if suddenly catching sight of something, holds her gaze steady, although she seems less to be looking outward than turning inward, trying to recognize what is in her sight.

Astonishingly, we now begin hearing the tune from the film's prologue, played tantalizingly softly. It is not possible for Félicie to hear this music, yet she seems to be trying to bring it to consciousness, or to place it. After the first musical phrase, she bites her lip, deep in thought, and looks back up, as if the space of the cathedral, with its high vaulted ceiling and glorious stained glass windows, might provide the answer. The tune is played again, and then again. As the music cadences, she once more looks forward, now seeming convinced she has found what she had been seeking. As the shot ends, she is pressing her lips together, resolute but a little sad. And then, as so often in the film, Rohmer cuts abruptly to a contrasting framing: a striking shot of the front door of Max's salon. A moment later, clearly anticipated by the camera, Félicie and Elise enter the frame and walk through this door.

It frequently happens in a Rohmer film that a state of affairs is first established by the camera and later becomes a subject of conversation. In this way, both Félicie's experience in the theater and her experience in the cathedral are both discussed at length in a remarkable conversation between Félicie and Loic, beginning in his car and continuing in his apartment, in which first Blaise Pascal and then Plato are invoked.

Félicie's account matches what we have viewed, except that she gives a name to what she was doing in those thirty seconds in which the camera was studying her face and the music was giving us an objective correlative, as it were, for what was transpiring within her: She was *praying*, she says, but not the way she was taught as a child. She was meditating, not thinking of God or asking anything of him. "Suddenly, everything was clear.... I saw I was alone in the world: it was up to me to act, and not be pushed around by anyone or anything."

"That won't help you find Charles," Loic interjects.

"I won't do things that keep me from finding him. Besides, I thought of something else in that second. Maybe you're right: Finding him's unlikely, he may be married, or doesn't love me. But that's no reason for me to give up."

"If even you admit your chances are nearly nil, why ruin your life for... "

"Because if I find him, it'll be a joy so great I'll gladly give my life for it. And I'm not ruining it: not everyone lives with hope."

When Félicie remarks that her reasoning must seem inadequate to a trained philosopher like Loic, he replies, "It's not stupid. Someone very bright said it earlier. Almost word for word... Pascal. He calls it a bet: If you bet on immortality, the stake is so huge it makes up for the long odds. Even if the soul isn't immortal, believing it is lets you live better."

"I believe the soul's immortal more than you do," Félicie replies. "You believe in it only after death, I say it exists before birth.... If the soul lives on afterward, why didn't it live before?... Why am I certain I love Charles? How can I be absolutely sure? When I met him, I felt I'd been through it before. How do you explain it unless we'd met in a former life?"

Once again, Loic identifies Félicie's thoughts with those of a major philosopher. Not Pascal, this time, but Plato. "The point is he reasoned just like you to prove the soul's immortal," Loic says, and goes on to read a passage: "'Your doctrine, that knowledge is simply recollection, if true, also implies a previous time in which we have learned that which we now recollect. This would be impossible unless our soul... had been in some place before existing in the form of man.'"

I have described this scene at such length because the dialogue is so delightful, and so particular to Rohmer. In this scene, Félicie, untutored in philosophy, is articulating what she calls her "intimate convictions," and Loic, trained in philosophy, is charting her thoughts in relation to those of philosophers of the stature of Pascal and Plato. Rohmer expects us, I take it, to accept Félicie's point that Loic differs from her by always checking his experience against books. And to accept that, although Félicie may be naive, by wanting to be herself, and by being prepared to risk sailing uncharted waters, she is more advanced, spiritually, even philosophically, than Loic.

Rohmer's films often revolve around women like Félicie who are admirable because they attend to their own experience with the kind and degree of attention necessary to know the thinking of major philosophers, but who follow their own hearts, not books. Yet Rohmer's films also include male characters, like Loic, who are trained in philosophy and are forever charting, through books, those women's ways of thinking and living. Evidently Rohmer himself is not unlike such male characters. He uses them to chart, through books, the ways of thinking and living of the admirable women who are at the heart of his films.

In *Tale of Springtime* (1990), there is an extended dialogue about Kant's transcendental philosophy. It occurs within a long scene involving the protagonist, no doubt the only woman in the history of film who is a sympathetic philosophy teacher; her teenage friend, who would like her father to become romantically interested in the philosopher; the friend's father; and a rather defensive woman who is a philosophy graduate student and also the father's present lover.

In writing about *It Happened One Night* in *Pursuits of Happiness*, Cavell finds deep connections between Kant and the art of film as Frank Capra understands and practices it. A comparable intuition of film's affinity with transcendental philosophy underlies the discussion of Kant in *Tale of Springtime*, I take it. There is this obvious difference, though: Whereas the Rohmer film incorporates an extended reference to Kant, it is only Cavell's writing about Capra's film that refers to Kant, not the film itself (I suppose I should say "the film *an sich*"). I must hasten to add, however, that the dialogue about Kant in *Tale of Springtime* incorporates an assertion by the film's philosopher protagonist that her young friend, who is just beginning to study philosophy and has not yet mastered Kant's vocabulary, nonetheless thinks and lives her life in ways that reveal her to be more attuned to Kant's transcendental philosophy than the more technically advanced philosophy student will ever be.

That a philosopher in a Rohmer film should invoke Kant is thus not surprising. And, given the women they are drawn to, and given those women's forms of life and ways of thinking, it is not surprising that Rohmer's philosophers often invoke Pascal, too. For there is an obvious affinity between Félicie's thinking, for example, and Pascal's.

Cavell calls the Cary Grant character in *The Philadelphia Story* a philosopher. But this "Emersonian sage," as Cavell also calls him, being American and unschooled in the history of Western philosophy, does not check his experience against books (although he is a reader, and his grandfather built the local library). If he had received a proper French education, he, too, might find himself lecturing the woman he loves about Pascal, as part of his effort to help her open her eyes, to plunge into uncharted waters, to take risks.

Almost without exception, Rohmer's films are romantic comedies. But although they are akin to the American comedies of remarriage Cavell has studied, they are not members of that genre. It is not hard to go through *Tale of Winter*, for example, and enumerate some of the features of the remarriage comedy that Rohmer's film negates.

- In *Tale of Winter*, Félicie's father is absent. Then again, she does not need a father, or any man, to help her to open her eyes; her eyes *are* open.
- Félicie's father is absent, but her mother is very present. And Félicie herself *is* a mother.
- It is not her true love Charles but her friend Loic whom Félicie feels she has known for so long – not only all her life, but all her lives – that she feels they are like sister and brother. (Hence *Tale of Winter* lacks the Oedipal dimension internal to remarriage comedies and their affinity with Freudian psychoanalysis, which the opening of *The Lady Eve* both acknowledges and mocks. In Rohmer films, cigars are just cigars, and a "*lapsus*," such as Félicie's fateful act of writing the wrong name of her home town and thus making it impossible for Charles to find her, is nothing but an inexplicable mistake with no hidden meaning.)
- The obstacle to the union, or reunion, of Félicie and Charles is external to their relationship. Their relationship does not stand in need of change.
- The perfect relationship between the lovers – whether they will literally marry is never explicitly at issue – is represented, within a film made up of an almost unbroken succession of conversations, as all but wordless, the music underscoring the sense of silence. (Charles speaks the prologue's only line of dialogue: "You're taking a risk.")
- Félicie, in finally arriving at a decision, does not change her way of thinking; she comes to see more clearly how she really does think.

We might take this last point, that Félicie is not called upon to change her way of thinking, to imply that she never achieves the perspective that the woman in a remarriage comedy achieves when she finally comes to recognize that her identity as a human being is not, cannot be, fixed. In a remarriage comedy, the woman longs to become the fully human being she is capable of becoming, but this is a process that is not yet and can never be completed. Félicie, too, feels it is her responsibility endlessly to perfect herself, but this quest calls for her not to change but to acknowledge how she thinks, whom she already is, whom she has always been.

Yet we might also take the fact that Félicie is not called upon to change to imply that from the outset she already possesses the perspective that the woman in a remarriage comedy must die and be reborn in order to achieve. Félicie's compass is fixed. But that is because she charts her course by her own heart. Then again, it is one of her "intimate convictions" that every human being has already died and been reborn innumerable times. (As the little girl in Renoir's *The River* puts it, "Babies can be born again and again, can't they?")

In her conversation with Loic, Félicie claims to his dismay that she is aware of her former lives, if only dimly, and that there is no other way to account for her certainty that the absent Charles is the man she really loves. Loic recognizes that she is thinking like Plato, but this way of thinking goes against his own "intimate convictions."

Most of Félicie's "intimate convictions" are principles that Rohmer has reason to expect viewers readily to accept. But does Rohmer believe – do we? – that people *are* aware of former lives, if only dimly, and that there is no other way to explain how people can be certain who it is they really love? Doesn't that belief make Félicie a bit flaky, a bit Shirley MacLaine-like?

Rohmer is well known for his idiosyncratic method of composing his screenplays. He conducts such extensive interviews with his actors and especially his actresses, touching on so many subjects – conversations that last for many months – that he is able to study how they speak, how they think, and can then model his characters' expressions, mannerisms, and gestures so precisely on their "originals" that they emerge with astonishing vividness, with the very breath of life. Charlotte Véry may well believe, as her character Félicie does, that souls are born again and again and that all knowledge is recollection. But what makes these beliefs – these "myths," as Loic calls them – meaningful within the film?

When in *The Lady Eve* Henry Fonda not once but twice tells Barbara Stanwyck that he has loved her in lifetime after lifetime since the beginning of time, the film is mocking – but also acknowledging that it is sucker enough to buy into – a myth of reincarnation that, the film suggests, is internal both to the concept of "romance" and to what movies are, to what makes them important.

Corollary to Félicie's belief in reincarnation is her belief that people are "types" and that it is natural for people who are themselves types to be attracted to some types but not others, or attracted to different types in different ways. In Rohmer, as in Renoir, nature underlies or underwrites tales of romance. But in Rohmer's films, as in Hitchcock's, people often act contrary to nature. Unlike Hitchcock, who often enjoys a perverse relation to his characters, however, Rohmer cherishes – and almost without exception rewards – characters who are truest to their nature, who dislike and oppose what is contrary to nature. Yet Rohmer also understands that in today's world the respect for nature his films exemplify and champion, hence nature itself, is endangered.

All of this is an open invitation for those who would think seriously about Rohmer's work to ponder Cavell's thoughts, in *The World Viewed* and amplified in "More of *The World Viewed*," about the role of types as film's means of rendering human individuality. And to ponder, as well, Cavell's understanding that film is a medium in which everything, and everyone, has a previous existence, as it were, and that human beings on film are capable of being reborn, reincarnated, again and again. No wonder Rohmer's philosophers find themselves invoking Plato as well as Pascal.

Although *Tale of Winter* is a romantic comedy, not a melodrama, it may seem to share more features with the films Cavell calls "melodramas of the unknown woman" than with comedies of remarriage. I am thinking, for example, of the facts, already mentioned, that in Rohmer's film the woman's mother but not her father is present and that she is herself a mother. To this I would add the crucial fact that, for all her conversations in the film, Félicie finds herself, in her lover's absence, in a state of isolation so profound as to appear to partake of madness. Perhaps the only real difference between *Tale of Winter* and, say, *Letter from an Unknown Woman* – but what a difference! – is that in Rohmer's film the man's love is as constant as the woman's. Through all his absence from Félicie's world, and from the film, Charles never forgets his love for her. And he never forgets *her*. After all these years, and without even a photograph to remember her by, he recognizes Félicie the moment he lays eyes on her.

Nonetheless it takes a miracle, or at least an astonishing coincidence, for these lovers to be reunited, for *Tale of Winter* to achieve the seamless joining of ideal and real, mythical and ordinary, supernatural and natural, that makes its ending so satisfying that even little Elise finds herself weeping tears of joy.

Late in the film, Félicie reminds Loic that it is Sunday and that to be true to his intimate convictions he should be at church. Sending him away, she asks him to pray for her. Her conviction is that she, alone, must take responsibility for her actions. It is against her convictions to ask God for anything. But it is not against her convictions for *Loic* to ask God for the thing she would ask for were it not against her convictions to ask for it: "Do it from the bottom of your heart," Félicie says seductively to Loic, and he says he will try. Félicie, amused, knows that Loic does not understand, as she does, that doing something from the bottom of one's heart is not a thing it is possible to *try* to do. Yet *Tale of Winter* pointedly leaves open the possibility that the "miracle" about to happen is God's answer to Loic's, or perhaps Félicie's, prayer.

But who, or what, in a Rohmer film, is God?

It is as true of a Rohmer film as it is of a Hitchcock film that one can walk in at any moment and know within seconds who the film's author is. Unlike the remarriage comedy or the melodrama of the unknown woman, the "Hitchcock thriller" cannot be defined, its underlying myth cannot even be told, without characterizing the role the figure of the author plays within its world. In a Hitchcock film, God is Hitchcock, the film's author. But in *Tale of Winter*, the author seems to be absent; God is the author of this world, it seems, not the author of this film. Yet it is not God, it is Eric Rohmer, who rewards Félicie and Charles for their faith by composing an ending that has the lovers meet again, by sheer coincidence, on a bus. For all his absence, Charles never stops being real within Félicie's world. Within *Tale of Winter*, the film's author never stops being real, for all his absence. Then again, the world on film, for all its absence, never stops being real, either. We might also say that the world on film, for all its reality, never stops being absent.

Cavell writes of the ending of *The Winter's Tale*:

> The resurrection of the woman is, theatrically, a claim that the composer of this play is in command of an art that brings words to life, or vice versa, and since the condition of this life is that her spectators awake their faith, we, as well as Leontes, awake, as it were, with her.[2]

For Shakespeare, we have said, theater is an art that "brings words to life, or vice versa," as Cavell puts it, and film, for Rohmer, is an art that brings *the world* to life, or vice versa. Then the words with which Cavell ends his essay on *The Winter's Tale* can also be applied to *Tale of Winter*, and they also provide a fitting conclusion to the present essay:

> The final scene of issuing in *The Winter's Tale* shows what it may be to find in oneself the life of the world. Is the life of the world, supposing the world survives, a big responsibility? Its burden is not its use but its specificness. It is no larger a burden than the responsibility for what Emerson and Thoreau might call the life of our words. We might think of this burden as holding, as it were, the mirror up to nature. Why assume just that Hamlet's picture urges us players to imitate, that it copy or reproduce, (human) nature? His concern over those who 'imitated humanity so abominably' is not alone that we not imitate human beings badly, but that we not become imitation members of the human species, abominations, as if to imitate, or represent – that is, to participate in – the species well is a condition of being human. Such is Shakespearean theater's stake in the acting, or playing, of humans. Then Hamlet's picture of the mirror held up to nature asks us to see

[2] *In Quest of the Ordinary*, p. 99.

if the mirror as it were clouds, to determine whether nature is breathing (still, again) – asks us to be things affected by the question.[3]

In Rohmer's *Tale of Winter*, in Charlotte Véry's Félicie above all, nature, in my experience, *is* – I am happy, even astonished, to say – still, or again, breathing. The film awakens me to the life of its world. And, I am also happy to say, I find myself deeply affected.

[3] *In Quest of the Ordinary*, p. 101.

CHAPTER 27

The "New Latin American Cinema"

In her important book *The New Latin American Cinema: A Continental Project* [here after abbreviated as *NLAC* (Austin: University of Texas Press, 1993)], Zuzana Pick argues that what has been called the "New Latin American Cinema" has been a continent-wide effort to create a cinema that speaks for and to Latin America as a whole. However, she argues that this idea of the movement, this idea of the New Latin American Cinema *as* a movement – it is her idea that this movement sees itself *as* a movement – emerged more and more explicitly as the movement evolved. This idea of the movement emerged hand-in-hand with the movement's developing practices, and hand-in-hand, as well, with the idea of Latin America as a distinct historical entity.

In Pick's view, the idea of a distinctive Latin America identity has emerged within a process, of which the New Latin American Cinema movement has been an integral part, of questioning the myths of progress that displaced the colonial legacy after Latin American countries consolidated themselves as modern nations. This idea of Latin America as a distinctive entity is based on a sense of a shared history and destiny, she argues, and also on a sense of a multiplicity of cultures that do not conform to state-defined allegiances and differences. "Latin Americans have assumed the history and envisioned the future of the continent," she writes, "in the layering of regional specificities (those inflected by locality) and through narrative negotiations of nation, class, race and gender. In this way Latin Americans have endowed themselves with a continental identity whose distinctiveness is precisely its composite character" (*NLAC*, p. 189).

The idea of Latin America endowing itself with a singular yet composite identity has served, in Pick's words, "to articulate regional autonomy and self-determination, countervailing the historical failure of countries to set up durable pan-Latin American political and economic organizations." The idea is "grounded in the desire of self-definition as well as the struggle for the control and autonomy of culture and identity . . . The search for means of representing national and continental realities, collective and individual identity, is the keyword" (*NLAC*, p. 192),

This idea of Latin America is a construct, an "imaginative and evolving projection," Pick acknowledges. But it also *produces* a sense of a community that recognizes itself through diverse variations. More than a utopian fantasy, the idea of Latin America is thus "a discursive formation whereby the history and imagination of the continent can be reclaimed" (*NLAC*, p. 190). This idea of Latin American identity, decentered yet historical, promotes critical discourses "aimed at locating, identifying and engaging with concepts of progress and projects of modernization, either to commend or censure them," Pick argues. (*NLAC*, p. 189). Thus it is an essentially modern idea, one that seconds the understanding expressed by Mexican cultural critic Carlos Monsivais, who insisted on the modernity (as well as the liberating agency) of social and cultural projects motivated by critical impulses. In Pick's view, the distinctive effort of self-definition that characterizes the New Latin American Cinema is a continent-wide attempt to assume, as an ideological foundation, this idea of a Latin American identity that is available in historical traditions yet still to be achieved through a modernist break with the past.

"At its inception in the 1960s," Pick writes, the New Latin American Cinema "broke with the national cinemas, such as those of Argentina and Mexico, that once dominated Spanish-language production. The manifestos and critical essays written by the filmmakers are polemical – even dogmatic – in their dismissal of what the filmmakers called the *old* cinemas of Latin America" (*NLAC*, p. 189). Through this "conscious rupture with traditional cinemas," as she calls it, the New Latin American Cinema from the outset defined itself as revolutionary. "The movement asserted the creation of new expressive spaces and the rejection of traditional genres. The movement challenged the hegemony of North American and European models" (*NLAC*, p. 190).

In the 1960s, the cultural politics of the movement converged with left-wing insurrectional tactics that spread throughout Latin America after the Cuban Revolution. Concurrently, "the movement debated the question of the appropriate filmic language for particular situations; the whole vexed question of what was a "national reality'; the uneasy relationship between filmmakers (largely middle-class intellectuals) and the 'people' they hoped to represent; and the nature of popular culture." In this manner, Pick argues, "the movement furthered critical and reflective approaches to cultural production and representation. It sanctioned an aesthetic capable of rearticulating itself into the collective by breaking hierarchical modes of address" (*NLAC*, p. 189).

Throughout the 1970s, the filmmakers of the New Latin American Cinema, often forced into exile or silenced by repression at a national level, assumed an increasingly explicit pan-Latin American character. Moreover, in the 1970s,

> Filmmakers also found in new institutional arrangements the possibility of relocating initiatives, previously supported only by the movement, into national practices. Their initiatives energized rather than weakened the movement and the New Cinema of Latin America integrated these national inflections into its supranational design. The films of the 1970s opted for narrative and aesthetic strategies, sometimes self-reflexive but always critical, capable of resolving the anachronism of underdevelopment. Moreover, the movement sought to expand its terms of reference . . . and set out to disengage its innovational goals from the confining rhetoric of the militant 1960s. The term 'Third Cinema,' for instance, often used to describe the politics of Latin American cinemas, was rearticulated to reflect its original impulse as a critically conscious and experimental agency of signification. (*NLAC*, pp. 188–9)

Again quoting Pick: "Although the anti-imperialist rhetoric and the cultural nationalism of the 1960s concealed the term *modernity* under the guises of Marxist theories of dependency and cultural resistance, the issue of modernity was not extraneous to the New Latin American Cinema. Filmmakers problematized either through their films or their writings what has been termed the 'discourse of present-ness,' a discourse that takes into account, ontologically, its own present-ness, in order to find its place, to pronounce its own meaning, and to specify the mode of action which it is capable of exercising within this present" (*NLAC*, p. 189).

In the New Latin American Cinema, in this picture, a self-declared community of activist filmmakers assumed the role of an artistic and political vanguard. Consistently preoccupied with questions of political agency, the filmmakers of the New Latin American Cinema denounced a modernity based on the self-aggrandizing claims and promises of progress made by nation–states. In Pick's view, however, this denunciation was always modernist, at least implicitly.

By the 1980s, the New Latin American Cinema much more explicitly declared its modernist aesthetic: "What Fernando Birri called the 'nationalist, realist, critical and popular' practices of the New Latin American Cinema in the early 1980s are 'a poetics of the transformation of reality . . . which through cinema aspires to modify the reality upon which it is projected.' At the basis of this poetics is a critical impulse that can reinvent itself in and through the heterogeneous elements and contradictory discourses of a continent at once unitary and diverse" (*NLAC*, p. 193).

Armed with a critical agenda and self-defined identity as a regional enterprise, the movement has been able to project its history into the future, Pick asserts, and thus has persisted as a valid political endeavor. "The movement's historical agency is grounded in a political and aesthetic agenda... As a discursive formation and a cultural practice, the movement has accommodated ideological and contextual realignments. The movement's specificity resides in the convergence of nationally based practices, including the infrastructural changes affecting filmmakers and their practices, with a pan-continental project. The movement's continental orientation, through a process of self-definition, controls the eclecticism of its cinematographic practices" (*NLAC*, p. 192).

Thus, in Pick's view, the movement constitutes

> ...a site of struggle between diverging, and sometimes contentious, processes of historical construction... By authorizing different approaches to production, distribution and exhibition, the movement has endorsed radical forms of filmmaking capable of revolutionizing existing social relations.... The New Latin American Cinema has served to reinterpret and redefine the place of film within the often contradictory realities of the continent. In a sense the movement is representative of what Rodolfo Parada calls the *mestizaje definitivo* of Latin America. ... The movement originates from an awareness and a sense of belonging produced at that 'moment of our history when we acquire the notion of our worth, and in which we decide to follow our ambitions. When we decide not to be imitators and followers, we begin to see the world in relation to who we really are, in relation to the Americas, as Latin Americans.' Paulo Emilio Salles Gomes described this process when he wrote about Brazilian cinema: 'We are neither Europeans nor North Americans. Lacking an original culture, nothing is foreign to us because everything is. The painful construction of ourselves develops within the rarefied dialectic of not being and being someone else...' This 'not being and being someone else'... is the principle upon which Latin Americans have challenged fixed notions and imagined new utopias. This principle conforms to a sense of forever-not-yet-being... which may constitute an identity in itself. Moreover, this principle implies critique and renewal and is profoundly attached to an unfinished experience of modernity whereby a yet-to-be-constructed modernity can be envisioned. As far as the New Latin American Cinema is concerned, this principle is exemplified in the movement's characteristic logic: its belief that its ideological project remains unfinished. (*NLAC*, pp. 196–7)

Never more than in this ringing peroration that is her grand finale, Professor Pick's writing expresses its own characteristic logic, its quite evident belief that *its own* ideological project *has* been finished. Throughout the book, there is an unacknowledged tension between the ideological project of the writing – to exploit the methodologies of American (that is, *North* American) academic film study to render fully explicit the New Latin American

Cinema's emerging idea of itself – and the ideological project it identifies as the movement's own. Rhetorically, the writing nonetheless endorses the movement's project, indeed, embraces it as if it *were* its own.

This tension suggests a double lack of critical perspective within the writing. The tendency to accept the movement's claims at face value suggests a lack of critical reflection on the movement the writing takes as its subject. It suggests, as well, a lack of critical *self*-reflection, as if there could be nothing problematic about the writing's own project, in particular its relationship to its subject.

This double lack of critical perspective is most apparent in the frequent slippages in the book's prose between *characterizing* – ostensibly objectively – and unquestioningly *endorsing* the claims of the movement.

- There is such a slippage, for example, in the passage in which Pick describes the idea of Latin American identity, an idea she believes to be at the heart of the movement's ideological project, as a "discursive formation whereby the history and imagination of the continent can be reclaimed." It is one thing to suggest that from within this "discursive formation" there appears a promise of "reclaiming" the "history and imagination of the continent." It is quite another to assert that this "discursive formation" actually possesses the power of effecting such a "reclamation" (whatever exactly such an achievement might amount to). The sentence smuggles this latter assertion in, as if its validity were beyond question.
- Another such slippage occurs when Pick writes that "the movement challenged the hegemony of North American and European models of cinematographic production and consumption. In this way, filmmakers advocated an oppositional and innovative cinema. They saw themselves capable of transforming the existing structures of filmmaking." The movement *claims* that historically there has been what can objectively be characterized as a "hegemony" of "North American models of cinematographic production and consumption." But the sentence simply assumes the validity of this claim, or, rather, set of claims, each of which is actually quite crucial to an assessment of the movement's achievements and failures, and each of which is also quite problematic, to say the least.
- When Pick argues that by debating certain issues "the movement furthered critical and reflective approaches to cultural production and representation," she slips in the assertion that these debates *furthered*, rather than obfuscated or otherwise obstructed, "critical and reflective approaches."
- Likewise, when she writes that the films of the 1970s "opted for narrative and aesthetic strategies, sometimes self-reflexive but always critical,

capable of resolving the anachronism of underdevelopment," she slips in the claim that these "strategies" are, in fact, capable of "resolving the anachronism of underdevelopment."

- Again, when she writes that the New Latin American Cinema "sanctioned an aesthetic capable of rearticulating itself into the collective by breaking hierarchical modes of address," she slips in assertions that are really matters to be decided on the basis of historical evidence, not theoretical fiat.
- Last, when Pick writes, "By authorizing different approaches to production, distribution and exhibition, the movement has endorsed radical forms of filmmaking capable of revolutionizing existing social relations," she slips in the assertion, yet again providing no evidence, that the forms of filmmaking the movement has endorsed possess the capability of "revolutionizing existing social relations."

In all these examples, and innumerable others I might have cited, Pick accepts the movement's leading claims on the movement's own terms, or on the terms she claims to be the movement's own. Never does she subject those terms – the terms in which, she claims, the movement claims to define itself – to critical questioning.

This is the basis of my earlier assertion that there is an unacknowledged tension between the book's ideological project and the ideological project it identifies as the movement's. Pick's idea of the New Latin American Cinema – her idea of its idea of itself – is that of a movement committed to a neverending process of critical self-questioning. Yet her writing never calls this idea into question.

Evidently, what makes Pick *wish* to accept the New Latin American Cinema on its own terms, what makes her *wish* not to question those terms, is the movement's claim to be radical. What makes the movement radical, in her view, is what she takes to be its radical capacity to define itself, to endow itself with an identity by defining itself in terms of an idea of Latin America that is itself emerging through a radical process of self-definition. But it is also her view that radical self-definition is commited to a neverending process of critical self-questioning. By this criterion, a movement that claims to define itself as radical cannot be radical. For such a claim exempts itself from critical self-questioning; it is a claim, a self-definition, that cannot critically be questioned. To question it is to deny it. And denying this claim is hardly on Pick's agenda.

In Pick's view, as we have seen, the movement's distinctive project of self-definition "assumes the idea of Latin America as an ideological foundation." But it is not possible to assume this idea of self-definition as an ideological foundation. It is an idea whose emergence can remain only an unfinished process, a process, furthermore, that has no "foundation."

Pick argues that the idea the movement assumes as a foundation is an idea of a Latin American identity that is already available in the form of historical traditions, yet still to be achieved in the form of a modernist break with the past. To assume such an idea as a foundation would be to assume as a foundation a modernist break with the past. But a specifically *modernist* break with the past is one that acknowledges the necessity, in order now to go on, of forgoing the wish for a foundation that the past is no longer capable of providing. A modernist break with the past must be *achieved*. Its achievement can never be assumed, never be taken for granted, never constitute a foundation.

Pick admits in passing that the movement's initial dismissal of the "old" Latin American cinema was dogmatic. She accepts unquestioningly that this rupture with traditional cinemas was defined from the outset as revolutionary (as if declaring oneself to be revolutionary is all it takes to *be* revolutionary). And, for all the dogmatic slumbers in which this rupture evidently was performed, she unquestioningly characterizes it as nonetheless a conscious break, indeed, a modernist one, as if were possible for a break with the past to be both dogmatic and conscious, both dogmatic and modernist.

Two crucial points are at stake here.

At its inception, the New Latin American Cinema dismissed the "old" Latin American cinema as traditional. Pick unquestioningly accepts the movement's term of criticism. Yet, in her view, the fact that the idea of a distinctive Latin American identity emerged within modernity implies that it is a modern idea, that it is on the side of modernity, as it were. She does not draw the obvious parallel: Film emerged within modernity, too; film, too, is on the side of modernity. In other words, there is no such thing as a traditional cinema (traditional as opposed to modern, that is).

Pick also accepts unquestioningly that the New Latin American Cinema broke with the "old" Latin American cinema not only for being traditional rather than modern, but also for imitating Hollywood rather than tapping into Latin American cultural traditions, for not challenging the "hegemony" of North American (and, to a lesser extent, European) models. The idea that Hollywood movies have been "hegemonic" has become an article of faith, a dogma, within my field of film study, as has the corollary idea that modernism in film means a conscious rupture with Hollywood's dominant codes.

To be sure, the idea of a distinctive Latin American identity is an idea of the difference between Latin America and what we in the United States are brought up calling simply "America." However, although Latin Americans, like North Americans, are not Europeans, they are no less Americans than North Americans are. In other words, the idea of Latin America – the idea of a distinctively *Latin* America whose distinctiveness is its composite character – is an idea of a Latin *America*. The idea of a distinctive Latin American identity is a distinctively American idea, an idea of America, an American idea of an America that is anything but hegemonic.

Thus it is no accident that, in the resounding words – some her own, some borrowed – Professor Pick invokes in her climactic grand finale, we can hear deep echoes of Emerson and Thoreau, who, in their aversion to the system building of European philosophal traditions, aspired to create a distinctively American idea of philosophical thought. Listen again to some of these words:

- When we decide not to be imitators and followers, we begin to see the world in relation to who we really are;
- Lacking an original culture, nothing is foreign to us because everything is;
- 'Not being and being someone else'... is the principle upon which Latin Americans have challenged fixed notions and imagined new utopias. This principle conforms to a sense of forever-not-yet-being... This principle implies critique and renewal.

And, finally,

- As far as the New Latin American Cinema is concerned, this principle is exemplified in the movement's characteristic logic: its belief that its ideological project remains unfinished.

Professor Pick's ideological project keeps her from recognizing the echoes of Emerson and Thoreau in her own words, the American-ness of her own voice. And it keeps her from recognizing the echoes of Emerson and Thoreau in the popular Hollywood movies whose dismissal as "hegemonic" she unquestioningly endorses. That these movies, in their American-ness, have aligned themselves with the idea of unity in diversity, have thus participated in the emergence of the idea of a distinctive Latin American identity, is a possibility she fails even to consider. In this she is representative of an American – that is, *North* American – field of academic film study that, repressing reflection on its own American-ness, for some years now has been bent on carrying out, without critical self-questioning, an ideological agenda of extending its own "hegemonic" doctrines and analytical models to films of every society and culture.

During the Nixon administration, the U.S. Surgeon General issued a report that appeared to lend scientific legitimacy to the widespread belief that violence in the mass media causes violence in society. The report concluded that mass media violence desensitizes people, makes them more hostile and aggressive and more likely to perform violent acts. In *Mass Media Violence and Society* [hereafter abbreviated as *MMVS* (New York: Wiley, 1975)], Dennis Howitt and Guy Cumberbatch scrutinized the research cited by the Surgeon General's report and demonstrated that none of the data actually constituted evidence that media violence significantly affects violence in society. Social scientists had compiled voluminous statistics, yet by and large they had assumed, rather than shown, that media violence causes real violence. The book went on further to conclude that the available data strongly supported the conclusion that media violence has no effect on, perhaps even reduces, the level of violence in society. That conclusion seems quite unjustified, though. Indeed, thinking in statistical terms may well hinder more than help in clarifying the roles mass media play in the diverse forms of life lived by Americans today. Our readiness to allow human beings to be reduced to statistical abstractions, I suspect, plays no small part in American society's obsession with violence.

Since its beginnings, the American cinema has been dogged by the belief that movies are harmful to society. In the early years of the twentieth century, New York's mayor tried to close all the city's nickelodeons, citing the "fact" that those "immoral places of amusement" were "liable to degenerate and menace the good order and morals of the people" (*MMVS*, p. 8). Chicago passed a law requiring films to receive permits before they could be exhibited. When two were denied permits, the Illinois Supreme Court upheld the Chicago edict, saying that those films "represent nothing but malicious mischief, arson and murder... and their exhibition would necessarily be attended with evil effects upon youthful spectators" (*MMVS*, p. 10). The U.S. Supreme Court concurred, endorsing the proposition that films were "capable of evil, having power for it, the greater because of their attractiveness and manner of exhibition" (*MMVS*, p. 11).

As such language suggests, the belief among film's earliest critics that movies caused harm to society was inseparable from a puritanical sense that movie viewing was in itself immoral. That moral judgment, in turn, was inseparable from a Victorian sense, as we might call it, that movies and moviegoing were *improper*. In the darkened movie theater, after all, women – some unescorted – sat shoulder by shoulder with men of all classes, viewing salacious scenes steeped in violence and eroticism. Film's turn-of-the-century attackers were fighting a rearguard action against a modern medium that they took – perhaps not wrongly – to be a threat to their moral values, which meant it was an affront to their sense of propriety. In America, the idea that movies have harmful effects has remained inextricably intertwined with the puritanical notion that movies are intrinsically immoral. And a Victorian moral outlook that equates what is morally right with what conforms to conventional social practices (especially sexual mores) remains deeply entrenched in American culture as well. Victorian moralists are hardly fashionable intellectual company, and I draw the lesson that we need to question our own motivations for being so ready to believe that movies cause our fellow Americans, but presumably not us, to lose their moral bearings. Another lesson is that we need to attend more thoughtfully to the origins and history of film and to the larger history out of which film emerged, so that we may stop drawing the morals of movies too hastily.

No one more fervently believed in film's capacity for evil than D. W. Griffith. Griffith's films were awesome demonstrations of the power of the new medium. Yet Griffith staunchly defended, against the attacks of Victorian moralists, his tapping into film's terrifying power. Griffith's early films couched his defense in terms of Victorian moral values. *The Drunkard's Reformation* (1909), for example, acknowledged that film was capable of intoxicating viewers and thus had the "power for evil." Yet he also believed, when he began his career as a film director, that the new medium possessed an unfathomable capacity to restore lost innocence. By the time of *The Birth of a Nation*, however, Griffith had lost his faith in film's capacity for redemption, his faith that tapping into the powers of the medium could be justified within the framework of Victorian morality. In the last third of *The Birth of a Nation*, the vengeful Ku Klux Klan, whose agency the film endorses, is no moral force, it is a nightmare inversion of Victorian moral values, no more capable of restoring America's innocence than movies are capable of saving America's soul. The American nation was born with blood on its hands, Griffith had come to believe. And so was the American cinema. Griffith envisioned film as possessing the power to whip viewers into a frenzied state, to cause viewers to lose their moral compass and give in to what is base in human nature. In Griffith's vision, movies have a voracious appetite for violence, as human beings have; violence is internal to film's nature, as it is internal to human nature.

The view that movies are inherently violent is at the heart of so-called apparatus theories, which emphasize film's supposed ability to force malignant ideological effects upon viewers. Indeed, it is a view that has surfaced again and again in the history of what we call "film theory," bridging otherwise opposed theoretical frameworks. Sergei Eisenstein famously insisted that montage, with its percussive, violent power, was the essence of the film medium, and he championed radically new kinds of films that would more fully exploit the medium's capacity to force its violent effects – visceral, emotional, intellectual – on viewers. Less famously, Eisenstein believed that every frame of every film had, as it were, the blood of the world on it because of the violence of the camera's original act of tearing a piece of the world from its "natural" place. The idea that the camera is an instrument of violence was taken up, at least implicitly, by André Bazin (If the film image is a "death mask" of the world, must not the camera be implicated in killing the world?), for whom Eisenstein's ideas were otherwise anathema, and, in turn, by Stanley Cavell (in its transformation into the world on film, the world undergoes a metamorphosis, or transfiguration, so profound as to be akin to death and rebirth). And the idea that film is inherently violent comes up again and again, and in a number of guises, in my own writings. It surfaces in *Hitchcock – The Murderous Gaze*, for example, when I characterize *Psycho*'s author, in the shower murder sequence, as unleashing murderous rage upon Marion Crane (Janet Leigh), and upon us, the film's viewers, or when, in my reading of that film, I suggest that Hitchcock is characterizing film – a characterization I embrace, at least rhetorically – as a medium of taxidermy.

Today's films are filled with images of arteries spurting, limbs mutilated or chopped off, faces exploding, flesh penetrated or torn, and so on. Thanks in part to the Production Code, such explicit, graphic images of violence, or of the effects of violence, were absent from the so-called classical Hollywood cinema, as were explicit, graphic images of sexuality. But there was violence, as there was sex, in classical movies. Without sex, after all, there could have been no romantic comedies or melodramas or musicals. Without violence, there could have been no gangster films, war films, westerns, private eye films, or horror films. In classical movies, as in Greek tragedies, however, violence was generally left for the viewer to imagine. When classical movies explicitly showed acts of violence or their effects, the camera refrained from dwelling on the gory details; the violence was not *eroticized*, as we might put it.

Two quite obvious distinctions complicate these matters.

First, when critics or theorists discuss film violence, they usually have in mind what we might call physical violence – killings, beatings, mutilations, and the like. Yet what we might call psychological violence, though lacking in gore, can be no less brutal and no less devastating to those subjected to it. In *Gaslight*, the Charles Boyer character does not set out to do his wife physical harm, but rather to drive her mad, to deprive her of a voice and, ultimately, even a mind of her own. Then, too, as Freud recognized, there can be violence in the most apparently innocent of actions. One might object that the violence in a joke or a slip of the tongue is merely symbolic, not real. As Freud also recognized, however, a clear boundary between real and symbolic violence is difficult or impossible to draw. "Real" violence can have symbolic meaning, and "symbolic" violence can have real consequences. In the Ophuls masterpiece, after all, a mere letter from an unknown woman proves quite literally death-dealing (if, perhaps, redemptive).

Second, in so-called fiction films, violence is generally simulated, not real. When a gunman shoots Liberty Valance, no one really dies, or, rather, no existing person dies. The most graphic images of violence (or of the effects of violence) are illusions created through the magic of makeup, tricks of photography and editing, and, increasingly, special effects. Violence in "live-action" movies is generally no more consequential than the violence in cartoons, such as the violence Wile E. Coyote suffers from the machinations of the Road Runner. When we view President Kennedy's head exploding in the so-called Zapruder film, by contrast, the violence projected on the screen is, or was, real. Yet John Kennedy, no less than Liberty Valance, is shot to death on the screen – which also means he has first been brought back to life on the screen – every time the Zapruder film is projected. Even in nonfiction films, death is not final, in the projected world, the way it is in the real world, the one existing world into which we are born and within which we are fated to die. On the other hand, if Kennedy had not met his death in the violent way he did, there would be no Zapruder film, as we know it; real violence is a condition of that film's existence. Luis Buñuel kicked a goat down a cliff in order to create one of the most memorable shots in his documentary, or mock documentary, *Land Without Bread*. In fact, the goat was already dead, but it *could* have been a living goat that Buñuel pushed to its death as a condition of his film's existence. And, in this regard, in the medium of film the distinction between fiction and nonfiction can be difficult, or impossible, to draw. To film a crucial sequence in *The Rules of the Game*, hardly a documentary, Jean Renoir directed a hunt in which dozens of rabbits were shot to death, the violence real, not simulated.

In writing about *Nanook of the North* in *Documentary Film Classics*, I argued that Flaherty's film equates filming with hunting. Such an idea often arises in discussions of nonfiction film. But if in Ernst Lubitsch's *To Be or Not to Be*, the "great, great Shakespearean actor" played by Jack Benny does to Shakespeare what Hitler did to Poland, what Flaherty does to Nanook by filming him hardly compares to what Nanook does to the walrus he harpoons, butchers, and consumes.The film *Night and Fog* asserts that the cameras of the Allied liberators were akin to the cameras of the Nazis, which were integral to the operation of the death camps, as guns were. But are cameras *generally* like guns?

To be filmed, a person must be in the world, a creature of flesh and blood. Filming people in the world, the camera does no real violence to them. It does, however, reveal their mortality, their vulnerability to violence. In the early years of photography, no one envisioned the making a photograph as a violent act. The introduction of Kodaks toward the end of the nineteenth-century, which made it possible for photographers to go out into the world and take snapshots of whomever they wished, coincided with the adoption of the violence-tinged language now universally applied to photography (calling the photographer's act "shooting," for example, or speaking of a person's picture as something a photographer *takes*). The emergence of the idea that photography has a violent aspect, the idea that cameras are like guns, coincided with the birth of motion pictures, which itself coincided with the birth of what we call modernity.

It is a strange idea, implausible on the face of it. Primitive peoples, we once were told, naively believe that cameras steal souls. Is it less naive to believe that cameras are violent? Unlike guns, cameras do not break bones (except, we now know, for x-ray cameras). In doing their mysterious work, cameras cause no physical harm. To be sure, photographs can be *used* in ways that harm their subjects, but in and of itself taking a photograph, like taking a look, has no effect whatever on the world. We may well have reasons to envision the birth of cinema, as we envision all births, as traumatic, violent. But every time the world is transformed or transfigured by being projected on a movie screen, every time the world is born again on film, re-created in its own image, the world no more suffers from the creation of its double than the cloned sheep suffers from the birth of Dolly. Furthermore, violence *within* the world on film, in and of itself, has no effect whatever on the real world. Insofar as film violence has no real consequences, it is not real violence at all.

Eisenstein insisted that to be true to their medium films should have as violent an impact as possible; viewers were to be hit on the head, as it were, by a series of percussive hammer blows. Apparatus theories, too, insist that movies do violence to viewers, although they deplore, rather than celebrate, this condition. And yet the train pulling into the station that would crush us to a pulp if we fell under its wheels is divested of its power to wreak violence on us when it is transformed into a train-on-film. Hence the popularity of the often-imitated Lumière film. Like all the earliest films, it vividly demonstrated to its original audiences a defining condition of the new medium, in this case the condition that the world on film differs from the real world by being exempt from real violence, by being unable to do violence to us and by being impervious to our capacities for violence. In *Hitchcock – The Murderous Gaze*, I argue that the shower murder sequence in *Psycho* declares Hitchcock's wish to murder the viewer, a desire it may be natural for anyone to feel who makes the classical role of movie director his or her own. But that sequence also declares it to be a condition of the film medium that the movie screen shields us from the world on film, shields the world on film from us.

Because it is not real violence, it would not be possible for film violence to harm us were it not for the massive ways we involve movies in our lives. In particular, film violence would pose no danger unless it were capable of causing real violence, whether by desensitizing viewers to real violence and thus neutralizing their inhibitions to performing violent acts in the world, by making real violence seem attractive, or by some other mechanism.

Viewing an action sequence in a John Woo film, we take pleasure in the fusillade of images purporting to represent the impact of high-power bullets on human bodies. Why it is so pleasurable to view graphic images of violence (or of the effects of violence), how viewing such images *can* be pleasurable, is a perplexing question. However we might go on to answer that question, though, we can agree that viewing such images *is*, or at least *can be*, pleasurable. We *have* an appetite for film violence, an appetite that film violence feeds, and perhaps creates.

Puritans condemn our appetite for film violence, as they condemn all our appetites, as sinful. Again, though, film violence would be capable of causing harm only if it had the power to lead viewers to crave real violence, not merely more film violence. Film violence would be capable of this if it had the power to lead viewers to believe, even if erroneously, that performing or suffering violent acts in the real world provides the kinds of pleasures film violence provides, or, especially, that the pleasures of film violence are only pale substitutes for the pleasures attendant upon the "real thing."

Again, a John Woo film offers innumerable images purporting to represent bullets causing mayhem to human bodies. Evidently millions of viewers all over the world have a taste for such images. Surely, though, one more readily gratifies that taste by viewing a John Woo film, in which camera placement, makeup, editing, and special effects ensure an optimal view of every bullet's bloody impact, than by getting one's hands on a high-powered rifle and raining bullets on human beings in the real world. (A taste for pornographic images is more fully gratified by viewing pornographic films than by brutalizing and raping women.) If our appetite for film violence were simply an appetite for *images* of violence (or of the effects of violence), in other words, film violence would not be likely to lead us – unless we were woefully misinformed – to perform real acts of violence. But films do not simply present us with images of violence (or of the effects of violence). They also represent violent *actions*.

In the climactic moment of *Raging Bull*, Sugar Ray Robinson hesitates, exhilarated and terrified by what he feels called upon to do, by his own desire to do it, and by his opponent's desire to have it done, before finally delivering the haymaker that busts Jake LaMotta's face but miraculously fails to knock him down. We experience this violence as something one character *does*, something another character *suffers*. We experience vicariously – that is, we imagine so vividly that we *all but* feel – the agony and the ecstasy Sugar Ray feels, within the film's fiction, as his fist smashes into the flesh and bone of Jake's face. We also *all but* feel the pain and the sweetness only Jake feels, within the fiction, as his already battered face erupts in a shower of blood. We *imagine* ourselves in Sugar Ray's place and in Jake's place. We *imagine* feeling what each character alone, within the film's fiction, is capable of feeling.

That is, we imagine that we are not merely viewing but living this exhilarating, terrifying moment of violence. (It is exhilarating because it is terrifying, but it is also terrifying because it is exhilarating.) We imagine that we are living this moment; we do not imagine we are merely imagining we are living, it. We might well find ourselves thanking our lucky stars, as we are viewing, that the medium of film separates us from the world Jake and Sugar Ray inhabit, that we are living our lives, not theirs. But we might well also find ourselves thinking, at this moment, that if it is so thrilling merely to be imagining throwing this punch and feeling its impact, it must be infinitely more pleasurable to be living what we are only imagining. If film violence has the power to motivate us to think such a thought, as in this celebrated instance it surely has, it *is* capable of stimulating, or even creating, an appetite for violence, a blood lust, that we imagine we can more fully gratify by performing or suffering real acts of

violence than by merely viewing violence (or the effects of violence) on film.

There is a continuum between cases, like this one, in which we experience violence on film as something a character does, as something a character suffers, hence as something we might wish to do or suffer and not merely view, and cases in which film violence is a mere abstraction with no power to move us to act or to suffer.

What Sugar Ray's punch does to Jake's face, within the film's fiction, one person does to another person. One's fist is part of one's body, part of oneself. But a fist is also a potentially lethal weapon of the "blunt instrument" persuasion. When Al Capone (Robert DeNiro) in *The Untouchables* smashes a flunky's head with a baseball bat, the bat is not literally part of his body. Yet within the fiction he can feel – and we can imagine feeling– the satisfying impact of wood on flesh and bone. What the bat does to this unfortunate man, Capone does to him by swinging the bat. But when Chow Yun-Fat shoots a hapless bad guy, the havoc the bullet wreaks on the bad guy's body, within the fiction, is not something that Chow does to him. To be sure, the bullet's impact immediately succeeds Chow's pulling of the trigger, and it has its impact on the particular bad guy he has targeted. The bullet acts at a distance, though, so that when Chow pulls the trigger, he can view the effect of the bullet's impact, but he cannot feel it as something he is *doing*, the way Sugar Ray feels his own punch or Capone feels the impact of the bat he is swinging. (Compare the images of Joan burning at the stake at the climax of Carl Dreyer's *The Passion of Joan of Arc*. Within the film's fiction, people must have built this pyre, bound her, and kindled the fire. But once their work is done, they, like everyone else, can only view as the flames, on their own, consume Joan's body.)

Nonetheless, within the fiction, Chow feels his finger pulling the trigger, and feels the gun's action as the trigger engages the firing mechanism. He feels this at virtually the same moment he views the havoc the bullet wreaks on the bad guy's body. To that extent, Chow feels the connection, as we might put it – and we vicariously experience his feeling of the connection– between his pulling of the trigger, which is something he does, and the violence the bullet causes, which is something the bullet does on its own, without human intervention. When he pulls the trigger, the violence follows automatically, the way a camera automatically takes a picture when someone presses the shutter release. A human being pulls the trigger, but a machine causes the violence, making it possible for the gunman, with no blood on his hands, to view, at a remove, effects that are, and are not, his doing.

When Chow views the world through the sights of his gun, all it takes is for him to pull the trigger for his target to become a bloody mess. Until he does pull the trigger, though, there is no sign at all, in the world he is viewing, of the impending violence. But violence threatens the bad guy Chow is targeting precisely because he is targeting him, because he is viewing him, at this remove, through this instrument of violence. At such a moment, too, we might well find ourselves thankful that the medium of film separates us from the world projected on the movie screen, thankful that movies make it possible to experience violence vicariously, thankful that film violence is not real violence. But, again, we might well also find ourselves thinking, as we are viewing, how much more pleasurable it would be to be pulling the trigger ourselves, how much more pleasurable it would be if the ensuing violence were real. Then we would be able to experience, and not merely imagine we are experiencing, the pleasure of making violence happen at a distance.

In fiction films, violence happens on cue, as if the camera were a gun, and the director, offscreen, were pulling the trigger. Violence the camera causes in this way is not real violence, as has been said, yet movies call upon us to imagine that film violence is real, and that is one key to the pleasure we receive from them. But they also call upon us to acknowledge that the world on film is separated from us by a barrier, hence that film violence is not real violence. This too is a key to the pleasures movies provide us.

Viewing the world on film, a world separated from us by an unbridgeable barrier, can stimulate our appetite for living *in* the world. A danger of film violence, as I have suggested, resides in the power of movies to motivate us to imagine that the pleasures of film violence are pale substitutes for the pleasures real acts of violence might provide us. Film violence is capable of motivating us to think that performing or suffering real acts of violence might make it possible to experience life more intensely, to exist more fully.

But living in the world can stimulate our appetite for movie viewing, too. As we go about the world, we feel removed, as if we were viewing our lives, not living them. How much better to be viewing a real movie! When we are viewing a movie, the conditions of the medium *automatically* place us outside the world on film, freeing us from the responsibilities of living within the world. Therein resides another, perhaps more insidious, danger of film violence. For if film violence can motivate us to think that real acts of violence might enable us to exist more fully within the world, it can also motivate us to think that real acts of violence might enable us to *detach* ourselves more fully from the world.

Some pundits say that when those two young men in Littleton, Colorado, undertook their terrible plan to blow up their high school and kill their fellow students, they were imitating acts of violence they had seen in movies, television shows, or video games. Others suggest that their goal was to become immortalized by the media, like Bonnie and Clyde. I picture them as undertaking, rather, to detach themselves from the world as they knew it, to repudiate the world endorsed by the media, a world of conformists and sports heroes and consumer goods. If censors had removed all representations of violence from the media, these youths would have felt more alienated from society, not less. By their violence, they felt they were rejecting America as it exists, declaring that society's conventions were not the measure of their existence. They were rejecting conventional morality too. Nonetheless, their violent act had a moral dimension. In their view, their commitment to being true to themselves made them superior – superior morally – to an America that lacked the moral standing to judge them, an America they felt it was their right, even their duty, to obliterate, at least symbolically. They felt they were elevating themselves above the fallen America they were condemning. Yet by embracing this view, they were unwittingly keeping faith with the moral outlook that has underwritten American movies since their beginning. Even during the period in which the Production Code forced movies to follow the letter of the Victorian moral law, they rejected the spirit of Victorian morality. American movies do not equate what is morally right with what conforms to society's conventions. In American movies, it is a moral imperative to quest for human fulfillment even when doing so entails refusing to accept the strictures of conventional morality; self-realization is a greater good than social acceptance. This moral outlook was not imposed on movies from the outside, the way the Production Code was, but is internal to the stories movies keep telling. It is the American cinema's inheritance of the transcendental philosophy of Emerson and Thoreau.

What movies are and what gives them their awesome power are mysteries that vexed America in the early years of film, and they have continued to vex our culture. What is it about the medium that is so frightening that it led film's earliest critics to believe – as so many continue to believe – that movies are "capable of evil, having the power for it"? And what is it about the medium that enables American movies to walk a moral path? The field of film studies has been reluctant to address, or even acknowledge, such questions. Despite the high priority it accords to what it calls – always choosing a pretentious term over a more humble one – "historiography," the medium's origins and history remain obscure to the field. That is because so much of its research has been ideologically driven, designed to confirm conclusions dictated in advance by currently fashionable theories rather than to put those theories to the test by discovering surprising new insights into mysterious matters that we prefer to believe pose no mysteries to us.

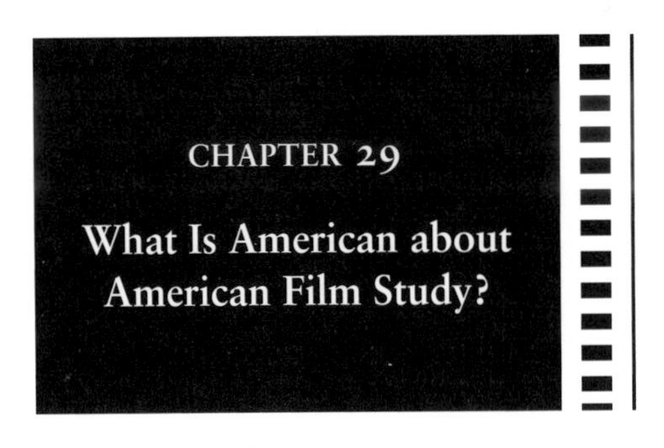

CHAPTER 29

What Is American about American Film Study?

For over a decade, the Hawaii International Film Festival has been the world's premier showcase for significant new films from Asia and for American films that, in whatever ways, contribute meaningfully to the enrichment of mutual understanding between Asia and America. Of all the exemplary features of the Hawaii Festival – the fact that all screenings are free to the community, for example – none has proved worthier than the annual Symposium in which we are all presently engaged.

I have had the pleasure and privilege of participating in three of these events. There is no way I can exaggerate their importance to my own education in Asian cinema (this also means my education in cinema, as every Asian nation, like every Western one, has participated in its own way in the international history of film).

The first was in 1985. At that time, I possessed little special knowledge of Asian films or the conditions of their production beyond what was expected of any conscientious American professor of film study. This was more than we were expected to know about Martian cinema, but not much more.

Apart from the *Apu* trilogy and perhaps one or two other films by Satyajit Ray, few among us, in 1985, knew the work of any "serious" Indian directors or were familiar, except by hearsay, with the vast subcontinent of the Indian commercial cinema. Other than martial arts films, few of us had seen a single film from Hong Kong, Taiwan, or mainland China. And it goes without saying that the cinemas of Korea, the Philippines, Indonesia, and Southeast Asia were completely unknown to us. There were excellent books on Japanese cinema in English, preeminently by Donald Richie, and a volume of brilliant essays by Sato Tadao, then hot off the press in English translation, was available under the title *Patterns of Japanese Cinema*.[1] But firsthand knowledge of Japanese films was restricted to a

[1] Sato Tadao, *Currents in Japanese Cinema*, trans. by Gregory Barrett (Tokyo: Kodansha International, 1982).

handful of postwar works (all great films, to be sure) by Ozu, Mizoguchi, and Kurosawa.

The paper I presented at the 1985 Symposium acknowledged a wish for an education in Asian cinema and declared an eagerness to participate in serious conversations about the relationship of film and culture.[2] It was, and is, my conviction that thinking seriously about film and culture does not mean applying a grand system of thought, what the field of film study calls a "theory." It means addressing this relationship concretely, as it works itself out in specific historical cases. And it means reflecting philosophically on the ways these cases illuminate each other.

To this end, my paper posed the question, "What is American about American cinema?" I understood this to be at once a question about history and a question about philosophy. Following up a number of remarks in Stanley Cavell's *Pursuits of Happiness*, then relatively recently published, the paper offered at least part of an answer: The American-ness of American cinema cannot be separated from the ways American movie genres have taken up and revised, made their own, the American tradition of philosophy founded by Emerson and Thoreau, an American way of thinking that it has also been an American tradition to repress (as the voices of Emerson and Thoreau have been repressed within academic philosophy in America, and as Cavell's voice has been repressed within American film study).[3]

In claiming this connection between American philosophy and American cinema, in claiming that American cinema had itself claimed this connection, I was also claiming the connection between my own way of thinking (for example, in entering that claim and also *this* one) and this American tradition of philosophical thought. I was making a claim as to who I am. And I was claiming the authority to enter such claims, to make such connections, not on the basis of an appeal to a "higher authority" but by appeal to my own experience, the way I actually find myself thinking. On philosophical principle, I was speaking in my own voice. That is what *is* American about my way of thinking.

At Hawaii, among the most thought-provoking developments for me was discovering the affinity between my American way of thinking and Sato

[2] William Rothman, "Hollywood Reconsidered: Reflections on the Classical American Cinema," *East–West Film Journal* 1(1): 36–47 (December 1986); reprinted in William Rothman, *The "I" of the Camera* (New York and Cambridge, England: Cambridge University Press, 1988), pp. 1–12.

[3] Stanley Cavell, *Pursuits of Happiness* (Cambridge, MA: Harvard University Press, 1981).

Tadao's Japanese way. Sato, too, in his critical writing and conversation about a film, characteristically makes a point of staking out a connection between the film and his way of thinking about the film, about the film's own way of thinking. And he, too, characteristically makes this connection by appealing to who he is, by speaking in his own voice, not by appealing to a higher authority.

I am not denying that Sato and I think very differently. His way of thinking, as I have said, is as characteristically – not "typically"!) Japanese as mine is American. Yet there can be no real conversation between voices that are not separate, different from each other. But neither can there be conversation if there is no common ground.

It helps in surveying the common ground between Sato and myself to keep in mind that he was a young man during the years of Japan's postwar occupation by America. And it helps to keep in mind as well that, although the Japanese films I knew were few, they had profoundly moved me. To be moved means for one's position, one's way of thinking, at least one's perspective on one's way of thinking, to be changed. Yet the Japanese films whose experience had changed my perspective, works such as Ozu's *Late Spring* (1949), Mizoguchi's *Ugetsu* (1953), and Kurosawa's *Ikiru* (1952) were themselves created during the American occupation of Japan or its immediate aftermath.

Like Sato's writing and conversation, films such as *Late Spring, Ugetsu*, and *Ikiru* embrace ways of thinking that may appear specifically American, as when they suggest that human beings deny their essential humanity every time they bow to society's pressures to conform. Yet they are not examples of cultural domination or equally pernicious cultural assimilation. For even as each film is affirming a way of thinking with which Americans find ourselves able to make connection, it is claiming, reclaiming, a specifically Japanese identity, recovering its own Japanese voice.

In their Japanese ways, these films are thinking for themselves. But thinking for oneself, speaking in a voice of one's own, what Emerson called "self-reliance," *is* the form Emerson and Thoreau envisioned philosophy in America taking. As Cavell has taught us, their affirmations of "self-reliance" did not mean that Emerson and Thoreau were relying on a preconstituted thing called a "self." It meant that they were calling upon philosophy – in their writing, philosophy was calling upon itself – to attain a new perspective on itself, to take a stand on its own identity. They believed that it was by working out philosophically the conditions that constitute philosophical thought that American philosophy could declare its own existence, its independence from the European philosophical tradition, and America could at last account philosophically for the fact that it had secured its political independence from Europe.[4]

Emerson and Thoreau, who were known as "Transcendentalists," after all, acknowledged their solidarity with the Kantians whose "Copernican Revolution" had transformed European philosophy from within. But Emerson and Thoreau no more simply inherited Kant's philosophical system than they inherited the systems that Kant's philosophy had overturned. The new philosophy they aspired to found in America called for a fundamental revision of Kant's guiding intuitions that reason has limits and that knowledge of the world is possible because what things "objectively" are cannot be separated from the forms of our subjectivity. What Emerson and Thoreau were proposing and exemplifying was not a competing philosophical system but a radically different understanding of what it means to think philosophically – an alternative practice of philosophy that breaks fundamentally with the European philosophical tradition that predominantly equates philosophy with system building. (Through Nietzsche, a close follower of Emerson's thought, this radical American alternative made its first decisive intervention within European philosophy itself.)

For Emerson and Thoreau, Western philosophy could be defined only by the dominant and dominating European tradition of philosophical system building. Thus they envisioned their way of thinking philosophically as an alternative that was, in a sense, specifically non-Western. Emerson and Thoreau were avid readers of the spiritual texts of Asia, eagerly awaiting each new translation. In their reading of every page, they felt confirmed in their conviction that their own way of thinking, which called for them to recognize their separateness from European philosophy, was attuned to Asian teachings. In turn, Emerson and Thoreau were read sympathetically in Asia, to world-historical effect. In India, for example, Tagore was a great reader of Emerson and Gandhi was a devoted student of Thoreau's writing (as, coming full circle, Martin Luther King was a follower of Gandhi's thought).

All peoples on earth stand on common ground. All human cultures are connected. But every human culture is also separate, different from every other. We cannot assume that the question of what is Indian about Indian cinema, the question of what is Chinese about Chinese cinema, or

[4] Compare Stanley Cavell, *The Senses of Walden*, expanded ed. (San Francisco: North Point Press, 1981); *Themes Out of School* (San Francisco: North Point Press, 1984); *In Quest of the Ordinary: Lines of Skepticism and Romanticism* (Chicago: University of Chicago Press, 1988); and *This New Yet Unapproachable America: Lectures after Emerson and Wittgenstein* (Albuquerque, NM: Living Batch Press, 1989).

Japanese about Japanese cinema (or, for that matter, what is French about French cinema or German about German cinema) are questions that call for answers of one single form.

To the question of what is American about American cinema, I had offered an American form of answer. Then what forms of answer, specific to each culture (that is, acknowledging ways of thinking internal to that culture, making its connection with those ways of thinking) might these questions call for?

When I returned from Hawaii, bursting with eagerness to pursue such thoughts, I embarked on a crash course in Asian cinema. In retrospect, it is clear that I had chosen a privileged moment to do so.

Had I attempted even one year earlier to begin in earnest my education in Asian cinema, I would have lacked access, in America, to too many crucial films. But in the spring of 1986, "Film *Utsav*" traveled to Los Angeles, where I was spending the year. This was a major exhibition, unprecedented in scope, focusing on the work of five Indian directors (V. Shantaram, Raj Kapoor, Guru Dutt, Ritwik Ghatak, and Mrinal Sen) virtually unknown in America. That spring, too, Chen Mei and Professor Cheng Jihua were for the first time conducting their legendary UCLA seminar surveying the history of Chinese film. And Chen Xiaolin, the woman newly appointed head of the China Film Import and Export Company in America, was in a position to lend me cassettes of the latest films from China.

Had I begun one year later, I also would have missed out on a decisive historical moment. For 1985 was the year the "Fifth Generation" of Chinese filmmakers made its initial spectacular impact on America and Europe. At the 1985 Hawaii Festival, *Yellow Earth* was on the program and Chen Kaige and Zhang Yimou were in attendance. *Yellow Earth* turned out to be the sensation of the Festival, as it was to be at film festivals all over the world. And it was followed, in the next several years, by a succession of stunning Fifth Generation films, each transgressing boundaries previously inviolable, each daring to push further the limits of expression.

From 1986 to 1989, as Director of the International Honors Program (IHP) on Film, Television and Social Change in Asia, I was responsible for fashioning a curriculum, putting together a small faculty, and personally leading groups of American college students on semester-long programs of study and travel in India, Hong Kong, China, and Japan (and sometimes Thailand). During the three years I was involved with the IHP, America's attention was being drawn ever more compellingly to Asia, to China above all. And in China, film was not only "writing history with lightning," as Woodrow Wilson is said to have said about *The Birth of a Nation*, it was making – and unmaking – history. What was most remarkable about the

Fifth Generation films, what riveted the attention of Americans who took an interest in them, cannot be separated from the breathtaking assurance with which these films claimed a leading role in the events of world-historical magnitude that were sweeping China. Film had not been in the vanguard like this, had not "manned the barricades," since the legendary events in Paris now known simply as "May '68" – and, to be truthful, not even then.

Americans studying Chinese film in this period found themselves swept up in these events and, indeed, called upon to play a role. Bearing witness to the Fifth Generation's struggle against villainous forces of repression, we were championing the films, taking their side. No doubt, the Fifth Generation filmmakers, shrewdly guided by their sage mentor Wu Tianming, head of the Xi'an Film Studio, were counting on us to arouse the conscience of the world should they find themselves brutally silenced.

In any case, as I mean my choice of words to suggest, like all Americans and like the Chinese themselves, Americans studying Chinese cinema in those years found ourselves envisioning events sweeping China as a grand historical melodrama (that these events constituted such a melodrama is a central intuition in Wang Yuejin's brilliant essay in *Melodrama and Asian Cinema*[5]). And we envisioned film in China, and ourselves as champions of Chinese cinema, as playing roles in this melodrama. The appeal of being swept up in a grand melodramatic struggle between virtue and villainy was inseparable from the appeal, for Americans, of studying Chinese cinema during this period (to varying degrees, this was true of studying the cinemas of other Asian nations as well). Swept up in such a melodrama, everything takes on cosmic significance. Nothing is merely academic. Not even film study (which by then had otherwise become, in America, all but completely academicized).

By the fall of 1989, when I attended my most recent Hawaii Symposium, the grand melodrama had taken a tragic turn. At Hawaii, the still-recent massacre in Tiananmen Square was fresh in everyone's mind. Yet again, China had failed in its struggle to free itself from its tragic past. The Fifth Generation had failed. Film itself had failed to fulfill the heroic role it had assumed.

As I am writing these words, it seems all too clear that a gloriously hopeful period in the history of Asian cinema has ended, its passing marked in China by Zhang Yimou's despairing *Ju Dou*, released last year in the West but not in China. And although I have been dwelling on the example of

[5] Wang Yuejin, "History and Its Discontent: Melodrama as Historical Understanding," in Wimal Dissanayake, ed., *Melodrama and Asian Cinema* (New York and Cambridge, England: Cambridge University Press, 1993), pp. 73–91.

China, what was a momentous historical period for cinema in other Asian countries, too, has likewise now ended. Among the events that mark the passing of this period, I am thinking of the deaths last spring of two great and irreplaceable artists, Lino Brocka in the Philippines and G. Aravindan in India.

It is equally clear, as we look back to the fall of 1989, that a formative period in the history of the study of Asian cinema, too, was then nearing its end. The study of Asian cinema, once marginal, has now become fully accepted by academic film study in America as an integral part of the field.

At the 1985 session of the Hawaii Symposium, most of the papers and discussions barely paid even lip service to the theoretical frameworks that were already paradigms for academic field study in America. Most of the participants were either Asian film critics with distinguished professional careers in their own countries but who were not based in the academic world (Sato Tadao and Chidananda Dasgupta, for example); "cultural interpretors" and champions of Asian cinema such as Donald Richie and Tony Rayns, who were likewise not academics; and Americans like myself who were indeed university teachers but who had come to Hawaii to take off our academic hats (caps?) and immerse ourselves in films and conversations solely for the sake of our own educations – we had not packed our academic axes, happy to be in a place where we did not have to grind them. (No doubt, viewed from the perspective of the academic field of film study, we were simply on vacation.)

At the 1989 session, there was no one like Sato Tadao, no one like Chidananda Dasgupta, no one like Donald Richie, no one like Tony Rayns – and no one like me as I was in 1985, no one all but completely lacking an education in Asian cinema. In 1989, the participating Americans, including myself, were academic film scholars who listed Asian cinema among our areas of professional specialization. And most of the Americans' papers – here I do exclude myself – paid more than lip service to the dominant paradigms of academic film study in America.

I am not denying that there is cause for celebration in the recent acceptance of Asian cinema by academic film study in America. But this development also has sobering implications.

In the late 1960s and early 1970s, when the case for the academic study of film was originally made to American university administrations and faculties, film study predominantly envisioned itself as a new field of criticism. The works to be studied were to encompass, but not be limited to, ordinary movies, in particular American movies of what the field has since come to call the "classical" period. The new field of film study predicated its claim for recognition on the conviction that the achievements of cinema, importantly but not exclusively including the achievements of American classical cinema, called for serious critical acknowledgment, and on the corollary conviction that no existing academic field was capable of the kind of criticism film called for. And just as Asian cinema's first large-scale acceptance within the field of film study coincided with the ending of the exhilarating period, all too brief, in which Asian cinema had captured the imagination of the world, cinema's first large-scale acceptance within the American university coincided with the definitive ending of the classical period of the American cinema.

This intriguing parallel makes it tempting to envision Asian cinema's acceptance by American film study as recapitulating film's own acceptance by the American university in the 1970s, and to envision both as comparable victories in comparable struggles. But there are two reasons to resist this temptation.

First, because Asian cinema did not *win* the acceptance of the field. There was no significant opposition, no struggle, hence no victory. It is closer to the truth to say that American film study simply annexed Asian cinema, as if it were its Manifest Destiny to do so.

Thus, for example, the Society for Cinema Studies (SCS), the major professional organization of the field in America, interprets the recent surge of interest in Asian cinema, which it sees as part of a broader concern with "issues of multiculturalism," as having been generated by considerations internal to the field's own priorities and agenda. This is clear from the language of the call for panel proposals that the SCS mailed to its membership in advance of last spring's annual conference:

> In the past several years, the Society for Cinema Studies has encouraged attention to issues of race, ethnicity, class, gender, sexual orientation and national origin. Thus it seems appropriate to ask in a more intense way critical, philosophical and historical questions about the notion of multi-culturalism in relation to the tradition areas of research in film . . . studies.

Why does it now "seem appropriate" to ask these unspecified questions? The statement implies that, given the steps the field has already taken, this is simply the logical next step. At no point does the statement reiterate what it takes to have justified the field in having taken those earlier steps, nor does it justify the present step beyond saying, in effect, "This simply *is* the agenda of the field of film study in America, these *are* the field's priorities, *this* is the way we do things."

No doubt it adds to the greater glory of film study in America to recognize the study of Asian cinema as a new branch of the field – on the condition that the procedures of this new branch conform to the field's existing priorities and agenda. But to accept the study of Asian cinema on such terms is to reject out of hand the possibility that Asian films may call for fundamentally different ways of thinking, ways of thought rooted in Asian cultural traditions, for example, if the films' own different ways of thinking are to be acknowledged. For film study in America to accept Asian cinema only as an object to be studied in accordance with already established procedures and doctrines is for the field to deny to Asian films, and to Asians, the status of subjects, subjects capable of thinking for themselves. It is to silence Asian voices, voices that are different from American voices, to suppress conversation between and among Americans and Asians.

For Asians wishing to study Asian cinema, the American field of film study, insofar as the Society for Cinema Studies speaks for it, envisions no option but to subordinate their own diverse ways of thinking to procedures and doctrines that it is assumed Asian films must yield to, not confront or challenge (or, for that matter, simply ignore). In truth, however, Americans studying Asian films are likewise offered no option but to subordinate our experience, too, to these procedures and doctrines. And it has long been one of the field's leading doctrines that American films and American ways of thinking must also yield to procedures and doctrines that themselves have been authorized by what the field recognizes as a higher authority.

This brings us to the second reason for resisting the temptation to envision film study's acceptance of Asian cinema and the American university's acceptance of film as comparable victories in comparable struggles: namely, the fact that the field of film study in America has never definitively won its struggle to secure its intellectual identity.

As I have said, in the late 1960s, film study was waging a struggle against powerful forces within the American university – I am proud to have played my modest part in this struggle – to win recognition that films were worthy of serious critical acknowledgment, and to win recognition as well that no existing academic field was capable of performing that acknowledgment. Film study's original struggle, as I understood it then and now, was at once to win recognition for film as an object of study and to win recognition for the study of film as an independent academic field.

No existing field was capable of studying film seriously, we were claiming, because the medium of film was different. Films were different in ways that called for the creation of new terms of criticism, new ways of thinking that acknowledged what was different about film's own different ways of thinking. Thus to back up its claim to exist as a field in its own right, the new discipline of film study we were envisioning would have to encompass a philosophical investigation of the ontology of the medium and the art of film, an investigation that would proceed, not by adopting a preexisting theoretical system whose authority the field accepted as given, but by reflecting on the testimony of films themselves, the testimony of critics' experience of films.

However, academic criticism in America, in departments of literature above all, was in the throes of radical transformation. One does not have to be a weatherman to know that since the 1970s, academic criticism in America has been swept by a succession of winds from the East – by structuralism, semiology, Althusserian Marxism, Derridean deconstruction, Lacanian psychoanalysis, and so on. Despite their mutual incompatibilities, and largely in disregard of the particularities of the French cultural contexts that motivated their original emergence, these theoretical systems became more or less collapsed, in America, into the single entity usually called simply "Theory."

When film study in America embraced Theory, it envisioned itself as thereby acquiring the authority, the certainty, of a science. But by taking this fateful step, a field that had aspired to intellectual independence denied its own authority and the authority of the films it studied and ceded its claim to be able to think on its own.

As I have said, film study in America had staked its claim to independence on the conviction that the field's mandate was to develop new terms of criticism capable of acknowledging film's own ways of thinking as importantly – but not exclusively – exemplified by classical American cinema. Theory underwrites a conflicting claim: Classical cinema does not exemplify ways of thinking that call for forms of critical acknowledgment unique to film; classical cinema is only a repressive ideological system, a system thoroughly implicated in the dominant and dominating social order.

Under the regime of Theory, the field takes itself to be authorized to endorse this doctrine that classical films exemplify ways of not thinking, not ways of thinking, that classical cinema is, indeed, a system for repressing thought. According to Theory, all there is about classical cinema for film study *to* study is the detailed working, semiologically and historically, of this system. This "study" is envisioned as a joint task for deconstructive readings and – more and more these days, but that is another story – what the field calls "historiography." Theory dictates not only the agenda but the results of this "study" whose mandate is not to paint an original portrait of the history of cinema but to fill in the outline Theory provides, to colorize Theory's picture.

The surest way for the field to test the doctrines of Theory would be by attending to the testimony of the films themselves, that is, by performing acts of criticism accountable to the critic's experience, and by reflecting on the implications of the readings that emerge from those critical acts. But Theory peremptorily dismisses all such testimony. Theory authorizes film study to deny *a priori* – for the field, Theory *is* this systematic denial of the authority of experience – even the *possibility* that a classical film or, for that matter, a critic testifying from her or his own experience, could be capable of "speaking" anything but ideology, could be capable of providing what could count – what Theory would count – as testimony.

A detailed historical account of the stages by which film study in America came to deny its own authority and that of the films it originally aspired to acknowledge would cite the reception of a familiar litany of French texts. But I think of the decisive moment, historically, as the appearance in 1971 of Cavell's *The World Viewed*.[6]

What made the publication of Cavell's brilliant little book of philosophy so decisive was not its subsequent influence on film study in America, its reception by the field, but its all-but-complete nonreception, the silence with which the field responded to the book. Historically, the moment film study in America turned to European theoretical systems in search of a foundation was also the moment it turned away from Cavell's American way of thinking philosophically – a way of thinking that denies the necessity, and the possibility, of any authority higher than experience, a way of thinking that, having been initiated by Emerson and Thoreau, had been embraced by Nietzsche, had profoundly influenced Heidegger and thus played a central role, historically, in the emergence of Theory itself. In Cavell's book, film study in America, which had already declared itself a separate field, had at last claimed to account, philosophically and historically, for its existence, its capacity to think for itself, had claimed a voice it could call its own. By bowing down to Theory, film study in America betrayed its capacity to think for itself and submitted to the suppression of its own voice.

To begin to understand how such a thing could possibly have taken place, it is helpful to think about what Americans least wish to think about, which is America's experience of the late 1960s, an experience that had opened, or reopened, deep wounds, wounds that have since festered, not healed. I think of America in those years as torn, I think of every American as torn – agonizingly, ecstatically – between thinking and repressing thought. When American academics in wholesale numbers turned to French thought at that traumatic historical moment, it was less to think more deeply about their own experience than to be released from thinking about it, to pull back from their own experience as if from the brink of a precipice.

[6] Stanley Cavell, *The World Viewed: Reflections on the Ontology of Film*, enlarged ed., (Cambridge, MA: Harvard University Press, 1979).

In the aftermath of May '68, French intellectuals, reflecting on their failure to effect a second French Revolution, had turned to Marx, to Nietzsche, to Freud, to Heidegger, at the same time turning their ways of thinking, not originally French, into philosophical systems that at once denied and, through the authority of that denial, reasserted the centrality of French thought. This is not the occasion for me to speculate as to whether these philosophical systems, within the French cultural context, primarily represented new French ways of thinking or new French ways of not thinking. But I do wish, on this occasion, to suggest that when Americans turned to these new French philosophical systems they primarily turned them not into new American ways of thinking but into new American ways of not thinking – new ways of not thinking about the way America since its creation has been torn, new ways of not thinking about the implications of the fact that America's Constitution declared the nation free while Americans were keeping slaves, new ways of not thinking about what was changing and what was unchanging in the relationships of men and women in America, new ways of not thinking about America's history of thinking and repressing thought. It was in quest of denying the necessity of thinking about itself, and the necessity of thinking for itself, I take it, that American film study embraced the still-dominant myth about its own origin – the myth that envisions the field as born, or born again, through its transfiguring faith in Theory. Within this myth, May '68, a historical moment America never experienced, is the decisive moment of the field's creation. This myth is a disavowal of America's own experience, a denial that the American experience was and is formative for film study in America.

Following the advent of Theory, film study in America felt authorized to dismiss American ways of thinking – for example, about democracy, individual rights, and freedom, but also about the conditions of the medium and the art of film – as having been completely discredited, unmasked as "dominant ideology," exposed as a system for repressing thought, as no way of thinking at all. Yet within the field of film study in America, Theory itself was a system for repressing thought, was no way of thinking at all, was "dominant ideology." This became comically clear the moment American academics, in wholesale numbers, suddenly began, in their professional capacity, to speak like committed Marxist/Leninists or Maoists even as they continued securing tenure, keeping their eye on mortgage rates, and, in general, taking for granted the privileges of membership in the American academic world.

Nonetheless, when China found itself swept up in the death throes of Maoism, so soon after the fall of the Berlin Wall signaled the annihilation, the self-immolation, of Marxism as an intellectually defensible position, all Americans who took an interest in Chinese cinema rejoiced, even those who were Maoists in Theory. In China at this time, only the villainous forces of repression viewed Americans as villains. The forces of virtue felt they shared common ground with us, with the American way of thinking. If Theory really held sway over their lives the way it does according to Theory, most American studying Chinese cinema would have found themselves on the side of the villains in China, not the heroes and heroines of the Fifth Generation.

The kind of melodrama – is it one kind? – I am invoking here hinges on a cosmic struggle between good and evil. That innumerable melodramas revolving around such cosmic struggles have been produced in every country of Asia as well as in America and Europe is one obvious justification for a symposium on the theme "Melodrama East and West." A subtler justification is that, as I have suggested, the appeal for Americans of studying Asian cinema has been, historically, inseparable from the way all actions, even the study of film, take on cosmic significance, when swept up in such a melodrama.

Within film study in America, the world "melodrama" is often used to refer to the so-called woman's picture. Characteristically, there is no villain in such a film, hence no cosmic struggle. In a woman's picture, the central struggle is a human one, a woman's struggle for selfhood, her struggle to speak in her own voice within a world in which no one knows her the way we do. That innumerable melodramas of this kind, too, have been made in Asia, as they have been made in America and Europe, is another obvious justification for a symposium on "Melodrama East and West." And it is another subtle justification that, historically, the experience of studying Asian cinema for Americans has had an appeal akin to that of the woman's picture. Swept up in the events of this kind of melodrama, too, everything is fateful, nothing merely academic – not because events take on cosmic significance, but because they assume a human dimension.

My experience of a particular Asian film – any film, for that matter – is a meeting, an exchange, between what I bring to the film (who I am, the way I think) and what I take away from the film (what the film teaches me, how its way of thinking changes the way I think). And my experience of an Asian film cannot be separated from what that film means to me as I experience it, my understanding of what the film means, that is, my understanding of how the film understands its own meaning. And that understanding – my understanding of the film's own understanding – is something I create in collaboration with the film itself and with all the people who have helped me, in whatever ways, to be the human being I am. The moral I draw from this is that for Americans there can be no meaningful study of Asian cinema – and, indeed, no meaningful study of cinema – that does not have a human dimension, that is not collaborative, dependent on conversations between flesh-and-blood human beings that bridge the gulfs that separate every person, and every culture, from every other.

When I reflect on the human dimension of my own education in Asian cinema, Gayatri Chatterjee is a person who springs immediately to mind. Each time I was in India leading a group of IHP students, this woman helped select films for us to view, interpreted moments of these films for us, answered countless small and large questions about their cultural and social contexts, explained innumerable matters, and so on. But she also facilitated my education in ways that went beyond anything she did by way of instructing me. Simply by being there for me, by being herself – which means, at times, by masking herself – in my company, by telling me anecdotes from her life's story, by letting me in on her thoughts and hence her ways of thinking, by becoming my friend and letting me be her friend, she enabled me to get to know two or three things about who she is, what type of human being, to gain glimpses of her subjectivity, the way she views the world – in short, to get to know her from the "inside" as well as the "outside," to know her the way Gayatri has gotten to know me, as a subject as well as an object, the way we know the "unknown woman" in a woman's picture.

Whatever else Gayatri has become to me, in India she served me a human reference point, an exemplar of the humanity of India, who enabled me to make connection with Indian films, to be open to their human dimension in a way that would not otherwise have been possible. And the Indian films her example helped open to me also helped open her to me as a human being, helped me appreciate her Indian way of being human, helped to render her form of life intelligible to me, yet also unknowable – not unknowable because she is alien, but because she is human, as I am. Human beings are not unknowable because there is something about them we cannot know, some particular piece of knowledge we happen to lack but which we can imagine possessing. Human beings are unknowable only in that they can never be possessed through what we call "knowledge." Human beings need to be acknowledged, not merely known. And what it is about human beings that needs to be acknowledged, acknowledged separately in every case, is that human beings cannot be possessed at all.

In China, Chen Mei similarly served as an exemplar of humanity for me. Becoming humanly attached to this witty, strong, passionate woman, who emerged from the nightmare of the Cultural Revolution unshakably committed to being her own person, helped me to experience China, and cinema in China, in ways that would otherwise not have been possible for me. Viewed from the perspective my relationship with Chen Mei helped me to attain, the cosmic struggle between virtue and villainy sweeping China was a backdrop to the struggles for selfhood of individual human beings. From this perspective, the fate of Chen Mei's quest meant more to me, was more momentous, than any merely cosmic struggle. It is not possible to attain this perspective, which is, again, the perspective of the woman's picture, without being attached to other human beings, and without acknowledging that we could not be so bound to others unless we were also separate, different, unknowable by other human beings and by ourselves.

Clearly the woman's picture is different, generically, from melodramas that revolve around cosmic struggles between virtue and villainy. The latter seems obviously to derive from the kind of nineteenth-century theatrical melodramas that are the focus of Peter Brooks's seminal study, *The Melodramatic Imagination*, a book that has wielded a powerful influence over studies of film melodramas.[7]

Brooks's book is heavily indebted to the new French thought, Lacanian psychoanalysis in particular. And it does, in the spirit of French thought, envision everything worthy of the name "melodrama" as originating in Paris, and only then crossing the English Channel to England and the Atlantic Ocean to America. In Brooks's account of melodrama's origin, it is the French Revolution, not the American one, that is formative, even for melodrama in America. No doubt, this conviction that the French experience was central, the American experience marginal, no less than Brooks's erudition and brilliance, helped *The Melodrama Imagination* attain the prestige it has enjoyed within the field of film study in America. Typically, studies of film melodrama unquestioningly endorse Brooks's claims about the emergence and history of theatrical melodrama and take for granted the validity of extending those claims to film melodramas as well.

For example, in "Melodrama/Subjectivity/Ideology," E. Ann Kaplan poses the question of how we can justify calling contemporary Chinese films "melodramas" when European and American melodrama "arose at a time when the bourgeois class needed to differentiate itself from the working and aristocratic classes," whereas the Chinese films "emerge within a nation dominated by the Communist Party's ideology of classlessness."[8] However, although the bourgeoisie's wish to differentiate itself from the aristocracy as well as the working class may or may not plausibly explain the rise of theatrical melodrama in France, it is no part of an explanation in

[7] Peter Brooks, *The Melodramatic Imagination: Balzac, Henry James, Melodrama and the Mode of Excess* (New Haven, CT: Yale University Press, 1976).

[8] E. Ann Kaplan, "Melodrama/Subjectivity/Ideology: Western Melodrama Theories and their Relevance to Recent Chinese Cinema," *Melodrama and Asian Cinema*, op. cit., 9–28.

the American case, as America, for all its class structure, had no aristocracy when it embraced melodramatic theater. And it is also no explanation at all for the emergence of *film* melodramas in the twentieth century – unless one assumes that stage and screen melodramas have one and the same form. The fact is, the relationship of the classical American woman's picture to what Brooks takes to be the historically specific theatrical form that is the focus of his study is no less obscure than is the relationship of nineteenth-century theatrical melodrama to recent Chinese film melodramas.

Brooks does not deny the obvious fact that forms sharing crucial features with the theatrical melodramas he studies have emerged in very different cultures at very different times. Yet by encouraging us to restrict the term "melodrama" to what he takes to be one historically specific theatrical form, Brooks is discouraging us from comparing other forms of melodrama with that form or with each other. I take it that Brooks means to discourage such comparative studies out of respect for the principle of historical specificity. But what is specific about a historical moment cannot be separated from how that moment is specified. The moment at which theatrical melodrama emerged in post-Revolution France is also a moment in the historical relationship between Europe and India, for example. Brooks does not choose to specify what he takes to be the moment of melodrama's emergence in Paris by making a connection between Europe and India in this way, presumably because he assumes that no such connection is relevant. Yet on what grounds can he dismiss out of hand the possibility that there is a historical connection as well as a formal relationship between, say, ancient or modern Indian melodramatic forms and the one theatrical form – if we assume it is one form – he is prepared to call "melodrama"? (The celebrated theatrical production of *The Mahabarata* recently directed by Peter Brook, Peter Brooks's near namesake, makes such a link seem tangible. Is this an illusion?) To rule out such a possibility a priori is to consign India and Europe to two completely separate worlds, as if they shared no common ground, and hence were not capable of conversation.

To assume that theatrical melodrama and film melodrama constitute one and the same form is to deny that film and theater are separate, hence to deny as well that there could be a conversation between *them*. Film and theater are, in truth, fundamentally different, and the nature of their difference has been, historically, one of film's central concerns.[9] But this means that the relationship between stage and screen melodramas is not knowable a priori, even in cases in which both hinge on cosmic struggles

[9] This is a central theme of the essays in the previous edition of my book *The "I" of the Camera*, as well as those in this edition.

between virtue and villainy. Brooks's book has actively inhibited film study from reflecting seriously on the relationship between theater and film as it has worked itself out in particular historical cases. It has also inhibited film study from meditating on the diversity of melodramatic forms in cinema, the diversity of their sources, the diversity of relationships these diverse forms of melodrama bear to one another. And those relationships cannot be separated from the historical specificity of each.

For example, in the case of the relationship of woman's pictures and film melodramas that revolve around cosmic struggles of virtue and villainy, it is by no means clear how these melodramatic forms are related to each other, generically or historically. Thus Cavell argues that the genre he calls the "melodrama of the unknown woman" derives directly from the remarriage comedy, a contemporaneous American film genre whose relationship to the theatrical melodramas Brooks writes about is far from direct.[10] In *Pursuits of Happiness*, Cavell suggests that Shakespearean romance is a central theatrical source for remarriage comedy, although the genre also has an important source in nineteenth-century theater, namely that most uncomical of playwrights, Ibsen.[11] If we look to the nineteenth century for a source of the unknown-woman melodrama, it would seem far more promising to turn first to Italian opera, rather than to French theatrical melodrama. And in working out the genre's connections with Italian opera, it is necessary to reflect on the ontological conditions of opera as well as those of film. It is necessary to keep in mind, for example, that although opera is performed on stage before live audiences, the medium of opera is fundamentally different from the medium of theater, as different as song is from speech, as different as both opera and theater are from the medium of film.

Maureen Turim's "Psyches, Ideologies, and Melodrama: The United States and Japan" is exemplary in its detailed demonstration of the fruitfulness of tracing the intricately crisscrossing historical lineages of the diverse forms of stage and screen melodramas in cultures as different as those of America and Japan.[12] Yet when Turim claims that Japanese and American film melodramas have both had to assimilate – or, rather, translate into

[10] Compare Stanley Cavell, "Psychoanalysis and Cinema: The Melodrama of the Unknown Woman," in *Images in Our Souls: Cavell, Psychoanalysis, Cinema*, ed. Joseph Smith and William Kerrigan (Baltimore: Johns Hopkins University Press, 1987), pp. 11–43; "Ugly Duckling, Funny Butterfly: Bette Davis and *Now, Voyager*" and "Postscript (1989): To Whom It May Concern," *Critical Inquiry* 16: 213–89 (Winter 1990).

[11] Cavell, *Pursuits of Happiness*, pp. 1, 20–4, 34, 47–51, 66–70, 103–4, 141–5, 153–60, 223, 260.

[12] Maureen Turim, "Psyche, Ideologies and Melodrama: The United States and Japan," *Melodrama and Asian Cinema*, op. cit., 155-78.

their own cultural terms and thus transfigure – an essentially French melodramatic tradition, even she allows the diversity of melodramatic forms, and the diversity of their sources, both of which she has taken such pains to elaborate, to collapse into a single form, a single source. In this collapse, the principle of historical specificity is one casualty. Another is the principle that the serious study of film cannot be separated from the task of acknowledging and addressing the ontological conditions of the film medium. Necessarily, to deny the latter principle is to deny the former. It is an unfortunate fact that the latter principle has been, since the advent of Theory, routinely denied by film study in America.

The woman's picture is the leading concern of Turim's essay, which invokes the impressive body of work on the American woman's picture that has been a central legacy of the powerful impact of the feminist movement on film study in America. The emergence of feminist criticism within the field, beginning with the publication of Laura Mulvey's "Visual Pleasure and Narrative Cinema," and feminism's subsequent rise to ascendancy, has surely been the most significant development since the advent of Theory – and the most encouraging.[13]

Feminism cannot be viewed simply as the latest in a succession of imported theoretical systems that American film study has incorporated into what the field calls "Theory." For one thing, although there are European feminists such as Julia Kristéva, Hélène Cixous, and Luce Irigaray who are figures to reckon with in the Parisian intellectual world, feminist film critics in America have not primarily been concerned with applying their theoretical systems or "translating" their work into the American context. Feminist film critics in America have made massive investments in French thought, as has virtually everyone in the field. But their primary allegiance and debt have been to feminism itself, not to Theory. And feminism is, in a sense, primarily an American movement. Its aspiration is to think for itself, to find its own voice.

Indeed, feminist film criticism in America has always been conscious that there is something problematic in its dependence on Theory. Already in "Visual Pleasure and Narrative Cinema," Mulvey recognized that feminism could not simply accept Lacanian psychoanalysis, say, because the Lacanian system envisions language – hence thought, hence psychoanalysis itself – as thoroughly implicated in the patriarchal system that feminism is struggling to overcome. Yet although feminist film criticism has recognized from the outset that Theory has a patriarchal aspect, the greater its investment in Theory, the greater its resistance to writing off this investment.

[13] Laura Mulvey, "Visual Pleasure and Narrative Cinema," *Screen* 16(3): 6–18 (1975).

Among feminist film critics, Mulvey's claims that all classical films are enunciated from the position of patriarchy and that the classical "codes" allow for no resistance to patriarchal ideology were almost immediately felt to be too extreme. Every leading feminist film critic, including Mulvey herself, has since tried a hand at revising this position. However, none of these attempts to negotiate a compromise between feminism and the rigid doctrines of Theory has engendered a response remotely comparable with the widespread excitement aroused by Mulvey's original formulations. Nor has any of these revisions achieved anything approaching large-scale acceptance. What has made it impossible for feminist film critics to arrive at a consensus as to how to revise Mulvey's original position, I take it, is that there is no possible compromise that *could* satisfy both the conditions of feminism and the conditions of Theory. Once Theory starts entering into compromises, once it acknowledges that it is fallible, in effect, its standing as a "higher authority" is lost. Then it has no authority at all.

Feminist film critics in America have never found themselves able simply to believe in Theory because Theory gives no answer or the wrong answer to feminism's most urgent questions. But if feminist film criticism has resisted Theory, it has never abandoned Theory completely, as if it were afraid of being abandoned *by* Theory. Thus feminist film criticism has never developed a comparably powerful system of thought it could call its own. Theory has its way of accounting for the unwillingness or inability of feminism to develop an alternative theoretical system, an account that envisions it as *impossible* for feminism to think for itself, to be anything but dependent on patriarchal systems of thought if it is not to be excluded from the realm of thought altogether. The feminist movement in America, committed to thinking for itself, has never actually credited Theory's account. Nor has feminism ever decisively challenged it, ever acknowledged that it has a feasible alternative to its continuing dependence on Theory.

In reality, the moment feminist film critics started considering exceptions to Mulvey's original position, the moment they started making distinctions, they found themselves turning for instruction to the films themselves, to the ways women – and men – experience them. The fact is, feminist film critics have been reading films without at every point depending on Theory. But they have still not looked down and discovered that the safety net of Theory is gone.

This then is feminist film criticism's alternative to remaining dependent on Theory: To acknowledge, on the basis of its own experience, that it is not necessary to possess a system of thought in order to be able to think seriously about film. The alternative, in other words, is to claim connection with the way of thinking philosophically that was founded in America by Emerson and Thoreau.

As I have suggested, the other face of film study's embrace of Theory has been the field's repression of this alternative to the dominant and dominating Western tradition of philosophical system building. Thus Cavell's work, which claims connection with this alternative philosophical tradition, remains repressed within the field of film study in America. In particular, the field has presented no grounds for rejecting Cavell's leading claim that the "melodrama of the unknown woman," like the "remarriage comedy" that was the subject of *Pursuits of Happiness*, itself inherits, meaningfully participates in, the alternative tradition of philosophy to which Cavell's own writing claims connection. (That film study in America is so constituted as to be able to dismiss philosophical alternatives without argument is part of what I mean by saying that the field has not yet secured its intellectual identity.)

In their aversion to the system building of Western philosophy, Emerson and Thoreau envisioned their alternative way of thinking as specifically non-European, hence non-Western, as I have said. By envisioning philosophy as the enterprise of constructing philosophical systems, Western philosophy has predominantly envisioned itself as a paradigmatically male activity, hence has understood itself as speaking, as needing to speak, in only a masculine voice. One of Cavell's guiding insights is that the dominant tradition of Western philosophy has excluded the feminine voice from philosophy, has disavowed – denied, suppressed – what is feminine in philosophy's own voice. As Cavell reads them, Emerson and Thoreau understood it to be a central aspiration of the new philosophy they were founding in America to be the recovery of the feminine aspect of the human voice apart from which it was not possible for philosophy in America to find a voice of its own with which to speak. By understanding the genres of American film that he has studied as aligning themselves with the philosophy of Emerson and Thoreau, Cavell understands these genres, as he understands his own writing, to be attuned to the goals of feminism.

There is an unbridgeable gulf between Cavell's way of thinking philosophically, which is repressed within film study in America as presently constituted, and the doctrines of Theory that claim to authorize this repression. But there is no gulf at all between Cavell's aspirations and the political aspirations of the feminist movement. Then why have feminist film critics not acknowledged or addressed Cavell's writing, why has feminism participated in film study's repression of Cavell's work?

In a letter to the editors of *Critical Inquiry*, Tania Modleski expresses outrage at Cavell's essay on *Now, Voyager*, and accuses Cavell of being unscholarly for not responding in detail to the dialogues and debates about the woman's picture among feminist film critics.[14] Cavell's reply, published along with the letter, refuses to accept this charge. To be sure, he does not, beyond the specific debts he acknowledges in his essay, take instruction from the extensive body of feminist literature about the genre of melodrama he is writing about. But, as he points out, his interest in these melodramas and his way of thinking about the genre go back to *The World Viewed* and, indeed, to even earlier writing he had published in the 1960s.[15] If there is a question of scholarly propriety – and why should there not be? – the question is not why Cavell has not systematically referred to feminist film criticism but why feminist film criticism has not referred to Cavell's writing. Feminist film critics have not only not offered detailed responses to Cavell's work but have not even acknowledged its existence, not acknowledged that it is *possible* to think about these films, about film, the way he does.

From Cavell's perspective, feminist film criticism's dependence on Theory has led it to remain fixated on doctrines that cannot be reconciled with the ontological conditions of film as he worked them out philosophically in *The World Viewed* (for example, the doctrine that in classical cinema the viewer's relationship to the film image can ever adequately be characterized by invocation of the psychoanalytic concept of the fetish). And its dependence on Theory has led feminist criticism to remain fixated on the denial, likewise irreconcilable with Cavell's way of thinking, that classical American film melodramas, written and directed by men, produced under "patriarchy," constructed in accordance with "codes" that are systematically implicated in dominant patriarchal ideology, could possibly be capable of thinking about the subjectivity of women in a way feminism could find fruitful.

A conversation between Modleski and Cavell is possible, a conversation that acknowledges and addresses the differences that separate them, only if Modleski acknowledges the common ground on which she and Cavell stand. It is not my concern whether Modleski and Cavell, personally, will prove willing and able to converse with each other. But it is my concern whether feminism and philosophy in America will prove willing and able to enter into conversation with each other. This is, for both, a fateful question. And the fate of film study in America, too, is at stake.

American film study cannot be a sisterhood any more than it can be a men's club. I wish a say in its agenda. I wish a say in whether the field

14 Tania Modleski, "Editorial Notes," *Critical Inquiry* 16: 237–8 (Autumn 1990).
15 Stanley Cavell, "Editorial Notes," *Critical Inquiry* 16: 238–44 (Autumn 1990).

acknowledges women's voices and men's voices and Asians' voices – and whether the field acknowledges *my* voice. And I wish a say in whether film study in America goes on envisioning itself as nothing apart from Theory or whether it acknowledges the voices it has repressed, revises its understanding of its own origin and history, and recognizes that there is a philosophical alternative to theoretical systematizing.

I seem to be proposing that film study in America replace one myth of origin (a myth about May '68 in Paris, about the advent of Theory) with another (a myth about late 1960s America, about the authority of experience). In any case, I do not believe that it was only at one historical moment, safely in the past, that the field submitted to the silencing of its own voice. What I believe is what the prevailing myth precisely denies, that film study in America came into being at a moment America was torn, and that the field has always been torn between acknowledging and denying film's capacity, and its own, to think for itself, between thinking and repressing thought.

This tension is clearly manifest in the statement recently mailed out to SCS members announcing the theme of the organization's forthcoming annual conference ("Oppression, Silencing and the Production of Diverse Voices"). The statement – like its predecessor, a classic of its genre – is worded so as to encourage SCS members to think of "silencing" and "oppression" as phenomena our field has *encountered* and as phenomena integral to the *subject* of film study. But the language of the statement never straightforwardly acknowledges the possibility that American film study itself, historically, may have been implicated, may still be implicated, in oppressive practices that silence diverse voices. The statement refrains from encouraging SCS members to think seriously about the relevance of the conference theme to the field's own practices.

For film study in America to awaken from its trance of Theory, to recover its own voice, all that is required is for the field to attain a new perspective, which is also an old perspective, on its own identity. What could be more fitting than for the field to come to itself in part through encounters with Asian cinema, and with Asians? Conversations about Asian cinema and about the diverse ways Asians have thought about cinema, conversations between and among Asians and Americans, can play a leading role in enabling the field ot attain this transfiguring perspective.

From such a perspective, it may be recognized not only that Asians and Americans, like men and women, are separate, different, but also that they stand on common ground, that conversation is possible. And from this perspective it may be recognized as well that American culture and film study in America have become all but completely estranged. Yet conversation is possible between them, too. They, too, stand on common ground.

Paul Willeman has warned against the danger, when reading "alien" films, of becoming "cultural ventriloquists," that is, believing we are allowing films to speak for themselves while it is really our own voices we are hearing. But for Americans, always needing to be reassured that we *have* voices of our own, it is an almost irresistible attraction of Theory that it appears to invest its practitioners with the marvelous power to cast their voices into the mouths of others. In America, the problem with Theory is not that it leads us to drown out the voices of others while believing we are having a real conversation, but that it leads us to imagine we are speaking in our own voices when we are really only moving our lips. Entranced by Theory, Americans do not become ventriloquists. They become dummies.

Index

Abraham Lincoln, 27
Adam's Rib, 5, 7, 56, 171, 173, 176, 200
Allen, Woody, 52n
American film, "Americanness" of, 1–10, 55–7, 146–7, 359–65, 372–80
Andrews, Dana, 134
Anger, Kenneth, 70
Antonioni, Michelangelo, 325
Apartment, The, 178–80, 185, 192, 193–205
Apu trilogy, 358
Aravindan, G., 364
Ascher, Steve, 283
Astaire, Fred, 170, 193
Astor, Mary, 69–73
Auerbach, Nina, 94–5
Austen, Jane, 30
Avenging Conscience, The, 22
Awful Truth, The, 5, 56, 170, 171

Bacall, Lauren, 114, 120, 158–9, 161–5
Baker, Carlos, 161
Ball of Fire, 113, 115, 119
Barbary Coast, 114, 118, 121
Barnouw, Erik, 3
Barrymore, John, 80, 84, 113, 114, 120, 298
Barrymore, Lionel, 24
Barthelmess, Richard, 24, 36, 298, 302
Batkin, Norton, xxx
Bazin, André, 131, 285, 322, 323, 325, 350
Beavers, Louise, 98, 100, 104, 105, 268
Beethoven, Ludwig van, 12
Bel Geddes, Barbara, 257
Bellamy, Ralph, 170
Beloved Rogue, The, 80
Belton, John, 111
Benny, Jack, 352
Bergman, Ingrid, 226, 255, 257, 298, 326
Berkeley, Busby, 170
Bhagavad Gita, The, 206
Big Sky, The, 114, 115, 116
Big Sleep, The, 112–4, 120, 121
Birds, The, 234, 242, 257
Birri, Fernando, 342
Birth of a Nation, The, xxix, 3, 11–16, 22, 29, 39, 78, 82, 83, 349, 362
Biskind, Peter, 7–8
Bitzer, Billy, 24–5
Blackmail, 20, 242, 258
Block, Mitchell, 297
Blonde Venus, 6, 55, 56, 59, 62–5, 302; role of African Americans in, 96, 100–2, 107
Blue Angel, The, 84
Bogart, Humphrey, 119, 120; in *To Have and Have Not*, 158–66
Bogle, Donald, 100, 101, 104, 105, 106

Boles, John, 91
Bordwell, David, 56
Boudu Saved from Drowning, 132
Boyer, Charles, 351
Brault, Michel, 281
Brennan, Walter, 119, 134, 159
Brenner, Gerry, 161
Bringing Up Baby, 5, 10, 110–5, 119–21
Brocka, Lino, 364
Broken Blossoms, 12, 29, 36, 79, 302
Brook, Peter, 373
Brooks, Louise, 114–15
Brooks, Peter, 58, 75, 87, 258, 372, 373
Brown, Joe E., 180, 189, 192
Brown, Karl, 23, 24, 25
Browne, Nick, 148, 153, 154
Buñuel, Luis, 351
Burch, Noël, 56
Burr, Raymond, 257
Buscombe, Edward, 141, 142, 143, 144

Cahiers du cinéma, 323, 325
Camille, 6, 96, 302
Capote, Truman, 290
Capra, Frank, 72, 169, 170, 177, 334
Carmichael, Hoagy, 159
Carroll, Leo G., 244, 255
Casablanca, 183, 297
Cassavetes, John, 197
Cavell, Stanley, xiii, xiv, xxvii, 2, 5, 6, 9, 10, 56–7, 82, 94–6, 99–100, 139, 221, 271–3, 275–8, 285, 292, 326–7, 334–8, 359, 360, 368, 374, 377, 378; *see also* comedy of remarriage; melodrama of the unknown woman; philosophy
Chandler, Raymond, 180
Chaplin, Charles, xx, 1, 4, 13, 193, 194, 198, 220, 298; and *City Lights*, 44–54
Chatterjee, Gayatri, 371
Chen, Kaige, 362
Cheng, Jihua, 362
Cherrill, Virginia, 46
Chienne, La, 131
Chopra, Joyce, 296
Chow, Yun-Fat, 355, 356
Chronicle of a Summer, 281
cinema-vérité, xxi, 8, 281–97, 304–6, 314
Circus, The, 46, 48
Citizen Kane, 178
City Lights, 4, 46–54, 193
Cixous, Hélène, 375
Clark, Paul, xxix
Coen, Joel and Ethan, 201
Colbert, Claudette, 5, 72, 106, 108
Collinge, Patricia, 108
Collins, Joan, 117
comedy of remarriage, 5–8, 82, 94, 95, 106, 139, 140, 157, 171–6; relationship to Billy Wilder films, 177–9, 191, 200, 204, 205; to cinema-vérité, 285; to *Tale of Winter*, 335–8; to *The Goddess*, 56, 57, 66; to Hitchcock films, 271–7; *see also* melodrama of the unknown woman; Stanley Cavell
Conversation Piece, 302
Cooper, Gary, 119, 298
Cotten, Joseph, 255
Coyote, Wile E., 351
Crime of M. Lange, The, 133
Crisis: Behind a Presidential Commitment, 286, 287
Crisp, Donald, 24
Cronkite, Walter, 286
Crosland, Alan, 80
Cukor, George, 177
Cumberbatch, Guy, 348
Curtis, Tony, 188, 192

Dalio, Marcel, 163
Dall, John, 258
Dasgupta, Chidananda, 364
Davis, Bette, 6, 96, 374
Death in Venice, 298–303

Delon, Alain, 302
DeMille, Cecil B., 169, 170, 186
DeMott, Joel, 283
DeNiro, Robert, 355
Derrida, Jacques, 367
Descartes, Rene, xv
Dial "M" for Murder, 252
Diamond, I. A. L., 200
Diaries 1971–76, 283, 284
Dickinson, Angie, 114
Dietrich, Marlene, 6, 100, 101, 147, 238, 298, 302, 330; and Ruan Lingyu, 58–64.
Dinner at Eight, 68, 84, 85
Dissanayake, Wimal, xxix
Doll's House, A, 5
Donat, Robert, 254
Double Indemnity, 7, 75, 76, 83, 177, 178, 180–5, 190, 192
Douglas, Kirk, 116
Dream Street, 27
Dressler, Marie, 84–5
Drew, Robert, 281
Dreyer, Carl, 13, 19, 84, 326, 355
Drunkard's Reformation, The, 13, 15, 326, 327
Dunne, Irene, 5, 102, 103, 172
Dutt, Guru, 362

Easy Virtue, 242
Eisenstein, Sergei, 13, 350, 353
El Dorado, 115, 116
Eléna et les Hommes, 122, 137, 220
Emerson, Ralph Waldo, films inheritance of philosophical perspective of, xv, 2, 5, 10, 55, 139, 170, 172, 177, 205, 240, 279, 338, 347, 357, 359, 360, 361, 368, 377

Family Portrait Sittings, xxi, xxxi, 304–20
Fargo, 201
femme fatale, 177, 185
feminist theory; *see* film theory
Fields, W. C., 62
Fifth Generation (of Chinese directors), 362, 363, 370
film criticism, xv, xvii, xxi–xxv, 9, 10, 99, 171, 270–4; relation to film theory, 321–4, 346, 364–7, 375–8
film noir, 173, 174, 177, 178, 180
film theory, xii, xv, xvi, 359; apparatus theories, xv, 350, 353; auteurism, 270–1, 321; feminist theory, 63, 176, 375–80
Flaherty, Robert, 282, 284, 352
Fleming, Victor, 67
Fonda, Henry, 196, 256, 336
Ford, John, 8, 13, 139, 141–56, 170, 177, 204
Foster, Barry, 261
Frege, Gottlob, xiii
French Cancan, 122, 135–8, 220
Frenzy, 255, 261
Freud, Sigmund, 59, 335, 351, 369

Gabin, Jean, 85–6, 135–8
Gable, Clark, 67–73
Gallagher, Tag, 141, 142, 146, 148, 154, 156
Gandhi, Mahatma, 361
Garbo, Greta, 6, 179, 298, 302
Gardner, Robert, 282
Gaslight, 6, 96, 297, 351
Gentlemen Prefer Blondes, 111, 113, 114, 115, 117, 120, 121, 179
Gertrud, 84
Ghatak, Ritwik, 362
Gilda, xiii
Girl in Every Port, A, 102, 114, 115
Gish, Lillian, 3, 24, 29, 30, 31, 32, 34–6, 62, 83, 179, 298, 302
Godard, Jean-Luc, 325, 326
Goddess, The, xi, 55–66
Golden Coach, The, 122, 135, 218, 220
Goldwyn, Samuel, 118, 119, 120
Gold Rush, The, 198
Gould, Timothy, 275–9
Grand Illusion, The, 85–6, 163, 208

Grant, Cary, 5, 10, 63, 94; 172, 190, 192, 204; 255, 257, 277, 288, 298, 302, 334; in Howard Hawks films, 110, 112, 114–7, 119–21; in *North by Northwest*, 241–53
Grapes of Wrath, The, 157
Great Dictator, The, 53, 193
Greed, 4
Grierson, John, 284
Griffith, David Wark, xx, xxix, 1, 3–5, 9, 11–16, 17–28, 29–43, 62, 78, 82, 83, 87, 88, 168, 169, 170, 220, 282, 288, 289, 295, 303, 326, 327, 349, 350
Guzzetti, Alfred, 304–20

Happy Mother's Day, A, 296–7
Harlow, Jean, 67–73
Harron, Robert, 17, 24, 29, 31
Haskell, Molly, 110
Hawks, Howard, xx, 8, 72, 110–21, 158–66, 170, 177, 179, 324
Hawthorne, Nathaniel, 2, 3
Haydn, Franz Joseph, 12
Haye, Helen, 256
Hayworth, Rita, xiii, 116, 121
Heche, Anne, 263, 264, 265
Hecht, Ben, 118
Hedren, Tippi, 181, 257
Heidegger, Martin, xv, 368, 369
Hemingway, Ernest, 158–63, 165–6
Hepburn, Katharine, 5, 10, 110, 112, 120, 121, 147, 173, 176, 204, 288, 298, 302
Hessling, Catherine, 131
His Girl Friday, 5, 79, 80, 114, 119, 120, 121
Hitchcock, Alfred, xxix, xx, xxii, 8, 13, 20, 74, 76–84, 108, 111–3, 116, 121, 135, 132, 143, 154, 178–82, 196, 200, 204, 216, 324, 328, 336, 338, 350, 353, 381; authorship of, 265, 268–80; and *North by Northwest*, 241–53; and *Vertigo*, 221–40
Hitchcock thriller, 272, 378; role of villains in, 254–63
Holden, William, 186
Home Sweet Home, 22
Hopkins, Miriam, 72, 114, 119
House of Darkness, A, 15
Hovey, Richard, 161
How Green Was My Valley, 147, 157
Howitt, Dennis, 348
Hurst, Fannie, 104
Huston, Walter, 24

I Was a Male War Bride, 114, 116
Ibsen, Henrik, 5
Ikiru, 360
Imitation of Life, 92, 104–8, 268, 269
improvisation, 289, 297
In Cold Blood, 290
Intolerance, 21
Irigaray, Luce, 375
Irma la Douce, 193
It Happened One Night, 4, 8, 56, 72, 106, 170, 171, 177, 334
It's a Wonderful Life, 172–4, 234
Ivens, Joris, 284, 304

James, Henry, 2
Jannings, Emil, 84
Jazz Singer, The, 102, 178
Jin, Xie, 61
Jones, Allan, 103
Ju Dou, 363
Judith of Bethulia, xxix, 11, 17–28

Kant, Immanuel, 334, 361
Kaplan, E. Ann, 372
Kapoor, Raj, 362
Keane, Marian, xxvii, 10n, 80n, 221, 231, 237
Keaton, Buster, 44–6, 53, 145, 179, 231
Kelly, Gene, 193
Kennedy, John F., 287, 288, 351
King, Martin Luther, 361
Kreines, Jeff, 283
Krishnaswamy, S., 3

Kristéva, Julia, 374
Krupa, Gene, 119
Kurosawa, Akira, 359, 360

Lacan, Jacques, xv, 271, 367, 372, 375
Lady Eve, The, 5, 76, 89, 171, 185, 335, 336
Lancaster, Burt, 302
Land of the Pharaohs, 114, 117, 118, 121
Landau, Martin, 255
Land Without Bread, 351
Lang, Doreen, 257
Lang, Fritz, 1, 115
Last Laugh, The, xiii
Late Spring, 360
Laughton, Charles, 179
Leab, Donald, 105
Leacock, Richard, 282, 283, 296, 304
Leigh, Janet, 181, 259, 263, 264, 350
Leigh-Hunt Barbara, 261
Lemmon, Jack, 179, 180, 188, 192–4, 200, 201
Leopard, The, 302
Letter from an Unknown Woman, 6, 7, 56, 96, 214, 238, 239, 337, 377
Lifeboat, 256
Little Match Girl, The, 131, 213
Little Theater of Jean Renoir, The, 122, 137, 138
Lodger, The, 77, 78, 79, 255, 256, 260, 261, 266, 273
Lombard, Carole, 113, 120
Lorentz, Pare, 284, 304
Louisiana Story, 148
Lubitsch, Ernst, 1, 169, 170, 177, 178, 179, 352
Lumiére, Louis, 353

MacDonald, Dwight, 325
MacLaine, Shirley, 179, 197, 199, 200, 201, 203
MacMurray, Fred, 7, 75, 180, 185, 192, 193
Madame Bovary, 6
Mahabarata, The, 373
Maltese Falcon, The, 70
Man Who Shot Liberty Valance, The, 141
Mangano, Sylvana, 302
Manhattan, 52n
Mann, Thomas, 298–303
Man's Favorite Sport?, 110, 115
Marnie, 119, 181, 238, 242
Marsh, Mae, 13, 14, 16, 17, 24, 78 82, 83, 87
Marshall, Herbert, 255
Martin, Dean, 116
Mary of Scotland, 147
Mason, James, 243, 255
May '68, 363, 369, 379
McCowen, Alec, 255
McCrea, Joel, 118
McDaniel, Hattie, 98, 100, 101, 103
McDormand, Frances, 201
McElwee, Ross, 283–4
McQueen, Butterfly, 98
Mei, Chen, 362, 371, 372
melodrama of the unknown woman, 6, 7, 56, 93–5, 96, 140, 221, 238–40, 271–5, 285, 338, 374, 377; *see also* comedy of remarriage; Stanley Cavell
Melville, Herman, 2, 3
Meyers, Jeffrey, 185
Mildred Pierce, 6
Miles, Vera, 196
Milland, Ray, 186
Mitchell, Thomas, 84
Mizoguchi, Kenji, 6n, 359, 360
Modleski, Tania, 274, 377, 378
Monkey Business, 114, 119
Monroe, Marilyn, 95, 113, 114, 120, 179, 189, 191, 192
morality, Victorian, 148, 204, 206, 348, 349, 357
Morgan, Frank, 84
Morgan, Helen, 84, 102, 103
Morgan, Kitty, xxvii, xxviii
Morin, Edgar, 281

Morocco, 101
Moss, Robb, 283
Mr. Deeds Goes to Town, 169
Mr. Smith Goes to Washington, 169
Mulvey, Laura, 9, 375, 376
Murder!, 231, 241, 255, 283
Murnau, F. W., 1, 13, 169, 170, 177, 324

Nanook of the North, 284, 285, 352
New Latin American Cinema, 340–7
New Wave, *see Nouvelle vague*
Nichols, Dudley, 141, 146
Nietzsche, Friedrich, xv, 361, 368, 369
Night and Fog, 352
Night of the Hunter, 179
Ninotchka, 178, 179
No Lies, 297
Noble, Peter, 104
Noonan, Tommy, 120
North by Northwest, 241–53, 255, 277
Notorious, 7, 226, 231, 242, 255, 256, 257, 277
Nouvelle vague, 281, 323, 325, 329
Novak, Kim, 222, 223, 224, 226, 265, 302
Novello, Ivor, 24, 77, 78, 79, 260
Now, Voyager, 6, 56, 96, 139, 173

O'Connor, Loyola, 29
O'Hara, Maureen, 147
Ondra, Anny, 258
Only Angels Have Wings, 84, 113, 114, 116, 119, 120, 183
Ophuls, Max, 1, 215, 351
Orphans of the Storm, 12
Ozu, Yasujiro, 6n, 56, 359, 360

Parada, Rodolfo, 343
Pascal, Blaise, 332, 333, 334, 337
Passion of Joan of Arc, The, 19, 326, 355
Peary, Gerald, xxx
Pennebaker, D. A., 304
Perkins, Anthony, 78, 79, 91, 119, 124, 125, 126, 128, 129
Percy, Esme, 255
Perez, Gilberto, 148n
Philadelphia Story, The, 5, 10, 56, 82, 94, 139, 171, 177, 204, 297, 302, 334
Philosophical Investigations, xiii, xv, xxv
philosophy: in American films, 55, 99, 177–8, 205, 220, 347, 359–61, 377–9; in *Death in Venice*, 298–303; in Hitchcock films, 254, 268–80; role in film study, xi–xvii, xxix–xxv, 6–12, 360–9, 359–61, 377–9; in *Tale of Winter*, 325, 333, 334; in writings of Eric Rohmer, 321–4
Pick, Zuzana, 340–7
Pilgrim, The, 49
Pincus, Edward, 283
Plato, 332, 333, 336, 337
Platt, Louise, 147
Poe, Edgar Allan, 2, 3
Primary, 281, 286, 287
Production Code, 4, 59, 67, 68, 72, 73, 350, 357
Psycho, 181, 196, 222, 223, 241, 242, 243, 255, 259, 262, 281, 297; place in Hitchcock's authorship, 263–4, 267, 269–70, 272; role of camera in,78–81; violence in, 350, 353
Psycho (Gus Van Sant remake), 128–34
psychoanalysis, xv, 63, 224, 262, 335, 367, 372, 375, 378

Raging Bull, 354
Rains, Claude, 255, 257
Rance, Mark, 283
Random Harvest, 6, 238
Raphaelson, Samson, 178
Rapper, Irving, 97
Ray, Nicholas, 8
Ray, Satyajit, 358

Raymond, Gene, 68, 69
Rayns, Tony, 364
Rear Window, 256, 272
Red Detachment of Women, 61
Red Dust, 67–73, 183
Red River, 114, 115, 116
Reed, Donna, 172–4
Reed, Elliott, 113
remarriage comedy, *see* comedy of remarriage
Renoir, Jean, xxx, xxxi, 13, 73, 85–6, 113, 122–9, 140, 141, 206–20, 324, 328, 336, 352; cinematic style of, 130–8
Ritchard, Cyril, 258
Richie, Donald, 358, 364
Rio Bravo, 113, 114, 119
Rio Lobo, 115, 121
River, The, xxx, xxxi, 206–20, 336
Robeson, Paul, 102–4
Robinson, Edward G., 114, 119
Rocco and His Brothers, 302
Rogers, Ginger, 119, 170
Rohmer, Eric, 321–4, 325–39
Rope, 258
Rossellini, Roberto, 324
Rozsa, Miklos, 181
Rouch, Jean, 281, 282
Ruan, Lingyu, 58, 59, 62, 64
Rules of the Game, The, 73, 163, 122–29, 130, 133, 134, 137, 140, 141, 352
Russell, Jane, 113, 115
Russell, Rosalind, 113, 121

Sabotage, 257
Saboteur, 242
Saint, Eva Marie, 245, 255, 257
Salles Gomes, Paulo Emilio, 343
Sarris, Andrew, 121, 178, 180, 193, 200, 201
Sato, Tadao, 358, 359, 360, 364
Scarface, 96, 116, 118
Schaetzel, Ann, 283
Schildkraut, Joseph, 24
Secret Beyond the Door, The, 115
Sen, Mrinal, 362
Seventh Heaven, 73
sexuality, xx, 5, 19–22, 24–5, 60, 61, 200, 265, 271, 282, 349, 350; in *Red Dust*, 67–73
Shadow of a Doubt, 108, 143, 255, 264, 272, 273, 277
Shakespeare, William, xv, 325, 326, 327, 329, 338, 352
Shantaram, V., 362
Shapiro, James, 227n
Sheridan, Ann, 116
Sherlock, Jr., 45, 53, 145, 231
Sherman's March, 283–4
Shop Around the Corner, 178
Show Boat, 84, 96, 102–4, 106
Sidney, Sylvia, 257
Simon, Simone, 73
Sirk, Douglas, 1, 8
Slezak, Walter, 256
Some Like It Hot, 179, 180, 188–92, 194, 196, 201, 205
Song Is Born, A, 113, 116
Southerner, The, 134
Spellbound, 115, 119
Stagecoach, 139–48, 157, 204
Stage Fright, 238
Stahl, John, 94, 108, 268
Stanwyck, Barbara, 5, 7, 75, 76, 88, 89, 94, 95, 115, 119, 147, 180–5, 336
Stella Dallas, 6, 7, 8, 56, 65, 76, 83, 87–95, 96, 98, 99, 102, 173, 185
Sternberg, Josef von, 13, 55–60, 66, 111, 100, 170, 177, 330
Stewart, James, 172, 173, 174, 221, 231, 234, 235, 256, 266, 288
Strangers on a Train, 255
Stroheim, Erich von, 4, 13, 186, 208
Sturges, Preston, 89
Sunrise, 4, 169, 177
Sunset Boulevard, 179, 180, 185–8, 202
Suspicion, 242, 244

Swamp Water, 134
Swanson, Gloria, 179, 186, 188
Sweet, Blanche, 19

Tagore, Rabindranath, 361
Tale of Springtime, 334
Tale of Winter, 325–39
Tearle, Geoffrey, 254
television, 167, 174, 175, 176, 286, 287, 288, 357
theater, xxi, 1, 13, 11, 32, 37, 39, 74, 75, 78, 79, 81, 130, 137, 156, 174, 179, 180, 189, 196, 197; in Hitchcock, 222–3, 237–8; relationship to cinema-vérité, 286–8; role in films of Renoir, 130, 137, 212, 213
theatrical melodrama, xxi, 15, 74–86, 258, 372, 373, 374
theory, *see* film theory
Thing, The, 114, 116, 121
Third Cinema, 342
39 Steps, The, 76–8, 83, 241, 242, 254, 257, 259, 328
Thoreau, Henry David, 2, 5, 10, 55, 170, 171, 338, 347, 357, 359, 360, 361, 368, 377
To Be or Not to Be, 352
To Have and Have Not, 114, 118, 119, 108–16
Toles, George, 201
Toni, 132, 133, 210n, 219
Tracy, Spencer, 5, 63, 173, 176
transcendentalism, 55, 139, 167, 170, 171, 177, 291, 334, 357, 381
Trevor, Claire, 147
Triesault, Ivan, 256
Trouble in Paradise, 179
Trouble with Harry, The, 200
True Heart Susie, 12, 21, 29–43, 208, 220
Truffaut, François, 255, 263
Turim, Maureen, 374, 375
Twentieth Century, 111, 113, 114, 120

Ugetsu Monogatari, 360
Untouchables, The, 355
utopianism, 168, 171, 172, 174, 17
176, 341

Van Dyke, Willard, 284, 304
Van Sant, Gus, 263–9
Vaughn, Vince, 263, 264, 26
Vertigo, 112, 179, 221–40, 241, 2
257, 258, 265, 267, 272, 273,
275, 277, 302
Vertov, Dziga, 284
Véry, Charlotte, 326, 336, 339
Vidor, King, 88, 99
villains and villainy, 62, 66, 107,
174, 254–62, 272, 363, 370,
374
violence, 66, 256, 272, 284, 348
virtue, cinematic representations
62, 66, 98, 102, 169, 258, 2
363, 370, 372, 374
Visconti, Luchino, 298–302
Vivre sa vie, 326

Walden, 171, 282, 361
Walker, Robert, 255
Walthall, Henry, 15, 24
Wang, Yuejin, 363
Wanger, Walter, 147
Warren, Charles, 238n
Way Down East, 12
Wayne, John, 115, 116, 148
Washington, Fredi, 104, 105
Whale, James, 102
White Rose, The, 21, 24, 38
Whitman, Walt, 2, 5
Wiese, Ellen, xxx
Wilder, Billy, 1, 179–205
Willeman, Paul, 380
Wilson, Edmond, 161
Winter's Tale, The, 94, 325, 3
338
Wiseman, Frederick, 282
Wittgenstein, Ludwig, xiii, xv,
276, 361
Woman on the Beach, The, 1